Capitalism, Colonisation and the Ecocide-Genocide Nexus

Critical Human Rights Studies

The *Critical Human Rights* Studies series is committed to investigating today's most pressing human rights issues from diverse interdisciplinary and intellectual perspectives. It embraces critically engaged scholarship, methodologies spanning the humanities and social sciences, creative non-fiction writing, co-produced approaches that bridge research and practice in human rights, and work that engages directly with policy. The series interrogates the human rights-related dimensions of phenomena such as colonisation, genocide, ecocide and environmental issues, migration, reconciliation projects, freedom of expression, digital rights, racism, poverty, indigenous peoples' rights, corporate power and extractive industries.

Published in association with the Human Rights Consortium and the Institute of Commonwealth Studies, this series is fully open access and welcomes new proposals in particular from those looking to bring perspectives and approaches from the humanities to address the series' central concerns.

Series Editor

Damien Short, Professor of Human Rights and Environmental Justice, Institute of Commonwealth Studies, University of London, UK.

Recently published

Refugee Reception in Southern Africa: National and Local Policies in Zambia and South Africa, Nicholas Maple (July 2024)
Mapping Crisis: Participation, Datafication and Humanitarianism in the Age of Digital Mapping, edited by Doug Specht (September 2020)
Reconciling Rwanda: Unity, Nationality and State Control, Jennifer Melvin (May 2020)

Capitalism, Colonisation, and the Ecocide-Genocide Nexus

Martin Crook

Available to purchase in print or download
for free at https://uolpress.co.uk/

First published 2024 by
University of London Press
Senate House, Malet St, London WC1E 7HU

© Martin Crook 2024

The right of Martin Crook to be identified as author of this Work has been asserted in accordance with sections 77 and 78 of the Copyright, Designs and Patents Act 1988.

This book is published under a Creative Commons Attribution-NonCommercial-NoDerivatives 4.0 International (CC BY-NC-ND 4.0) license.

Please note that third-party material reproduced here may not be published under the same license as the rest of this book. If you would like to reuse any third-party material not covered by the book's Creative Commons license, you will need to obtain permission from the copyright holder.

A CIP catalogue record for this book is available from The British Library.

ISBN 978-1-912250-58-5 (hardback)
ISBN 978-1-912250-59-2 (paperback)
ISBN 978-1-912250-61-5 (.epub)
ISBN 978-1-912250-60-8 (.pdf)
ISBN 978-1-912250-67-7 (.html)

DOI https://doi.org/10.14296/lsbs7954

Cover image: Photo by redcharlie on Unsplash.

Cover design for University of London Press by Nicky Borowiec.
Series design by Nicky Borowiec.
Book design by Nigel French.
Text set by Westchester Publishing Services UK in
Meta Serif and Meta, designed by Erik Spiekermann.

Contents

Acknowledgements	vii
List of abbreviations	ix
1. Introduction: ecological inequity, 'exterminism' and genocide	1
2. Australia then: the architecture of dispossession	27
3. Australia now: the architecture of dispossession	67
4. Kenya then: the architecture of dispossession	103
5. Kenya now: the architecture of dispossession	143
Conclusion: a neo-Lemkian ontology in the age of the Anthropocene	181
Bibliography	193
Index	253

Acknowledgements

First, I want to thank my infinitely patient and generous wife, Viktoriia, without whose unwavering support and sacrifice I would not have been able to muster the strength and determination to finish the book. My infinite gratitude extends to all my family. My parents never stopped believing in me. My friends, who, like my family, forgave my neglect, as I devoted myself to this project, and patiently waited and extended their generosity of understanding, who offered me hugs, advice, love and solidarity. I thank you with all my heart.

I am deeply grateful and indebted to Professor Damien Short and his excellent and invigorating intellectual insights, sage advice and the time he generously shared with me. I want to extend my gratitude to Dr Padraic Gibson and Professor Paul Burkett, whose stimulating discussions cast light on my research topic that proved invaluable, and all the figures who are no longer with us, without whose pioneering and fearless work I could not have written this book.

Above all, I want to dedicate this work to those Indigenous people who contributed to the book and to all those resisting all forms of oppression. It is their struggle that offers us a beacon of hope in a world under a pall.

List of abbreviations

AAL	Australian Aborigines League
AAPA	Australian Aboriginal Progressive Association
ABD	Accumulation by Dispossession
ACHPR	African Commission on Human and Peoples' Rights
ACtHPR	African Court on Human and People's Rights
AI	Amnesty International
ALRA	Aboriginal Land Rights (Northern Territory) Act of 1976
APA	Aborigines Progressive Association
ATC	Aboriginal Treaty Committee
ATSIC	Aboriginal and Torres Strait Islander Commission
BBOP	Business and Biodiversity Offsets Programme
BDO	Biodiversity Offsetting
CAR	Council for Aboriginal Reconciliation
CARA	Council for Aboriginal Reconciliation Act 1991
CDEP	Community Development Employment Program
CEMIRIDE	Centre for Minority Rights Development
CMP	Capitalist Mode of Production
COB	The United Nations Convention on Biological Diversity
CPA	Communist Party of Australia
CSG	Coal Seam Gas
EROI	Energy Return on Investment
EU	European Union
FPIC	Free Prior and Informed Consent
FPP	Forest Peoples Programme
GDP	Gross Domestic Product
GHGs	Greenhouse Gas Equivalents

LIST OF ABBREVIATIONS

ILUA	Indigenous Land Use Agreement
IMF	International Monetary Fund
IPCC	Intergovernmental Panel on Climate Change
IWGIA	International Work Group for Indigenous Affairs
JI	Joint Implementation
KFS	Kenya Forest Service
LALC	Local Aboriginal Land Council
LTV	Labour Theory of Value
MP	Mode of Production
MRGI	Minority Rights Group International
NLC	National Land Commission (Kenya)
NNTT	National Native Title Tribunal
NRMP	Natural Resource Management Program
NSW	New South Wales
NSWALC	New South Wales Aboriginal Land Council
NTA	Native Title Act of 1993
OPDP	Ogiek Peoples' Development Program
PES	Payments for Ecosystem Services
REDD	Reducing Emissions from Deforestation and Forest Degradation
RNTC	Registered Native Title Claimants
SAP	Structural Adjustment Programme
UN	United Nations
UNDP	United Nations Development Programme
UNDRIP	United Nations Declaration of the Rights Indigenous Peoples
UNEP	United Nations Environment Programme
WaTER	Water Tower Protection and Climate Change Adaptation Programme
WTO	World Trade Organisation

Chapter 1

Introduction: ecological inequity, 'exterminism' and genocide

A spectre is haunting the globe in the twenty-first century – the spectre of ecological collapse. The rising tide of ecological destruction portends the destruction of the biosphere, and with it the natural bases for life on earth. Given humanity's dependence on the biosphere and the dependence of organised human existence on its biotic and abiotic environment, this rising tide poses a threat to all group life and must therefore be recognised *as a primary driver of genocide*. Indeed, the preponderance of evidence demonstrates emphatically that unless the global community and political and diplomatic elites involved in climate governance change course dramatically and wean us off fossil fuels and an economic system predicated on perpetual growth (Hickel, 2017, 2020), ecological catastrophe awaits us. With climate change and a looming ecological crisis casting an ominous shadow over planet earth, the systems and institutions that support life – food production, energy production, biodiversity and ecosystems – face collapse. It stands to reason therefore that what I term 'ecologically induced genocide' (Crook and Short, 2014) will become in the twenty-first century the preponderant form of 'group death'.

Unfortunately, there is no sociological or socio-ethically agreed definition of what constitutes an act of genocide; there are as many theories of genocide as there are cases or instances of it. Passions boil over inevitably among scholars of genocide, understandably since we are by definition a part of the object that we are studying, the epistemological trap that bedevils the human or social sciences. Subjectivity cannot extricate itself from the object it studies. This is what Smith (1990, pp. 205–6) calls the inescapability of standpoint, a fact which obliges us to adopt a 'reflexive critical inquiry'. This does not mean that a clear distinction cannot be made between the intent of study and the object of study. Despite the embeddedness of the subject with the object, the study of human rights as *social facts* can still be pursued. By being aware of one's epistemological limitations we can only strengthen claims of truth on social phenomenon. Therefore, we must adopt what Powell (2011, ch. 1) calls a 'critical sociology' and acknowledge that one is in effect taking sides wittingly or otherwise when conducting studies of social phenomenon. Never has this been truer when studying the value-laden, inherently normative subject of human rights, or one corner of its varied and contentious field: genocide. Arguably, this explains why the 'value free' methodological and ontological prejudices of classical sociology, particularly in its *positivist* guise, which sought to maintain the pretence of scientific impartiality and objectivity and thus not engage in normative critiques, were so slow to analyse genocide (Short, 2010b, p. 831).

It is with this in mind that the study of the Indigenous groups such as the Sengwer, in the former British colony of Kenya, and the Gomeroi, Githabul, and Wangan and Jagalingou nation in Australia – another former British colony – was embarked upon. The book intends to explore the genocidal effects of climate governance and market environmentalism on Indigenous peoples in Kenya and forms of energy extraction on Indigenous groups in Australia – united by, among other things, a discourse of 'developmentalism', as well as ontologically, since efforts to mitigate climate change (in Kenya) would not be necessary absent modes of energy extraction that drive climate change (in Australia) – and to deepen and enrich our knowledge of genocide and the eco-genocidal nature of colonisation and the capitalist mode of production more specifically, which underpins developmentalism. Fundamentally, it attempts what I have called a political economy of genocide, which through the synthesis of a variety of theoretical traditions, seeks to explicate the manner in which material forces, on local and global scales, underpin and give rise to (though not reducible to) ever evolving relations of genocide. To be clear, by political economy of genocide I mean an understanding of genocide as inherently rooted in the structures of economies and their relation to the political environment and systems of government, or more specifically, how a particular mode (or modes) of production, and their corresponding forms of class (and social) struggle and laws of motion influence historical processes more generally and genocidal processes more specifically. In essence, I use material conditions as the focal point and proceed dialectically, in an attempt to identify the laws of motion of 'genocidal societies' (Barta, 1987, pp. 239–40).

Hitherto, the study of genocide has for the most part, even when it adopts a sociological sensibility, stopped short of explaining relations of genocide as rooted in political economies, or when they do, it is done so superficially, or in a rudimentary manner. Instead, this book seeks to introduce greater political economic rigour to our understanding of relations of genocide and grapple with the dialectic between the logic of capital accumulation and the logic of Indigenous elimination, understanding how these two logics, neither wholly reducible to the other, interact and often conflict. The former logic refers to the central driving motive, the *raison d'être* of capitalism, namely the extraction of value from labour (and nature) to produce capital at ever expanding scales (Marx, 1976a). This forms a crucial structural part of the *political economy of genocide* under settler-colonial contexts (Crook and Short, 2014; Crook, Short and South, 2018; Crook and Short, 2019). Capitalist political economy and capitalist ecology, since any consideration of the political economy must also incorporate an understanding of how nature is (re)shaped and (re)made, gives rise to the ecocide-genocide nexus for two fundamental, structural reasons, or what might be otherwise understood as the dual character of capital accumulation. Firstly, due to what is known as the *value-contradiction* in radical political economy, intertwined with the various industrial (and financial) processes operating within the circuits of capital. This is the 'normal' functioning of capital once the generalised commodity system has been established alongside its various institutional legal and governance structures that guarantee private property and money as a store of value. Here accumulation proceeds 'under conditions of "peace, property and equality"' (Harvey, 2003a, p. 144). The value contradiction, between use value, the utility of an article, product or service, which is qualitative and thus varied and diverse, and exchange value, a signifier for abstract social labour time of an article, which must be uniform, equivalent and homogenous in a system of generalised commodity production, is the primary driver of the eco-destructive tendencies of the capitalist mode of production because it blindsides capitalism to the contribution to value production derived from nature, given the fixation solely on labour's contribution to value. Critically, due to the necessity for homogeneity and uniformity to facilitate exchange in a market system, the formal abstraction of exchange value leads to an obliteration of qualitative differences in commodities and 'abstracts' from the complex, delicate and intricate web of ecological interconnections and diversities.

In essence, the narrow horizon of exchange value, combined with the insatiable drive to accumulate capital and ceaselessly expand through the force of competition, has a number of pertinent ecological implications.

Firstly, the commodification of ever greater spheres of nature. What White (2015, p. 214) described as the four elements of nature – water, air, earth (land), sun (energy) – are transformed into value for the capitalist class. Secondly, as shown in more detail in the discussion of environmental sociology and Marxist ecology below, a rift or a breakdown in the 'social metabolic order' is created (Foster, 1999, p. 383). Moreover, under capitalism, arguably for the first time in history, nature is biologically and physically remade on a *global* scale, into a 'capitalist nature' (Smith, 1984, p. 77),[1] with all its attendant ecological contradictions perhaps most cogently expressed in the notion of the Anthropocene (Zalasiewicz et al., 2015; Steffen et al., 2015). Capitalist nature, probing the very limits of these ecosystemic laws, and destabilising the biosphere itself in its ceaseless drive to accumulate capital, could cause the ecological collapse of human civilisation and even trigger an auto-species extinction event or omnicide (Levene and Conversi, 2014, p. 282). Thus, the new metabolic order can be, and invariably is, genocidal for those social groups living on the margins of the capitalist world. It is precisely at the borders, or what Kevin B. Anderson (2016a) called the 'margins' between the ever-expanding sphere of capitalist production, trade and investment and the 'social vitality' of the non-capitalist world, inhabited by socially and culturally distinct Indigenous and territorially bounded peoples that the contradictions of capitalism become most violent and pronounced.

The second key structure in the political economy of eco-genocide is any extra-economic coercive process of naked plunder or theft that alienates a social group from their lands as the capitalist system expands into non-capitalist territory, 'into a world dense with cultural difference' (Smith, 2002, p. 79), beyond the circuits of capitalist production and *outside* the realm of ordinary 'expanded reproduction'. This occurs through processes of enclosure that logically *precede* the later eco-destructive industrial farming, mining, extractive and other industrial projects captured in the first structure that compound and deepen domicidal severance – in a word: colonialism. The central economic mechanism, otherwise known as primary accumulation, is the name given to the violent and predatory process that originally transformed feudal relations of production into market relations dependent on the commodification of the means of economic subsistence (Marx, 1976a, chs. 25–32; Glassman, 2006). Primary accumulation was a historical process which was the necessary precondition for the rise of the capitalist system *and* its continual expanded reproduction (De Angelis, 2001). Critically, this entailed the creation of a population with no other means of subsistence through their violent separation from their social means of production (Marx, 1976a, pp. 874–5);

the capital-relation presupposes that separation (Marx, 1976a). It is this forcible separation which serves simultaneously as a key historical precondition for the expanded reproduction of the capitalist system to forcibly incorporate or 'enclose' materials, resources and labour not yet subject to the laws of generalised commodity production, the global accumulation process and the realm of exchange value, *and* a technique of genocide bringing about social death or domicidal severance.

To be clear, the second structure, namely primary accumulation, chronologically speaking precedes the first structure only at the site at which domicide and separation take place, namely at the borders between the outer frontier of the expanded reproduction of the global circuits of capital and Indigenous territory. This is because it is the value contradiction, the first key structure, that gives initial impetus to the expansion into that territory. The work of, *inter alia*, Rosa Luxemburg (1963) and Vladimir Ilyich Lenin (1996) did much to expand the scope of Marx's analysis which, with exceptions in the form of some of his rather voluminous unpublished notebooks, manuscripts, letters[2] and his journalistic writing on colonialism (Marx, 2012) and 'pre-capitalist' societies (Anderson, 2016a), examined the capitalist system as a 'closed system' confined to a 'national framework' and did not take into its purview capitalism as a global system (Harvey 2003a, p.144; Wood 2006, p.2). Lenin (1996) recognised that overseas territories would become important as sources for the export of capital given the overaccumulation of capital at home. Harvey (2003b, p.65; 2003a, ch.3) more recently also recognises the importance of geographical and temporal dimensions as 'escape' avenues or 'release valves' for the resolution of contradictions within capitalism, specifically the overaccumulation of capital, neither of which can be profitably employed, when he coined the term 'spatio-temporal fix' 'as metaphor for solutions to capitalist crises through temporal deferment and geographical expansion'.[3] Luxemburg (1963, p.452), who understood both the necessity of capitalism having something 'outside itself' to offset its own internal contradictions and the dual character of capital, stressed the importance of recognising the necessity of capital through its encounter with what she called 'non-capitalist modes of production' via 'colonial policy, an international loan system and war', to facilitate continued accumulation on the *international* stage between nations. Harvey (2003b; 2005, pp.137–82), picking up where Luxemburg left off, stressed the continued importance of 'accumulation by dispossession' (ABD) in the period of neoliberal globalisation, recognising it as a permanent feature of the dual character of capital accumulation processes operating not just outside of capitalism understood as closed system on the international stage, but also as a continuous process operating *within* many countries as well. It is this latter dynamic that underpins what political scientist James Tully (2000, p. 39) has called internal colonialism.

The second key structure consolidates *de facto* and ultimately *de jure* control of Indigenous land; in the latter case, 'facts on the ground' are consolidated and entrenched by creating the necessary legal and institutional architecture in the form of private property regimes (Busbridge, 2017), aided and abetted by neo- and settler-colonial courts, legitimised by the constitutive logic of various colonial discourses and enforced by the political jurisdiction and ultimately violence of the relevant settler-colonial state (Goldman, 1998). It is this second key structure that secures *de facto* and *de jure* control, what the founder of the discipline of settler-colonial studies, Patrick Wolfe (2006a), called 'the logic of elimination', or ongoing permanent systems of setter colonialism, present in both case studies in this book, which in essence systematically eliminates Indigenous peoples through various techniques and modalities (*inter alia*, mass killings, biocultural assimilations, spatial technologies), to secure their land, resources and sometimes their labour. They are a series of structures designed to extinguish Indigenous sovereignty and secure the aforementioned separation of Indigenous people from their land and social means of production.

The observation that settler colonialism is a permanent structure rather than a fleeting ephemeral moment, reminds us that it is not consigned to the past, but, as will be made painfully obvious in the two case studies under examination, persists to the present day. It is, as Elkins and Pedersen (2005, p. 3) observe, 'the foundational governing ethic of this "new world" state'. It also draws attention to its multifaceted systematic nature. The effort to extinguish Indigenous alterity and self-determining sovereignty, the foundational governing ethic, is continually re-enacted through labour, land and population policies. Consequently, settler-colonial society is 'marked by pervasive inequalities usually codified in law' and structural inequities, or 'settler privilege' at every level of society, including the economy, politics and criminal justice (Pedersen, 2005, p. 4). Physical destruction and cultural assimilation were for Wolfe on a continuum of techniques that produced the same eliminatory outcome. For Wolfe these techniques or strategies could include a 'whole range of cognate biocultural assimilations' and spatial removal technologies, and were therefore not limited to physical destruction (Wolfe, 2006a, p. 388). In fact, Wolfe (Wolfe, 2006a, p. 402) insisted that those who accept the settler-colonial paradigm are obliged, precisely because it is a structure and not an event, to chart the transmutation of the logic of elimination, from the initial frontier violence phase through its various 'modalities, discourses, and institutional formations', its continuities and departures. This book will precisely do this but go one step further than 'chart'. It will attempt to dialectically explain what Strakosch and Macoun (2012, p. 44) describe as the shifting 'structural target of the settler colonial logic of elimination', or what in Lemkian terms might be described as the evolution of genocidal techniques, by undergirding this transmutation with political economic drivers and the evolving imperatives of the Australian and Kenyan settler-colonial economy on the one hand, combined with Indigenous resistance to those imperatives, on the other. After all, Australia and Kenya are not just settler-colonial states but *capitalist* states as well. By examining the nature of the unfolding of this dialectic through time in both of these two sites of relations of genocide, I hope to deepen understandings of the 'history of the present' (Foucault, 1995), as a means of revaluating contemporary phenomena (Garland, 2014). By understanding how genocidal structuring dynamics were set loose and entrenched in the past, we can shed more light on how they continue to reproduce themselves in the present, and indeed how they have changed and evolved, and so, given the inherent structural nature of colonial genocides, better trace the transmutation of the logic of elimination, through its various continuities and departures, 'modalities, discourses, and institutional formations' (Wolfe, 2006, p. 402). It is precisely what Garland (2014, p. 373) described as the 'historical conditions of existence upon which present-day practices depend' that I will first set out to establish in the initial chapters of both case studies, before going on to delineate the manner in which those conditions manifest in the present historical juncture, in mutated form.

Taken together, these structures, properly understood, can be read in their totality as the political economy of genocide that invariably underpins settler-colonial societies. It is these two structuring dynamics, broadly conceived: ecocidal logic of capital on the one hand, and the settler-colonial logic of elimination on the other, and their dialectical interaction, which was earlier cited as under theorised and under researched in the genocide studies field. It is precisely this under researched nexus that Mohawk scholar Audra Simpson (2016, p. 440) beseeched scholars to illuminate further. The proposed model of a political economy of genocide is designed to address this gap.

Moreover, I aim to incorporate a greater understanding of *socioecological dynamics*. In other words, I want to address the lacuna in the study of genocide and shed light on what will become in the twenty-first century arguably the most important vector of genocide: ecocide. There is now a much needed 'ecological turn' in genocide studies that acknowledges the material 'extra-human environment' as critical to the biological and cultural integrity of distinct social groups (Crook and Short, 2014, 2019, 2020, 2023; Crook, Short and South, 2018; Short, 2016; Lindgren, 2017; Dunlap, 2017). This is particularly pertinent where Indigenous groups are concerned, as they are invariably what Abed (2006, p. 326) has termed *territorially bounded* groups whose cultural and spiritual vitality is inextricably bound up with the land, in particular, culturally and ecologically vulnerable Indigenous and place-based groups who are subject to an array of ecological and cultural genocidal coercive pressures, such as land grabs in the service of economic development projects, like energy extraction in Australia (Short, 2016, ch. 5), or in the service of conservation and the environment in Uganda (Lyons and Westoby, 2014), Kenya (Crook and Short, 2021, 2023) and elsewhere (Böhm and Dabhi, 2020). Such projects will render them 'socially dead even if non-lethal coercive means are used' (Abed, 2006, p. 326). To Indigenous and place-based peoples, land embodies their 'historical narrative', their 'practises, rituals and traditions', as well as their political and economic cohesion. Therefore, by ecologically induced genocide, I mean scenarios where environmental destruction results in conditions of life that fundamentally threaten a social group's cultural and/or physical existence (Abed, 2006). In short, as Wolfe (2006, p. 387) astutely observed, 'land is life'.

By synthesising the critical developments in radical political ecology with a political economic approach, my analysis addresses this gaping lacuna by drawing attention to the critical role that the destruction of ecologies plays in the genocide of Indigenous and place-based peoples, and indeed humanity more generally. It is my contention that ecological destruction should be considered the ninth technique of genocide, added to the eight first delineated in the path-breaking book *Axis Rule in Occupied Europe*, written by the neologist and founder of the genocide concept Raphael Lemkin (1944, pp. 82–90). This is my contention given the ecologically embedded nature of all human life and the risk posed to ecology and the biosphere by the capitalist economic system discussed below. I define the ninth technique as: *the destruction of, or severance from, the eco-systemic habitat of the group.* Indeed, the case studies examined in this book will demonstrate that this technique is driven by what I (Crook, Short and South, 2018) have previously called the 'eco-criminogenic' nature of the capitalist mode of production (CMP).

The genocide – ecocide nexus

As yet there are only a few papers in the canon of genocide scholarship that attempt to theorise the material 'extra-human environment' as, what

Lemkin termed, an *essential foundation* of a social collective (1944). Raymond Evans (2008) is one such example. In his contribution he specifically calls for a theoretical reorientation on the pivotal importance of environmental destruction to the continued survival of a social group. Echoing this sentiment, Damien Short and I (2014, p. 319) have called for a paradigm shift and a new 'ecological turn' in genocide studies. Short has done much to drive this turn, spearheading a reappraisal of the changing shape of the engine that now drives and underpins what he called (2010b) 'settler colonial expansionist land grabs' and their attendant genocidal consequences. His work on Indigenous people in Australia and First Nation Americans in Canada are cases in point. Short (2010b, pp. 837–8) elaborates:

> Driven by corporate agendas governments frequently dispossess Indigenous groups through industrial mining and farming, but also through military operations and even national park schemes – all of which routinely take no account of core Indigenous rights. But of all such activities it is industrial extractive industries which pose perhaps the biggest threat to Indigenous peoples' survival, for it is not just the accompanying dispossession which they bring but also the 'externalities' of pollution and environmental degradation.

Thus, the central focus of my book will be to illuminate the nexus between the two socioecological phenomenon and join the chorus of a nascent yet growing body of literature in genocide studies dubbed the 'environmental turn' (Churchill, 2002; Huseman and Short, 2012; Crook and Short, 2014, 2020, 2023; Lindgren, 2017; Dunlap, 2017; Crook, Short and South, 2018). I, however, want to go beyond this body of literature and attempt a synthesis of the sociology of genocide and environmental sociology into a new theoretical apparatus. Previous literature has by and large merely sought to empirically observe and document the necessary connection between these two phenomena and assert a socio-ethical critique condemning capitalism for its ecocidal and genocidal 'externalities'. If they move beyond an empirical and ethical critique, they invariably identify the prevailing socio-economic system, unbridled neoliberal globalised capitalism, wrongly narrowing the historical scope of capitalist production's eco-destructive period to this late phase of neoliberal market fundamentalism and/or point to the industrial expansionist drives of capitalism in vague abstract, ahistorical terms. In his critique of 'green theory' and 'ecocentrism' as a critique of the anti-ecological nature of the capitalist system, Foster (2016b) made much the same critical observations, arguing that 'abstract notions like growth, industrialism, or consumption take the place of investigations into the laws of motion of capitalism as an economic and social order, and how these laws of motion have led to a collision course with the Earth system'. Heeding Foster's warning, I seek to illuminate the political-economic drivers and mechanisms couched in an ontology that recognises the co-evolution of nature–society relations and accounts for the rise of ecologically induced genocide in its various iterations as a necessary function of capitalist production. As we will see, this encompasses the pastoral economy in the early history of Australian settler capitalism, or more recently fossil fuel extraction, including its particularly virulent form 'extreme energy' or unconventional fossil fuel extraction, or the Kenyan context and the commodification of nature, pursued under the euphemistic guise of the conservation of nature. The new theoretical apparatus will illuminate the nexus that binds all of these ecologically destructive practises in a common sinew of mutual destruction: *the ecocide-genocide nexus*. The form that this co-evolution of mutual destruction takes is, of course, an expression of the crisis-prone socioecological contradictions of the global capitalist system at any given particular historical juncture.

The book will argue that a radical political economy and ecology can help explain the destructive drive of the *extractive industries* and the drive to commodify nature through the institutional matrix of *neoliberal climate governance* and, more importantly, the fundamental contradiction between the capitalist production and its extra-human environment. It is the contention of this author that the capitalist system, propelled by the necessity to accumulate capital, in the form of industrial agriculture, neoliberal climate governance, industrial extractive industries and more recently even renewable energy (Dunlap, 2017), are the *sine qua non* of modern genocide. In other words, it is precisely these industries that constitute the dominant delivery system for the genocidal technique *par excellence*: ecological destruction.

However, to understand how settler-colonial states mediate the laws of motion of the capitalist system and express its drives, I will also draw on the rich storehouse of insights from settler-colonial studies, critical race studies and critical Indigenous studies to make sense of the diverse and complex ways in which the genocidal techniques, underpinned as they are by the aforementioned logic of capital, become manifest at the various levels of the settler-colonial and (post)colonial formation. In other words, the lacuna in the genocide studies literature which this book attempts to address is the failure to illuminate and explicate the manner in which the ecocidal logic of capital intersects with the settler-colonial 'logic of elimination' (Wolfe, 2006a, p. 387). I will combine this with the sociology of genocide as understood through a neo-Lemkian colonial settler lens, within which the master concept of culture is retained and where genocide is understood as a structure or process, unfolding through time, over many decades if not centuries, that cripples the essential foundations of a group by breaking up or stifling the relations of solidarity that bind a group together (Card, 2003; Short 2010a, 2010b; Barta, 1987; Curthoys and Docker, 2008; Docker, 2008; Kreiken, 2004, 2008; Moses, 2002; Powell, 2007). In essence, a Lemkian ontology understands social collectives as held together by its common culture, which secures its structural integrity and ultimately its physical well-being (Schaller, 2008a; Van Kreiken, 2004). The flipside of this ontological coin is that genocide is not an assault on the individuals *per se*, but rather an assault on the very structures, or essential foundations, of the group itself, weakening the integrity of the group and its capacity to successfully reproduce. Therefore, genocide is not limited reductively to 'Nazi-like extermination policies' or mass death. As Woolford and Benvenuto (2015, p. 379) remind us, a 'people can be placed in precarious conditions that threaten its survival as a group without gas chambers or concentration camps'. Accordingly, forms of cultural destruction can result in the liquidation of the social group, just as surely as physical destruction, both ultimately leading to 'social death' (Card, 2003, p. 63; Short, 2003, p. 48). By social death, Claudia Card (2003, pp. 63–79) argued that the 'social vitality' of the group, which is secured through inter-generational *and* contemporary relationships and the formation of group identity which gives meaning to life, if disrupted or thwarted, would lead to social death. Where what Moses (2002) dubbed the 'liberal' approach, adopting a more legalistic interpretation, equates genocide with mass killing, intentionality, state actors and holocaust uniqueness, the 'post liberal' approach seeks to decolonise the discipline and focuses on the points of continuity between the Holocaust and colonial and postcolonial regimes and structures, both theoretically and ontologically, and in country-specific case studies such as Canada, Australia or Israel (Dunlap, 2017, pp. 555–6). Moreover, for Lemkin, and myself, genocide is necessarily a dimension of colonial settler societies, best summed up in Lemkin's (1944, p. 79) keen abstraction:

> Genocide has two phases: one, destruction of the national pattern of the oppressed group: the other, the imposition of the national pattern of the oppressor. This imposition, in turn, may be made upon the oppressed population which is allowed to remain, or upon the territory alone, after removal of the population and the colonization of the area by the oppressor's own nationals.

Of course, today, in a 'postcolonial' world, where modern sovereign nation states with internationally agreed borders rarely, with a few notable exceptions, invade and annex other territory, colonialism and the colonial settler/Indigenous relations reproduce themselves and endure in modified form; the colonial modality referred to as 'internal colonialism' being a more apt category which captures the lived experience of vulnerable Indigenous groups who continue to suffer from systematic legal, political and social oppression and discrimination at the hands of the colonial state machine (Tully, 2000). It is through this Lemkian colonial settler lens, combined with Marxist ecology, political economy, settler-colonial studies, critical race studies and critical Indigenous studies that we can illuminate the ongoing imposition of genocidal structuring dynamics in the case studies that will form the focus of my book.

A synthesis of the sociology of genocide and environmental sociology

The contribution Marxist ecology and historical materialism can make to the field of genocide studies is twofold: first, by helping us theorise ecology and the material 'extra-human environment' as the *ninth essential foundation* of a social collective and its vital importance for biological and cultural integrity of any social collective (Crook and Short, 2014; Crook, Short and South, 2018).[4] Historical materialism as a theory of society and historical change is rooted in an understanding of the centrality of social production of wealth or use values to the rise and historical evolution of social relations. This production, a universal requirement for all societies, includes basic requirements of food, shelter and clothing, as well as cultural and aesthetic needs. Crucially, this material requirement includes ecology. As Marx asserted, 'The first premise of all human history is, of course, the existence of living human individuals. Thus, the first fact to be established is the physical organisation of these individuals and their consequent *relation to the rest of nature*' [emphasis added] (Marx and Engels, 1998, p. 37). Therefore, Marx ecologically embedded all human societies, recognising the co-evolution of human and natural history.

Secondly, Marxist ecology attempts to identify the causes of ecological degradation under the capitalist system, locating it in the manner in which the capitalist class have both historically monopolised control of the means of production, including the land, and the manner in which social production is carried out, both of which degrade the extra human environment, causing a metabolic rift (Burkett, 2014; Foster, 1997a, 2000). Briefly, Marx (1976a, p. 198) described as 'social metabolism' the ecological processes that govern the continual exchange of materials and energy between all life and its environment and allow for the regeneration and continuation of the ecological life-sustaining web, only mediated through the social relations of any given society, thus ecologically embedding all social formations. The key mediator of the life sustaining metabolic relationship, where human societies are concerned is labour (Marx, 1976a, p. 283). Every distinct social order or mode of production produces its own corresponding metabolic order, since each mode is distinguished by the manner in which labour and the other forces of production are organised. Contrary to prevailing Western environmentalist thinking which is broadly predicated on an empirically erroneous 'nature-culture dualism' (Braun, 2002, p. 10), society and nature are inevitably brought together in a dialectical relationship (Harvey, 1996). In other words, the metabolic interaction is socially mediated by the historically structured social relations between producers and between producers and appropriators of the surplus product (Crook and Short, 2014, p. 300), to produce a 'social nature' (Braun, 2002, p. 10; Smith, 2008). As Marx (1973, p. 85) was keen to stress, 'some determinations belong to all epochs, others only to a few'. Indeed, what Smith (2008) called the 'production of nature' is common to all systems of social production. The concern of this book, however, will be the capitalist system, and the role it has played in restructuring socioecologies of much of the world through the 'colonial encounter' of European empires from the seventeenth century onwards (Grove, 1995, 1997; Crosby, 2004) with their colonised territories and what might be called the 'production of colonial nature'. It is in the production of *colonial* nature that the book will tease out those 'few' determinations unique to capitalist production.

These theoretical and historical insights can be fruitfully incorporated into our understanding of ecologically induced genocide. If we accept the ontological reality that all social groups are ecologically embedded, and expand Lemkin's techniques to include ecological destruction, Marxist ecology offers a very fruitful set of tools to illuminate eco-genocidal processes in settler-colonial spaces *where the capitalist system plays a central role*. As I will demonstrate, these case studies will make the ecocidal properties of the capitalist system painfully apparent.

Governmentality, colonial discourses and the constitutive logic of race

Colonization invent[ed] the colonized.

—Bhambra, 2014, p. 132

Much has been written to finesse understandings of how, alongside the material practises that facilitate the logic of elimination, various discursive, ideological and biopolitical techniques have been employed to pursue the erasure of the Indigenous *genos*. Critical race studies have done much to illuminate the ways in which socially constructed, racialised differences and the uneven racialised landscapes they create enable the material reproduction of the economic system in colonised spaces and ultimately the accumulation of capital, on local, national and international scales. There is a rich and important literature that identifies the critical role colonialism and its corollary, racial oppression and expropriation play in the expanded reproduction of *racial capitalism*. Works such as C. L. R. James's (2001) *Black Jacobins* and Cedric Robinson's (2000) *Black Marxism* stand as testament to this. The structuring power of racial categories facilitate the expanded material reproduction of the capitalist system by cheapening the labour of 'othered' bodies (Pulido, 2016), and structuring racialised landscapes that enable the accumulation process, such that the associated environmental externalities differentially impact white and non-white communities and restrict access to environmental benefits (Pulido, 2016). More recent work develops and deepens the work of such seminal thinkers like Cedric Robinson in this vein, showing that racial capitalism has played a pivotal role in environmental history and the transition to the Anthropocene, or the *Racial Capitalocene* (Vergès, 2017), dovetailing with the ecological Marxist insights discussed above. The role of racial capitalism will become painfully apparent in both case studies.

Of critical importance to developing a heuristic understanding of the symbolic violence and biopolitics that accompanies the material reproduction of the colonial political economy and racial capitalism are processes of 'internal territorialisation' (Vandergeest and Peluso, 1995, p.387). They hinged on modern state technologies or 'spatial practices' such as, *inter alia*, mapping, cadastral planning and surveying, which were crucial to state formation as well as capital accumulation. These cadastral technologies that facilitated the expansion of the colonial state and regulated the behaviours and conduct of subject populations were both enabled and enablers of the cultural erasure and (re)inscription of colonised spaces which are central to relations of genocide in both sites of settler colonisation. As Peluso and Lund (2011, p.673) have argued, territorialisation is 'no less than power relations *written* on the land' [emphasis added].

Of course, as Indigenous scholar J. Kēhaulani Kauanui (2016) reminds us, we mustn't conflate indigeneity with race or ethnicity. As alluded to already, the histories of othering, settler-colonial violence, subjugation, relationship to place and subject positions are not identical for all racialised groups. Influenced by what is often described as the 'discursive turn' within postcolonial studies and post-structuralist school, scholars working within the critical Indigenous studies and settler-colonial studies tradition have applied concepts and categories borrowed from within this tradition to better understand what was earlier referred to as the shifting structural target of the settler-colonial logic of elimination. Key to the discursive turn is the notion that knowledge and power are mutually constitutive of each other, a notion attributed to the French philosopher, historian and sociologist Michel Foucault, first formulated in his path-breaking work *Discipline and Punish: The Birth of the Prison* (1995). Referring to the evolution of the penal system, Foucault (1995, p. 23) observed that 'a corpus of knowledge, techniques, "scientific" discourses is formed and becomes entangled with the practise of the power to punish'. This ontological nexus between 'the deployment of force and the establishment of truth' (1995, p. 184) was extended to a development of an understanding of how modern governments (including colonial ones, as we will see), exercise their power. In particular, Foucault's notion of 'biopolitics' and 'governmentality' (Foucault et al., 2014): the former referring to the notion that in the modern age, entire populations and their 'improvement', in arenas such as public health or economic productivity, have become the object of government, requiring new bodies of knowledge, including, *inter alia*, the macroeconomic, bio-scientific and statistical. The latter referred to the 'art of government', which he broke down into 'rationalities' or discourse that governments employed and various 'technologies' that governments deploy to ensure that the objects of government conform or 'normalise'. This alternative model of state power to the traditional top-down, juridical, hierarchal notion, creates 'regimes of truth' which, via disciplinary institutions, such as hospitals, psychiatric institutions, schools and the like, allow for the more efficient social control of whole populations as they internalise those discourses or norms of behaviour (Foucault, 1998, p. 140). Edward Said, one of the founders of postcolonial studies, would apply this framework to an understanding of colonial relations of power, arguing (1994, p. 9) that the latter was not simply constituted through 'accumulation and acquisition' but that '[b]oth are supported and perhaps even impelled by impressive ideological formations that include notions that certain territories and people require and beseech domination, as well as forms of knowledge affiliated with domination'. Sadly, this insight will prove highly redolent to this book.

Even human and Indigenous rights, and by extension, progressive efforts to reconcile with and recognise Indigenous people, function as forms of governmentality that act to discipline those to which they have been extended and neutralise Indigenous political challenges to settler-colonial states (Moreton-Robinson, 1999b; Alfred, 1999). Mohawk scholar

Taiaiake Alfred (1999, p. 58) argues that 'reconciliation' efforts and the legislation of new rights for Indigenous peoples is nothing more than the continuation of colonial relations by other means, arguing that the granting of 'rights' is one of the weapons in the arsenal of colonialism given the role of the colonial settler state in shaping and defining them. Glenn Coulthard's (2014) path-breaking work *Red Skin, White Masks* argues much the same, describing the 'recognition paradigm' as the new *modus operandi* of colonial power (Coulthard, 2014, p. 4). Where colonial power is not primarily reproduced through violence, the structure of dispossession is secured through psycho-affective discourses that forge a 'colonial subject' (Coulthard, 2014, p. 4). More specifically, Alfred argues that to aspire to secure rights through the colonial state is to implicitly accept the authority of the colonial state in the first place. Even when the 'liberal' human rights academic and policy communities champion Indigenous rights and argue in favour of 'collective rights' (as opposed to rights couched in Lockean or Benthamite terms of the individual), advocated by William Kymlicka (1995) and Charles Taylor (1995), which protect persistently disadvantaged individuals *as* members of minority communities, they are still insidiously plagued with colonial notions. For all the eloquence and merits of the 'collective rights' arguments, they are predicated on the liberal settler state's jurisdiction over Indigenous nations (Tully, 1995, p. 53).

The liberal politics of 'recognition' flounders when it conflates the status of immigrant minority communities who have, voluntarily and with consent, chosen to become citizens of any particular nation-state and Indigenous peoples who invariably consider themselves as not only culturally distinct, but crucially, dispossessed First Nations, who did not give their consent, nor willingly hand over their land or relinquish their self-determination (Short, 2008, p. 19). The consequent focus on 'internal citizenship' as a solution to Indigenous rights claims subsumes Indigenous self-determination and political autonomy to the overarching authority of settler state authority and consequently becomes a form of *internal-colonialism* (Tully, 2000, p. 39). It is precisely these colonial assumptions, discursive manoeuvres, forms of governmentality and psychoactive affects that we will see deployed to great effect by settler and (post) colonial administrations in Australia and Kenya respectively.

The import for the purposes of the argument of this book is that these forms of discursive violence, racialisation and biopolitics help us comprehend the manifold ways in which, through various cognate biocultural assimilation projects, social death is achieved.

The case of Kenya and Australia as sites of continuing genocide: the logic of comparison

In the case of Australia, we witness a process of continuing genocide that can be broken down into phases, beginning with the much studied and discussed 'dispersal' extermination campaigns of the 1800s, the biopolitical assimilation programmes that followed in their wake, such as the 'protection' regimes and the reserve system, the more recent 'reconciliation' process and the bowdlerisation of Indigenous rights as part of an assimilationist nation-building agenda (Moran, 2009; Short, 2003, 2008). Now in the current phase, we witness the continued settler-colonial land grabs which enable the rampant mining of Australia, in what Short (2016) has described as resource-based ecological genocide and more recently extreme energy known as coal seam gas (CSG) production.

In Kenya, the dynamic genocidal structure – not singular event – as Wolfe (2006) described, was set in train during the initial colonisation phase under the auspices of the Imperial British East Africa Company in 1888, which principally involved, above all else, land grabbing, followed by what I (Crook, 2013, pp. 31–5) called the second concentrated phase of genocide during the emergency period from October 1952 to December 1959, which organised the brutal suppression of the resistance to land alienation (Anderson, 2005; Elkins, 2003, 2005a). In this new third phase, in Kenya's postcolonial period and the age of climate change and the Anthropocene, ecologically vulnerable Indigenous groups are being menaced by a multitude of ecological and cultural genocidal coercive processes of social change, among which the most salient are land grabs, market environmentalism and neoliberal conservationism. The forces that underpin these processes are the Kenyan post-independence state and its drive to develop the economic base of its economy in a sharply competitive globalised economy, restructured along neoliberal lines (Kwokwo, 2014, ch. 4). The ecological fallout from these development agendas threatens the cultural integrity of forest dwelling peoples like the Sengwer by both severing their connection with their land, the land which embodies their cultural identity and spiritual vitality, sustained through inter-generational and contemporary relationships (Card, 2003, pp. 63–79).

In essence, my book seeks to deepen the attempt to understand the structural roots of 'genocidal societies' as Tony Barta (1987) called them, as national entities and in their many political economic connections with broader global structures, and reveal their political economic underpinnings. This attempt to give the study of genocide sociological rigour was given a new lease of life with Barta's (1987) path-breaking piece

Relations of Genocide: Land and Lives in the Colonization of Australia, in which he coined the phrase 'relations of genocide', a concept which was obviously inspired by his Marxist leanings, and gave the phrase 'genocidal society' a much-needed shot in the arm, after Irving Horowitz used it misleadingly, as Barta (1987, pp.239–40) argues, to describe a state apparatus seized by the Nazis for the purposes of systematic structural elimination of social groups. For Barta (1987) genocidal societies were distinct from genocidal states, because as he put it:

> the whole bureaucratic apparatus might officially be directed to protect innocent people but in which a whole race is nevertheless subject to *remorseless pressures of destruction inherent in the very nature of the society*. It is in this sense that I would call Australia, during the whole 200 years of its existence, a genocidal society [emphasis added].

In is in this vein and this tradition that my book seeks to illuminate the inner structural connections between capitalist social formations and cultural and ecologically induced genocide in order to repudiate the notion that genocide is somehow an aberration of the social and political system, a pathological breakdown of the normal functioning of our society's institutions of economy and government.

The central contention of this book is that the continuing genocide of, *inter alia*, the Sengwer in Kenya and the Gomeroi, Githabul, and Wangan and Jagalingou in Australia, is the necessary product of the expansion and imposition of the colonial occupant's capitalist system, a system inimical to the Indigenous way of life. Herein lies the ultimate structural root of the cultural genocide of the aforementioned Indigenous groups. It also succinctly and eloquently captures what Short (2016, p.37) has urged other genocide scholars to do above all else, which is to examine and reveal 'the *context* and *manner* in which Indigenous cultures are "changing" in the face of continuing settler colonial expansionist projects driven by global capitalism and a "logic of elimination"' [emphasis in original].

Kenya and Australia share a history as former colonies of the British Empire, which will provide illuminating similarities and contrasts. Above all, it is this shared heritage as former British settler colonies that will set them both on the path to genocide and see them unleash Lemkin's two-staged process. The precise historical manner in which the logic of settler-colonial capitalism will manifest as the 'logic of elimination' in the respective colonial spaces and the corresponding points of similarity and difference is what interests us here. Above all, it is this shared heritage which I will demonstrate unleashed genocidal structuring dynamics in the past and laid down a legacy that continues to reproduce those dynamics in the here and now. The precise manner and trajectory of these genocidal structuring dynamics in both sites is what will be traced.

Firstly, we must consider the manner in which both settler colonies were forcibly integrated into the international division of labour and the imperial chain of global capitalist production, investment and trade. This has left a lasting legacy in how both countries are currently governed and incorporated into the global economy, which has implications for the continuing genocidal structuring dynamics in both countries. Moreover, as alluded to earlier in the case of Kenya, both countries have recently gone through similar processes of *neoliberalisation*, which have not only deepened (and to some extent transformed) their historic role in the international division of labour laid down during the period of the British Empire, but have played a crucial political economic role in the current phase of their respective genocidal structuring dynamics.

As well as having their fates tied by the British Empire, the manner in which they exhibit genocidal processes as a function of their political economies is also tied in another sense. The role that the Australian economy now plays as a major exporter of primary goods in the form of minerals and fossil fuels is not only, arguably, a legacy of its origins as a settler-colonial adjunct of the British Empire, but also a major contributor to 'anthropogenic forcing', changing the Earth's energy balance and total atmospheric concentrations of CO_2. Australia is in fact an outlier as an atmospheric polluter and carbon emitter (Morton, 2021), which of course is destabilising the biosphere's carbon cycle characteristic of the Holocene. This, in turn, drives climate change and plays a crucial part in the general ecological crisis. Without this crisis there would be no rationale or pretext for the intellectual, ideological and political economic enterprise previously described as market environmentalism and the green economy. Without this enterprise, the avenues for green accumulation that it forced open would not have come to pass, since there would not be an ecological crisis to manage. The fact that the anti-ecological properties of the capitalist system drive the destabilisation of our climate and the Anthropocene more generally, which is now, through intergovernmental institutions and a whole array of other actors and stakeholders, being turned into an opportunity for capital accumulation through various market environmentalist schemes, ties the fates of Indigenous peoples in Australia and Kenya in yet another way.

This leads to the next fascinating point of comparison: the peculiar and tragic turn of events which brings the fates of Indigenous peoples together across the two case studies, via the shared planetary carbon cycle, has given rise to two distinct and seemingly opposing forms of the capitalist mode of production. On the one hand, in the case of Australia, as we will see, a mode of economic organisation which, shaped by the imperative to accumulate capital and produce value, extracts Earth's resources in an ecologically destructive and unsustainable manner. On the other hand, a mode of production in Kenya, which seeks also to accumulate capital and produce value as narrowly defined by the capitalist system, but this time in order to *conserve* rather than destroy. The latter has been described as a *conservationist mode of production* (Brockington and Duffy, 2010). In essence, while one genocide machine causes ecological ruptures, another, spawned by the first, seeks to 'fix' them.

Finally, the cases exhibit interesting similarities and differences in the way that indigeneity is coded and instrumentalised by both settler-colonial forces and those resisting them. The legal, normative symbolic and social scientific meaning of indigeneity presents interesting differences across the two case studies both historically speaking and in the present juncture. Consequently, these differences and their political and ideological import will have material and political implications for the genocidal structuring dynamics and the resistance to them.

Methodological considerations

The truth is the whole.

—Hegel, 2006, p. 81

The methodology of this book will consciously adopt an activist perspective in the full recognition that 'knowledge is vital to social action – as to individual ethics – [which] has long been recognized. Thinkers have been doers (contrary to stereotype). And reflection on successes, failures and unexpected consequences of social action has been a vital source of new understanding' (Hale, 2008, p. xiii). In the past the positivist 'objective' forms of anthropology and social science which studied Indigenous communities often served to exclude Indigenous peoples from the production of knowledge and impose and thus perpetuate colonial forms and categories which condemned Indigenous peoples to a static and primitive form of existence and reproduced the colonial discourse that did so much to consolidate their subjugation. As Hale (2008) points out: 'Anthropologists have lately engaged in much soul-searching over complicity in colonialism, but anthropology was also recurrently the basis for efforts to mitigate harmful colonial practices'. It is in the spirit of this latter sense that this study was undertaken. The voice of the victims of genocidal processes are accorded equal evidentiary weight, as will be explained below, given the inherently phenomenological dimension of the crime of genocide.

In essence, my methodological approach could be described as 'mixed methods'. On the one hand I am using, following the structural or colonial genocide school, a 'radical structural approach' (Burrell and Morgan, 1979, pp. 33–4) which takes as axiomatic the existence of external objective structures independent of our cognition, but which also seeks to identify the contradictions and tensions within those structures to bring about radical change. It is 'committed to radical change, emancipation, and potentiality, in an analysis which emphasises structural conflict, modes of domination, contradiction and deprivation' (Burrell and Morgan, 1979). On the other, the collection of qualitative data, in particular interviews with Indigenous people that capture the lived experiences of structural violence and the meanings that they attribute to the various losses and social harms they experience. This is often referred to as the 'interpretive approach' (Burrell and Morgan, 1979, p. 30), which seeks to understand how actors make sense of their experiences and in the case of social groups, reach intersubjective or collective understandings of their situations (Putnam and Banghart, 2017, p. 2–3), which, given the recursive relationship between action and meaning construction, play a critical role in shaping future interactions.

However, I seek to move beyond what are often mutually exclusive approaches and, following the genocide scholar Christopher Powell (2010, p. 8–9), adopt a *relational* approach that eschews both what he called the *objectivist* and *subjectivist* strategies outlined above, and which avoids reductively erasing the significance of agency as mere epiphenomenon from history but seeks to understand it dialectically in conjunction with structure, as part of a larger rich totality; 'The truth is the whole' as Hegel famously observed (2006, p. 81). If therefore, we take seriously Lemkin's understanding of genocide and his methodology – in particular, his privileging of culture as the 'master concept' – then we must acknowledge that group life and its destruction manifest both at the level of the objective, such as the destruction of for instance the ecosystems that physically and biologically support the integrity of group existence, which exist independent of our sense perceptions and can indeed be recorded and even quantitatively measured. They also manifest at the intersubjective or phenomenological level, in the sense that the trauma and cultural significance of such a phenomenon and its impact on the 'social vitality' of group life (Card, 2003, p. 63) – the contemporary and intergenerational relationships and connections people have within a genus – is inherently a *lived experience*, which can only be fully understood through the intersubjective meanings that the victim groups attribute to the social and cultural harms visited upon them. It therefore stands to reason that the verbal testimonies of those who have experienced 'social death' are crucial to understanding it. As Wise (2017a, p. 4) argues, by focusing on the experiential dimensions of genocide, we introduce a vital 'complementary phenomenological layer of understanding' which can enrich our comprehension of an experience which, by its very nature, eludes the grasp of most, and help us better appreciate the distinctive harms associated with genocide.

The aim of this research is therefore to document the experiences of predominantly the Sengwer and Kikuyu in the former British colony of Kenya and predominantly the Gomeroi, Githabul, and Wangan and Jagalingou nation in New South Wales (NSW) and Queensland, Australia, not because they are the only groups experiencing ecologically induced genocide, but because their experiences are indicative of the nature of relations of genocide in both countries. Where I do refer to the experiences of other groups, again, it is because they shed further light on the genocidal structuring dynamics that are the focus of this book. Through a comparative approach, the research seeks to identify and tease out the commonalities and fascinating differences in the unfolding of the genocidal structuring dynamics due to the imposition of the capitalist mode of production, or what I have elsewhere described as a *mode of eco-genocidal destructive production* (Crook, Short and South, 2018), in two different sites of colonisation, united by their connection to the British Empire and the global political economy it helped construct. By mode of eco-genocidal destructive production, I am referring to the manner in which the capitalist mode of production, in order to expand production and generate capital, must first destroy extant forms of material culture and forms of organising economic production. The effect is eco-genocidal. As we will see later, this two-stage process involving first destruction followed by expanded capitalist production mirrors the two stages of colonial genocide explicated by the founder of the concept of genocide, Raphael Lemkin (1944). The precise manner in which this happens is the subject of this book.

The field research included over thirty semi-structured interviews with participants across multiple sites of extraction and 'conservation' in predominantly Queensland and NSW in Australia and the Cherangani Hills in Kenya. The aim was to carry out interviews with those recruited via existing contacts with Indigenous and non-Indigenous activists made by myself using purposive sampling, with a view to expanding this participant group via snowball sampling. After beginning with general biographical questions, I asked broad open-ended questions about how they were impacted by various development projects, about the various forms of loss and social harms experienced on a personal and collective level due to those projects and their associated forms of (colonial) governance. I explained from the outset that the aim of my research was to draw attention to the experiences of the victim groups and to understand the nature of these harms. In almost all cases the participants would use, if not the language of genocide itself, an idiom that connoted genocide or cultural destruction. The limitations of relying on snowball sampling, such as selection or referral biases, were to some extent mitigated by the triangulation of the data with analysis of documentary evidence and other primary sources, such as statutes, court rulings, government documents, NGO data and relevant secondary literature.

In the identification of the techniques used to bring about genocide I will use Lemkin's eight techniques (1944, pp. 82–90), to which I add the ninth, the ecological foundation. They are the following:

1. Political: involves the cessation of self-government and destruction of political institutions followed by the imposition of administration by the colonial occupants; all local political organisations are dissolved and imposition of parties of the occupant originating from the colonising power.
2. Social: involves the annihilation of leadership, abolition of local courts and the imposition of the legal system of the occupant.
3. Cultural: ban on the use of native language, imposition of colonial education and the rigid control or restriction/prohibition of cultural activities, for example, art, theatre, music and so on.
4. Economic: destruction of the foundation of economic existence.
5. Biological: interdiction of the reproduction of the group by decreasing the birth rate or the apprehension of the children and their assimilation into the group of the occupant.
6. Physical: mass murder and endangering of health.
7. Religious: disruption of religious influence, destruction of religious leadership.
8. Moral: creation of an atmosphere of moral debasement.
9. Ecological: the destruction of, or severance from the eco-systemic habitat of the group.

Finally, it is helpful to use the internationally recognised rights of Indigenous peoples as found in *United Nations Declaration of the Rights Indigenous Peoples* (UNDRIP) (UNGA, 2017) as useful proxies for measuring the extent and unfolding of relations of genocide. Their relative retardation, violation and degradation are in inverse proportion to the unfolding of the genocidal structuring dynamics, since the denial of these rights make meaningful group existence untenable. They will be particularly useful for gauging the extent of genocidal structuring dynamics in the modern period given their dominance and prevalence in the discourse and struggle surrounding the subject of this chapter. In particular:

1. Free, prior and informed consent (FPIC) (Article 19).
2. Rights to self-determination (Articles 3 and 31).
3. Rights to land (Article 26) which are pivotal to their cultural integrity and the remedial rights that allow them to protect said rights.

The denial of FPIC on development projects or the right to self-determination *prima facie* constitute existential threats to the cultural integrity of a social collective or group that is uniquely susceptible to the crime of genocide (Abed, 2006, pp. 308–30), namely 'culture producing' groups (Moses, 2010, p. 23), who consent to a life in common, whose culture is comprehensive and whose membership cannot be easily renounced (Abed, 2006, pp. 308–30). The denial of the first two are cultural genocidal coercive processes, in addition to constituting arguably political and social techniques, since the *genos* or social group 'exists by virtue of its common culture' (Lemkin quoted in Moses, 2010, p. 25), a social structure, like all social structures that must be understood diachronically (Elias, 1978, pp. 113–16), where change is integral to its flourishing. Ergo, genocide is the forcible disruption or interdiction of the process of cultural change or reproduction of the *genos* (Powell, 2007, p. 538). Cultural change emanating from the group itself cannot take place if and when the denial of the first two rights takes place. The denial of the right to land, or indeed its destruction through ecologically destructive practices, also menaces the collective existence of a group, particularly where Indigenous groups are concerned, who are, by definition, *territorially bounded* and whose cultural and spiritual vitality is tied to the land (Abed, 2006, p. 326). The denial of land rights is so fundamental to group integrity that it most probably impinges on all nine foundations of group existence listed above.

Through a comparative analysis of the two loci of genocide, I aim to illuminate and tease out the fascinating similarities and differences that comparison affords. This will underscore the utility of a political economic approach otherwise defined as neo-Lemkian above. Finally, by employing theories of global political economy, such as those drawn from radical political economy and geography traditions,[5] the inner connections of global capitalist economic and geo-political structures with the Australian and Kenyan colonial sites will be illuminated.

Chapter outlines

This work consists of six chapters. Chapters 2 and 4 will begin with an analysis of the political economic, legal and discursive context of the genocidal and ecocidal processes of the Indigenous groups that form the focus of my study in Kenya and Australia respectively. Chapters 3 and 5 will go on to analyse and dissect the lived experience of the aforementioned Indigenous groups in the current period and try to grasp, both in their own words and through the application of the synthesised apparatus outlined above, the ecocidal and genocidal impacts of both extreme energy and the extractive industries and their associated forms of governmentality and the institutional matrix of neoliberal climate governance, being careful to illuminate the structuring dynamics of the colonial settler/Indigenous relations. Further, these chapters will trace the origins of ecologically induced genocide, in both the local structural matrix between the capitalist state and the national economy and the related categorical imperatives of capitalistic production and its structural relationship to the *larger international forces of capital accumulation, trade and investment*, belying what Wise (2017b, p. 34) calls the 'domestic fallacy', the tendency in genocide studies to privilege state-centric causes which lead to 'inadequate International Relations analyses of the production of genocide' (Shaw, 2012, p. 2).

The concluding chapter summarises the findings of the book; arguing that in essence, the settler-colonial–Indigenous relation, in the age of the Anthropocene and a global ecological crisis, is characterised by the genocide-ecocide nexus (Crook and Short, 2014, 2020). Furthermore, the chapter will attempt to underscore the interlinkages between Indigenous struggle and the broader struggle against the ecological crisis, which the preceding analysis has pointed to. It will expound a way, in the age of ecocidal capitalism, that can forge a generalised climate resistance, leading us beyond the rotten machinery of ceaseless economic expansion, accumulation of (exchange) value and the insatiable exploitation and raping of the planet for the aggrandisement of an ecological elite governing a planet stricken by the greatest existential threat to organised human existence in history.

Notes

1. The remaking of nature leads to what O'Conner (1994, p. 165) described as 'the second contradiction of capitalism', as the eco-destructive mode of production undermines the conditions of the (re)production of the capitalist system itself.

2. Much of it is only now being translated via the MEGA project (Marx-Engels-Gesamtausgabe).

3. Harvey (2003b, p. 64) defined 'spatio-temporal' in the following manner:

Overaccumulation within a given territorial system means a condition of surpluses of labour (rising unemployment) and surpluses of capital (registered as a glut of commodities on the market that cannot be disposed of without a loss, as idle productive capacity, and/or as surpluses of money capital lacking outlets for productive and profitable investment). Such surpluses may be absorbed by: (a) temporal displacement through investment in long-term capital projects or social expenditures (such as education and research) that defer the re-entry of current excess capital values into circulation well into the future, (b) spatial displacements through opening up new markets, new production capacities and new resource, social and labour possibilities elsewhere, or (c) some combination of (a) and (b).

4. Marxism has often been accused of Eurocentrism and a stagiest' 'evolutionary' or unilinear theory of history, of a type with developmentalist thinking that had grave consequences for the Indigenous and colonised all over the world (Churchill and Larson, 1992; Samson and Short, 2005, p. 7–8). However, many scholars have disputed this characterisation, showing Marx evolved in his thinking and in many respects matured beyond a Eurocentric, unilinear understanding of history (Anderson, 2016a, ch. 5).

5. See for instance Smith (2006, 2008); Callinicos (2009); Harvey (2001, 2003a, 2003b).

Chapter 2

Australia then: the architecture of dispossession

The colonial structures which have yet to be dismantled have persisted throughout the history of Australia (and Kenya) as a colonial settler state, in various modalities and historically specific phases; the long chain of genocide mutates and evolves through time. In other words, as with any social phenomenon, it has a history. There are common threads and sharp breaks, continuities and discontinuities. The task is to identify and trace the varying modalities, discourses and institutional formations (Wolfe, 2006a, p. 388). Wolfe (2006a) argued 'genocidal outcomes have not manifested evenly across time and space', referring to native title in Australia or Indigenous sovereignty in the US, which were 'hardly equivalent to the impact of frontier homicide'. Though the preceding exploration in Chapter 1 of social death does not imply a normative hierarchy of genocidal techniques, nevertheless, this 'unevenness' is suggestive of an evolution and mutation of genocidal techniques, which will be placed within a broader context of the imperatives of the respective settler colonial economies and their corresponding political economy.

It is precisely this unevenness that I aim to show in the following chapters, illuminating the manner in which these genocidal processes are continually shaped by the changing structural imperatives of the Australian political economy and its relationship to the global capitalist chain of trade and investment; that is to say, both the continuity and breaks in the nature and form of relations of genocide, showing how at each turn, the eco-genocidal process is shaped by the structural imperatives of the settler colonial capitalist system. Above all, I show how the nature of relations of genocide in Australia in the past and today and the shifting 'structural target of the settler colonial logic of elimination' (Strakosch and Macoun, 2012, p. 44) are conditioned by the dialectical interaction between eco-cidal logic of capital on the one hand, and the settler colonial logic of elimination on the other, and Indigenous resistance to both logics.

Australian society on the cusp of colonisation

It is beyond the scope of the book to describe in any detail the nature of precolonial contact Indigenous societies.[1] The section on Indigenous socie-ties at the threshold of colonisation serves *only* as a heuristic device to bring into sharper focus the varying impacts of European expansion and its correlate, settler colonial relations of genocide on the essential founda-tions of Indigenous social formations, as well as cast light on how and why some Indigenous social formations were able to adapt to Australian settler capitalism at various stages in its history and geography. Ultimately, it seeks therefore to shed further light on what was once poignantly described as 'the great Australian Silence' – the unacknowledged relation between two social groups *within a single field of life* (Stanner, 2009, p. 189) [emphasis added]. What I sketch here, and it is only an imperfect sketch given the inherent pitfalls when using Western epistemologies and frames (Attwood, 1994), is what Sansom (1988) called 'Aboriginal commonality': those features of social and cultural life held in common by all Indigenous social formations or nations. The Indigenous of Australia have occupied the continent for at least 65,000 years, arguably the oldest civilisation on earth. Their mode of production, or economic figuration in the language of neo-Lemkianism, could be described as hunter-gatherer. By this is meant a mode of subsistence characterised by 'the absence of direct human control over the reproduction of exploited species, and little or no control over other aspects of population ecology such as the behavior and distri-bution of food resources' (Panter-Brick, Laydon and Rowley-Conwy, 2001, p. 2). Whether the forces of production, the means of production combined with labour, can strictly be characterised as hunter-gatherer, is open to debate, with some arguing that, at least in some territories, the Indigenous economic figuration not only changed their environment through burning to 'manage' migration of herbivorous herds but also reached a techno-logical peak in eel farming (Butlin, 1993, p. 56; Broome, 1995, p. 124). It has also been speculated that Indigenous societies were on the cusp of agriculture, gardening and the domestication of animals (Tindale, 1974, p. 94). Rhys Jones (1968) and palaeontologist Duncan Merrilees (1968) independently argued Indigenous societies of Australia had for millennia practised a form of 'fire-stick farming', which shaped the flora and fauna of 'The Biggest Estate on Earth'. Heather Goodall (2008, p. 16) has gone as far as to say that *no* Indigenous society relied solely on 'nature', but rather used various techniques and strategies (productive forces) to increase the carrying capacity of their lands. In any case, what is pertinent for the study here is the fact that Indigenous material culture did not, unlike the capitalist system that would be violently imposed on the Australian continent, violate the regulative ecosystemic laws leading to a metabolic rupture, in the fashion described in the section on capitalist ecology in Chapter 1 (Peck, 2013, p. 230).

In fact, the Indigenous social formation's superstructure, juridico-political and ideological relations, or what Keen (2003, p. 2) refers to as institutional fields such as religion, marriage, cosmology, kinship, governance structures and so on, alongside Indigenous production relations, was embedded in kinship relations which enabled the local clans to ecologically sustain themselves and mitigate the material vicissitudes of the hunter-gather mode, in innumerable ways. Remarking on pre-contact Indigenous social formations in the region of the state of Victoria, Broome (1995, p. 123) noted the significance of ecological responsibilities embedded in the religious world views and kinship systems of Indigenous people:

> Each clan owned particular stories about the journeys and creations of the great ancestral beings. The natural world was shaped by, and still contained, the power of these great ancestors. People, land and ancestral beings were bound together in a oneness through a totemic relationship. *Each person through their totem had power and responsibility to care for land and living things.* [emphasis added]

In Indigenous philosophy, the beliefs in mythic beings who create and shape the natural world is usually referred to as 'Dreamtime' or 'the Dreaming', primordial forces or totemic ancestors who created the world and its landscapes (Dreaming) and left behind ancestral law that Indigenous societies must follow. This ancestral law, is in a manner of speaking, mapped onto the land, rivers, plants and animals, by 'songlines', which traces the trails taken by the sacred spirts of the Dreaming, who left behind marks on the landscape as they created it, imbuing it with spiritual significance, creating a 'mythic geography' (Servello, 2010, p. 673). This totemic and animistic philosophy imbued the natural landscapes with religious significance and invested features of the natural world with souls, ensuring that living in harmony with natural rhythms and natural metabolic cycles was a preeminent moral duty (Servello, 2010, p. 672). Sadly, this Indigenous figuration would be violently disfigured and absorbed into the Australian colonial political economy, preserving those aspects that were functional and amenable to its imperatives.

The various phases of genocide that would unfold shortly after the arrival of European, mainly British colonists, broadly speaking can be defined as firstly: *Frontier violence*, where open and direct physical confrontation and violence was the principle genocidal technique used to bring about the pacification of Indigenous people and suppression of Indigenous sovereignty as a means to securing access to land. The period of frontier violence depended on the region and colony, but it lasted right up until the end of the nineteenth century and even into the beginning of the twentieth in Australia's Northern reaches: Northern Queensland, the Northern Territory and the Western Australian Kimberly region (Russell, 2005, p. 108). Secondly: *Protection (welfare) regimes*, wherein colonial authorities increasingly resort to institutional and bureaucratic measures, primarily though 'protection boards', to pacify Indigenous people and extinguish Indigenous sovereignty. This phase is defined by attempts to biologically or culturally 'absorb' Indigenous people into a homogenous settler-colonial culture, designed to breed out the 'Aboriginal problem' (Edmonds and Carey, 2017, p. 380) – at times segregation and concentration are the predominant techniques and at other times 'integration', but all serving the ultimate purpose of extinguishment. Finally, *the recognition phase*, broadly speaking from the late 1980s onwards, and perhaps best symbolised by the High Court ruling which 'granted' native title rights to Indigenous people, known as *Mabo & Others v State of Queensland* (now on in Mabo), will be the main focus of Chapter 3, the second chapter focused on Australia as a site of relations of genocide. In this period Indigenous civil and land rights and eventually self-determination are recognised and even legislated for, but in a manner conducive to the continued (re)production of the settler colonial political economy.

Each stage of the colonial project would need to be legitimated and supported by a system of colonial discourses, representations and racial categories which possess a constitutive logic and structuring power, designed to impoverish meaningful land rights and sovereignty and reduce Indigenous rights to that of occupancy and usufruct (Wolfe, 2006a, p. 391). These colonial discourses ranged from what Moses (2000, p. 9) described as an 'optimistic Enlightenment anthropology' to what I descibe as a 'cynical enlightenment anthropology'. It was optimistic because the position of Indigenous people on the lowest rung of civilisational development was due *not to race but environment*, rooted in more 'benign' abolitionist and evangelical notions of protection, which considered Indigenous people at best itinerant 'savages' living in a state of nature, bereft of permanent social structures. This was an 'optimism' that still conceived of 'civilising' assimilationist initiatives to make

Indigenous people adopt the large-scale sedentary farming and grazing of the white colonist. It was cynical once the colonial discourses embraced social Darwinist ideologies which categorised Indigenous people as 'the lowest link in the connection of the races' (Banner, 2005, p. 108), and 'child-like' and intellectually inferior, where inferiority was attributed to *immutable* racial characteristics. If the discourse didn't outright condone extermination and 'final solutions' it simply accepted the inevitability of the eradication of Indigenous peoples as their population numbers collapsed due to disease, despair, starvation and other social and psychological dysfunctions caused by the various processes of dispossession and domicide (Moses, 2000, p. 96) – the 'doomed race' theory as it was known (Moses, 2000, pp. 95–7; Reynolds and May, 1995, p. 176). This was an increasingly influential theory among colonial administrative circles, which took hold in the latter half of the nineteenth and early twentieth century, along with biologically determinist notions of race (Stepan, 1982), peddled by notable explorers and colonial administrators like Sir Harry Johnston (1902) and perhaps best epitomised by the work and 'humanitarian ethnography' of Sir George Grey (1840, 1841; see also Lester, 2016). What this entire spectrum of thinking had in common, whether it was optimistic or cynical, was the assumption that their inferiority pushed systems of governance, or indeed Lockean property, beyond their reach (Strang, 1996). In particular, the British believed that the land was *terra nullius*, or a land without landowners or even civilised beings, and so the land was there for the taking (Lloyd, 2010, p. 26).

The rosy dawn of relations of genocide

However, it is important to understand that the manner in which the genocidal structuring dynamics today, just as they were during the 'rosy dawn' of Australian settler capitalism, are ever being conditioned, in the final analysis, by the imperatives of capital accumulation and the global chain of capitalist production and trade (Marx, 1976a, p. 915). In essence, the relations of genocide and settler–Indigenous relations from the outset, and as they passed though the various phases or regimes of genocidal structuring dynamics, were at each historical juncture conditioned by: firstly, the capitalist system and its attendant laws of motion and the corresponding chain of global capitalist production and trade, and the place within the global division of labour that Australian settler capitalist economy would assume; secondly, the balances of social forces between 'the rapacious alliances in the settler states and capitalist landed, mining and financial classes in all the settler zones' and the various Indigenous nations resisting their total annihilation and colonisation (Lloyd, 2010, p. 29). Put simply, the historical road to the architecture of dispossession now in present-day Australia and its corresponding genocidal structuring dynamics were conditioned dialectically by the nature and imperatives of Australian settler capitalism, embedded in a global political economy, and the resistance to it in the lead up to the watershed moment of the Mabo case, which would usher in the modern phase of relations of genocide.

I will briefly explicate the manner in which each phase of genocide was conditioned by the above dialectic. The capitalist system was implicated in the ecocide and genocide inflicted on the Australian continent and dispossession of the Indigenous population long before the British Empire first arrived on the Australian continent in 1788, with its first fleet of officers and convicts. The colonisation of NSW and Van Diemen's Land was driven by the need to offload a surplus population of convicts, vagabonds, prostitutes and, generally, the immiserated and pauperised social layers filling British prisons; the deportation of this 'surplus' population acted as a social and political pressure valve (Lloyd, 2010, p. 24; McMichael, 1980, pp. 315–16). This penal settlement became all the more important with the loss of the American colonies in the 1770s. The initial impetus on the part of the British empire to establish a penal colony in Australia as a depository for criminals and then later political criminals, which ultimately set in train a historical process that would unleash ecocidal and genocidal forces, can be explained by the laws of motion of the capitalist system: in particular the general laws of capital accumulation (Crook and Short, 2019). Fundamentally, the drive to cheapen the factors of production and increase the productivity of labour (Marx, 1976a, p. 773) in the long run produces a surplus population or 'reserve army of the unemployed', who at various moments in the production cycle can no longer be profitably employed (Marx, 1976a, ch. 25). It would be these layers of society, 'the lowest sediment ... [that] dwells in the sphere of pauperism' (Marx, 1976a, p. 797), which would commit crimes against the sanctity of property and fill the jailhouses of Great Britain and eventually the fleets sailing to Port Jackson (Sydney). In essence, the population dynamics unique to the capitalist system gave fateful impetus to the establishment of a penal colony on the other side of the globe.

Once the penal colonies had been established, of course, they would have to become self-sufficient, just as the Kenyan colony would have to be, as we will see in Chapter 4. In the beginning this proved difficult, and when it became clear that the settlers were there to stay and competing for game, land and water, low-intensity guerrilla warfare broke out between the Indigenous population and the colonists. It is at this point that we witness the beginning of the phase of frontier violence. By its close towards the end of the nineteenth century, according to one historian as many as 20,000 Indigenous of Australia were killed in a century of resisting the expanding frontier, 10,000 of those killed in Queensland alone (Murray, 1996, p. 19; Reynolds and May, 1996, p. 178). In the same period, Indigenous resistance to colonisation exacted a death toll of 3,000 Europeans and 3,000 more wounded (Reynolds, 1987, p. 133). The combined impact of land seizures, deprivation of food and water sources, exotic diseases and frontier massacres would have devasting effects on population numbers. By some accounts, pre-contact population size was as high as anywhere between 300,000 to 1,500,000 (Bourke, 1998; Butlin, 1993). By the end of the first century of colonial occupation that number had fallen to as little as 100,000 (Kiernan, 2007).

With the onset of the nineteenth century, two logics of imperialism dialectically interacting but distinct (Callinicos, 2009; Harvey, 2003b) would breathe new life into the ailing colony and simultaneously unleash a devasting wave of genocidal destruction on the continent. *Firstly,* the logic of geo-political competition, or what Harvey terms the *territorialist logic* of state, and, *secondly,* economic competition or the politics of production, exchange and accumulation. London was concerned to see off imperial rivals in the region, principally the French (Thorpe, 1992, p. 89). Moreover, the colonies in NSW served a strategic importance, in that they would stymie efforts by the French empire to set up a Pacific trading hub on the Australian continent. In fact, the acquisition of the Australian continent allowed the British to strengthen trading links with its most important colony, India, as well as the Far East and the Pacific, and resume large scale transportation of convicts (Thorpe, 1992). This is a geostrategic logic that, as we will see in Chapter 4, drives the initial colonisation of Kenya, as well.

The logic of capital would eventually get a foothold on the Australian continent with the take-off of industrialisation across north-western Europe (Lloyd, 2004, p. 4). This would drive an increase in trade on the international markets and a rapidly growing surplus population of convicts, a much-needed supply of labour for the burgeoning capitalist economy, and give the Australian colony a renewed significance and importance to the British Empire. The Australian colony, like many others, would become an important outlet for over-accumulated capital and, through geographical expansion, a means of orchestrating what Harvey (2003a, p. 139) called 'spatio-temporal fixes' to the capitalist system's contradictions, and provide an 'outside' for British capital (Luxemburg, 1963) seeking higher returns on investment and overseas markets for its capital and consumer goods as well as cheaper inputs, in the form of primary agricultural goods and mineral and fossil resources.

It is in this political economic connection that we find the structural drivers of the frontier violence phase and the otherwise obscured logic of its pacifying role, for it was the thirst for land, wool and minerals that drove accumulation by dispossession (Harvey, 2003b, 2005, pp. 137–82) and the '"creative destruction" of pre-capitalist [Indigenous] ecological-political orders' (Havemann, 2016, p. 186; Coulthard, 2014). In other words, it was the developmental priorities of the nascent colonial state that proved fatal to Indigenous life: a nascent colonial state rooted in the emergence of a form of Australian settler capitalism, land-extensive and capital intensive, hitched to the rise of the world market created by the European empires and European industrialisation; a world market that involved both flows of capital and labour and manufactured goods into Australia and flows of strategic raw materials out of Australia. This would include the discovery of minerals and base metals such as copper and later gold, tying the fortunes of the burgeoning colonial economy to the 'industrial-ising effects of raw material exports' and yet another form of capitalist extractivism (Lloyd, 2010, p. 27). The temperate climate and extensive grasslands of NSW and later Tasmania and Queensland lent itself to European-style agriculture, and crucially sheep and cattle grazing; wool becoming a crucial export, supplying the textile mills in the colonial metro-pole (Lloyd, 2010). The thirst for wool in the heart of the empire would drive a land grab throughout Australia from the early nineteenth century to the early twentieth that would dispossess the Indigenous population and deprive them of access to their means of subsistence and their way of life more generally (Thorpe, 1992; Rowley, 1970). The 'sheep and cattle were the shock troops of empire' (Russell, 2005, p. 77). By the 1860s, 400 million hectares of land in the south-east had been occupied by 4,000 Europeans with 20 million sheep (Moses, 2000, p. 96). This wasn't just genocidal but ecocidal.

In this connection is revealed the global interconnectivity of the structure of genocide with a larger chain of global capitalist production and trade. Wolfe (2006, p. 394) remarked that settler colonialism:

> presupposed a global chain of command linking remote colonial frontiers to the metropolis. Behind it all lay the driving engine of international market forces, which linked Australian wool to Yorkshire mills and, complementarily, to cotton produced under different colonial conditions in India, Egypt, and the slave states of the Deep South.

The forging of the global chain was driven by the *extensive* expansion of the British Empire, with Australian settler colonisation representing the 'development of a global process of "primitive accumulation"' (McMichael, 1980, p. 309).[2] As argued in the previous chapter, this process embodied both the *first stage* of the political economy of genocide, namely the extra-economic processes of plunder, fraud or theft, from *without* the circuits of production and capital accumulation that alienate social groups from their lands through processes such as 'enclosures' or imposed private ownership, ultimately reconfiguring new global value chains (Harvey, 2003b, pp. 63–88), which leads to the *second stage*, what is known as the value-contradiction in radical political economy embedded within the various industrial (and financial) processes operating *within* the expanded reproduction of the circuits of capital, what Harvey (1981, p. 10) referred to as 'capitalism's inner dialectic'. These two stages correspond with Lemkin's two-stage process of genocide, 'the destruction of the national pattern of the oppressed group: the other, the imposition of the national pattern of the oppressor' (Lemkin, 1944, p. 79). The development trajectory of Australian settler capital and its agents, wool growers or the 'squattocracy',[3] must be seen as part of a global process, anchored in *Pax Britannica*, in which, under the doctrine of imperial trusteeship, the Australian colonies were consolidated as regions structurally incorporated into a world imperial division of labour. In short, a mercantilist free-trade system ensured the British imperial economy a steady supply of wool and shaped the developmental trajectory of a settler economy hitched to the export of primary goods exports. And so 'in the first fifty years the Australian colonies were built on the sheep's back of the squattocracy' (Davidson, 1987, p. 203).

The ecocidal nature of rapidly expanding pastoral frontier must not be overlooked. In fact, stock farming not only shifted or expanded frontiers rapidly but also annexed and exploited the resources that hunter-gatherer societies depended on for their survival, consuming water and grazing at a rate beyond the capacity of the ecosystems to regenerate themselves. Moreover, the influx of livestock wrought havoc on the itinerant flows of hunter-gatherer communities, who were, ecologically speaking, as well as from the vantage point of indigenous ontology, a part of the local ecosystems as much as any other form of life. Barta (2010, p. 303) observed that land 'was something to which they in many profound ways belong, rather than something which belongs to them'. Their hunting, fishing and gathering activities were disrupted, with herds of game, a critical source of food, displaced and edible plants trampled on. This is what the anthropologist Birdsell (1970, p. 117) described as 'ecological completion', adding '[t]his is a classic ecological replacement situation in which protected animals and dispossessed men competed directly for a wide variety of food staples necessary for the existence of both. In Australia the animals always won' (1970).

Of course, it was the animals not Indigenous to the land that won. Here, we can vividly see Lemkin's second stage of genocide, the imposition of the cultural pattern on the occupied space, possessing an *ecological* dimension. The remorseless process of capital accumulation, in this context unleashed onto the fertile plains of Indigenous land through the conduit of the international markets, would drive the extraction of resources at a rate that the land would struggle to absorb, requiring more and more of a 'throughput of materials and energy', leading to a metabolic rift. The imposition of what Barta (1987, p. 239) called an 'alien economic, social, and political order' or what Alfred Crosby (2004) called 'ecological imperialism' on the Australian continent would have predictable ecocidal consequences. This was what I earlier defined as a mode of eco-genocidal destructive production. In fact, the ecocidal consequences of the pastoral system would have devasting impact on Indigenous life modes, a system which in its wake imported a variety of diseases, microbes, weeds, domesticated plants and animals, or what Crosby (2004, p. 89) described as 'portmanteau biota'. This in turn, weakened the ability of the Indigenous figuration to *fully* reproduce itself on the now remade colonial ecologies, furthering the severance of Indigenous people from the land and simultaneously deepening the process of primary accumulation.

Though the balance sheet of genocide in Australia involved the destruction of the vast majority of the over 500 distinct Indigenous nations, after the violence of the frontier phase of colonisation (and the associated theft of land, massacres, ravages of disease and miscegenation) died down by the close of the nineteenth century, *some* nations or Indigenous groups, partially destroyed, nevertheless managed to maintain some connection to their land and their culture. This would be determined by their outward articulation with the colonial economy and the degree to which they could adapt to its imperatives. What is at issue here is the dialectical and contradictory relationship between the logic of capital accumulation and the logic of Indigenous elimination. To the extent that Australian settler capitalism could find use for its Indigenous population, their modes and ways of life would be spared, at least partially. What Schaller (2008a, 2008b) has previously called *situation coloniale*, which under some circumstances necessitated the retention of Indigenous labour even if as a group they continued to experience genocidal forces, is evidenced in some parts of remote Australia towards the latter half of the nineteenth century. Due to institutional and academic inertia, a recognition of what is referred to as 'Aboriginal participation' in Australian economy has taken time to filter through various disciplines, even Australian labour history taking relatively long to acknowledge Indigenous involvement in the settler economy (Irving, 1994).[4] What is sometimes referred to as 'hybridisation', in which elements of both settler capitalist or market relations and the concomitant forces of production and technologies are fused with the largely nomadic Indigenous mode of production (Altman, 2005), was not the general rule. It was the product of varying degrees of coercion and was confined to those industries that were to some extent 'compatible' with those Indigenous communities who, as a necessary precondition, were already partially destroyed by colonisation and its associated techniques of land theft, violence and disease.

The industries that were compatible with the Indigenous mode of life were so because they relied on intermittent and seasonal labour which allowed Indigenous peoples to maintain a conditional though warped connection to their traditions and land. The preeminent example of this form of hybridisation from the mid-nineteenth century were pastoral and cattle stations, where the landholdings, particularly on the land extensive developments in the northern semi-arid zones, could be as large as a million hectares, thus allowing Indigenous workers to live on the land on the pastoral stations, in the forms of family camps. Indigenous people were able to materially subsist, at least in part, by, for instance, going 'walkabout' or wandering off the pastoral stations in the Northern Territory and Queensland to hunt bush meat and flora during the wet season (Lewis, 1997, p. 7; Anthony, 2004, p. 126; May, 1994, p. 87). This would permit the maintenance, on colonial terms, of connection to land and of spiritual and ceremonial rites and obligations (Castle and Hagan, 1998, p. 30). In other words, cultural survival (Curthoys, 2015, p. 220). The fact that they were not fully and completely severed from their relationship to the land and thus not fully integrated into the circuits of pastoral capital, their notions of work defying 'capitalist penetration' (May, 1994, p. 87), made Indigenous labour suitable to the seasonal nature of the work *and* increased further the surplus that could be extracted from their labour, since the capitalist agricultural industry didn't have to concern itself with the *costs of their reproduction* (May, 1994, p. 88). Some industries required Indigenous labour, such as pearling in western Australia until the late 1880s, but did so in a form that separated Indigenous people from their country and social group (May, 1994, p. 219). Where Indigenous labour was not required, for instance in the south-eastern colonies like NSW which possessed incipient industrialising economies with a relatively high level of technological development of production relations, incarceration in missions and reserves far removed from their traditional land, or domicide, was the norm (Thalia, 2003, p. 279). However, as we will see, a small minority of Indigenous people would be 'proletarianized'. Indigenous 'bush skills' were generally not required for the burgeoning industrial economy in regions like NSW, which instead turned to the much larger pool of white settler labour (Edwards, 1992, p. 190).

In a landmark essay, Bob Thorpe (1992, pp. 157–221) argued that Indigenous people were kept alive to the extent that they could be profitably employed as 'colonised labour', using this framework to analyse Indigenous participation not just in the nineteenth but also twentieth century, whether it was employment in the remote pastoral stations or employment, underemployment and mass unemployment in the most menial jobs in the late twentieth century. Anthony Thalia (2004) has argued that in fact the relation between the pastoralists and Indigenous people in the Northern Territory, and their otherwise competing land claims, are better understood as feudal relations of power and dependence. By not paying them, their mobility in the market was restricted, and instead they were forced to work on the stations and rely, at least in part, on food rations given to them by the station owners and the land they camped on. Thalia (2004, p. 119) rightly rejects the argument forwarded by Ray Evans (1984) that they were slaves, pointing out that their ability to maintain 'moral communities' meant they were far from the 'natally alienated' plantations in North America and the Caribbean.

These examples serve to underscore the relationship between the form and severity of genocidal techniques and the changing imperatives of the Australian settler colonial economy. For to the extent that Indigenous production relations and lifeways were compatible, they would be partially preserved. Once the terror and violence during the frontier violence phase had settled down, the squatter pastoralists slowly realised that Indigenous people had skills and knowledge of the terrain, hunting and tracking skills that could be harnessed in the cattle industries (Rowse, 1987, p. 84; Thalia, 2004, p. 123). In fact, Indigenous people would be hired as horse breakers, shepherds, stockmen, guides, diplomats and property managers (Reynolds, 1990, pp. 84–6; Russell, 2005, pp. 84–6; Goodall, pp. 66–88). These skills of course, derived from what was earlier described as their hunter-gather mode of production in precolonial times.

To the extent that this relationship prevailed, a system of *internal colonialism* existed where the Indigenous figuration continued to exist in an asymmetrical relation with the colonial pastoral industry. Pierre-Philipp Rey (cited in Foster-Carter, 1978, p. 218) argued that in what was earlier described as the 'margins' between the ever-expanding sphere of capitalist production, trade and investment and the 'social vitality' of the non-capitalist world, when capitalist imperial forces colonise a new territory, rather than immediately destroy any proceeding pre- or non-capitalist mode, instead it reinforces those modes precisely to ensure the continued provisioning of labour, goods or resources. Harvey (2003a, p. 146) argued similarly that on occasion primitive accumulation or accumulation by dispossession, the first key structure in the political economy of genocide, even when co-extensive with proletarianisation, involved some degree of *preservation* and co-opting of pre-existing cultural and social structures. Wolpe (1980, p. 248), ruminating on the dialectical interplay between two modes of production in a colonial context, observed in South Africa that 'The capitalist sector benefits from the means of subsistence produced in the non-capitalist MP to the extent that it is *relieved of paying a portion of the necessary means of subsistence by way of indirect wages'* [emphasis added].

This observation is apt for our purposes here and mirrors the relationship of Indigenous workers with their pastoral masters on the stations and bears a striking resemblance to the *situation coloniale* that will be explored in the Kenyan settler colonial space. Philipp Rey (cited in Foster-Carter, 1978b, p. 218) identified three stages in the articulation of the capitalist system with other modes. They were:

1. An initial link in the sphere of exchange where interaction with capitalism reinforces the pre-capitalist mode.
2. Capitalism 'takes root', subordinating the pre-capitalist mode but still making use of it.
3. The total disappearance of the pre-capitalist mode.

These stages can be adapted to the present case study. The initial link here was of course the theft of land but also, at a later stage in some regions, the exchange of labour for payment in kind or wages and access to pastoral land for cultural and subsistence reasons. This would lead to the second stage where the Indigenous mode is subordinated, though not entirely destroyed. The third stage is of course arguably the most disturbing and chilling since it posits the complete disappearance of the Indigenous mode for some Indigenous groups at least, with perhaps the caveat that it may survive at the superstructural level, or their culture or cosmology, in the manner suggested by Moreton-Robinson (2009a, p. 11). It is a contradictory process where the articulation undermines *and* perpetuates the Indigenous figuration in distorted form. The question, when we turn later to the present juncture in Australia (and Kenya) is, do we still find evidence of the second stage, or has this articulation already begun moving towards the third, the *total* disappearance of the pre-capitalist mode?

This experience is better captured by a theory of a dialectical articulation between *two* modes of production, under conditions of internal colonialism, in what Laclau (1977, p. 33) called an economic system and what I refer to as a *social formation*: really existing, historically determined societies in their totality, often made up of many coexisting economies. Rarely, in the history of capitalism, if at all, has the capitalist system existed in pure unadulterated form. Afterall, capitalism itself arose out of the womb of feudalism within the boundaries of the nation-state. Marx (2002) observed such a scenario with multiple coexisting modes of production in nineteenth century France, in his historical treatise *The Eighteenth Brumaire of Louis Bonaparte*, where capitalist, feudal, patriarchal and petty commodity production existed side by side. In all such concrete social totalities, the ultimate character of the social formation is determined by the dominant or hegemonic mode, the 'general illumination which bathes all the other colours and modifies their particularity' (Marx, 1973, pp. 106–7) and gives it its laws of motion or operation. The concept of internal colonialism serves to remind us of two things about this articulation. Firstly, that this articulation was performed under conditions of asymmetric, colonial power relations. Secondly, that this articulation served to develop the settler colonial society at the expense of the Indigenous social formation. This formulation is arguably superior to what was earlier described as hybridisation, since the latter serves to obscure the asymmetric colonial power dynamic. Moreover, the articulation between modes of production framework allows us to identify the laws of motion of each respective mode of production and the social relations that dominate this relationship.

Hartwig (1978, p. 129) argues that the articulation of two modes does not revolve around the extraction of surplus labour alone, but may include:

1. The *extraction of commodities* in different ways.
2. The extraction, not of the product, but of labour-power. In both these instances the associated political policy is likely to turn on the domination and conservation of the non-capitalist societies.
3. In other instances the particular mode of economic exploitation may be accompanied by a policy aimed at or having the effect of destroying the non-capitalist societies, such that the producers are 'freed' of the means of production. [emphasis added]

In light of my research, the 'extraction of commodities', includes raw materials such as fossil fuels or subsurface minerals, and even in some cases factors of production such as land itself, and does under specific historical circumstances entail the partial preservation or 'domination and conservation of the non-capitalist societies' as we will see when we examine present day Australia. In essence, those circumstances hinge on a number of factors, but most crucially Indigenous resistance, which shifted the terrain of settler-Indigenous relations onto the field of recognition politics.

With the subsumption of labour to capital, a key moment in the institutionalisation of the capitalist system and the penetration of the labour process by the social relations of production, in its growth out of the womb of feudalism and, I would argue, as it metastasises around the world, it does so 'on the basis of the technical conditions within which labour has been carried on *up to that point in history*' (Marx, 1976a, p. 425) [emphasis added]. The subsumption of labour consists of two stages. First is *formal* subsumption, where capital subsumes labour on the basis of the technical conditions in which it historically finds it, where labour carries on much as it had done prior to subsumption, or for our purposes, prior to colonisation. This is then followed by *real* subsumption, where the labour process and social relations are fully transformed through the application of science and technology. The former is based on the extraction of *absolute* surplus value, the latter, through the application of machinery and technology, *relative* surplus value. Although Marx spoke of formal and real subsumption in connection with *wage labour* only, it is, I would argue, applicable to all production relations in which capital extracts, directly or indirectly, surplus value from labour on the basis of 'the technical conditions in which it finds it'. This may include the semi-feudal relations found on the pastoral stations in Australia, or those we will see on white settler farms in the White Highlands in Kenya in Chapter 4, where again African peasants would negotiate access to settler land in exchange for working on their fields. In a similar fashion, Hardt and Negri broaden the scope of formal and real subsumption to embrace all forms of pre-capitalist production relations, with clear implications for colonial scenarios where two economic systems are forcibly conjoined in the manner argued above. They argue 'the richness of the category of formal subsumption is indeed that it reveals the economic and cultural differences of labor, land, society, and community that have been subsumed within capitalist production *but maintain their connection to the territory and the past*' (Hardt and Negri, 2017, p. 182) [emphasis added].

The important ontological point is that to the extent capital in its forcible articulation with the Indigenous mode can utilise Indigenous labour (or in certain specific concrete historical junctures as we will see when we discuss present day Australia, Indigenous land and resources), and extract surplus value given the *technical conditions in which it historically finds it*, that social figuration will be preserved at least partially in a deformed state. Thus, for the vast majority of Indigenous people who were not employed in the pearling or pastoral industries for instance, they would be murdered or corralled and concentrated on the reserves and missions, trapped, as we will see below, in a Lefebvrian 'grid'. Those whose 'foreign processes of production' (Hardt and Negri, 1994, p. 15) could not be adapted to the needs of capital would be deemed biopolitically unfit and subject to the most extreme genocidal techniques. This will be underscored by the Kenyan settler colonial experience in Chapters 4 and 5.

The 'closure of the frontier' and the beginning of what I term the *Protection (welfare) regimes* phase of relations of genocide, would see the colonies turn to bureaucratic and legislative measures to control and regulate the lives of Indigenous people (Edmonds and Carey, 2017, p. 378). The purpose was to 'protect' Indigenous people by either segregating them or assimilating them into the white settler population. The foundation of these bureaucratic regimes would be the protection boards and protection acts, passed over a period of forty years at various stages across the six colonies. By the turn of the twentieth century, all the six colonies would have protection regimes in place. Although they differed in detail, in essence they severely restricted the freedoms of Indigenous people, controlling everything from where they could live and work, whom they could marry and even who was and wasn't officially 'Aboriginal' (Evans et al., 2003, p. 138). Some protection systems, such as the Queensland model laid down in the *Aboriginals Protection and Restriction of the Sale of Opium Act 1897*, placed a greater emphasis on segregation, forcing Indigenous people to live on reserves or missions. By the 1930s, legislation would emphasise instead cultural 'assimilation' and 'biological absorption', fuelled by a fear of a rising demographic 'time-bomb' of mixed race or 'half-caste' and 'octoroon' Indigenous people that might one day become the demographic majority and presumably upend their colonial supremacy, a fear which weighed heavily on the minds of the white settler population (Chesterman and Douglas, 2004). A national policy emerged across the various state and Territory administrations to deal with the 'problem' of 'half castes' which sought to forcibly integrate them and 'make the "Aboriginal problem" and Indigenous people disappear' (Edmonds and Carey, 2017, p. 379). In light of the aforementioned 'cynical enlightenment anthropology', only those who were not entirely of Indigenous descent had any hope of becoming 'civilised'. Tragically, these bureaucratic regimes and the policy of forced assimilation would lay the foundation for the 'Stolen Generations' (Tatz, 1999, p. 333), the many thousands of Indigenous children, in particular those deemed 'half-caste', removed from their families to be raised and 'educated' on church led missions, reserves or compounds.

Eventually, policies that sought to control the fertility and offspring of Indigenous women, as well as stipulations regarding who Indigenous people could marry, would become increasingly the focus of the various protection regimes. With the passing of the federation of the six Australian colonies into the newly born Australian nation, this system of protection regimes would endure, with its logic of miscegenation as a technique to eliminate the Indigenous problem by forcibly incorporating 'half-caste' children into the body of white settler society. What one historian described as a 'surveillance and control network' would persist until the 1970s (Kidd, 2007, p. 13). Fundamentally, the control regimes constituted an example of what Lemkin understood as biological destruction". However, the import and intended effect of the control regimes was not limited to biological destruction.

Indeed, the role it played in the reproduction of the settler colonial economy was a just as crucial, if poorly understood, function of the protection regimes. For instance, in Queensland, the *ad hoc* Indigenous labour arrangement on the cattle stations was formalised under the auspices of the protection regime. An amendment to the protection legislation was passed in 1904, giving powers to protectors to regulate Indigenous labour by requiring a formal contract in which part of the wage would be paid into a trust account. This administrative system determined how Indigenous people could spend their wages as well as who they could work for, thus functioning as a means of enforcing cultural assimilation (Castle and Hagan, 1997, p. 66). However, it would also diminish labour costs and thus facilitated the reproduction of the pastoral system. Alongside the economic and cultural 'adaptability' of Indigenous labour to the needs of the pastoral economy and its ability to reproduce itself, at least partially outside the circuits of pastoral capital, the racialised exploitation of Indigenous labour through the 'protection regimes' played a crucial role in the viability and reproduction of the pastoral system. In fact, these regimes were designed not just as a solution to deal with the 'demographic problem', either as system of racial apartheid or biological absorption, but as a prop to the pastoral industry.

First and foremost, by concentrating and incarcerating the Indigenous population 'the land outside the reserves could productively be utilised by pastoralists, miners, settlers and agriculturalists' (Jackson, 2018, p. 82) and resistance more easily managed (Edmonds and Carey, 2017, p. 378; Maddison, 2017, p. 428). In this sense they were yet another technology of planning – a form of 'social spatialisation', what Fields and Fields (2012, p. 18) call *racecraft* or what I call 'racial spatialisation', central to the reproduction and expansion of capitalism (Lefebvre, 1974). These are technologies or spatial practises such as segregation and concentration of a racialised population enabled through mapping, cadastral planning, surveying and ultimately issuing of Crown land under various forms of licences and leases. The control regimes and their associated spatial practices perform two vital functions for the settler colonial regime. Firstly, they were key to erasing the cultural maps of Indigenous societies, reconstituting land as a blank map bereft of settlement and 'ripe for the taking'. Secondly the defining, controlling and regulating of spaces with prescribed relations that governed who could and couldn't utilise the land and the forms of social life that could flourish within them (Jackson, pp. 72–3). These processes, termed 'internal territorialization' by Vandergeest and Peluso (1995, p. 387), were necessary for both the consolidation of the colonial state formation *and*, in the final analysis, the rebranding of geographical space with the hot iron of exchange value, essential to facilitate the expansion of the capitalist system, throughout the history of the colony, to the present day. As Blomley (2003, p. 127) sharply observed, 'maps and cadastral surveys are generally treated as the handmaiden of property'. In the final analysis, the protection regimes and their systems of concentrating Indigenous people on reserves were a crucial part of racial spatialisation and ensured Indigenous struggle for sovereignty and land were 'contained and defined in their spatiality and *trapped in its "grid"*' [emphasis added].

But the utility of the protection regimes did not end there. They were a disciplinary technology, a form of biopolitics that would acculturate Indigenous people to the new work ethic and work patterns of a capitalist economy and society (May, 1994, p. 75). Among the many control measures were included stipulations regarding Indigenous property, work and payment of wages, which implicitly, and sometimes explicitly, condoned non-payment. Often the wages were diverted into state-managed accounts held in trust for Indigenous workers, though often these wages would be misappropriated and never returned to Indigenous workers (Kidd, 2007, p. 8). This system of fraud and embezzlement, would eventually be replicated right across Australia (Kidd, 2007).

Ultimately, having already driven the push to find a dumping ground for a swelling convict population, a mode of eco-genocidal destructive production would eventually manage to gain a foothold on the Australian continent, which once consolidated, would unleash a structural logic of its own: *a logic of elimination, driven by a logic of accumulation*. The combined necessities of 'exiling politically and socially dangerous convicts from all parts of the Empire and of finding raw materials formed the dynamic of Australia's development' (Lloyd, 2004, p. 4). But the logic of elimination, driven by a logic of accumulation, is just one side of the dialectic of the settler–Indigenous relation. One important legacy of the structural logic would be to forge a new historical actor, in the form of the 'Indigenous proletariat' that would have huge consequences for the political economy of genocide in Australia and usher in the recognition phase. The road to the reconciliation period, which we are still living through, where the state formally began a process of seeking redress for the crimes of settler colonialism, was paved with Indigenous resistance; a resistance qualitatively influenced by the emergence of this new historical actor.

Indigenous peoples for itself

It is beyond the scope of this book to offer a detailed account of the history and evolution of Indigenous struggle. However, a brief sketch of this topic and its most salient features will help us appreciate the role it played in shifting the terrain of relations of genocide onto the terrain of reconciliation and the emergence of a new Indigenous historical actor. As we saw earlier, resistance began almost immediately, and attempts at redress, cynical or not, began very early in the life of the settler colony. What would eventually become articulated as 'land rights' in the modern vernacular of human rights were from the very beginning opposed by those who gained most from the dispossession of Indigenous people. They were, broadly speaking, the pastoral industry, landed interest and settler colonists (and through trade, moneyed interests and industrialists in the metropole) and, as shown below, mining interest or the mineocracy (Foley and Anderson, 2006, p. 83). Resistance during the frontier violence stage of the colonisation of Australia was low-intensity armed struggle or guerrilla warfare. Occasionally it consisted of large, pitched confrontations, but usually it consisted of small low level 'stealthy revenge expeditions' that killed shepherds, speared sheep and cattle and ransacked settlers' property (Goodall, 2008, p. 78). With the eventual closing of the frontier and the shift to more bureaucratic means of control, resistance did not simply cease. Despite the draconian and totalitarian measures imposed on the reservations and missions on Indigenous life, many still continued to resist. In fact, the reservations and missions were often the locus for the transmission of culture and sites of resistance (McLisky, 2007). Those who would escape the clutches of the protection regimes would do so for a variety of complex reasons, with circumstances differing from state to state and region to region.

With the nature of 'control' shifting between segregation and cultural assimilation or biological absorption across region and time, conditioned by the vagaries of local and global economic and political events, various 'push' and 'pull' factors would compel the migration of some Indigenous people to the towns and cities. The self-explanatory desire to escape the draconian conditions of the protection regimes could be compounded by exogenous factors, such as increasing pressures on land and increasing social and cultural hostility from nearby white settler communities. Just such a confluence of factors would prove fateful for resistance to relations of genocide and the birth of the Indigenous land rights movement.

In short, the combined 'push' of the desire to escape the draconian protection regimes and by the beginning of the twentieth century, lawfully mandated protection board dispersal policies that sought to break up Indigenous communities surviving under colonial terms in the reservations and cattle stations, where they previously practiced their culture, traditions and rituals, and maintained links with their ancestral lands and the wider kingship network, abetted by mutable definitions of indigeneity (McCorquodale, 1987), and the 'pull' of demand for labour during and after the First World War, led to the exodus of 'lighter caste' Indigenous people from reserves (Read, 1994, p. 55). For instance, in NSW, according to Goodall (1995, p. 76) '[t]he Board believed it was necessary to *push adult Aborigines into the white working class* as isolated labourers and aimed to make them live independently of government and separate from any other Aborigines' [emphasis added]. This was primarily motivated by fears of a fast-growing population of 'full-blood' Indigenous people that would irrevocably 'pollute' the Anglo-Australian culture and of course, shift the balance of power (Goodall, 1995, p. 76).

This sort of forcible assimilation would for some lead to their migration to the bigger cities looking for employment where they would join the ranks of an industrial workforce. It would be their forcible integration into the body of the Australian working class, in a manner not too dissimilar from the enclosures in England that played a very significant role in both the development of Indigenous political consciousness and the consequent form the resistance would take throughout the twentieth century. This would pave the road to the period of recognition of land rights, native title and the period of 'reconciliation'. It was with the rise of modern civil rights and equal citizenship campaigns, and with it the demand for land, in the 1920s and 1930s, stretching into the 1960s, that we saw the birth of the modern Indigenous land rights movement (Foley and Anderson, 2006). This new Indigenous movement would leave behind the tactics of guerrilla war and adopt what Russel (2005, p. 130) described as 'European political technologies'. Critically, this new modality of struggle involved building alliances with sections of the white settler community. These collaborative struggles were in part a function of the creation of what historian of Australian labour history and Indigenous history Padraic Gibson (author interview, 10/02/2017) calls the 'Aboriginal proletariat' in the urban sectors in the towns and big cities.[5] This development was crucial in the transmission of these 'European political technologies' back to the rural areas and building links with sections of the white community and ultimately the rise of a pan-Indigenous consciousness and identity central to the Indigenous land rights movement.

The vast majority of Indigenous people, even in the more industrially developed regions of Australia such as the South East, lived and (until very recently) still do live in remote rural areas. A significant number became agricultural workers with important implications for later forms of Indigenous struggle. In fact, in the period of the birth of the modern civil rights movement in the early twentieth century, the majority of Indigenous labour was deployed in the pastoral and agricultural industries or on the missions and stations (Rowley, 1971b, pp. 217–348). However, despite its numerical size, it was the conditions of class formation in the cities, and of course the impetus given to industry by the capitalist economic mode that led to the rise of an *urban* Indigenous proletariat and thus the basis for new forms of political struggle. To coin a phrase, the settler colonial bourgeoisie produced their own Indigenous gravediggers. Indeed, Heather Goodall (2008) and John Maynard (2007) have shed light on the pivotal role Indigenous activists forged in the crucible of industrial capitalism in the towns and cities played, especially Melbourne and Sydney. In fact, Indigenous proletarians – two NSW Indigenous wharf labourers, Fred Maynard and Tom Lacey, in particular – were key to founding the first Indigenous political organisation of the twentieth century, the Australian Aboriginal Progressive Association (AAPA), formed in the 1920s (Foley and Anderson, 2006). The 1930s saw the emergence of the Aborigines Progressive Association (APA) in NSW and Australian Aborigines League (AAL) in Victoria. Again, Indigenous wage workers were key (Horner, 1994, pp. 38–41). Bill Ferguson, who was a founder of the APA, was heavily involved in union activism, being a member of the Australian Workers Union (AWU), and in organising unemployed Indigenous *and* white workers in the Depression hit 1930s (Goodall, 1996, p. 19). The dialectical relationship of influence moved in both directions. For instance, the role of these organisations in fostering a pro-Indigenous sentiment within parts of the union movement and the broader workers' movement was important (Horne, 1994, pp. 105–16).

This is not to ignore the immediate drivers of the formations of these organisations: the above-mentioned policies of forcible disbursement and assimilation and the consequent sharp reduction in Indigenous reserve land and the nature of the draconian protection boards. In fact, the consequences of these policies were threefold. Firstly, the emergence of a minority of Indigenous proletarians who were forcibly dispersed by (or willingly escaped from) the regimes of control as part of the authorities' population transfer policies into 'the white working class' (Goodall, 1995,

p. 76) and mainstream society more generally, in an attempt to destroy Indigenous alterity. Secondly, by this process was brought about the creation of historical subjects, 'black émigré' communities in cities and towns across the country that would retain organic connections with their communities and their ontological relationship to land and who could not only leverage their new found structural power by virtue of their proletarian relation to capital but transmit back to the rural communities forms of political organisation developed in the cities (Russell, 2005, p. 132). For instance, Fred Maynard, the founder of AAPA, whilst he worked on the docks in Sydney, maintained his connection to his community. It was the issues of land theft, child removal and the tyrannical nature of the boards in the rural areas that motivated him to form the AAPA (Maynard, 2007, p. 17). But it was the lessons he learned as a dock worker involved in radical trade unionism with the Waterside Worker's Union that taught him how to agitate and organise (Russell, 2005, p. 132). Thirdly, and crucially, it was their lived experience in the cities as workers, workers who were connected to the rest of the world through an international chain of capitalist production and trade that exposed them to international networks involved in anti-colonial struggles and the radical and revolutionary traditions of the global labour movement that allowed them to garner a generalised awareness of the plight of Indigenous people right across the country (Goodall and Cadzow, 2009, pp. 142–50).

These new organisations, which gradually built regional networks that fostered organisational and ideological connections between Indigenous communities, undoubtedly played an important role in fostering a sense of pan-Indigenous identity, an *Indigenous peoples for itself*, symbolised most potently by the Day of Mourning protest in 1939, a protest which reflected an awareness of the common struggle to resist colonisation and invasion (Russell, 2005, p. 135). This pan-Indigenous nationalism would be further bolstered in the post-Second World War period by a growing resistance from Indigenous proletarians in the rural and pastoral industries, most notably the Pilbara strike of 1946 and the Wave Hill Strike of 1966. In the former, Indigenous stock workers in Western Australia took strike action which impacted 6500 square miles of pastoral land and was supported by dozens of trade unions and trade and labour councils. One trade union, the Australian branch of the Seaman's union, banned the transport of wool from affected areas (Foley and Anderson, 2006, p. 86). Their action would inspire the later Wave Hill strike. In 1966, 200 Gurindji stockmen in the Northern Territory walked off the station, due to the decision to delay the granting of equal pay under the federal industrial awards in 1965 (Chesterman and Galligan, 1998, p. 194; Goodall, 1995, p. 383) and the refusal of international meat-packing company Vestey Brother to pay out wages. The Gurindji would eventually set up an independent camp in Wattie Creek twenty kilometres away, closer to the community's sacred sites. This was a symbolic act that represented the wider aims of the action beyond mere industrial equality and a bold demand for the return of ancestral land. The dispute would run for seven years until the coming to power of the Labour Whitlam government, a radical administration by the measure of Australian politics, determined to establish Indigenous land rights. The Gurindji dispute played a significant role in hastening the passing of the Aboriginal Land Rights (Northern Territory) Act 1976 (ALRA), a cornerstone of the modern legal land rights regime, as did a series of (failed) legal challenges to commercial development in Indigenous land in the post Second World War era, including most notably what became known as the *Gove* case, in which Indigenous *Yolngu* people in the Gove region took the Commonwealth and the mining corporation Nabalco to the Supreme Court, seeking an injunction to prevent the opening of a mine on their lands. Sadly, Mr Justice Blackburn ruled that the plaintiffs had no case since there was no basis for native title in Australian law.

This was also the period of a global anti-colonial movement and an international post-war regime traumatised by the horrors of the Second World War, in large part rooted in 'the almost metaphysical obligation to rule subordinate, inferior, less-advanced peoples' (Said, 1994, p. 10). The response from the West was a faltering belief in their 'metaphysical obligation' and a growing awareness, driven by the wave of anti-colonial struggle around the world, that universal principles would need to form the basis of a new world order, one which cast notions of racial hierarchy and civilisational superiority, if not into the dustbin of history, at least in a light that was more palatable. A new global political space was emerging, grounded in emerging global information technologies and the rise of new international political fora like the UN, couched in the ideological and legal rhetoric of human rights. Naked exercise of imperial power was no longer tenable and an accommodation to a growing decolonisation movement could not be avoided.

The new international order was and still is flawed, however. Not least due to which is the maintenance of a global political economy that all but reproduced relations of imperial and (neo)colonial domination, a global political economy that we will examine more closely when we consider the fate of modern Kenya in Chapter 5, and an international legal and political architecture that lacked teeth (Alston, 1998; Carraro, 2019, p. 1081), and did little to bring substantive and concrete change to those who were once described as the 'Fourth World', Indigenous peoples. Despite the commitment from the UN to decolonisation and self-determination, the latter being a core principle enshrined in the UN Charter motivated by the desire from most of its member states to create obstacles to the exercise of imperial or colonial power, this commitment would have limits. In what become known as the 'blue water' thesis, the new decolonisation regime would be restricted to overseas territories formerly ruled by European states and stop short of applying to Indigenous peoples subject to continuing forms of internal colonisation, for fear it would encourage secessionist movements (Iorns, 1992, p. 212). It could only apply to *aggregate* populations of independent states and not any of its 'substate' groups (Anaya, 2004, p. 77).

Nevertheless, arguably without the changes the new regime wrought, and the international pressure exerted on Australia, later legal and political reforms such as the Mabo case discussed below could not have been possible (Russell, 2005, p. 135). But this new international environment did not just consist of a new international legal and political architecture founded by sovereign states, but of course was buffeted by the winds of the anti-colonial movement which, as earlier, continued to transmit its ideological radicalising influences. The new wave of Indigenous activists of the 1960s and 1970s were increasingly influenced by the black power movement, just as their counterparts in the 1920s had been, this time by the likes of Malcolm X and the US Black Panther Party (Foley and Anderson, 2006, p. 88). Again, just as it was in the 1920s and 1930s, the loudest voices calling for the return of ancestral lands to Indigenous people were the thousands of Indigenous activists based in the major cities like Sydney, Brisbane and Melbourne, who by virtue of their location and class position were situated at the crossroads of radical class politics, the radicalising influences of the black power and anti-colonial movement of overseas, whilst maintaining connections with their communities in the rural areas. Some of these rural areas now began to organise a 'homelands movement' in central Australia, leaving reservations and missions and returning to set up camps on their ancestral land (Foley and Anderson, 2006, p. 91).

Rattled by this groundswell of resistance on multiple fronts, the prime minister at the time in a forced error made a statement on Indigenous land rights that would have consequences for decades to come. Prime Minister McMahon chose the occasion of 26 January 1972, 'Invasion Day', to issue a statement repudiating the very idea of Indigenous rights to land. Almost immediately, Indigenous activists assisted by the CPA embarked on the journey to the capital to set up the 'Aboriginal Tent Embassy' (Short, 2003, p. 33). What the Tent Embassy demonstrated in bold and poignant relief was, despite regional differences, the maturing of an idea; the intersubjective notion of a united pan-Indigenous movement (Bennett, 1991, pp. 13–14). This movement would increasingly focus on the necessity to claim land and assert self-determination.

Given the lack of a history of treaty making with its Indigenous population, unlike the histories of Indigenous settler relations in Canada, North America and New Zealand, the notion of treaties between Indigenous nations and the settler colonial state began to acquire increasing importance within the Indigenous political movement (Short, 2008, p. 33). With the commencement of a campaign for a treaty between Indigenous peoples and the state adopted by the National Aboriginal Conference in 1979, a forum established by the federal government in 1977 for the expression of Indigenous views, and shortly after the Aboriginal Treaty Committee (ATC), a think tank made up of white academics whose establishment credentials and social capital gave the campaign a degree of respectability it had hitherto not had (Short, 2008), then Prime Minister Bob Hawke was presented with the *Barunga Statement* (AIATSIS, n.d.) by representatives from the Central and Northern Land Councils, statutory bodies established by the aforementioned ALRA.

The statement called for the granting of the full range of civil, political, religious, economic and social and cultural rights, the same rights pronounced with such fine lofty words on the treaties and declarations that were promulgated in the UN human rights system in the post-war era. But more than this it demanded compensation for lost lands, access to sacred sites, the right to be educated in their own language, culture and history and the respect for Indigenous identity, and the rights to manage their own affairs, but above all it demanded a system of Indigenous land rights. What followed was the bowdlerising of these demands and their watering down, as they filtered through the corridors and chambers of Australia's political system, until gone was the language of land and justice and in its place the language of education and reconciliation, epitomised by the *Council for Aboriginal Reconciliation Act of 1991* (CARA). That created the *Council for Aboriginal Reconciliation* (CAR), formed to lead the reconciliation process. This act established a ten-year reconciliation process, which would redirect the lobbying efforts and political energy of the Indigenous treaty movement towards what Short (2008, p. 1) described as 'a more equivocal open ended "reconciliation" initiative'. According to the Hawke government at the time, the Australian people would not accept a treaty till they were first educated. The era of recognition and reconciliation was born.

In this new phase of relations of genocide, the *modus operandi* of colonial power takes on a new form, recasting settler–colonial Indigenous relations and effecting accumulation by dispossession through forms of *discursive* and *administrative* genocide made possible by the colonial-settler state (Alfred, 2009; Povinelli, 2007). Now relations of genocide operate primarily through forms of colonial *governmentality,* or what Coulthard (2014, p. 3) described as 'asymmetrical exchange of mediated forms of state recognition and accommodation'. In other words, state recognition and accommodation are used to reproduce settler colonial relations, not attenuate them (Reinhardt, 2016, p. 54). Nevertheless, despite the 'cunning of recognition' (Povinelli, 2007), it was the dialectic of resistance that forced the settler colonial state onto the plain of recognition politics, shifting the relations of genocide into this new phase. This new phase in the relations of genocide will be epitomised by the passing of the *Native Title Act of 1993* (NTA), legislation that ostensibly offered land rights to all Indigenous people across Australia on a federal level, but in practice did so in a manner that only deepened colonial relations of genocide.

The rise of the mineocracy

The forcible integration of the Australian colony into the global economy would bequeath a legacy that is crucial to illuminate if we are to understand the present juncture in the history of Australian relations of genocide. Firstly, an Australian political economy which although not subject to underdevelopment and relations of dependency that other former colonies of the European empires in the Global South still suffer from, including Kenya, nevertheless through its integration into the British-led global imperialist chain of capitalist production and trade (Scammell, 1968, p. 126), would become an export-orientated extractivist state significantly dependent on the overseas sale of primary goods; in particular, as we will see, the extraction of fossil fuels. What I call the 'mineocracy', the hegemonic mining fraction of the Australian ruling class, will play a crucial role in shaping modern relations of genocide. Secondly, due to the above examined Indigenous struggle dovetailing with a global decolonisation movement and the rise of a global human rights regime (Arfat, 2013), as well as the rise of the mineocracy, a period of *ostensible* reconciliation with Indigenous communities and recognition of their rights would take place in a form that would denude and disembowel those rights (Samson, 2020), in large part due to the mineocracy. It is crucially, the convergence of a resurgent mineocracy shaped by global political economic dynamics with the shifting terrain of settler Indigenous struggle brought about by Indigenous resistance that will determine the present historical juncture and the nature of relations of genocide in today's Australia. Having discussed the role of Indigenous resistance in the previous section, we will now turn to the second of these dialectically interwoven legacies.

The reorganisation of capitalism known under the 'rubric of neoliberalism' (Harman, 2007) was an essential background enabling factor for the continued dominance or resurgence of the mining lobby or fraction of capital in Australia, the mineocracy. One which reorganised capital, on a global and national scale, and its conditions of expanded reproduction, to attempt to restore profitability to a system that had suffered systemic crises from the mid-1970s onwards. Chief among them was the long-term decline in the rate of profit, beginning as early as the late 1960s (Choonara, 2013), combined with rising oil prices, reaching a dramatic peak with the 'OPEC' oil shock of 1973–4. These structural and proximate causes would combine to give rise in the US, UK and, to a lesser extent, other OECD countries to 'stagflation'; neoliberalism, in policy and governance circles, was the response (Harman, 2007).

As a form of reorganisation of capital, or in effect class warfare, it involved two dimensions. Firstly, a regime of orientation/war of manoeuvre which involved a frontal assault on the labour movement and dismantling of embedded social democratic institutions (Davidson, 2010, 2013). To that I would add frontal assaults on all communities who, as Wolfe put it dryly (2006, p. 388), are simply 'in the way', most pertinently for this book, Indigenous people. Secondly, a regime of consolidation/war of position, which involved a molecular process of gradual *commodification of new areas of social life* and the construction of neoliberal institutions (Davidson, 2010, 2013; Bargh, 2007) [emphasis added]. This commodification process will, as we will see below, implicate Indigenous territory and when we turn to focus on Kenya in Chapter 5, previously 'unconquered' spheres of nature in new forms of neoliberal environmentalism.

Finally, these two logics of neoliberalism manifest as government policies in response to the aforementioned structural crisis. They include, *inter alia*, privatisation of state industries, commodification of services (for example water or energy), or even pollination or carbon molecules (Chapter 5); financial deregulation; flexible labour markets; removal of protective tariffs and subsidies and exchange controls (domestically and internationally, in the latter case leading to globalisation); monetary policy; regressive taxation and even policies that could be described as forms of accumulation by dispossession (Harvey, 2003a, p. 145). Indeed, as Gordon (2006, p. 18) argues, neoliberalism involves 'the intensification of ... accumulation by dispossession' for Indigenous peoples. In essence, the reworking of state–market–civil society-relations to facilitate expanded reproduction, extended accumulation and the extension of the commodity form to hitherto untapped spheres of nature–society relations (Heynen et al., 2007, p. 10), necessarily involves another round of 'enclosures' of Indigenous land (and occasionally labour) at what was previously called the 'margins' of the capitalist world (Anderson, 2016a). These processes of enclosure, understood as the termination of complex assemblages of communal rights, under neoliberalism are, as we have seen in Australia and will see in Kenya, merely extensions of historical processes that stretch back many hundreds of years justified by and which gave shape to John Locke's moral defence of private property (Heynen et al., 2007, p. 10). Increased penetration of land, and in some cases commodification of Indigenous labour, are key to the success of the neoliberal project (Gordon, 2006).

What Sassen (2013) has described as the 'disassembling of national territory', to make it more amenable to global corporate interests and thus facilitate land grabs for extractivist purposes, involved transforming nation-state ownership over land and resources, undermining national sovereignty and driving new struggles over land. Territoriality is *still* settler colonialism's specific, irreducible element, only this time, rather than foreign colonial powers violently seizing land through military occupation, it is achieved through global economic regimes of trade, investment, privatisation and financialisation, which oblige states both in the Global South *and* the Global North to implement neoliberal reforms in a race to the bottom. The role of what Harvey (2003a, pp. 127–30) calls 'mediating institutions' like the IMF or World Bank, through the manipulation of credit and debt management, is crucial to understanding how the prescriptions of neoliberalism can be imposed globally. As Sassen (2013, p. 27) avers, 'formal sovereignty can easily coexist with coloniality'.

The intended effect of this reorganisation of capital and the associated policies was of course to restore levels of profitability to the preceding post-war boom that lasted from the end of the Second World War to the late 1960s (Campbell, 2005). The success of these manoeuvres and policies have been contested and arguably have been mixed (Brenner, 2006; Davidson, 2013). Nevertheless, a necessary outcome of this political process was the reorganisation of global economic governance along neoliberal lines. Critically, where Australia is concerned, this is enabled by an unholy alliance between *global* corporate interests and resources or 'extractivist states', restructured by foreign capital for the purpose of territorialisation of Indigenous land for extractive purposes (Bebbington et al., 2008; Howlett et al., 2011; Lyons, 2018).

What concerns us here is the impact this has had on capitalist extractive development and the co-extensive land grabs in Australia in the twenty-first century. Australia has always been dependant on mineral development; not long after initial colonisation, it assumed its role in the international division of labour as a political economy based not just on colonial pastoralism but, particularly towards the latter half of the nineteenth century, also *the extraction of minerals and fossil fuels* (Crook and Short, 2019; Howlett and Lawrence, 2019, p. 822). Indeed, the roots of the extractivist state, in its 'developer' role (Davis et al., 1993) and its pact with the mineocracy, which has endured to this day, were laid in the early nineteenth century (Howitt, 2001). Through processes of neoliberal globalisation, what Howlett et al. (2011, p. 317) described as the 'largest expansion of mining and energy' in its history took place, worth AUD $190 billion per annuum or 15 per cent of the economy (Cleary, 2011, p. 5), the proximate cause, made possible by globalising forces, which Clearly (2012, loc. 187)[6] calls a resources 'super-cycle' – the influx of investment tied to the industrialisation of China and India. In recent years, the commodity prices boomed, which saw prices become treble what they were in 2004 (Clearly, 2012, loc. 205), and fuelled the resource rush in Australia. These have now started to show signs of waning, explained in part by a global energy transition to renewables spurred by international agreements through the UNFCC (Lyons, 2018, p. 1). Nevertheless, it seems rising global demand for energy, combined with the slow-paced nature of that energy transition on the supply side (in part due to perfunctory efforts on the part of governments in international agreements), means higher energy prices are here to stay for the foreseeable future (Sen, 2021).

This has catalysed and deepened the process of state-corporate-led land grabbing and extractivism. In Australia, regulation of the extractive industries is not handled by independent statutory bodies but overseen by state government departments who directly report to ministers. In turn, these governments, given their dependency on royalties from energy extraction, have a financial interest to approve proposed developments and feed their 'growing addiction to mining revenue' (Cleary, 2012, loc. 270, 880), particularly if one considers Australia's unique fiscal arrangement where the Commonwealth will receive the lion's share of tax revenue, leaving states dependent on royalty payments from various forms of mineral extraction (Howlett and Lawrence, 2019, p. 823). In fact, its regulatory regime is so streamlined and optimised for the enticement of foreign direct investment in its energy sector that the Behre-Dolbear Group (2014), one of the oldest mineral industry advisory firms in the world, ranks Australia as only second to Canada in terms of leading investment destinations, due to the minimal 'political risk' (2014, p. 1) posed by its regulatory and legal regime. No doubt its 'auspicious' Indigenous land rights regime, forged in the crucible of the neoliberal restructuring of Australia, goes someway to minimising this 'political risk'. According to United Nations' criteria, Australia's commodity exports are so dominated by mineral and energy resources that Australia is classified as a *mineral-dependent economy* (Altman, 2013, p. 132). As Cleary (2012, loc. 45) observes with a palpable sense of alarm '[i]n less than a decade, the frenzied pace of Australian resource development has tipped the balance of coexistence to the point where mining dominates our society, our economy and even our political system'.

In the current world division of labour, Australian settler capitalism is positioned within it as a major exporter of mineral and fossil fuels. According to many, the mineral export trade is in the 'national interest' (Cleary, 2011, p. 5). Arguably, this global economic connection as a mineral-dependant exporter, historically and especially in the current period, emboldened the Australian settler-state as a colonial institution and delayed its demise on the ash heap of history, giving it a new lease of life and obstructing meaningful decolonisation, begun in the late 1960s as discussed above; the fabrication of a national crisis in the wake of Mabo and the institutionalisation of Indigenous land rights under the *Native Title Act of 1993* (NTA) testify to this structuring dynamic.

Beware of genocidaires bearing gifts: the phase of recognition

Understood dialectically, history is characterised by both continuities and sharp breaks with the past. Settler–Indigenous relations, or relations of genocide, are no less subject to historical change: architectures of dispossession have a history (Crook and Short, 2019). Since the dawn of the land rights era in the 1970s, inaugurated with the passing of the ALRA, and arguably brought about by Indigenous struggle as argued above, the mineocracy, insolubly woven into the global chain of capitalist investment, production and trade, has persistently and effectively reconfigured the state to diminish the substance and leverage of those rights in any negotiations with Indigenous nations (Altman, 2012); the social construction of a 'national crisis' mounted to enfeeble the NTA (discussed in detail below) would not be the first such campaign in Australian history (Altman, 2012, p. 54). The ALRA was the first of several important land titles to emerge in the land rights era. Passed by the Liberal-Country Party Fraser government, but given important impetus by the previous radical Labour Whitlam administration in the wake of mounting pressure from a resurgent Indigenous land rights movement and an increasingly militant Indigenous proletarian movement in the rural and urban areas examined above, the ALRA was stripped down to make it more acceptable to the mineocracy.

That is not to say that in its own terms it did not mark a significant advance of Indigenous land rights. Firstly, it created a new category of inalienable land title known as 'Aboriginal freehold'. This land would be held by land trusts on behalf of Indigenous landowners and managed by statutory bodies known as Land Councils (Altman, 2013, p. 122). Moreover, these Land Councils, funded by mining royalties, are statutorily empowered to advocate on behalf of the relevant Indigenous community in negotiations with commercial interests and claim land. The councils using the royalties to provide Indigenous communities with a degree of financial independence from the government is an interesting innovation (Altman, 2012, p. 54). Critically, ALRA would enable the legal and political architecture, and more specifically *a degree* of self-determination and self-governance that supported what would become known as the 'outstation movement', where Indigenous people in large numbers left their former reserves and missions to reclaim ancestral land (Austin-Broos, 2009, pp. 185–93).

However, although the ARLA (limited to the Northern Territory) does, at least ostensibly, ensure that Indigenous landowners have FPIC on any commercial building on the land, and, moreover, the right to refuse or veto, as well as receive compensation in the form of royalties, the statute stops short of conferring subsurface mineral rights. Justice Woodward, who had provided legal counsel for the Yolgnu people in the Gove case, was commissioned by the government, in what became known as *The Woodward Land Rights Commission* (Woodward, 1974), to establish a legal architecture for the realisation of Indigenous land rights. It was this legal architecture that became the basis for the ALRA. He advised against the inclusion of mineral rights to placate the mining lobby. Moreover, the right of veto is confined to the 'exploratory stage' with no second veto during the 'mining stage' (ALRA, 1976, Part IV), a restriction again due to industry lobbying (Rumler, 2011, p. 8) and limited where the 'national interest' case exception applies (ALRA, 1976, Section 40(b), Section 43). The exact meaning of national interest is left nebulous and opaque, open to interpretation in a manner conducive to vested interest. In the event that agreement is not concluded within the allotted time it can go to arbitration where again, no veto right applies (ALRA, 1976, Section 46(7)).

This legal architecture therefore structures an asymmetrical field of negotiation which institutionalises *unequal bargaining power,* a form of what Comaroff (2001, p. 306) described as 'lawfare', 'the effort to conquer and control Indigenous peoples by the coercive use of legal means', or what I call 'colonial lawfare'. It played a seminal role in giving shape to the current political economic and discursive landscape of settler colonial Indigenous relations and the struggles that followed. Indeed, the current historical juncture in the relations of genocide in Australia are better understood as what Coulthard (2014) calls in the Canadian context the 'recognition paradigm', or what Singh (2014, p. 49) describes as 'recognition from above'. Coulthard (2014, p. 3) argues:

> The now expansive range of recognition-based models of liberal plural-
> ism that seek to 'reconcile' Indigenous assertions of nationhood with
> settler-state sovereignty via the accommodation of Indigenous identity
> claims in some form of renewed legal and political relationship with the
> Canadian state. Although these models tend to vary in both theory and
> practice, most call for the delegation of land, capital, and political power
> from the state to Indigenous communities through a combination of
> land claim settlements, economic development initiatives, and self-
> government agreements, where colonial relations of power are no lon-
> ger reproduced primarily through overtly coercive means, *but rather
> through the asymmetrical exchange of mediated forms of state recogni-
> tion and accommodation.* [emphasis added]

Once again, the precise form and modality of genocide would be shaped
by the imperatives of the settler colonial capitalism. But it is important to
note that the terrain upon which settler colonial–Indigenous struggle is
fought is the political terrain of *reconciliation* and *recognition*. The forma-
tive influence of the ARLA gave significant shape to this terrain.

In the Australian reconciliation process, we see precisely the continuation of accumulation by dispossession through this beguiling modality
of 'recognition' politics and the granting of 'rights' to land and procedural rights which merely act to enable the continued dispossession and
colonisation of Indigenous peoples and the expanded reproduction of
Australian mining capital. In this current post-Cold War historical juncture
characterised by the salience of the human rights regime and human rights
discourse in international diplomacy (Arfat, 2013), such a reconfiguration
of settler state–Indigenous relations and the political economy of genocide
became a necessary ideological cloak to secure the expanded reproduction
of *Australian mining capital*, a fraction of the Australian ruling class key
to understanding settler colonial–Indigenous relations in the current
juncture. Recall Mohawk scholar Taiaiake Alfred's (1999, p. 58) warning
that the legislation of rights for Indigenous people is a legal and discursive weapon of the settler colonial state as it plays a central role in shaping and defining them.

To secure the interests of any particular fraction of the ruling class, and
by extension political power and the active consent of those ruled (a necessary prerequisite in Western-type societies with a developed civil society) – the Italian Marxist philosopher Antonio Gramsci argued this would
happen, not solely through the exercise of brute strength and coercive fore
of armed bodies of the state such as the police or army, but by the exer-
cising of influence through the private institutions of civil society, which
would play an educative function and through which the active *consent*

to the hegemonic order could be secured. This extension of the class state into the realm of civil society Gramsci called the 'integral' or 'extended' state (Liguori, 2016, pp. 1–25). This entailed two processes. Firstly, some concession to the interests of other social groups would be necessary. This would call for at least some sacrifice of the 'corporate' interests of mining capital: conceding procedural and consultation rights to affected Indigenous groups under the NTA. Secondly, the elaboration of a sophisticated ideological discourse that could unite disparate class fractions and other social groups: The construction of the 'recognition' and 'reconciliation' paradigm. The reconciliation process is an exemplary exercise in securing the hegemony of mining interests.

Freeman's (2002, p. 85) dictum regarding the institutionalisation of human rights is pertinent here. As he argued, human and other rights are the products of balances of power (Freeman, 2002, p. 85), such that during the process of institutionalisation, they are so, in a manner which eviscerates and emasculates them and makes them less able to challenge the structures of power they originally arose to address. We should not be surprised since, as Samson (2020) has so ably demonstrated, the antecedents of latter-day human rights discourse (and I would argue their associated forms of biopolitics and governmentality) are rooted in a constellation of intellectual traditions, namely the Western Enlightenment tradition, nineteenth century liberalism and the American and French revolutionary traditions, all of which were moulded to, and fundamentally shaped by, the prevailing imperatives and exigencies of European colonialism and slavery. As we saw in the encounter of Enlightenment thought with Indigenous people in Australia and will see in the following chapters devoted to Kenya, these roots, given nourishment by notions of 'cultural hierarchy' (Samson, 2020, p. 21), would bear poisoned fruits of racialised exception, elision and exclusion to the much-vaunted universalism of human rights.

Reflecting on this tradition, the great postcolonial thinker Aimé Césaire (1972, p. 3) put it more succinctly, perhaps better than anyone, when he inveighed against what he called 'pseudo-humanism', describing it as 'narrow and fragmentary, incomplete and biased and, all things considered, sordidly racist'. By the same token, the discursive manoeuvres woven into the fabric of human rights talk operating through racialised disciplinary knowledges and the 'outwardly raceless legal prose' (Samson, 2020, p. 12) make what Aileen Moreton-Robinson (1999) calls 'whiteness' invisible, as well as the epistemic, social and political privileges that it confers. This is so, above all, because the Lockean *individualist* construction of rights rooted in notions of alienable private property (which made possible the colonisation of Indigenous land and domicide in the first place), in their *colonial* form, presuppose the legitimacy of settler colonial sovereignty, which elides the long history of structural violence that continues to (re)produce the vast inequities on every conceivable social indicator (Samson and Short, 2006, p. 173; ABS, 2018a, 2018b). It is what Samson (2020) describes as the 'colonialism of human rights', infused with 'forms of knowledge affiliated with domination' (Said, 1994, p. 9) that enables the reproduction and maintenance of colonial relations of power. It is this process of institutional bowdlerisation and pseudo-humanism with all its exceptions and elisions that will characterise the period of recognition that as a phase has yet to come to a close.

This process of emasculation of human or Indigenous rights is aptly demonstrated by what is known as the Mabo case Australia, a pivotal turning point in the history of relations of genocide in Australia.[7] In 1992, the High Court handed a judgment that acknowledged the rights of Indigenous peoples to native title on land that had not already been forcibly annexed via colonisation. The devil is always in the detail, however. Despite ostensibly appearing to be a great concession on the part of the colonial state, native title could only be asserted if and when the concerned Indigenous groups could prove ongoing 'traditional connection' through Indigenous laws and customs and still occupy the land in question, meaning, of course, those who had already been dispossessed no longer had any claim (Short, 2016, p. 131). Short (2007, p. 859) invokes Freeman's warning when evaluating the nature of the native title regime in Australia and its requirement that Indigenous people pass a series of colonial tests. Wolfe (1999, ch. 6) described this as 'repressive authenticity': proof that your nation or clan have maintained occupancy and traditional governance structures since original colonisation in 1788, or that you still practise a culture considered 'traditional' and authentic. This was despite the preceding history examined above of mass killing and population collapse wrought by frontier violence, followed by the involuntary population transfers under the 'protection regimes' designed to separate Indigenous peoples from the rest of the population, and 'smooth the pillow' for a 'dying race'. Altman (2012, pp. 52–3) aptly describes this repressive authenticity as a discursive logic that either traps Indigenous people in a pre-contact fiction of essentialised 'traditionality' 'as if untouched by colonial history', or conversely a 'modernity' which disqualifies their claims to land, and so ultimately denies the intercultural reality of many Indigenous people. This form of thinking, correctly labelled 'repressive authenticity', will raise its ugly head once more in the later chapters examining the plight of Indigenous people in Kenya in the modern period.

To add insult to injury, even those who qualified under all the onerous and highly selective preconditions would not have the right of veto over development on their land, the latter due to laws introduced by the Howard government, the NTA, under the pretext of 'agrarian reforms' – once more, a colonial discourse of development that facilitated domicide, forcing them into an unenviable 'colonial dilemma'. This was a choice between refusing to be party to the ecological destruction of their land but risk having the land expropriated by the relevant state authority any way, if it was deemed in the 'national interest', and thus not benefit from any potential royalties (Short, 2007, 2010a),[8] or embark on the 'Right to Negotiate' provisions laid out in the NTA and enter into an Indigenous land use agreement (ILUA) for the proposed development known as a 'future act'. In recent years the federal government has required that resource developers fund the negotiations themselves, including the payment of travel, accommodation and sitting fees and paying for meetings (Burnside, 2008, p. 57). For the resource developer to fund the negotiations constitutes a conflict of interest and undermines the impartiality of the future act process and fundamentally alters the power dynamic (O'Faircheallaigh, 2006, p. 5). If after six months no agreement is secured between the concerned Indigenous party or 'registered native title claimant' and the resource developer, it goes to arbitration, a process or colonial dilemma that generally favours mining interests (Corbett and O'Faircheallaigh, 2006; Ritter, 2009), and often drives a wedge into Indigenous communities and fosters intercommunal conflict (Bebbington et al., 2008). Predictably, in the wake of the 1992 Mabo decision in the Australian High Court and the subsequent NTA passed one year later, native title across large swathes of land was extinguished either by 'valid grants of interests' by the Crown (O'Faircheallaigh, 2011), or to validate existing commercial titles that may have fallen foul of the Racial Discrimination Act (RDA) 1975, which gave legislative effect to the United Nations Convention on the Elimination of All Forms of Racial Discrimination (CERD) (Short, 2007, pp. 862–3).

In the *Wik Peoples v The State of Queensland*, brought to the High Court in 1996 by the Wik peoples, an Indigenous nation from western Cape York Peninsula in northern Queensland, the Court recognised that pastoral leases did not extinguish native title and did allow dual occupancy by both pastoral lease holders and Indigenous peoples. The decision, in fact, balanced the rights of the pastoralists and the rights of Indigenous peoples. Nevertheless, the alleged threat led to yet another socially constructed existential threat to health of the nation. Subsequently, the then Howard government introduced new legislation in the form of the 'Wik 10 Point Plan', which the deputy prime minister at the time claimed had 'bucketfuls of extinguishment' (cited in Short, 2008, p. 79), further extinguishing native title on vast swathes of pastoral land and narrowing the scope of native title rights in innumerable ways.[9] Short (2016, pp. 130–31; see also

Samson and Short, 2005, p. 11) argues that these reforms were introduced due to the exertion of influence by powerful commercial interests and in particular the extractive industries, who employed 'a campaign of misinformation' grounded on fear and spurious arguments about the greater good of development. Critically, this process of institutionalisation of native title was achieved through the construction of native title as a national crisis that jeopardised the wellbeing and future prospects of the Australian nation, largely orchestrated by the Mining lobby and aided and abetted by the national press and executive and legislative branches of the Australian government (Short, 2007). The purpose of the confected national crisis was clear. Short (2016, p. 131) explains:

> The 1993 Native Title Act's primary purpose was the validation of existing commercial titles and the provision of guarantees that future land negotiations would be conducted within the parameters set by existing colonial power inequalities – thus ensuring that the native title regime would offer Indigenous peoples no protection from settler colonial expansionist pressures powered by the engine of global capitalism.

It must be stressed that not all Indigenous groups resist forms of capitalist development on their land, and not all are necessarily coerced, in the strictest sense of the word. Some freely engage with the market or straddle both market and kinship relations in a form of hybridity (Altman et al., 2009). Lemkin was keen to stress the difference between cultural genocide and 'cultural diffusion' (Docker, 2008, p. 96). The former might be described as forced assimilation, which for him still equalled a technique of genocide. The latter involves a gradual, relatively spontaneous or voluntary process of cultural exchange and slow adaptation to new events and outside situations where the weaker culture adopts cultural practises that are considered more efficient or advanced (Docker, 2008, p. 11). Determining which it is can only be done empirically. Nevertheless, the denial of veto power amounted to a repudiation of effective Indigenous sovereignty and *de facto* extinguishment of native title, a right considered foundational under FPIC provisions of UNDRIP (UNGA, 2017). As Justice Woodward (1974) remarked, 'to deny Aborigines the right to prevent mining on their land is to deny the reality of their land rights'. Moreover, as we will see in the case studies below, very often those within Indigenous communities who choose to engage with the NTA, ILUAs and so on, and in effect adopt the market 'as the path to development' (Altman, 2013, p. 132), do so under conditions inherited from the past. Due to a history of dispossession, population transfer, dispersal campaigns, cultural assimilation, mass murder and ultimately forcible articulation with the settler colonial economy, Indigenous communities are already far progressed on the path to its 'freeing' from the means of production (Hartwig, 1978, p.129). Inversely, its precolonial mode and lifeways are increasingly less capable of supporting them (if at all), such that they are through the 'dull compulsion of economic relations' (Marx, 1976a, p.899) compelled to choose employment in the 'real economy'.

Perhaps even more troubling is what Burnside (2008, p.57) argues is the accompanying broader discourse of 'crisis', in which mining companies play a role in 'alleviating' the social and economic marginalisation and disadvantage of Indigenous people, which is recast as pathologies, dysfunctions and a 'culture of poverty' (Burnside, 2008, p.55). In a clear manifestation of neoliberal biopolitics (Foucault et al., 2014), the developmentalist discourse or *rationality*, as it has done in the past, reconstructs the Indigenous as a subject requiring, as the former Howard government desired, intervention on the part of resource developers. These mining companies are empowered with an 'industry mandate' to 'implement a certain vision of the good Indigenous society' where Indigenous people 'participate in the "real economy"' (Burnside, 2008, p.57). The vision: to transform kin-based societies into market-based ones (Altman, 2007, p.308). In essence, the hegemony of the mining fraction of capital in Australia and neoliberal global forces embodied in the form of transnational corporations configure a political economy that coerces Indigenous people to embrace globalisation and the market relations (Altman, 2013, p.132), and thus, in terms of their development, 'close the gap' between themselves and the rest of Australian society. In other words, Indigenous people who seek to maintain their cultural and spiritual connection to their ancestral land in Australia are forced to negotiate with extractive and other development interests, aided and abetted by the various lands rights legislation like the ALRA or NTA and the corresponding statutory bodies set up under such legislation, like the Aboriginal Land Councils erected under the Aboriginal Land Rights Act (1983).[10] These have a statutory duty to prudently manage and invest what are called Statutory Investment Funds, various Indigenous assets and mining royalties from various development projects, increasingly in an *entrepreneurial* vein.[11] Consequently, they face the prospect of being transformed into entrepreneurs and rent seekers acquiring a share of royalties from development projects on their land and assimilated into the system of Western, Lockean property regimes and generalised commodity production for the market. In the words of former Minister for Families, Housing, Community Services and Indigenous Affairs Jenny Macklin, 'native title is a right which must be used as a tool to bring about positive change for social, cultural, economic purposes ... it must be part of our armoury to close the gap between Indigenous and non-Indigenous Australians' (cited in Altman, 2009b, p.2). This process functions as a means of 'neoliberal assimilation' or interpellation (Althusser, 1994, p. 129), what Rose (2004, p. 276) described as the 'internalising role of property', where resource companies prepare Indigenous people for greater participation in what Australian policy makers call the 'real economy' and ween them off the 'poison' of welfare payments (Pearson, 1999, p. 32).

This political decision to tie the fortunes of Indigenous communities to mining royalties and Statutory Investment Funds and ultimately capital accumulation, is redolent of a form of neoliberal governmentality with neoliberal characteristics (Foucault et al., 2014), of the kind discussed in Chapter 1. This time Indigenous populations will be 'improved', through arenas like public health or *economic productivity*, requiring new bodies of 'expert' knowledge. In this case, the rationality of government is a neoliberal one which understands the path to improvement is tied to the market and the commodity form. The disciplinary institutions, which function as technologies of government ensuring conformity to new 'neoliberal' norms, include not just the broader state government and its various ministries and departments supervising the various resource development projects, but also the institutions and agencies created by the native title and land rights legislation such as the ILUAs and Land Councils.

A similar process can be detected when examining the broader neoliberal reforms to the provision of Indigenous welfare and administration of Indigenous affairs. Where once during the height of the era of the land rights movement in the 1970s federal policy had been predicated on notions of self-determination and the provision and allocation of funding of services accordingly devolved to Indigenous controlled bodies, the revisionist Howard government sort to shift the logic and nature of welfare provision to one that would no longer encourage 'separatism' but instead 'mainstream' service delivery (Howlett et al., 2011, p. 11). That is to say, no longer would Indigenous services and infrastructure be predicated on the recognition of Indigenous alterity. A major step in that direction was taken by the Howard government when in 2004 it abolished the Aboriginal and Torres Strait Islander Commission (ATSIC) and the public works scheme known as the Community Development Employment Program (CDEP) which involved welfare payment in return for labour, the former being the only body that represented Indigenous people on a pan-national level and one expressly designed to give Indigenous people a representative voice in the self determination of Indigenous policy (Walter, 2007, p. 158). The intention, therefore, was to end the policy determination to foster self- determination of Indigenous people as a people. Now in the age of neoliberalism, for people in general and Indigenous people specifically, individual self-reliance is the only viable and moral course for development (Martin, 2011, p. 209), and unemployment attributable to individual failure. Therefore, welfare provision must be restructured to force those Indigenous people languishing in a state of welfare dependency into self-reliance (Neale, 2013, p. 180). Indigenous welfare recipients who are not deemed to fit the neoliberal ideal of the rational moral life of independence and self-reliance (Martin, 2011, p. 209) are cast as deviants (Moreton-Robinson, 2009b, p. 70).

This reframing of Indigenous people as lazy or work-shy for not imbibing a European work ethic under neoliberal discourse, is of course consistent with early colonial discourse (Moreton-Robinson, 2007, p. 91). This is the rationality of government, the reconstituting of Indigenous people as pathological individuals within the neoliberal framework. The governmental technology and its disciplining institution in this context is what is known as 'income management', where state imposed restrictions on welfare payments discipline Indigenous people to conform to imposed norms of behaviour, what Altman (2013, p. 92) calls 'neoliberal assimilation'. Ultimately, Indigenous communities who participate in the ALRA and NTA process and through the biopolitics of income management and neoliberal welfare are subject to pressures to internalise the corresponding discourses or norms of behaviour (Foucault, 1998, p. 140) that rationalise globalisation and the market as the path to development (Altman, 2013, p. 132; 2009, p. 41).

The reconciliation period that began with the 'reconciliation' initiative and the creation of CAR under Hawke's government in 1991, as a response to the growing demands for a treaty, quickly followed by a succession of Court decisions and laws that failed to provide restitutive justice or acknowledgement of past wrongs as other reconciliation projects had typically done, and rendered land rights effectively meaningless and impotent, presents us with a clear example of administrative genocide. In other settler colonial societies such as Canada, if treaties and other forms of arrangements and agreements were negotiated and signed, they were not worth the paper they were written on as they were often signed under duress, under false pretences, within positions of unequal bargaining power and asymmetrical knowledge and with settler appointed Indigenous 'leaders' who held no such rightful claim. Under conditions of asymmetrical exchanges of mediated forms of state recognition and accommodation under the socio-legal regime of the NTA, the very same conditions pertain. What Short (2008, p. 3) describes as a *prima facie* paradox, namely, a state-sponsored process of recognition and reconciliation with the ostensible aspiration to address Indigenous disadvantage, the theft of lands and the suppression of Indigenous sovereignty, nevertheless undercut by government actions and legislation which effectively precluded such aspirations, can be made intelligible once the political, legal and economic – in short, structural – impediments or relations of genocide that lie buried beneath the surface are excavated.

Notes

1. For more on this topic see Crook (2021).

2. Bukharin (1929, p. 29) makes this distinction between extensive and intensive expansion of the world economy.

3. Those that simply took land without formal Crown authorisation.

4. Two pathbreaking studies in Australian historiography which help unearth the history of Indigenous participation in the settler economy are Rowley (1972a) and Henry Reynolds (1990).

5. I am deeply grateful to Dr Padraic Gibson, historian of Australian labour history and Indigenous History, Sydney based anti-racist activist and trade unionist and Senior Researcher at the Jumbunna Institute for Indigenous Education and Research, University Technology Sydney, whose thoughtful comments and insights on this topic were immeasurably helpful.

6. I use the format 'loc.' for citations when citing mobi formatted books.

7. *Mabo and Others v Queensland* (No 2), 1992.

8. Under the later amendments to the NTA, section 39(1)(c) states that if no agreement between Indigenous community and the resource developer is reached, the resource developer has the right to move to arbitration through the Native National Title Tribunal (NNTT), which must take into account 'the economic or other significance of the act to Australia, the State or Territory concerned'.

9. Native Title Amendment Act 1998 (Cth) [Australia]. No. 97, of 1998.

10. Aboriginal Land Rights Act (1983) [Australia]. No. 42 of 1983.

11. Take for instance the New South Wales Aboriginal Land Council (NSWALC, 2011), which in a rather typical annual report explained their investment philosophy:

> The funds to provide compensation for future generations. Prudent financial management is essential to maintain growth. A less risk-averse strategy could increase returns but could clearly increase the risk of losses ... changes to the legislation in 1990 allowed LALCs [Local Aboriginal Land Councils] to sell or mortgage their land under certain conditions, Land Councils are developing a more *entrepreneurial approach to their land assets*. [emphasis added]

Chapter 3

Australia now: the architecture of dispossession

The play of powerful forces incarnated in the form of capitalism and the nexus between it and the duplicitous (neo)colonial settler state is clear. The dialectical interaction between the ecocidal logic of capital on the one hand and the settler-colonial logic of elimination on the other, and Indigenous resistance to both logics, paved the road to the birth of the land rights movement, Mabo and eventually the institutionalisation of Indigenous land rights, shifting the modality of relations of genocide and the structural target of the settler-colonial logic of elimination onto the terrain of state recognition and accommodation under the socio-legal regime of the NTA. Of course, recognition is always on colonial terms. Indeed, whichever path laid down by the NTA Indigenous people take on the crossroads of the colonial dilemma, both negotiation or refusal to negotiate in slightly divergent ways illustrate Frantz Fanon's (1967, p.84) observation that colonisation (and genocide) operate on both a material and discursive or intersubjective level. The material level was succinctly summarised by Short (2016, p.131) when he referred to the 'engine of global capitalism'. Both pathways would entail the incorporation of Indigenous land into circuits of capitalist production and exchange. Both pathways form a part of Fanon's (1967) 'psychological' or intersubjective terrain of colonialism with all the harmful implications for identity formation and reduced mode of being that the misrecognition entails. Although both pathways compel a degree of *recognition* of the supremacy and authority of the colonial institutions, the former pathway is more insidious, since it entails elements of assimilation which allow for *de jure* control of Indigenous land by Indigenous peoples *but on colonial terms.*

It is through the former pathway that the potential for interpellation or the internalisation of the 'values secreted by his masters' (Fanon, 1967, p. 221) are greatest. Of course, none of this is inevitable. The objective and subjective dimensions of colonialism are not tautologies that guarantee cultural assimilation and interpolation of Indigenous subjects, as we will see when we examine Indigenous resistance towards the end of this chapter.

The extractivist mode of production in Australia today

Capitalist ecology gives rise to the ecocide-genocide nexus for two fundamental, structural reasons:[1] firstly, the extra-economic processes of plunder, fraud or theft, from without the circuits of production and capital accumulation, that alienate social groups from their lands; secondly, the value-contradiction embedded within the various industrial (and financial) processes operating within the expanded reproduction of the circuits of capital – what I earlier referred to as a political economy of eco-genocide. These structures are particularly pertinent where settler-colonial contexts form the backdrop.

In the case studies below, we will see the *first stage* of primary accumulation in the repeated attempts to domicidally sever Indigenous people from their land and then secure mining rights to extract subsurface minerals to facilitate the process of capital accumulation (the second stage). This first stage will be facilitated through the modality of recognition politics and land rights as once again a form of 'hybridisation' (Lloyd, 2010, p. 33), in which state-sponsored land grabs facilitated by the modality of land rights that erect uneven fields of negotiation make the Indigenous societies 'ready' for fusion through the 'cunning of recognition' (Povinelli, 2007) with settler capitalist or market relations. This corresponds with Hartwig's (1978, p. 129) first mode of articulation of the settler-colonial and Indigenous figuration, first discussed in Chapter 2, namely the extraction of commodities in different ways. In this case the commodity will be coal and gas.

The second key structure at the second stage is shaped by the *law of value* under capitalist production which from the beginning of settler colonisation in Australia, and as I have argued in Canada (Crook and Short, 2014), explains the ecologically destructive forces unleashed by capitalist extractive industries. For it blindsides capitalists, economic theorists and the various intellectuals that would seek to 'rationalise' the capitalist system to nature's contribution to value production. Commodities, as exchange values, embody or measure the quantity of abstract socially necessary labour time expended in their production. Their qualitative differences, as objects in the material world with use values, are erased, so that they may be made commensurable. Money, as the general equivalent of value, as the measure of general wealth, is necessary, precisely because of the 'contradiction between social generality and homogeneity of [exchange] value versus the material particularity and *qualitative variety* of commodity use values' (Burkett, 2014, p. 84). Ecological connections and diversities are lost in the abstraction of exchange value. As I have argued elsewhere: 'The formal abstraction under exchange value therefore tends towards the simplification and homogenisation of nature as well as its artificial divisibility or fragmentation into either elements of the natural conditions of production or as commodities themselves' (Crook and Short, 2014, p. 302). In other words, value and money, not only abstract from the web of ecological interconnections and diversities but through the pricing of aspects or parts of nature, enable its fragmentation and carving up into discrete vendible articles for sale or as elements of the means of production. Marx (1973, p. 141) sharply observed, 'as value, every commodity is equally divisible; in its natural existence this is not the case'.

Concretely, this means the extraction, processing and distribution of these elements or natural commodities, such as mineral resources, fossil fuels or produce, is conducted in a manner that disregards its relationship with the ecological whole and disembodies and dislocates these natural commodities. In essence, the narrow horizon of exchange value combined with the insatiable drive to accumulate capital, understood as an ecological process, requires more and more of what ecologists describe as 'throughput of materials and energy' (Burkett, 2014, p. 112) – a continual exchange necessary for the regeneration and continuation of the ecological life-sustaining web (Marx, 1976a, p. 290). As we saw on the Australian pastoral frontier and will see below at the sites of fossil fuel extraction, this places an ever-greater strain on the social metabolism of the capitalist system and therefore on nature and the biospheric web – eventually causing 'metabolic rifts' (Burkett, 2014; Foster, 2000, 2005; Stretesky et al., 2013).

Value analysis is perfectly capable of accounting for all forms of what have become known as 'extreme energy' as well, a form of extractivism which will feature in the case studies below, given its name due to the much higher levels of ecological destruction and energy consumption needed to extract the mineral resource in the first place, a term first coined first coined by Michael T. Klare (2013). Unfortunately, extreme energy has opened up a new and rapidly expanding front in the relations of genocide and Indigenous resistance in Australia today. What elsewhere I described as 'a nadir of the anti-ecological dysfunction of exchange value' (Crook and Short, 2014, p. 302), extreme energy is an umbrella term for particularly virulent forms of ecologically unsound industrial energy extraction. These include, for instance, mountain-top removal, deep-water drilling and hydraulic 'fracking' or CSG, as it is known in Australia. However, although describing them as simply more intensive and environmentally destructive forms of energy extraction is helpful, it still leaves unclear how extreme this form of energy needs to be in order to qualify under this umbrella term. Instead, Lloyd-Davies (2013) argues extreme energy should be understood *as a process* in which the energy resources easiest to extract are first targeted, such as those sources of oil or gas conveniently concentrated in larger pockets and relatively easy to drill down into and access, which largely characterised the 'halcyon days' of energy extraction in the early twentieth century. This is then followed by the resort to the extraction of increasingly difficult, complex and energy-intensive sources of mineral resources. Critically, the increase in effort is correlated with an increase in environmental degradation.

One of the central ecological contradictions of the capitalist system is that between the exponential increase in the throughput of materials and energy associated with the treadmill of accumulation and the *natural limits of production* (Crook and Short, 2014, p. 302). Given the disequilibrium between capital's ferocious pace in the throughput of energy and materials and nature's laws and temporal rhythms and metabolic cycles, eventually capital provokes 'materials-supplies disturbances' (Marx, 1968, p. 515). This results in an inevitable shortage of materials and an accumulation crisis.[2] The result, as dictated by the operation of the law of value, is that the price of the relevant raw material will go up as the amount of socially necessary labour time objectified in each individual product or use value rises in relative terms. Marx (1968, p. 515) analysed this phenomenon through the prism of an agricultural crisis:

> A crisis can arise: 1. in the course of the reconversion [of money] into productive capital; 2. through changes in the value of the elements of productive capital, particularly of raw material, for example when there is a *decrease in the quantity of cotton harvested. Its value will thus rise.* [emphasis added]

This rise in the value of constant capital, as opposed to labour, could become so costly it starts to disrupt the process of the reproduction of capital, as the profit realised in the sale of a whole plethora of commodities, of which the various raw materials are a constituent part, no longer covers the costs of the elements of production. This process is exemplified by extreme energy as the supply of fossil fuels begins to run up against natural limits, thus raising the relative amount of objectified labour in a given quantity of fossil fuel leading, in the medium to long term, to a rise in the average price of fossil fuels. Indeed, within the process of extreme energy, where more complex and costly techniques are required for the extraction of ever-scarcer sources, the very same process unfolds. This is precisely a manifestation of materials-supply disturbances, or *natural limits* in modern parlance, as a form of accumulation crisis. Furthermore, the resulting rise in the price of raw materials engenders, under conditions of competitive accumulation, a number of competitive responses. These include increased production from suppliers (therefore accelerating and intensifying the metabolic strain on the environment and exacerbating the aforementioned contradiction) and the use of *previously unused substitutes* (Marx, 1991, pp. 118–19). Extreme energy 'as a process' is both an expression of material shortages engendered by the contradiction between 'nature's time' and 'capital's time' and a competitive response, through the operations of the market, to correct the imbalance through the extraction of ever more extreme substitutes. The net metabolic effect on the social metabolism is to put further pressure both on local ecosystems and the biosphere more generally. Even what is known as the 'energy return on investment' (EROI) profile of forms of extreme such as CSG, where less net energy is acquired due to the more intense and complex forms of extraction required, can be explained by value analysis, since under a capitalist economy (and ecology), all other considerations, in particular ecological imperatives of sustainability, conservation and energy efficiency, are subordinated to exchange value. We will return to the wave of ecological fragmentation and dislocation wrought by extreme energy when I examine the case studies more closely. Suffice to say, with 'peak oil' having been passed most likely in the first decade of the twenty-first century (Murphy, 2010), it seems likely we will continue to occupy this stage of the process for the foreseeable future.

Although in the past, particularly in the nineteenth and first half of the twentieth century, colonial capitalist development and state formation relied on both land *and*, to an admittedly lesser extent, Indigenous labour, where the mineocracy and extractivism are concerned, at the sites of extraction and its associated political economy, the *colonial-relation* is of greater weight than the *capital-relation*, when considering what Coulthard (2014, p. 11) described as the 'subject position of the colonized vis-à-vis the effects of colonial dispossession'. To be clear, the capital relation is still constitutive in the sense that at the time of writing in Australia, over 40 percent of 'Aboriginal and Torres Strait Islander people' live in urban centres (Australian Bureau of Statistics, (ABS, 2024) and as many as 56 per cent of those in major cities are part of the labour force (AIHW, 2023) and thus will be exposed to the kinds of political influences and structural forces delineated in the previous chapter when discussing the rise of the new historical subject, the Indigenous proletariat. Moreover, under many

Indigenous Land Use Agreements (ILUA), entered into between mining companies and Indigenous people (discussed in more detail below), there are requirements to employ Indigenous labour, on paper at least. However, in practice it doesn't always materialise, either due to chronic underfunding of various Indigenous institutions provided for under legislation to represent Indigenous interests in negotiations with resource companies (O'Faircheallaigh, 2007, p. 31), or a general historical underinvestment in social and physical infrastructure for Indigenous communities, leaving them ill prepared to take advantage of potential employment opportunities (Howlett et al., 2011, p. 319).

Although the collective or cultural memory of the struggles that grew out of the intersection of the capital and colonial relation still endure to this day,[3] nevertheless, in a more immediate or direct sense, the employment of Indigenous labour in the extractive industry *today* plays a far smaller role, given the relatively minor degree of Indigenous employment in the extractive industry. Despite the hollow promises offered by industry spokesman, Indigenous labour is not central to this process of accumulation by dispossession (Altman, 2018, p. 354). Therefore, in this current juncture, the colonial relation will figure more greatly in the determination of the case studies examined below. The case studies will exemplify the 'nadir of exchange value', which will take form as the extractivist mode of production controlled by the mineocracy, made possible by an unholy alliance between global corporate interests and resource or 'extractivist states' for the purpose of (re)territorialisation of Indigenous land for extractive purposes (Bebbington et al., 2008; Howlett et al., 2011; Lyons, 2018), just as the pastoral industry did in the nineteenth and twentieth centuries, only this time through the governmentality and discourse of 'recognition'.

Wangan and Jagalingou Traditional Owners Council versus the mineocracy

One case which exemplifies the mode of administrative genocide arguably more than any other in Australia, in the name of development and driven by an alliance between the extractivist state and resource developers, is the continuing struggle waged by the Wangan and Jagalingou (W&J) Traditional Owners Council, manifest in their campaign 'Adani, No Means No'. W&J are seeking to prevent Indian-based industrial conglomerate Adani Enterprises' proposed Carmichael Mine, which, if developed, would be the world's largest open-cut coal mine, covering 30,000 square kilometres in a region known as the Galilee Basin, Central Queensland. This is a region which possesses the largest untapped coal deposit in the country and is considered key by state and federal governments to be Australia's future resource revenue prospects; this is Australia's new coal frontier (Lyons, 2018, p. 2). The project, which also includes extensive air, rail and port infrastructure, crosses the homelands of four different Indigenous nations, including W&J ancestral homelands governed by W&J for 'untold thousands of years' (Burragubba, 2018, p. i). The potential environmental externalities of the project are considerable. They include: contributions to climate change, with an estimated generation of 4.6 billion tonnes of greenhouse gases (GHG) emissions, which will be approximately 0.5 per cent of the entire remaining carbon budget for the country assuming we hold global temperature rises to 2 degrees Celsius above preindustrial levels (Taylor and Meinshausen, 2014); damage to the Great Barrier Reef World Heritage Area; biodiversity loss; and the destruction of sacred cultural and spiritual sites for the W&J, including the Doongmabulla Springs Complex, all of which have been the subject of legal action in the Australian Courts (Environmental Law Australia, n.d.). Explaining the importance of the Doongmabulla Springs Complex, W&J Council spokesperson and Indigenous community leader Adrian Burragubba (W&J FC, 2019) said:

> The mine would pollute and drain billions of litres of groundwater, and obliterate our ancient springs ... The water is our life. It is our dreaming and our sovereignty. We cannot give that away ... Water is central to our laws, our religion and our identity. It is the Mundunjudra, the water spirit, the rainbow serpent.

In a submission written to the United Nations Special Rapporteur on the Rights of Indigenous Peoples, W&J Family Council members Adrian Burragubba and Murrawah Johnson (2015) made clear the genocidal implications. If the development of the Adani mine went ahead:

> It would permanently destroy vast swathes of our traditional lands and waters, including a complex of springs that we hold sacred as the starting point of our life and through which our dreaming totem, the Mundunjudra (also known as the Rainbow Serpent) travelled to form the shape of the land. We exist as people of our land and waters, and all things on and in them – plants and animals – have special meaning to us and tell us who we are. *Our land and waters are our culture and our identity. If they are destroyed, we will become nothing.* [emphasis added]

This would qualify as the ninth genocidal technique defined in Chapter 2, an ecologically induced genocide. Nevertheless, Adani have almost too predictably framed the development of this coal mine in developmentalist language that promises to lift millions out of poverty in India by supporting electrification projects; their main home page is daubed with the Orwellian slogan 'growth with goodness' (Adani, n.d.).

Adani has reached agreement via ILUAs with Indigenous communities, but given the colonial structure of the NTA, which favours mining interests (Corbett and O'Faircheallaigh, 2006), and the colonial dilemma it poses, those same agreements have driven intercommunal conflicts, as they often have (Bebbington et al., 2008); a division emerges between those who are persuaded of the potential for employment and economic development, often out of desperation or due to economic marginalisation and exclusion, and those who seek to protect country and sacred cultural and spiritual sites, divisions I will return to when I examine the fates of the Githabul and Gomeroi. Given the various structural disadvantages of the NTA which skew the negotiating field in favour of the extractive companies and the resource state, including a threat to extinguish native title, compulsory acquisition of their land and denial of any compensation or royalties *if they refuse to negotiate or choose to resist any ILUA*, their sustained campaign is both rare and quite remarkable (Bebbington et al., 2008). Indeed, it is precisely due to these skewed and asymmetrical forms of negotiation under the present legal frameworks discussed above that a wedge is driven within communities between those who seek to defend country and protect the environments and those understandably drawn in by promises of economic development and employment opportunities. Sadly, those opportunities constitute arguably the worst deal offered in history for Indigenous peoples under ILUAs and their equivalents (Robertson, 2017).

The conflict between W&J and Adani revolves around the highly controversial ILUA agreed with the W&J. The ILUA is necessary to 'surrender' native title over a 2,750-hectare area necessary for the development of the mine and associated infrastructure. Despite numerous refusals of proposed ILUAs by the Native Title Claim Group dating back to 2012, Adani applied to the National Native Title Tribunal (NNTT) for a determination under the NTA for a mining lease.[4] In an interview with the W&J Council's official advisor and long-time collaborator Anthony Esposito (author interview, 10/02/2017), he explained that the failure to reach initial agreements prior to the resort to arbitration under the NNTT was the inauspicious circumstances under which the W&J registered native title claimants (RNTC) were required to reach an agreement:

> The native title act is designed to make sure the window shuts on 'em pretty quickly ... they have a right to negotiate but if they don't do it quickly enough it gets slammed on them anyway. Generally, people want ILUAs. At the end of the day, it's a sensible path for most people to take and even though there are time limits, good proponents will actually spend time on building agreements, and good claimants [RNTCs] will spend time working back and forth with their community members and carrying on negotiations. And in the more positive circumstances you do end up with an agreement that could probably pass the free prior and informed consent test.

When asked why the negotiations did finally breakdown, he responded (author interview, 10/02/2017):

> It didn't pass the test because firstly, the offers on the table weren't adequate. Secondly, the negotiating style was poor even down to the level of 'look if you don't agree we'll go and get what we want anyway' – so effectively coercion. It broke down because of insults. It broke down because of lack of resources to enable proper and meaningful consultation. The company provides information, and the traditional owner group is expected to get across ten technical reports, feasibility studies, complex legal documents to do with agreements, all in a period of time, so the odds are really stacked against them ... *they are trying to cover all this over with the veneer of consent.* [emphasis added]

Indeed, under such onerous conditions, where (lack of) time, resources and technical knowledge create asymmetrical terrains of negotiation, it is understandable when some applicants within the RNTC agree to the ILUA – most notably perhaps of the seven, Patrick Malone and Irene White. In fact, until Adrian Burragubba was appointed as a member of the RNTC in August 2014, the dominant position within the claimant group accepted the mine on Indigenous land and was willing to negotiate on the condition that it would return long-term intergenerational benefits to traditional owners. Their withholding of consent was conditional on acquiring benefits that were satisfactory to the whole community. However, given the unequal power dynamic and onerous conditions present within the negotiations of the ILUA illuminated above, many within the former faction arguably acquiesced rather than willingly embraced the inevitability of the mine. As Patrick Malone conceded: 'Even though some [Wangan and Jagalingou] people didn't like the idea of the mine, most knew it would probably go ahead and it was best to take the opportunities for our people, to get jobs for the next generations' (McKenna,

2015). In 2015, the NNTT concluded that despite the failure to reach agreement with the Indigenous community the mine could go ahead under what is called the 'expedited procedure' system,[5] of the NTA. This was a system that now favoured resource or mining interests even more under the Howard government amendments to the NTA and his 'Wik 10 Point Plan'.[6]

As Ritter (2002, p. 1) dryly observes to Indigenous people, 'this colonial euphemism [...] is merely a coded way of the Government saying "the resource interest does not have to talk to you about the grant of this tenement"'. Ritter (2002, p. 5) astutely argues that processes like the NNTT are bedevilled by bureaucratic pathologies in which a type of hyperactivity is manifested in the needless proliferation of rules and procedures which are 'the opiate of the bureaucrat' (Hogwood and Peters, 1989, p. 52). Needless to say, this procedural labyrinth is compounded when invariably both the NNTT and the Federal Court are funded to a greater extent than native title parties (Hogwood and Peters, 1989, p. 6). This further skews an already asymmetrical field of negotiation, which is concealed by an overgrowth of 'bureaucratic ideology' that claims to interpret the application of the expedited procedures in a rational and impartial manner, transforming what are political decisions into technical questions that can only be solved by bureaucrats. This amounts to an 'imposition of colonial truth, in the guise of objectivity, upon the Indigenous populace' (Hogwood and Peters, 1989).

An appeal against this decision brought by the W&J was dismissed,[7] as was an appeal from that decision.[8] This power to effectively annex the land by fiat demonstrates the colonial dilemma discussed above and the total evisceration of the three key rights under UNDRIP defined in Chapter 1. In April 2016, Adani, in collusion with the states Coordinator General, organised yet another meeting with Native title claimants wherein they secured agreement, with seven out of the twelve registered native title claimants (RNTC) agreeing to the mine. What W&J advisor Esposito (author interview, 10/02/2017) described as the 'veneer of consent' is still preferable to the appearance of forced annexation. Despite a further meeting in 2017 with Adani rejecting any agreement, this ILUA stands as the legal basis for the Carmichael Mine. However, according to W&J spokesperson Adrian Burragubba, the agreement was only secured during the April 2016 meeting after repeated rejections, through a concerted campaign of bullying by the Queensland Government and Adani (Lyons, 2018, p. 3).[9]

In essence, the W&J argue (Esposito W&J advisor, author interview, 10/02/2017), in a scenario repeated again and again with members of

Indigenous nations across the country in my field interviews, that, in the meeting in question, some who attended were not actual members of the native title group nor ever identified as members of the W&J. Moreover, Adani stood accused of paying bribes to some of the native title claim group to vote in favour of the mine (Esposito W&J advisor, author interview, 10/02/2017; Robertson, 2017). These payments were ostensibly made through what was earlier described as the 'industry mandate' where resource developers are encouraged by the government to fund the ILUA negotiations. The exacerbation of the already existing uneven power dynamic this creates is demonstrated by this case study (Esposito W&J advisor, author interview, 10/02/2017; Burnside, 2008; O'Faircheallaigh, 2006, p.5). It also resonates with Lemkin's second genocidal technique: *social*, which recall, involves the annihilation of the national leadership and the imposition of the legal system of the occupant. Sadly, this technique will be evident in the case of the Githabul and the Gomeroi, examined below.

Despite the native title group being split almost down the middle, with one native title claimant who originally voted in favour in the April 2016 meeting switching sides, the ILUA was ruled valid by the full bench in an appeal hearing at the Federal Court, 'notwithstanding any deficiencies which might have tainted the validity of the certification', noted Justice Melissa Perry (Smee, 2019). But as Adrian Burragubba (Smee, 2019) pointed out in response:

> The decision [hinged] only on the question of whether the certification and registration of the Adani ILUA were administered according to the legal requirements of the Native Title Act ... It will not pull back the veil on the ... process leading up to and after the authorisation meeting. Nor will it confirm whether in fact the people in attendance at the Adani meeting were entitled under the laws and customs of Wangan and Jagalingou people to make that decision to sign away W&J rights in land for monetary compensation.

In a graphic demonstration of the power wielded by the mining lobby, the Queensland government moved to pass a series of policies and expedited approvals to mitigate any risk to the Carmichael mine and associated infrastructure. This included the 'Galilee Basin Development Strategy', a policy developed by the Queensland government in 2013 to expedite planning approvals and land acquisition and remove any requirements to pay government royalties (The Queensland Cabinet and Ministerial Directory, 2013). In 2016 the Adani development was designated as 'critical infrastructure', which again enabled the fast-tracking of approvals for the mine as well as the curtailing of community consultation, which clearly transgresses FPIC. Lyons (2018, pp. 6–7) argues the significance of these and other strategic and policy manoeuvres, including the granting of environmental approval, despite the aforementioned environmental impacts of the proposed mine and even the rewriting of the *State Water Act* (Environmental Law Australia, n.d.), was to provide a statutory mandate to hasten the compulsory acquisition of Indigenous land and extinguishment of native title. In the context of the history of Australian settler–Indigenous relations, encounters between extractive interests, the state and Indigenous peoples, and the history of Indigenous land rights in Australia, it is hard to disagree.

To underscore the nature of the genocide machine in the era of 'recognition' politics, the federal government would go on to force through amendments to the NTA, referred to mockingly as the 'Adani amendment' by the W&J Council (Stockwell, 2017), to overturn a key 'McGlade' High Court decision on 2 February 2017.[10] This decision recognised traditional Indigenous collective decision-making structures which required unanimous support for an ILUA to go ahead. This threatened to invalidate Adani's ILUA, given only seven of the twelve registered native title applicants signed. Within weeks the federal government would introduce an amendment to the NTA: Indigenous Land Use Agreements Bill, 2017. Whilst the bill was being expeditiously drafted and passed, the Attorney General intervened in the Federal Court to delay the McGlade order. As before, with the NTA and the Native Title Amendment Bill (1997) that followed it, the legislation retroactively validated any ILUAs considered under threat by McGlade, again fuelled by government and mining lobby claims that it jeopardised the future of the mining industry. In keeping with previous attempts at recognition and reconciliation (Short, 2007, 2008), the consultation process was severely curtailed with stakeholders and effected communities allowed only two weeks to make a submission to a Senate Inquiry, assuming they had the legal expertise to make sense of the complex legal amendments, again begging questions regarding meaningful FPIC. Ultimately, in August 2019, the Queensland government extinguished native title over 1,385 hectares of W&J country and granted Adani exclusive possession freehold title over large swathes of land, which included sacred cultural sites used for ceremonial purposes (Doherty, 2019). As we shall see when we turn to the Githabul and Gomeroi resisting CSG and extreme energy below, the manipulation of the ILUA process, buttressed by neoliberal assimilation and a historical legacy of dispossession and genocide discussed above, is sadly not uncommon and will be evident in the experience of the Githabul and Gomeroi faced with the advancing wave of extreme energy.

The Githabul and Gomeroi in gasland

Another front has opened in recent years in Australia's 'resource rush' (Cleary, 2012). The rise and rapid expansion of CSG, a virulent form of extreme energy sometimes referred to as 'unconventional energy' (Trigger et al., 2014, p. 176), is like a tsunami sweeping over land rights, rights to self-determination and FPIC. Like a tsunami it scars the landscape, destroys animal habitats and washes away the original inhabitants of the land. Unlike conventional forms of extraction, CSG involves the development of technologies that enable access to previously inaccessible resources, particularly methane, which is trapped within coal seams. Unlike conventional gas, the pockets of gas are relatively small and diffuse, requiring a large number of wells spread across the landscape, driving an industrialisation of the countryside and giving it a large footprint. If we then consider the associated infrastructure above the surface of roads, pipelines, water treatment facilities, gas compression stations and the drill pads themselves, it's not difficult to appreciate its transformative impact on land cover change alone. In Queensland there are approximately 40,000 square kilometres of land leased for the development of CSG wells (Trigger et al., 2014). Whereas conventional larger gas domes are found thousands of metres below, suitable coal seams are usually only a few hundred metres below and rarely thicker than a metre. The relatively lower levels of EROI that define extreme energy, due to the more intense and complex forms of extraction discussed above, are an attendant feature of CSG as well, since, in order to extract the gas, the balance in the coal structure must be changed by 'dewatering' and often, if not always, hydraulic fracturing. An inordinate amount of water must be extracted to facilitate this process. For instance, in the Surat basin 400,000 litres of water per day were extracted (Keogh, 2014). The coal seam will then be primed with potassium chloride and hydraulically fractured under a high-pressure pump of water, sand and a number of other abrasive chemicals. It is this forcing open of the coal seam that allows the gas to flow. In essence, as Short (2016, p. 147) pithily observes, 'CSG production is a landscape altering phenomena of some magnitude', leaving behind what Cleary (2012, loc. 268) wryly refers to as the 'footprints of giants'.

Like other forms of extreme energy, CSG production produces a range of negative environmental externalities such as toxic water contamination, air pollution and methane migration driving increased carbon emissions and, as elucidated above, a vast industrialisation of the countryside. CSG specifically also drives a depletion of the water table and potentially subsidence, given the extraordinary quantities of water that must be extracted to facilitate the process. This in turn leads potentially to the contamination of freshwater aquifers and ground water by coal seams, if it is porous and they are connected. A paper commissioned by the Queensland government assessing the risk that CSG posed to the environment argued there was a risk of subsidence which could lead to the fracturing of aquifers and the altering of 'hydraulic connectivity' (Moran and Vink, 2010, p. 4). The potential for resulting contamination from either the dewatering process and resulting flow of gas, or the abrasive chemicals used is substantial, quite apart from the collapsing water table and its implications for farming and subsistence practices more generally. The scale of ecological destruction is clear and for those Indigenous people and the broader community living on or near the sites of extraction, the environmental and social impacts are grave.

In states like Queensland and NSW in the east, invariably these forms of extraction cross paths with prime farmland (Cleary, 2012, loc. 205), which, as we will see towards the end of this chapter, has played a crucial role in the forms of solidaristic resistance that it has given rise to. We will first explore these impacts as indicative of the environmental and social harms of CSG before fully attending to Indigenous peoples resisting this form of extraction. One farmer I interviewed named John Jenkyn who lives in Chinchilla QLD, part of the Western Downs region in the heart of the gas fields in the Surat basin, arguably the epicentre of CSG in Australia, described a rather typical experience, explaining to me a whole plethora of environmental and social impacts due to the imposition of drilling sites and wells on his farmland. He explained that due to the use of the local dam water, he, his wife and two children experience skin rashes, constant headaches, nausea, vomiting, dizziness, hair loss, nose bleeds and sore eyes and depression and anxiety (author interview, 02/03/17). Much of rural Queensland is a water catchment area, so residents rely on collected rainwater, local wells and dams. He now believes that this is also being caused by air pollutants caused by both the contamination of ground water and air pollutants. The latter, he suspects, are caused by a combination of factors typical to CSG projects. Firstly, the dumping of the saline and most likely radioactive water by water trucks on roads adjacent to his property. This contaminated water will then, particularly on hot days (in Chinchilla QLD, in the summer it can reach upwards of 50 degrees Celsius) evaporate and come back down as precipitation on their land and in their water tanks. Indeed, he explained that in a matter of weeks they had lost eighteen cows due to providing water from the rainwater tanks. Add to this the huge 'tailing ponds' that collect the wastewater, which stretch for 700 acres near his land. They too will eventually gas off and come back down as rain. The other sources are fugitive gas emissions from nearby pipes and nearby gas flares, which leave a bright orange glow on the night-time sky.

To compound the air pollution levels, Jenkyn has to contend with local, giant water treatment facilities like the QGC's Kenya Water Treatment Plant, the gas company responsible for the local gas fields and associated infrastructure, which is tasked with treating the contaminated water. These and other facilities involved in the conversion of coal-seam gas into liquefied natural gas (LNG) are responsible for emitting a whole array of what Dr Mariann Lloyd-Smith, senior advisor to Australia's National Toxics Network, described as a 'toxic soup' (author interview, 26/01/17), including volatile organic compounds (VOCs) which can cause irritation to eyes, nose and throat and damage to the central nervous system, and other chemicals known to cause cancer, such as benzene, formaldehyde and nitrous oxides, which impact respiratory health and particulate matter. In fact, Jenkyn complained of a loss of sense of taste due to a constant 'metallic taste in the mouth ... which overpowers everything'. To add further to his family's woes, he argued that, above all, his family suffers due to sleep deprivation and the constant noise from construction work, which he stated was '24 hours a day'. He averred that due to the cumulative environmental impacts all local wildlife has disappeared. This can only be described as ecocide. He now hangs a banner on the edge of his farm property emblazoned with the words he claims were used by QGC representatives in closed town meetings with local government officials and the local Chamber of Commerce to describe the areas impacted by their operations: sacrifice zone.

In an interview conducted with a local GP, Dr Geralyn McCarron (author interview, 09/03/17), who had studied the health impacts of CSG development for many years, her data underscores the sacrificial nature of this form of extreme energy. She explained to me that she had conducted interviews with 113 local residents of the Western Downs region, approximately 200 km west of Brisbane, a territory encompassing much of the land most impacted by the development of CSG wells and associated infrastructure in QLD, including local towns like Chinchilla, Tara and Condamie, she catalogued an alarming array of symptoms. CSG development first began approximately 2007 onwards in this region. The symptoms included, *inter alia*, 'nose bleeds, eye irritation, coughs, skin irritation, joint pain, and muscle spasms'. Children reported 'pins and needles, funny feelings in their hands, funny movements' (author interview, 09/03/17). She added that over time people have begun to report 'unusual cancers, and unusual patterns of cancers ... there's one area [*sic*] seems to observe pancreatic cancer'. As she explains, this is a relatively uncommon cancer with on average 11.6 in 100,000 developing this cancer (Loveday et al., 2019, p. 826). And yet in one area she explains with a 10 km radius, an area that is not a densely urbanised area, there were three people with pancreatic cancer. Dr Geralyn McCarron also spoke to residents of the Tara estate, an area known not only as a major site for CSG development in QLD but also for its high levels of social marginalisation and poverty where many of its residents known as 'blockies' suffer stigmatisation. The social and economic decline are due in part to its marginal agricultural success given the inauspicious climatic and environmental conditions (Makki, 2015, p. 124). In one family interviewed opposite this estate adjacent to a water tailing pond, two of the children had cancer, one had leukaemia and the other a rare form of tissue cancer known as sarcoma. In the family next door, one child also had leukaemia. As Dr McCarron put it frankly, 'in terms of "hit rate" that's not what you would expect at all' (author interview, 09/03/17). The aforementioned practice of water trucks dumping wastewater on local roads in fact happened throughout the Tara state. As Dr McCarron explained to me (author interview, 09/03/17), in one lane in particular, out of six families, five of them have cases of cancer.

In an interview conducted with one Tara Estate resident, Dianne Glenda Parker, who lives only 500 metres from the nearest CSG well, who was also an Indigenous women stolen from her parents in what was earlier referred to as the 'stolen generations', she described (author interview, 03/03/17) how shortly after moving to Tara, in 2014, her husband was diagnosed with 'micro bacterial disease', dying shortly after in 2015. She suspected it was partly due to potential toxins collecting in her rainwater tank. She also explained that many residents suffered from runny and sore eyes, constant headaches, bloody noses and tiredness 24/7. Rainfall, called 'black rain' by a local reporter, would strip paint from her car. She added that the reporter who filled the report regarding the 'black rain' lost her job and the story disappeared off the internet. She added:

> The smell that's in the air sometimes will make you wanna vomit and you're just sick all the time ... When it is 50 degrees outside in the heat, you can't go outside because it stinks – it gets to smell like rotten eggs. And then you get this metallic taste in your mouth. So, you get in your car and go somewhere you can breathe. It's terrible.

Some nights she has to wear a face mask to filter the air so she can sleep. She described moreover that she can't drink any of the water from her three rain tanks because they are contaminated. The water is so bad she told me that the local government would fine her for releasing the water on her front yard. The local CSG company supplies them with bottled water instead. She added, with sobering frankness, 'I'm just existing.' She later explained that if it were not for her friend, our interlocutor, she would have killed herself.

In Dr McCarron's investigations, including information she personally received from the Darling Downs Hospital and Health Services, the region of Queensland which encompasses Western Downs, she informed me that between the years 2007, just on the cusp of the beginning of CSG development, and 2012, the population grew by 7 per cent. However, acute hospital admissions for respiratory conditions increased by 124 per cent, hospitalisation for heart problems rose by 114 per cent, diagnosis of invasive cancer by 14 per cent and rates of admission for attempted suicide rose by 50 per cent. Of course, this is just correlation and not conclusive proof of a causal connection, but it does at the very least demand further investigation. Arguably, the anti-ecological impacts of CSG on their sacrifice zones are genocidal not just potentially for Indigenous people but for all communities within its ecological 'blast radius'.

To return to our besieged Jenkyn family in the heart of the gas fields, in experiences that would mirror those of many other farmers and pastoralists across the country (see Cleary, 2012, loc. 131), the Jenkyn family had little choice but to accept the wells on their farmland. In a manner reminiscent of the asymmetric fields of negotiation constructed by the NTA and other Indigenous land rights legislation described above, state laws in NSW and QLD empower gas companies to acquire access to farmlands in as little as ten business days with an 'Entry Notice' to pursue exploratory 'preliminary activities' (Department of Resources, 2021, p. 9). This cannot be refused by the landowner. In twenty business days, the minimum negotiation period, the resource company can acquire permission to conduct 'advanced activities' such as drilling (Department of Resources, 2021, p. 20). If no 'Conduct and Compensation Agreement' is reached, by a total of fifty days, the resource company can turn to the local Land Court, which has the legal authority to overrule the landowner and order land access to develop production wells (Department of Resources, 2021, p. 21). This facilitates the swift speed at which the CSG projects are spreading across Australia's rural areas. When one considers that recent enabling legislation where, for example, QLD is concerned, such as the Mines Legislation (Streamlining) Amendment Bill, 2012, was passed with minimal consultation, in only six days, three of which were over a weekend during the Olympics, a bill that concerned at least sixteen other pieces of relevant statues, the average community resident would hardly have the time to consider it properly.

Jenkyn (author interview, 02/03/17) also spoke of what he felt was a breakdown in local community solidarity, with those in the local community who felt the CSG industry would bring much sought after prosperity to a region long suffering social and economic decline, showing hostility to him and those like him who opposed the CSG industry. Indeed, in research conducted by Luke et al. (2018) on the intersection between historically rooted place identity and the propensity to resist forms of resource extraction, although many farmers in the Western Downs felt that gas extraction was incompatible with historically rooted understandings of land productivity given the threats it posed to the land identified above, some farmers expressed a position that unconventional gas was not necessarily incompatible with farming, as long as it didn't interfere with how they connected to their place. In other words, many felt that the Western Downs was already an industrialised landscape and so unconventional gas could coexist with agriculture (Luke et al., 2018, p. 8). Intriguingly, some farmers embraced the changes wrought by unconventional gas, due to associations with more prosperous times in the past (Luke et al., 2018). Indeed, some farmers considered it a way to escape current economic hardships brought on by many years of drought and declining productivity and fertility of land (Luke et al., 2018). This again has echoes of the 'colonial dilemma' imposed on besieged Indigenous communities described above.

Moreover, as John Jenkyn explained to me, the process whereby environmental impacts are measured is invariably done by the resource companies themselves, as is common across Australia (Cleary, 2012, loc. 179). These tests, which monitor levels of various heavy metals, toxins and dust in the environment, are taken when weather conditions like direction of wind or rain are most favourable to the resource companies (Cleary, 2012). This is precisely the experience Jenkyn relayed to me. Jenkyn described incidences where test samples and results were tampered with, sabotaged or the results simply disappeared. For instance, Jenkyn explained that the autopsy results taken from his dead cows sent off by the local veterinarian to a government approved laboratory in Toowoomba, QLD, were 'inconclusive'. When he asked to see a copy of the report, the laboratory claimed it had disappeared. In another incident, when Jenkyn organised a toxic report for his rainwater tank, once the laboratory discovered where the samples had come from, Jenkyn argued they refused to proceed. He explained that this laboratory worked closely with the CSG industry and did not want to sour relations with its biggest market. He informed me that associates of his who knew employees working for said laboratory firm explained it was common practice to 'leave the lid off water samples or even dilute them to get the desired result'. In a moment of exasperation, Jenkyn, referring to an institutional environment that frustrated and stymied his attempts to empirically ascertain the environmental hazards produced by CSG in his farm, said sardonically, 'do I have to become a scientist to live in my own home?'

This type of malpractice and corruption conditioned by a political economic environment dominated by the mineocracy is far from unique in Australia gas and coal country (Cleary, 2012, loc. 179). Further, with such a legal and political economic matrix conditioned by the hegemony of the mineocracy, able to force the submission of the white settler population, many of whom are the descendants of pastoralists and farmers, whose cattle once formed the 'shock troops of empire' (Russell, 2005, p. 77), the ability of the mineocracy to continue to colonise Indigenous land and suppress Indigenous alterity shocks but does not surprise.

Among the countless examples that exemplify such a phenomenon is the story of the Githabul nation, who in 2007 successfully secured a consent determination recognising them as native title holders over 1,120 square kilometres in nine national parks and thirteen state forests in northern New South Wales (NNTT, 2007). Five years later they had to contend with the arrival of CSG on their land when the New South Wales Aboriginal Land Council (NSWALC) put in an application for CSG prospecting in the Tweed and Byron Shires (Farrrow-Smith, 2012). When asked what risks CSG posed to their communities, one Githabul elder responded (no. 4, author interview, 23/01/2017):

> It's killing our spirituality. Our connection to country is spiritual ... each one of us when we were born were given our piece of water. And we had to learn how to sing to that water and that water called for us. This is our law. Our ancestors lay in the landscapes according to our law.

Githabul elder no. 2 pointed out, 'we still get our bush tucker from the water. If they bloody well come in with the mining and the gas, we've got nothing! Our culture's gone, it's finished, it's over.' The impact on water due to CSG production and potential for contamination was clearly seen as a major existential threat.

Turning to the land rights and native title system, one leading Githabul elder explained in an interview (no. 1, author interview, 23/01/2017) that he and many other rightful native title holders and elders were not consulted and their traditional decision-making structures of tribal council or eldership were marginalised or ignored entirely. In fact, the New South Wales Land Council, a statutory body legally empowered to assist traditional owners in negotiations with resource developers (Altman, 2012, p. 53), had actually arranged the deal with the CSG company, bringing into question how these bodies are unduly influenced by the power of mining interests, resource states and the political, legal and economic reality of asymmetric colonial terrains of negotiation.

Indeed, the Githabul elder explained (no. 1, author interview, 23/01/2017) that the broader socio-legal terrain of NTA and the preceding civil and political reforms discussed in Chapter 2 are designed to reproduce colonial relations. After stating that the NSW state was trying to force them into an ILUA over a CSG development with Metgasco on their ancestral land, he added:

> We have been basically at loggerheads with the Native Title Tribunal … this process of Native Title is ethnically cleansing us … the recognising us into the constitution (after the 1967 referendum) was a reverse psychology issue. It wasn't about them recognising us, it was getting us to recognise their laws and governance over us. And to recognise is to say you accept.

This notion of reverse psychology is one that chimes with the arguments elucidated at the beginning of this chapter and would be very familiar to Fanon (1967, p. 84) and his argument that colonialism operates at both the level of the objective and the subjective and indeed Althusser's (1994, p. 129) arguments pertaining to the *interpellation* of individuals via the recognition function of ideology.

Referring to the NTA and the way in which the various pressures and financial enticement drives wedges in the communities, another Githabul elder argued (no. 2, author interview, 23/01/2017), 'it is so damaging, it destroys relationships between families, it divides. That's what the government is all about: divide and conquer'. Alluding to both the inherent ecological dangers posed by CSG and the financial enticements offered through the ILUAs and the associated mining royalties, he added, 'they chuck a bit of money on the table to one of our mob, they run with it … We don't want the money; the land is precious to us.' Githabul elder no. 1 concurred adding (author interview, 23/01/2017) 'we are strong witness against some of those in our community who are prepared to take the dollar and run'. Githabul elder no. 2 (author interview, 23/01/2017) stated categorically there were three documents that divided Indigenous communities: 'Aboriginal Land Rights Act, the Native Title Act, and religion'.

The NSWALC CEO Geoff Scott has publicly taken issue with this stance, arguing that signing the ILUA would be the only way to end their community's welfare dependency, avowing (Code, 2013), '[d]o you want to get benefit from it or do you want to continue to get the scraps off the table? Do you want to continue to rely on government for your livelihood? I think we owe our children better than that.'

Indeed, there is a logic to this, if one accepts the structural realties of Indigenous co-existence within the settler-colonial social formation, dominated by capitalist production. And yet, this is the very colonial dilemma discussed above, what Short (2016, p. 149) described as a 'stark choice between a settler-colonial rock and a hard place; a native title system devoid of veto power and extreme energy "solutions" being presented, counterfactually, as environmentally safe and the only realistic lifeline for economically disadvantaged Indigenous communities'. In fact, Indigenous communities rarely benefit from the much-vaunted employment opportunities provided by CSG production (Trigger et al., 2014). Moreover, this is the financial and structural compulsion to negotiate examined earlier, which assumes the market *as the path to development* (Altman, 2013, p. 132, 2009a, p. 41), with all its biopolitical and interpellating implications regarding what was earlier referred to as neoliberal assimilation (Altman, 2013, p. 92).

Turning to the broader institutions set up under the NTA and the NSW ALRA (1983), Githabul elder no. 1 averred (author interview, 23/01/2017) that the Aboriginal Land Councils, despite being statutory bodies empowered to advocate on the behalf of Indigenous communities, were indeed being instrumentalised as a colonial weapon with genocidal implications. He explained:

> They're using State Land Councils under the persona of being an Aboriginal organisation and supposed to be holding our properties in trust, and they've been using the state to come down to force local tribes into 40-year land lease agreements over the properties upon which our people suffered, where we have our language and our ceremonies and our connection to Bush ripped away from us ... It's using the persona of the word Aboriginal to represent us as a people, when it's basically a land office belonging to the state doing business for mining companies ... the State Land Council is just one office that is utilised to try and fulfil the process of *wiping us away as a culture.* [emphasis added]

Githabul elder no. 1 even suggested that those who chose to agree to the ILUA, enticed by the financial rewards, played their part as unwitting pawns in their genocidal destruction: 'It's not just the State Land Council. It's some of our own mob who've been sitting up there quite comfortably living off our suffering.' He caveated this by explaining that it was due to their already impoverished and marginalised status that this sort of co-opting of members of their community was possible. Indeed, as I argued above, the history of forcible articulation with the settler-colonial economy has, through the 'dull compulsion of economic relations' (Marx, 1976, p. 899), left many Indigenous people with little choice but to seek development though the settler-colonial economy on colonial terms.

The use of Land Councils as colonial instruments, he explained, was commonplace: 'that isn't just happening on the Northern Rivers. This is happening right across every tribal system in the area.' Referring to the

Indigenous group Boggabilla, he explained how they had been manipulated into an agreement:

> They were forced because they were ignorant of the English language. They were fraudulently conveyed the 'truth' and they signed off on a 40-year lease, and the next thing they knew they had one big hell of a road going straight through their old reserve to a mining spot. People have been evicted.

Referring to these evictions and the inevitable displacement that comes with ILUA agreements and the extinguishment of native title, he added:

> This is just a way of forcing us out of these old concentration camps that are a reminder to the old Commonwealth of their past history. And if they can close these places down and assimilate us into the broader community then the tribal structure that stands here is fragmented and gone!

This is of course of a piece with the racial spatialisation central to the reproduction and expansion of the capitalist system (Lefebvre, 1974) discussed in Chapter 2.

He stressed that in order to compel his community to acquiesce to an ILUA, the Aboriginal Land Council would threaten to deny the local Indigenous community funding that they receive to provide essential services for Indigenous communities. This was a 'bargaining chip'. He continued:

> Do you know the saying? To rob a strongman, you must first bind him. Once you bind him you can rob him of all that he has. Well, this is what the government is about. Binding us legally to an agreement knowing that we are honourable peoples, erm, into these agreements with the Commonwealth.

This use of the Land Council constitutes a violation of the right to self-determination (Articles 3 and 31) under UNDRIP (UNGA, 2017).

Moreover, the cunning of recognition would not stop there. In a story of manipulation, deception and fraud that will be echoed when we examine Kenya and their attempts to assert their sovereignty in their negotiations with the (neo)colonial government, the Githabul elder explained (no. 1, author interview, 23/01/2017) that, in order to secure the ILUA, an Indigenous community member turned native title applicant was prematurely released from a seven-year prison sentence to sign the ILUA 'and do this business'. Moreover, Githabul elder no. 1 explained, 'the government, if you don't already have a system of governance set up, will impose one on the community'. In the Northern Rivers that was the 'Bundjalung', which translates as 'black man on country'. He affirmed 'we will not come under a fictitious tribal council known as "Bundjalung"!' Explaining the function of this fiction of representation, he added, 'all the endeavours of the Crown and State [are] to basically usurp and ethnically cleanse us of our country'. Githabul elder no. 4 clarified (author interview, 23/01/2017) that the new tribal council was 'literally put together so the government doesn't have to talk to all the different tribal systems ... to do their business on country'. When asked who constituted this new Bundjalung tribal council, Githabul elder no. 1 explained that they were black pastors, men of the cloth from the Northern Rivers who had good standing in the Indigenous community due to their knowledge of the Gospel. He clarified that these black pastors believed they were doing good for the community, but ultimately embroiled them in a colonial deal through the ILUA. This imposition of illegitimate representative structures clearly violates FPIC (Article 190) and rights to self-determination (Articles 3 and 31) under UNDRIP (UNGA, 2017). These testimonies, once again, as we saw with W&J and their struggle with the Adani mine, exemplify asymmetric fields of negotiation and unequal bargaining power where agreements are signed under duress and with settler-appointed Indigenous 'leaders' who held no such rightful claim. It is evident from the fields interviews that those Githabul interviewed felt that both the land rights and native title system, as well as the anti-ecological nature of extreme energy, posed a genocidal threat.

Unfortunately, these forms of political, legal and economic asymmetries in the colonial terrain of negotiation are evident in the experiences of another Indigenous nation at the forefront of the struggle for sovereignty and alterity against the rapidly advancing frontier of extreme energy. Gomeroi country, by some estimates, spans 75,000 square kilometres, tipping over into the southern border of QLD as far as the MacIntyre river, and extending all the way down to the northernmost reaches of the Tongo State Forest and Goulburn River National Park in NSW. Assailed on multiple fronts by various mining projects in the north-west of NSW, there are currently multiple conventional coal mines on the Liverpool plains operated by Whitehaven coal, with two at Werris Creek, one in Gunnedah, two Whitehaven mines close to Boggabri, an open-cut Tarrawonga Mine near the township of Narrabri and another, also near Narrabri operated by Boggabri Coal Pty Ltd. (Norman, 2016, p. 243). The Tarrawonga Mine and another mine, Maules Creek Mine, also run by Whitehaven Coal, operate in the vicinity of Leard State Forest, whilst the Boggabri mine impinges on large areas of the forest (Norman, 2016). The Leard Forest contains at least 11 Indigenous sacred sites that face destruction due to the operation of the mines (Hunt, 2016). This is aside from the cumulative environmental hazards that are generated by multiple mining operations in close proximity to each other that can exponentially accumulate and reach 'tipping points' which bring about qualitative shifts in ecosystems (Clearly, 2012, loc. 287). These cumulative impacts are rarely measured or 'picked up' by environmental impact assessments in Australia which invariably only examine mines in isolation (Clearly, 2012, loc. 269).

To add to their woes, the Gomeroi now face a CSG project known as the Narrabri Gas Project operated by gas company Santos on portions of the Pilliga Forest. The proposed project will span 98,000 hectares, encompassing Crown and private land as well as the Pilliga Forest, and impinges on Gomeroi registered native land. It will have 850 coal-seam gas wells (Knaus and Cox, 2021). Despite many years of protests from various communities, both Indigenous and non-Indigenous, and many legal battles to shut down or suspend the CSG project, the NSW Land and Environment Court issued a judicial review decision upholding the initial decision of the NSW Independent Planning Commission to go ahead with the proposed CSG project. In fact, in yet another indication of the power of the mineocracy, the incumbent Australian Prime Minister Scott Morrison announced the Narrabri gas project would be among fifteen other projects given fast-track approval to accelerate Australia's economic recovery in the wake of the Covid-19 crisis (Knaus and Cox, 2021).

The Pilliga Forest also holds powerful cultural significance to the Gomeroi, with many significant sacred sites (MEHI Centre, 2021), thus placing an important cultural obligation of custodianship and stewardship on Gomeroi elders over the land and waters of the Pilliga. To date, Santos have drilled eight exploratory wells in addition to one core hole. Aside from the 1,000 hectares it plans to clear from the forest for well sites, tracks and pipelines, which will have devastating impacts on the habitats of the koala bear (which includes thousands of hollow-bearing trees) and the Pilliga mouse, the internal fragmentation of the forest will facilitate the penetration of weeds and exotic animals throughout the forest (MEHI Centre, 2021). Once up and running, the CSG project will have all the ecological and social harms associated with this form of extreme energy detailed at the beginning of this section. The eco-genocidal threat to the Gomeroi is clear.

One Gomeroi elder (Gomeroi elder no. 1, author interview, 27/02/2017), who is now part of the registered native title group, conveyed the threat that CSG poses:

> Throughout our nation there are many areas that were used for initiation for our men and women, for example Bora rings. In the Pilliga Scrub there are men's areas as well as women's. They are very sacred places,

with us six generations before colonisation. There are many endangered species of animals that are in that area, scarred trees that are a major part of our songlines.

Recall that these aspects of the landscape were in Chapter 2 referred to as 'mythic geography' (Servello, 2010, p. 673). He continued:

They told people where to eat, where to camp and what type of food was in area, and with 850 wells going in there, they will certainly knock those out … and most certainly it will kill the water. It [the CSG project] sits above the Artesian basin. The hot water baths have come out of the ground [*sic*] are healing water … water is life … the spirit of our land has already been killed by mining projects and this here project will do it even more.

After explaining the threat to local river systems and linking extractivism to climate change, he was quick to add that by far the biggest threat to the land and environment came from CSG:

The biggest threat out there I believe, if you know what I mean, is the CSG. The Great Artesian Basin with underwater aquifers that runs into the Surat [basin] and that runs into Galilee basin, and that's where they're going to build the Carmichael Adani coal mine. It will be a 'flow on effect' … that will go through three states: New South Wales, Victoria and South Australia. People down South are going to face the full effect of it as well. That will affect millions of people, not hundreds, not thousands, but millions.

Not only is he demonstrating a detailed understanding of the complex hydraulic system and the threat posed to it by CSG, but he is alluding to cumulative impacts right across the country and their relationship to other resource developments such as Adani coal mine, which was the subject of the case study above. Regarding the Pilliga Forest, which is the site of the proposed Santos CSG project, he said 'there are 13 endangered species within that forest alone there … the endangered species that are in there are our totems. Some totems are plants, some are trees. There are box trees, there are burial sites within that area.' Another Gomeroi elder (author interview, 21/03/2017) concurred:

With all the wells that are going in there, we have the Great Artesian Basin and the underground water systems that run through Pilliga Forest where Santos is planning on putting 850 wells for starters, and a pipeline stretching out for miles and miles and miles. We're concerned with the groundwater obviously and the impact that will have on all the animals and the vegetation within the forest and the cultural impacts of that. You know many of those animals are our totems, those animals are our totems ... they are our spiritual connections ... We're supposed to look after them to ensure that they have continuation of life, so that they don't become extinct. We look after them and they look after us, and we can't do that when we have the threat of coal seam gas and mining on our country.

Recall that what Keen (pp. 1, 15; Birdsell, 1970) referred to as 'totemic geography and totemic identity' plays a key role in organising kinship relations and the sustainable management of land, air and water. One Gomeroi elder (author interview, 27/02/2017) explained that those sites included the aforementioned Bora ring ceremonial and initiation sites through which younger members of the nation would be given knowledge. He explained the gravity of destroying those sites which the CSG gas wells threaten to do:

> Social structures that we had back then, the colonisation process has broken them up, you see. But with our land still intact, and our knowledge keepers still being able to go out there and teach the younger generation, if they say, knock them out, that's another part of our history and nation lost.

In this sense these sites are essential for the successful transmission of culture. By destroying them those intergenerational relationships, which Card (2003, p. 63) recognised as essential to social vitality, would be lost.

Turning to the issue of cultural heritage and the protection of sacred sites, which has been as a central mobilising issue for Indigenous communities like the Gomeroi who face resource and development projects on their land (Norman, 2016, p. 243), he (author interview, 27/02/2017) told me 'they never ever ever look at our sacred sites in the same way that they look at a church'. One Gomeroi elder (author interview, 21/03/2017) elaborated on the vexatious problem, expressing doubts about the feasibility of avoiding damage to sacred sites in the course of resource extraction and poured scorn on the myopic methods used, which demonstrate a fundamental lack of cultural understanding or sensitivity:

> People like Santos and Whitehaven Coal, they think that you can mitigate everything. You can't mitigate everything. They say, 'we'll go around this, we won't destroy this'. They think it's just about a little artefact on the ground. There might be a knife edge on the ground, but it's much more than that ... it's the connection of all those things to each other, in the place they are. It's the significance of all these things, the relationship they have with each other, not just a singular item. It's how they relate to everything else in the landscape. To remove it from an area

then that's desecration ... how would you like chopping up the Great Wall of China!

This is precisely the sort of mechanistic thinking discussed at the beginning of this chapter that sees nature, refracted through the commodity form, as bearer of exchange value, which can be fragmented, disembodied and dislocated in a manner that pays no heed to its relationship with the ecological whole. Reflecting on this problem, Harvey (1993, p. 10) mused 'Newtonian mechanics and Smithian economics may be adequate to building bridges, but they are totally inadequate in trying to determine the ecosystemic impact of such endeavours'. One incident she conveyed exemplified the colonial nature of the cultural heritage laws. A request for protection under the cultural heritage laws for a sacred site on the grounds of a Whitehaven coal mine was rejected by the relevant federal minister because although the government recognised the cultural significance and sacredness of the site, apparently it didn't meet the requirements of the act: 'This is a white fellas act we're talking about. How does a non-Aboriginal person know what's sacred and what's not sacred to an Aboriginal person?'

Turning to the problem of NTA and the ILUA process, when asked if during the negotiation process with the CSG company one Gomeroi elder (author interview, 27/02/2017) felt his community had been properly consulted and given the right of FPIC (Article 19). He explained:

> With native title, look it's a government construct, to benefit them and mining companies. Everyone knows that. There are ways around that with unity. Now, let's say for us with the Gomeroi nation we have 17 or 16 [native title] applicants who speak on behalf of 32,000, that is the estimate of how many Gomeroi people there are out. So, if you have just 16 people going in there, just talking on behalf of everyone else, that's not informed consent, is it?

As for the institutions set up under the other land recovery regime, the ALRA, and the associated LALCs, one Gomeroi elder (author interview, 27/02/2017) averred 'they allow mining, they were one of the first ones! Look here, when they first set up the Local Aboriginal Land Councils, they were supposed to be the governing body for the communities, but they went away from that.' When I asked why this was the case, he argued this was due to corruption and manipulation. Referring to the Narrabri LALC which has responsibility for the Pilliga Forest, he said wryly that 'last year Whitehaven and Santos threw them a Christmas party last year'. Referring to the work undertaken by the LALCs to identify sacred sites under the provisions of the Aboriginal and Torres Strait Islander Heritage Protection

Act 1984 (Cth), he observed with keen dryness, 'If you have registered Aboriginal parties who go out there and do cultural heritage, then just sign off and say, "no no no, it's not significant", they will go straight in there and do it. And they [resource companies] got people there in the Land Council doing it'.

Venessa Hicki, a Gomeroi woman living in Walgett, NSW not far from the site of the Santos CSG project, conveyed a similar experience, arguing (author interview, 06/02/17) that their local LALC were 'out for themselves'. She explained that when she asked if they would do anything about the Santos CSG project on the Pilliga Forest, they would typically retort, 'that's got nothing to do with us'. But she exclaimed, 'we are all Gomeroi'. Arguably, here, the architecture of the Indigenous representative institutions can act as a fragmentary force, weakening potential solidarity on broader geographical and indeed cultural scales. Her persistent questioning at the LALC eventually granted her a meeting with a member of the State Land Council, who told her, 'we're doomed if we do and we're doomed if we don't. But it's up to us Aboriginals to get in, because if we don't get in, white man is going to get it all.' This is as a clear a statement of the colonial dilemma as any I have recorded. Recall that earlier it was argued that tying the material fates of the various institutions erected under the Indigenous land recovery legal regimes to that of the resource companies through mining royalties would compel those institutions to function as technologies of government ensuring conformity to new 'neoliberal' norms. On a more fundamental level, though it may ensure fiscal independence from the government, it does not ensure fiscal independence from the mineocracy. Moreover, this alleged fiscal independence from the government conveniently side steps the fact that the government itself, under the political economy dominated by the resource sector, is not structurally independent.

Turning to divisions within his own community, one Gomeroi elder (author interview, 27/02/2017) said there were people who were helping the mining companies to destroy their landscapes and threaten their culture, 'they ought to be ashamed of themselves'. One Gomeroi elder (author interview, 27/02/2017) added, 'and that's why we voted the old boys out ... and we'll go in there as a unified force and deal with Santos'. This is a reference to the fact that the original Gomeroi native title claimant group, who had once taken a strong stance against CSG and mining more generally, in 2015 signed two ILUAs with Whitehaven Coal. The agreement was criticised by a number of Gomeroi for being conducted and negotiated behind closed doors and largely in secret, stressing the lack of consultation with the broader community (Norman, 2016, p. 249). One Gomeroi elder (author interview, 21/03/2017) told me:

They made a deal with Whitehaven Coal that none of us were privy to ... they signed off on a deal without any of the [Gomeroi] nation knowing what that deal entails. They were not supposed to sign off on any deals until it was brought back to the nation and agreed to by the nation.

When I asked why, she responded bluntly:

There's money involved. As far as I'm concerned it comes back to dollars and cents, [*sic*] being able to look after themselves rather than the nation as a whole. It's not just jobs going into the future, because it's not just about money. First and foremost, it's got to be about protection of country. That goes without saying for Aboriginal people, or it should.

Again, it must be stressed that not all Gomeroi are opposed to mining. Some, as Norman (2016, p. 248) in her fieldwork found, hope that it will offer opportunities for desperately needed investment in their communities. The quote above and the reference to 'jobs' clearly speaks to this desire, as well as the tension and division created by the need for development assistance and the manner in which it is provided by the settler-colonial state. And care must always be taken to avoid falling into the discursive trap of reifying an 'ideal type' of Indigenous person that will naturally sacrifice all in the name of the environment and see those that do not as somehow embodying a 'corrupted' form of indigeneity, as the Left and the environmental movement are sometimes guilty of (Vincent, 2016, p. 223). But again, as with the Githabul above, this is a position taken not in historical isolation, not devoid of historical context, but one informed by a history of forcible articulation with a settler-colonial economy and centuries of systemic violence and chronic underfunding in their communities, leaving many with very little choice in practice. These are issues recognised in the literature (Trigger et al., 2014), but all too rarely are they historicised within a context of settler colonialism and relations of genocide. Ultimately, a new leadership group were voted in, replacing the former applicants, despite legal attempts to have the election declared illegitimate (Murphy, 2016). Suffice to say those attempts failed.[11]

The stories of the Wangan and Jagalingou, the Githabul and Gomeroi demonstrate empirically Freeman's (2002, p. 85) warning that we must always pay attention to the manner in which rights are institutionalised. Indeed the 'shifting structural target' of the settler-colonial logic of elimination has been found to reside within the discursive, normative, legal and institutional landscape of human and Indigenous rights, ironically violating those very rights enshrined in UNDRIP and menacing the group life of those Indigenous communities. Indeed, the rights codified under the complex land recovery regimes in Australia continue to ensure the partial destruction/reproduction of Indigenous societies and economies so that they can be 'made ready' for fusion with settler capitalist or market relations and articulated with the broader imperatives of Australia settler-colonial economy. In turn this nourishes and supports the Australian economy's role in the international division labour as a key site of fossil fuel and mineral extraction. The system of rights in the age of recognition and reconciliation serve not only to reproduce a particular form of articulation between settler-colonial and Indigenous societies and economies, one which ensures the *extraction of commodities in different ways* (Hartwig, 1978, p. 129), but also subjects the target Indigenous populations to remorseless structural pressures to conform and assimilate to the 'real economy' and in so doing foster their 'development'. However, the success of these processes is not a foregone conclusion. These are not economically deterministic processes but shaped by struggle. The driving force of history has always been struggle, which is decided in the political sphere (Bedford and Irving, 2000, p. 94). It is to this struggle we now turn.

Resistance to the relations of genocide

The Githabul and Gomeroi case is notable for another reason. Their struggle against forms of extractivism has involved building alliances with non-Indigenous communities. In the case of the Githabul, after years of struggle, and a series of direct actions, including blockades of drilling equipment and CSG drilling sites, in alliance with a broad grassroots community and environmental movement in the Northern Rivers region, culminating in the Bentley Blockade in 2014 (Luke, 2018), they successfully denied the CSG firm a 'social license' (Luke, 2017) and shut down the development project. The Gomeroi have also recently built emerging alliances with environmental groups and local farmers. It offers a glimmer of hope that, through what has been dubbed the green-black alliance (Vincent and Neale, 2016), the colonial terrain will not inevitably succeed in subduing and pacifying Indigenous peoples and that, depending on the balances of forces, it can be restructured to favour Indigenous peoples resisting colonisation.

Invariably, the state of green-black relations has been cast in a negative light with the discourse assuming an inescapable and irreconcilable conflict between the values of the environmental movement and those underpinning Indigenous land rights (Ritter, 2014). It is wise to caution against those who would automatically assume a natural affinity between the two causes (Langton, 2004). From the beginning of what can be called the modern environmental movement from the 1970s, in Australia there have been cases where environmentalists have used problematic language and imagery not too dissimilar from that which will be examined in the following chapter when we turn our attention to the British occupation of Kenya: that is to say, an imagery and discourse that depicted nature as a 'natural wilderness' bereft of people, Indigenous or otherwise (Neumann, 1996). And even if, today, these discourses have largely been rejected, in part due to the influence of Indigenous movements and eco-centred spirituality, problems remain in what Vincent and Neale (2016, p. 4) describe as the 'sticky problems of fostering relationships across racialized difference in a settler colonial setting'. Vincent (2016, p. 213) pithily summarises the 'unstable relations' between 'black and green' when he observes 'non-Indigenous desires for contact with Aboriginal people, reification of cultural otherness, and post-colonial guilt combined to shape, constrain and sometimes wreck these relations'. Indeed, these relations can be fraught and complicated by virtue of living in what was earlier referred to in Chapter 2 as *a single field of life* structured along colonial lines. Nevertheless, what the interview data shows is that despite these tensions and historically informed complex entanglements, there are promising alliances in which what Vincent and Neale (2016, p. 5) call Indigenous 'greenies' and non-Indigenous environmentalists are not only succeeding in common goals to halt and sometimes reverse the tide of resource extraction and environmental degradation, but are dialectically mutually transformed and constituted by each other (Vincent and Neale, 2016, pp. 4–5). Of particular interest is the potential for the transformation of broader layers of Australian society towards a greater level of ecological consciousness.

The case of the Githabul typifies and illuminates these issues. With the CSG industry rolling out rapidly since 2009, predominantly in QLD, the state of NSW took a more cautious regulatory approach. More importantly, experiences and issues faced in the neighbouring state of QLD, and overseas in the US, stimulated community-level discussions in a number of rural areas in New South Wales and elsewhere (Luke, 2017, p. 266). These discussions would sow the seeds of an anti-CSG movement across rural Australia called 'Lock the Gate Alliance' (Lloyd et al., 2013). Critically, this alliance would be constituted by farmers, rural residents, environmentalists and ultimately some Indigenous nations and activists. The anti-CSG movement in the Northern Rivers, spanning between 2011 and 2015, involved not just the blockade of wells and drilling sites, but included petitions, marches, protests and landholder visits to parliament (Lloyd et al., 2013). Although not the only protest movement in Australia, the movement in the Northern Rivers was arguably the most successful, since it both halted the development of CSG by the resource company Metagasco in the area (Hawke, 2015) *and* built alliances with the local Indigenous nations.

The Githabul elder explained (author interview, 23/01/2017) his involvement in the Northern Rivers movement against CSG starting with the now infamous blockade against the CSG company Metagasco's building of a drilling pad on their land back in 2014:

> I think my first platform was 'Doubtful Creek'. We got involved because the mining company coal seam gas implicated us in a deal that we were not aware of. So, we had to stand our ground and say there was no dialogue between the mining company and the original peoples. They may have had some contact with some individuals that were prepared to sell out but when it comes down to the crunch, they didn't recognise tribal council and eldership, so we had to step it up.

In other words, it was because of what they believed to be a fraudulent ILUA as well as the threat to country that CSG posed, that he and a number of other Githabul elders decided to get involved.

> We had nothing to do with the mining, so we seized the opportunity to take the platform to be a tribal voice within our own country that was acceptable to the rest of the community, and that was the safety of land for the young. If we destroy it then we destroy our children's future.

Githabul elder no. 3 concurred, stressing when referring to Doubtful Creek and the Bentley movement (author interview, 23/01/2017), 'it wasn't Lock the Gate that got me there, but the conscious decision to be there for Mother Earth'.

A number of Githabul seemed to agree that forging an alliance with non-Indigenous communities, such as those engaged in Lock the Gate, is crucial to successfully resisting ecological and genocidal threats to land and ecosystems. Githabul elder no. 3 argued, 'if the broader community can understand why sovereignty can be there for all of us … we built good relations with the broader community'. Githabul elder no. 1 agreed and added (author interview, 23/01/2017), 'and we maintain them. I don't think black fella and white fella can no longer stay apart while the Commonwealth is about to rip this country apart'. Githabul elder no. 3 added:

> I think the government thought they had us with regards to 'separation'. They thought they had the majority of the Githabul under their thumb, but when we united with our brothers and sisters, our white brothers

and sisters, we came as one. When we came as one, we were powerful. It was untouchable. Because them two cultures standing together, black and white fighting for one thing, and that was to save Mother Earth.

Githabul elder no. 2 (author interview, 23/01/2017) explained that the Bentley blockade, the culmination and high point of the long-running resistance movement against CSG in the Northern Rivers, and perhaps the high point of the black-green alliance, was a powerful and unique occasion: 'it was something that was displayed as white and black fellas coming together to defend country. I don't think that this sort of campaigning has ever been done before in Australia, it's quite unique'. Reflecting on Bentley and the anti-CSG multi-ethnic protest movement, Githabul elder no. 1 (author interview, 23/01/2017) said, 'It was a gathering of minds, it was a gathering of social structures within our society that normally wouldn't come together except for in the extreme emergency for the safety of the land.' Githabul elder no. 3 (author interview, 23/01/2017) agreed, saying, 'what I saw at Bentley was the collective knowledge of all colours coming together: hippies, farmers'. Here there is a clear recognition that the jeopardisation of the land and the life supporting ecosystems united otherwise disparate and historically divided communities.

Speaking of his nation's struggle against CSG on the Pilliga, one Gomeroi elder (author interview, 27/02/2017), after acknowledging the settler-colonial role of farming and pastoralism in particular, conceded that he and a number of other Gomeroi elders decided they had no choice but to unite with white farmers:

> We co-exist at the moment. Sure, history is not that good, but we've gone to a couple of meetings with Lock the Gate Alliance and they believe that working together and forging a new path, a new history from this point ... colonisation in Australia started 229 years ago. Let's say we go forward and in 229 years we can look back and say *we came together* to stop the evil threat of CSG in NSW. [emphasis added]

In one interview with local carpenter Ian Gaillard from Lismore in the Northern Rivers, involved in anti-CSG demonstrations against Metagasco and one who worked closely with members of the Githabul, the very first thing he reflected on was this fraught and complex history (author interview, 23/01/2017):

> Just around here in Lismore there are very powerful places now being taken over for housing or bulldozed and developed and the significance of them to the local people [Indigenous communities] is huge. So how can they even begin to trust people of European descent? And they are,

> in some ways, in fights like the gas. It's been a bridge for a lot of people
> to get involved.

The carpenter demonstrated a deep sensitivity to the privileges inferred to himself and the settler community repeatedly throughout my interview. Discussing the NTA regime he described it as 'white man's thinking'. A recognition of white privilege and the history of settler colonialism is not uncommon to the environmental movement in Australia (Vincent, 2016), but, at least in the Northern Rivers, is evidently spreading even to the rural community, and those like himself who wouldn't traditionally be involved in environmental activism. This is arguably due in part at least to his relationship with Indigenous communities in organising against CSG. Demonstrating an ecological awareness that is clearly influenced by his relationship with Indigenous communities as well as a respect and deference, he said:

> You hear farmers in Australia, and it makes me sick to the core to hear
> it, 'we have the right to do what we want in our land'. Fuck you man,
> it's not your land! It [the land] belongs to the land, it's not ours. We might
> be custodians ... I'm 65 years old and I've done quite a lot of time with
> Indigenous people, but I'm still a novice ... if I was sitting here with an
> [Indigenous person] they would cut me to ribbons.

Mariann Lloyd Smith, alongside her role as senior advisor of Australia's National Toxics Network and expert on the environmental impacts of CSG, as a local resident played a central role in the Northern Rivers anti-CSG movement. She took part in various local town meetings and door to door awareness raising campaigns, campaigns across NSW and in the various successful blockades that took place. These included at Doubtful Creek and Bentley. Speaking of Indigenous participation in the anti-CSG campaigns, she spoke eloquently of the young Indigenous activists who gave strength, comfort and solidarity to those non-Indigenous who had no experience in blockading. She stressed (author interview, 26/01/17), 'they had a very spiritual role, as well as an informative and active role'. Speaking of the tensions historically between the environmental and Indigenous communities, she said:

> I've been involved in a lot of campaign issues and other than campaign
> issues that were specifically to do with Indigenous people, I've not seen
> that coming together with the environment movement, because the
> environment movement and Indigenous people have had a rocky his-
> tory ... fishing and hunting where there has been a clash of cultures. But
> this [anti-CSG] seemed to break down the barriers.

The threat posed by extractivism in Australia is laying the historical soil for the forging of alliances across communities that historically were alienated from each other. The influence of Indigenous ecocentric spirituality on the broader communities opposed to ecologically destructive development projects from the interview data is clear, as well as the greater efficacy of building extra-parliamentary direct action, rather than limiting the struggle to legal resistance, as the case of the Wangan and Jagalingou nation and the entire legal edifice of the land recovery regimes in Australia demonstrates. Arguably, what Marx called the 'superior relations' of production (Smith, 2005, p. 75), by which he meant Indigenous relations, play an important role in the struggle against ecological degradation. It is in the mutual constitution of the Indigenous, rural and environmental communities that the influence of Indigenous ecocentric and animistic cosmology plays an important role. It is this enduring ontology that offers hope for a resistance to a capitalist society irrevocably alienated from nature.

Notes

1. Of course, it should be stressed that the Soviet Union, in its quest for rapid industrial expansion and the 'overcoming of backwardness', also played a major role in driving the Great Acceleration and the Anthropocene. For its ecocidal history, see Feshbach and Friendly Jr, 1992; Peterson, 1993.

2. Marx's analysis of accumulation crisis brought on by materials-supplies disturbances operates on two levels: first, focusing on the conditions of crisis caused by fluctuations in the value of the materials in question brought on by shortages, and the second, relating to the indirect fluctuations in 'prices' brought on by the resultant competition, speculation and the credit system. See Karl Marx (1968, p. 515).

3. Gibson, author interview, 10/02/2017.

4. The NTA is constituted by an extremely complex array of institutions that includes Native Title Representative Bodies who represent native title claimants and the NNTTs which register native title claims heard in Federal Courts and also facilitate ILUAs and 'future acts', which refer to the necessity of resource developers to negotiate with native title parties, if they are impacted by new mineral development. Finally, once the native title is legally determined, Prescribed Bodies Corporate will be the legally recognised holders of that title in perpetuity.

5. This falls under Section 237.

6. Previously, the expedited procedure system contained in section 237 of the NTA had stated that an act attracts an expedited procedure if:

a) *the act does not directly* interfere with the carrying on of the community or social activities of the persons who are the holders of native title in relation to the land or waters concerned; and

b) *the act does not interfere* with areas or sites of particular significance, in accordance with their traditions, to the persons who are the holders of native title in relation to the land and waters concerned; and

c) *the act does not involve* major disturbance to any land or waters concerned or create rights whose exercise is likely to involve major disturbance to any land or waters concerned.

In the Howard amendments each condition would now begin with *is not likely to*, making it more difficult for Indigenous groups to object to the expedited procedure under the NTA.

7. *Burragubba v State of Queensland* [2016] FCA 984.

8. *Burragubba v State of Queensland* [2017] FCAFC 133.

9. The ILUA was the subject of further legal challenges in the Supreme Court of Queensland based on NTA grounds: *Burragubba & Anor v Minister for Natural Resources and Mines & Anor* [2016] QSC 273; *Burragubba & Ors v Minister for Natural Resources and Mines & Anor* [2017] QCA 179.

10. *McGlade v Native Title Registrar* [2017] FCAFC 10

11. The original Federal Court ruling to have the applicants replaced affectively recognising the decision of the Gomeroi community (*Gomeroi People v Attorney General of New South Wales* [2017] FCA 1464) was appealed (*Boney v Attorney General of New South Wales* [2018] FCAFC 218) but failed.

Chapter 4

Kenya then: the architecture of dispossession

As argued in the Australian context, genocidal processes in Kenya are determined by the changing structural imperatives of the Kenyan political economy and its relationship to the global capitalist system, where again continuities and breaks in the nature and form of relations of genocide are shaped by the structural imperatives of the settler-colonial capitalist system. Once again, the dialectical interaction between ecocidal logic of capital on the one hand, and the settler-colonial logic of elimination on the other and Indigenous resistance to both logics will prove decisive. Kenya and Australia share a history as former colonies of the British empire, which will provide illuminating similarities and contrasts. Above all, it is this shared heritage as former British settler colonies that will set them both on the path to genocide and see them unleash Lemkin's two-staged process. The precise historical manner in which the logic of settler-colonial capitalism will manifest as the 'logic of elimination' in the respective colonial spaces and the corresponding points, similarities and differences is what this entire book sets out to illuminate, and by way of comparison will bring into sharper focus. A historical examination of Kenya's colonial past will illuminate how the nature and precise techniques of genocide *evolve over time*, in articulation with the imperatives of capital accumulation and the global chains of capitalist production and trade.

Kenyan societies on the cusp of colonisation

If we can better understand the nature and form of social and ethnic groups before contact with colonial forces, we can better understand the varying impacts of European expansion and its correlate, settler-colonial relations of genocide on the essential foundations of Kenyan social formations, and why some Kenyan societies were better able to adapt to settler capitalism. As before, the objective is not to write a comprehensive history or anthropology of *all* pre-contact Kenyan societies but rather to illuminate the relations between multiple ethnic and social groups *within a single field of life*. In Kenya, societies varied in their production relations as well as culture, a distinction that would prove devastating to those forced to inhabit a rung on the civilisational ladder imposed on them by their colonial occupiers. Unlike Australia, where Indigenous societies varied in their particulars but could be said to possess features of social and cultural life, including their production relations, *held in common* by all, in Kenya there were qualitative and marked differences between their production relations and forms of property. As we will see shortly, this will have existential consequences for the social and ethnic groups concerned. Indeed, I have chosen to focus on the Kikuyu and Sengwer, precisely because their history under British settler colonialism, and the impact of settler colonialism post-independence, helps illuminate the *uneven* nature of relations of genocide in the Kenyan colony and beyond and in so doing reveals the structural contours and causal relations between the former and the political economy of genocide.

Prior to the arrival of British colonists, what would become known as the British East Africa Protectorate until 1926 (from which time it would become known as the Colony and Protectorate of Kenya), was a culturally and ethnically diverse landscape. In fact, as many as forty-two separate ethnic groups existed in precolonial Kenya, all with their distinct histories and political and social structures and historical intercommunal relations (Agbese and Kieh Jr, 2007, p. 128). Moreover, invariably, the social structures were broadly ordered according to egalitarian principles, unlike their Ugandan neighbours, whose societies were characterised by hierarchical kingdoms and chieftainships (Agbese and Kieh Jr, 2007). Social collectives in Kenya were predominantly clans and lineages based on common descent, organised vertically according to age sets which, though by and large equal, had distinct rights and duties (Berg-Schlosser, 1994, p. 249). The generational system was the preeminent social and political institution. Finally, precolonial ethnic groups lacked any centralised bureaucracies, and certainly a centralised state (Ochieng, 1985, p. 44).

The Kikuyu were predominantly a horticultural and agricultural people, as were the majority of Indigenous Kenyans, such as groups like the Kamba, Luo or Nandi, herding livestock on land they had cleared from forests in the Kikuyu plateau. Such groups would be 'granted' land on reserves and coerced into furnishing labour for the settler farms. Their mode of life not only made them compatible with the demands, disciplines and rigours of settler agriculture but they would be deemed sufficiently 'civilised' according to the racial taxonomy of the colonial elites. The basic unit of social organisation of the Kikuyu was the family or *nyumba*, consisting of the father, mother and children (Muriuki, 1974, p. 110). This could extend into the 'joint' family if the father was wealthy enough to support another wife and furnish another hut for her to occupy with her children. Families who had the same provenance aggregated into sub-clans or *mbari*, clans or *moheregu* and ultimately the tribe as a whole (Jackson, 1969, p. 14). The Kikuyu reproduced themselves through fission, growth and population dispersal, what Sahlins (1961) described as a *segmentary lineage system*, where the reproduction and the stability of the social relations of the Kikuyu depended on succession into subgroups and expansion into newly settled lands. With polygamy being the rule, the larger the clan the more sons there were, meaning in turn more livestock, wives and offspring. This was the principal measure of wealth and influence. In fact, the manipulation of family relationships, especially through marriage, was a key mechanism that facilitated expansion by providing access either to more cattle in exchange for daughters, or through marriage, sons who could provide labour, both necessary when seceding from existing clans, venturing forth into new lands and establishing a new settlement (Bates, 1987, p. 6). There is dispute among scholars about the degree to which egalitarianism existed within the Kikuyu (Kershaw, 1997, pp. 26–8, 61–8), the debate hinging on the nature and distribution of property and production relations, suffice to say that there *were* degrees of inequality. A large and wealthy clan (or particular *mbari* and in turn *nyumba* or family within it) would augment its authority by attracting non-clan or alien elements to their fold, in the fashion of a magnet, some eventually being completely absorbed and thus enlarging the clan, while others would remain *ahoi* or simply tenants of the respective property-owning clan or *mbari* (Muriuki, 1974, p. 114). Since the number of your offspring was in part a function of the size of your *mbari* or kin group and that in turn determined access to land and cattle, which in turn secured the material means to offer 'bridewealth' for the forging of wider kin networks, wealth, as measured in livestock, wives and offspring, was dialectically constituted through this 'virtuous circle'.

Within what is known as the *kiama* system (Gathigira, 1952, pp. 63–8; Benson, 1964, pp. 6–7); Lambert (1965, ch. 9), the highest authority in Kikuyuland, vested with judicial and executive powers, those families with significant land holdings and thus formidable capacities to furnish cattle and other food stuffs would be accorded greater access and influence on the *kiama* councils, with the need to pay fees to ascend the ranks of the *kiama* system being an obligatory precondition (Kershaw, 1997, pp. 65–6). The *kiama* system fulfils key political, social and judicial functions and can perhaps be better characterised as the *social relations of kinship*. Therefore, the *social relations of kinship* can be seen by the end of the nineteenth century to possess in embryonic form certain class characteristics. What we have here is the mode of production shaped by the conditions of social production determining the social relations of kinship in the *kiama* system.

The purpose of this brief exposition of the ethnography of the Kikuyu is to help us better understand the nature of the genocidal structuring dynamics: if the Kikuyu suffered any attenuation, restriction or deprivation of land ownership, then their ability to rear cattle and other foodstuffs, to expand out into new fresh virgin territories, and ultimately *to operate as a segmentary lineage system*, what Kanogo (1987) termed the 'Kikuyu expansionist dynamic', is undermined. This in turn would lead to the stymieing of the ability of Kikuyu tribesmen and women to perform initiation ceremonies, progress through the various status grades, rear a family and of course ultimately enter the stage of elders and partake in the political and social organisation of their society (Kenyatta, 1938, p. 26; Routledge, 1910, p. 154). In other words, it would inflict a fatal blow on their ability to practise their culture (Kilson, 1955, p. 104). Jackson (1969, p. 103) concurred when he asserted '[a]ny significant loss of land by the Kikuyu people, in addition to threatening their basic means of subsistence would *threaten a fundamental aspect of the foundation of their socio cultural system*' [emphasis added]. It is the obstruction and interdiction of the reproduction of the segmentary lineage system with the arrival of white settlers (Jackson, 2017 p. 237), what Bates (1987, p. 8) described as a massive exogenous shock, and I describe as the unleashing of genocidal structuring dynamics, that would drive a radical reconstitution of the factors of production on land, giving rise to acute shortages of the former that would fuel the anticolonial resistance against British occupation. By the same token, it is this same radical reconstitution of the political economy of Kenya to meet the imperatives of the metropole that would unleash genocidal structuring dynamics on forest-dwelling peoples like the Sengwer, orchestrating their removal from their ancestral dwellings and their forcible assimilation on the reserve system.

The unevenness with which genocidal structuring dynamics impact the various ethnic groups in Kenya will come into sharper focus once we examine the fates of those who were disparagingly labelled as 'Dorobo'. The fate of the Sengwer would be qualitatively different to that of agriculturalists like the Kikuyu. The Sengwer, like the Ogiek, would be deemed by the colonial authorities as not compatible or conducive to the extraction of surplus value and not civilised enough to warrant continued existence as a social collective in its own right. These were the hunter-gatherer societies, who would arguably, from a Lemkian perspective, suffer the most devastating and comprehensive social death, since their mode of life was not deemed fit for incorporation, in any form, into the political economy of the colony.

The archaeological and anthropological sources show there existed pre-colonial contact place-based forest-dwelling communities that possessed a forager/hunter-gatherer mode of production (Sutton, 1973; Lunn-Rockliffe, 2018). The Sengwer, like the Ogiek, who they have sometimes been confused with, have a predominantly hunter-gatherer economy and society with a subsistence strategy orientated around beekeeping, honey storage, hunting in the forest and herbal medicine (Kenrick, 2020a, p. 238), taking advantage of various altitudes to exploit different ecological niches in the forest glades of the Embobut Forest in the Cherangani Hills in different seasons. Although towards the end of the nineteenth century the Sengwer would begin to (re)adopt elements of food production, or farming, through contacts with Arabs and the Maasai, testifying to the fluid and historical nature of group life (KNCHR, 2018, p. 23). Today, in fact, the Sengwer still rely to some extent on food production or 'mixed economies' in the form of family gardens in the forest glades and keeping of cattle (Kenrick, 2020a, p. 238). Furthermore, the evidence points to their occupation of their land for at least 250 years, long before the period of colonisation began, a historical reality that is overlooked or ignored by those who adopt an 'instrumentalist frame', perhaps most notably Lynch (2016). By instrumentalist, Lynch and her acolytes suggest that Indigenous group identity, like that of the Sengwer's, is strategically forged to curry favour with the British colonial authorities. Oral testimonies taken form Kalenjin populations, including the Marakwet (Davies and Moore, 2016), Pokot and, most pertinently, the Sengwer, attest to their arrival in the Cherangani Hills at least 250 years ago (Lunn-Rockliffe, 2018, p. 54), though my own interviews date it as far back as 500 years (anonymous Sengwer, author interview, 15/12/2020).

As already stated above, like all the other forty-two ethnic groups before colonial contact, their social structure was ordered according to egalitarian principles, lacking any centralised bureaucracies, with their social formation organised around clans and lineages based on common descent, organised vertically according to age sets with distinct rights and duties (Berg-Schlosser, 1994 p. 249). The Sengwer are made up of twenty-one clans in the Embobut Forest (Kenrick, 2020a, p. 238). The descent group (the kinship system) would, as it did with Australian Indigenous societies, play an important superstructural function. Their superstructure would mediate inter-clan, biological, environmental and ecological tensions. In pre-capitalist societies, particularly hunter-gatherer figurations, production (and procurement) relations were embedded within kinship networks and their corresponding obligations and commitments. The kinship system determined your relation to others and the corresponding obligations to them, the land and natural resources. For instance, each clan or extended family lineage had a designated forest territory, usually marked out by topographical features like hilltops in glade clearings, named after founding elders (Lunn-Rockliffe, 2018, p. 156). Within Embobut, three glades, Koropkwen, Kaptirbai and Kapkok, are recognised as the ancestral homes of the Sengwer (Lunn-Rockliffe, 2018, p. 127; anonymous Sengwer, author interview, 28/12/2020), though according to today's political geography, the Sengwer reside predominantly in three administrative districts of modern-day Kenya: Trans-Nzoia, West Pokot and Elgeyo-Marakwet (Kenrick, 2020a, p. 238). This practice of using topography to mark out clan territories is a widespread practice documented among other neighbouring ethnic groups such as the Marakwet and Pokot (Moore 1986; Davies, 2009). These territories contained valuable animal and plant resources crucial to material subsistence strategies. The clan system ensured that hunting, foraging and bee keeping could only take place within your clan's designated forest territory (anonymous Sengwer, author interview, 28/12/2020), further ensuring ecological sustainability.

In fact, their relationship with the bee population is described by Lunn-Rockliffe (2018, p. 165) as a 'companion species' meaning that they have a symbiotic relationship, as part of a larger forest ecosystem, ensuring that the forest is protected and habitats are created for the beehives, which in turn promotes pollination. Here, in an analogous way to that which we found with Indigenous superstructural relations in Australia, the ascription of supernatural forces to nature, or the biome in which they inhabit, is the backbone of the Sengwer religion. The Sengwer lifeway also reproduces itself in accordance with ecological cycles and environmental rhythms, a sustainable relationship that is regulated through its religion and spiritual ontology. What is sometimes referred to as 'animism', the belief that spirits inhabit and animate all living things including flora and even the abiotic environment, accounts for the existence of taboos and totems which help preserve the life of species native to their forest dwellings. For the Sengwer, spirits inhabit the trees themselves, so that whenever a tree is felled for cultural or religious reasons they must first pray (Mamati, 2018, p. 38). In the case of totems, this involves the designation of special status and even membership of the tribe to certain animals, which contributes to environmental conservation (Mamati, 2018, p. 28). For one participant and member of the Sengwer, the interviewee stated that their clan totem was a hawk or *sirere* (anonymous Sengwer, author interview, 28/12/2020).

A key component of the religious world view is the belief in ancestors as living dead members of the community who still play a key role in the life of the community as spiritual guides. Not conserving the resources of the forests can anger the spiritual ancestors, or *Assis* (the Sun), the divine creator or God, and *Illat* the god of thunder and rain, and so it was the duty of the community to live in sustainable co-existence with the environment (Mamati, 2018, p. 37; anonymous Sengwer, author interview, 09/12/2020). Ultimately, it was the council or clan elders who were sanctioned by deities to ensure their forest dwellings were looked after, though there was a strong emphasis on communal or collective decision-making responsibility, for instance the requirement to share the proceeds of a hunt. This collectivism was in part derived from their shared belief that they all descended form a common ancestor called 'Sengwer'. Through oral literature and initiation practices, Sengwer from an early age were initiated into and taught environment management practices, which stressed that they were custodians of the forests, mandated by Assis (Mamati, 2018, p. 34). Aside from the oral historical and anthropological evidence presented above of the residence of the Sengwer within the Embobut Forest in the Cherangani Hills as hunter-gatherers for at least 250 to 500 years, which would of course predate the arrival of the British colonists, we also have British colonial records which testify to the Sengwer status as hunter-gatherer societies at the eve of the twentieth century. It is to those early records that we will turn in the discussion of the Sengwer's tragic and fateful entanglement with settler-colonial relations and their corresponding genocidal structuring dynamics in the following section. What the above analysis has shown is fascinating parallels with Indigenous groups in Australia who also possessed a fusion of hunter-gatherer production and superstructural relations, with an emphasis on collectivism and reverence and respect for nature. Given the intimate socio-cultural and economic attachment to the forests that the above has illuminated, the severance of the Sengwer from their forest dwellings would induce social death, the *sine qua non* of the crime of genocide.

The genesis of relations of genocide

The genocide of the Sengwer, Kikuyu and other ethnic groups in Kenya would not have taken place but for the operation of socio-economic and geo-political structures that extended far beyond the boundaries of Kenya itself. Therefore, it is necessary to analyse those structures that led to the British government's involvement in and colonisation of Kenya and established the *situation coloniale*. Ergo, an analysis that illuminates the *global dimension* will be outlined in order to draw attention to the larger socio-economic and political forces that conditioned the colonisation of Kenya and the resultant genocidal process. This provides a mechanism that can demonstrate Lemkin's assertion that genocide and colonisation are ineluctably bound up with each other. More specifically, this latter connection will help explicate the imposition of the foreign economic system on Kenya's Indigenous population.

Once again, as with the establishment of the Australian colony explored in Chapter 2, there are two 'logics of power' dialectically interacting but distinct. Firstly, economic competition or the politics of production, exchange and accumulation and secondly, the logic of geo-political competition or the territorialist logic of state, dialectically interacting but distinct (Callinicos, 2009; Harvey, 2003b). Between 1873 and 1896 the world economy experienced what is commonly known as the 'Great Depression', the first great economic contraction in the life of the capitalist global system (Callinicos, 2009, p. 153). Arrighi (2007, pp. 116–20) compares this to what he describes as the 'long downturn' of the twentieth century, both periods characterised by intensified competition and stagnation. In the last few decades of the nineteenth century Marxist economists have argued that the global economy suffered from a system-wide crisis of profitability determined by the rising organic composition of capital and a consequent deleterious effect on the rate of profit (Harman, 1984, pp. 51–4). The response of Britain was distinct. Unlike the 'organised capitalisms' of Germany and the US, where a state-led process of cartelisation and rationalisation took place, Britain preserved the relatively decentralised business structures that had arisen during the industrial revolution and instead embarked on a phase of overseas investment, from £700 million in 1870 to £2 billion by 1900, upwards of £4 billion by 1913 (Callinicos, 2009, p. 153). Critically, the growing expansion of US manufacturing exports and increasing competition from the US and Germany in Latin America, and a consequent relative decline in Britain's competitiveness, compelled Britain to abandon its 'imperialism of free trade' and foster its growing surpluses with India, Australia and the new colonies in Africa (Gallagher and Robinson, 1953). Moreover, the areas that would eventually be annexed in the African continent would broadly coincide with those regions that were the recipients of European capital (Good, 1976, p. 602). What we see here at work is the operation of the structural logic of a socio-economic system shaping the world economy, forging a world division of labour that ensnared agricultural suppliers of food and raw materials. This is precisely what we saw unfold in the Australian colonial space in Chapter 2, where Australia became a key exporter of wool to the British textile factories and later beef and other foodstuffs.

The global economic context was set for Britain's intrusion into the west African region that would come to be known as Kenya. This was the beginning of what has become known as 'the scramble for Africa' (Pakenham, 1991), so called because it entailed the movement of the great powers of Europe to carve up Africa (Elkins, 2005a, p. 5; Whittlesey, 1953, p. 81; Robinson, and Gallagher, 1961, p. 308). This began at the Congress of Berlin 1884–5 where the division of Africa into forty-odd colonies and protectorates that paid no heed to ethnic groupings would later serve the template for the modern states of present-day Africa. Britain would assume control of the East African Protectorate in 1886 in a deal concluded with Germany and the Sultan of Zanzibar (Moon, 1973).

But why did Britain annex what was known at the time as the East African Protectorate, in addition to all of its other colonial dependencies? Britain at the time was concerned that French inroads into Eastern Africa towards the Nile and German encroachment south of the British foothold of Mombasa on the coast would ultimately pose a risk to its control of the Suez Canal, which was pivotal to Britain's access to the trade routes to India and more specifically the captive market for British industrial goods that India represented (Cain and Hopkins, 1993, p. 334; Jackson, 2017, p. 232; Good, 1976, p. 602). If the Suez was choked off or, worse still, annexed by a rival power, then access to the markets of India and the Far East would be cut off. According to one chargé, British officials told French diplomats, 'take all you want in Africa, provided that you keep off the valley of the Nile' (Robinson and Gallagher, 1961, p. 333). The logic, according to British state planners, was their rivals, especially the Germans, might dam up the Nile head waters to desiccate Egypt and eventually force the withdrawal of British troops around the Suez Canal area due to the resulting ecological disaster (Elkins, 2005a, p. 2). This paranoid logic would entail a foreign invading power importing the necessary manpower and equipment to not only dam the White Nile but all of its tributaries. A railway stretching from the coast to Uganda was therefore proposed; quite a considerable engineering and logistical feat for the time, given the topography of that region, not to mention an onerous burden on the purse strings of the British government, to the tune of £5 million (Jackson, 2017, p. 233). This would provide the means for the British army to quickly mobilise its forces in response; a sceptical British public would dub the railway, and by inference, the British government's convoluted logic, the 'Lunatic Express' (Miller, 1971). In an effort to keep hold of the territory, the British government encouraged immigration, namely white settlers, and thus, wittingly or otherwise, set in train a series of events that led to the formation and imposition of a foreign or 'settler/estate' economic system. Once again, we see a striking parallel with the Australian settler-colonial space, in that both can trace their origins to geopolitical imperatives.

And so, we see the intersection of economic and geo-political competition in the context of a global economy that by the last third of the nineteenth century may not have been fully capitalist but nonetheless was knitted together through an interlocking nexus of trade and investment under the hegemonic sway of the capitalist mode of production (Hobsbawm, 1975) located in the western hemisphere with Britain standing at its apex (Saul, 1960). This was facilitated by the rise of key technologies such as rail and steam power and most importantly driven by the ceaseless competitive drive to accumulate, the *raison d'être* of capitalism (Marx, 1967a, ch. 25). It is at this intersection that we find the global mechanisms that conditioned Britain's intervention in East Africa, which would have disastrous genocidal consequences for those Indigenous denizens of what became known as Kenya.

Architectures of dispossession then: land and labour

As with the establishment of the Australian settler colony, in order to establish the colony, British forces would first have to embark on a war of conquest akin to the frontier wars explored in Chapter 2. Although the East Africa Protectorate was declared in 1895, the war of conquest lasted from 1894 till 1912, a period coterminous with fortress building and survey mapping (Marx, 1967a). In order to develop the land between Imperial British East African Company (IBEAC)-controlled Uganda and the coast, with ultimately a view to protecting the head waters of the Nile, work began in 1896 on the 582-mile Uganda railway (Good, 1976, p. 602), called so because it linked landlocked Uganda with the rest of the world, financed and directed by the British government. It would eventually span 582 miles from the coastal port of Mombasa all the way to Lake Victoria (Elkins, 2005a, p. 1). Once the railway neared completion and the final cost of the railway became clear, the drive to establish an economically viable colony would in part be motivated by the necessity to pay off the debt incurred by the British taxpayer (Elkins, 2005a, p. 3; Brett, 1973; Wolff, 1974, p. 134).

The geography of the Eastern African Protectorate was laid down in embryo by the IBEAC, to whom British commercial activities had been delegated prior to the construction of the railway. As they moved deeper inland, driven by a desire to secure the Swahili caravan trade to Uganda, IBEAC built a series of fortifications strategically placed running all the way back to the coast. As Jackson (2017, p. 232) observed 'these would form the geography of the embryo settler state. Fortifications provided the necessary facility for safety and replenishment in the days when it took a month to get from Mombasa to where Nairobi now stands and a full ten weeks to reach Lake Victoria'. It was from these fortifications that punitive raids were launched by the IBEAC in an effort to secure the trade routes, put down resistance and ensure access to supplies when they were not forthcoming. This extended to burning down entire villages, stealing livestock and massacring hundreds of men, women and children at a time (Jackson, 2017). But this strategy also involved building alliances with agreeable Africans brought under the patronage of the corporation. In this initial phase of the colonisation of Kenya therefore, we see the beginning of the colonial authority's 'pacification' programme and war of conquest against recalcitrant ethnic groups (Ogot, 1968, p. 259), and through its alliance-building, what would become a core component of the colonial state's administrative logic of co-option of local 'tribal' leaders. The pacification programme would continue as the railway reached completion, reordering the demographic landscape, displacing those who lived near it, particularly the Kikuyu, and unleashing a pattern of racial violence that would endure for the lifetime of the colony (Elkins, 2005a, p. 2).[1]

The formation of the colonial state in Kenya was a volatile, contradictory and haphazard one (Berman, 1990, chs. 1–2). In essence, it involved, and played a crucial part in (Berman and Lonsdale, 1980, p. 56), the drive to link metropolitan capital with Indigenous societies and seize effective control of African labour and production, restructuring them to meet its needs (Berman, 1990, pp. 34–5; Berman and Lonsdale, 1992, pp. 101–22; Brett, 1973; Wolff, 1974). This, the *global* connection and its role as an economic adjunct of the metropole, was not unique to Kenya but common to the political economy of colonialism in Africa more generally (Amin, 1974; Wallerstein, 1976), and indeed, as we saw in the previous chapter, the formation and territorialisation of the Australian settler-colonial state. It was a process of *articulation*, very similar to the one we witnessed in the Australian context, where two different and often inimical and incompatible economic systems and modes of life are weaved together, leading to the uprooting, dislocation, transformation and, paradoxically, destruction *and* partial preservation of the figurations of Indigenous societies. In essence, as with the Australian colony, it was a logic of elimination, driven by a logic of accumulation. Only, what distinguished the Kenyan case was that the articulation and partial preservation of the Indigenous mode only occurred with those Indigenous groups considered, in today's parlance, 'developed' enough. Whereas those who were at the very bottom of the civilisational ladder, were forcibly subsumed into other social groups.

In order to furnish the needs of land and cheap labour that settler production so desperately needed, the colonial state, as it did in Australia, embarked on a form of primary accumulation and its corollary, the creation of a ready supply of cheap black labour. To achieve these aims the colonial state had to 'destroy the cycle of simple reproduction of the Indigenous domestic economy via the monetization of at least some elements of material reproduction' (Berman, 1990, p. 37), by introducing a complex set of laws and regulations. The policies and regulations discussed below materially obliged African peasants to either seek work on the settler farms or sell or supply agricultural commodities. Here we see a process remarkably redolent with that which occurred in Australia, where the Indigenous mode of life was partially destroyed and made ready for a forcible process of what Lloyd (2010, p. 33) described as 'hybridisation', in which after a war of pacification, and a state sponsored land grab, the Indigenous societies would be 'made ready' for fusion with settler capitalist or market relations. This corresponds with two of Hartwig's (1978, p. 129) three modes of articulation of the settler-colonial and Indigenous figuration, first discussed in Chapter 2, namely the extraction of commodities in different ways and the extraction of labour power. For the vast majority of the Kikuyu, the latter was the predominant form of articulation, driving the formation of a nascent Kenyan working class (Ochieng, 1992, p. 262). The renowned political economist Colin Leys (1975, p. 171), reflecting on the profound significance of these polices, singled out one transformative process above all: 'of all the ways in which capitalism wrought transformations in the pre-existing modes of production, the employment of wage labour stands out as the most far-reaching'.

The former mode of articulation confined to those privileged or tenacious few, who managed to negotiate the labyrinthine system of regulations and restrictions we will discuss below, was designed to retard African peasant agriculture. In other words, the destruction of the Kikuyu figuration was not uniform and in fact some elements were transformed into nascent centres of commodity production for the market. The imposition of a foreign economic system led to the emergence of an internal transition towards a petite bourgeoisie class of farmers whose ranks would be bolstered by the creation of a social layer of teachers, clerks, domestic servants, lawyers, interpreters and skilled workers who due to their income and security of employment would be given the appellation petite bourgeoisie (Leys, 1975). Combined with the rise of a new working class, this would unleash contradictions between two competing capitalist production relations within Kenya (Berman, 190, ch. 9). The third mode of articulation, namely the destruction of non-capitalist societies, and the 'freeing' of producers from the means of production, was the fate of the Sengwer and all other hunter-gatherer societies, since by virtue of being materially hunter-gatherer, its structure cannot so easily be adapted, as we saw in the Australian context, to producing value for settler-colonial capitalism and supporting the accumulation of capital and ultimately the expanded material reproduction of the capitalist system. The hunter-gatherer mode of Indigenous people and their knowledge of the Australian plains was well suited to assisting the pastoral and cattle stations. The hunter-gatherer mode of forest-dwelling people did not prove as useful to white settler farmers in Kenya. In another respect, there is a notable difference with the Australian colonial space, in that forcible monetisation did not, on the whole, force Indigenous people to produce cash crops for the market, but instead forced their entry into the labour market, either on pastoral farms and stations or, to a lesser extent, their participation in the various industries in the growing cities from the early twentieth century. This meant that, unlike in Kenya, the destructive articulation of two alien economic systems did not nurture an incipient petit bourgeois Indigenous farmer class of Australia.

So how did the colonial-settler state supply land and cheap black labour for settler production? Firstly, the colonial state embarked on a massive programme of land alienation and the *forcible* relocation of the dispossessed Kikuyu and all other ethnic groups to 'native reserves', equivalent to the homelands in South Africa under apartheid, the Indigenous reserves in the United States and the reserves or missions examined in Chapter 2 in nineteenth- and twentieth-century Australia. The laws alienating huge swathes of Kikuyu land which were *forcibly* imposed were varied and complex, beginning with the land regulations of 1897 (East Africa Protectorate, 1897), and ultimately culminating after years of bitter and protracted negotiation in the Crown Lands Ordinance in 1915 (East Africa Protectorate, 1915; see also Kilson, 1955, p. 114; Berman, 1990, p. 56). The latter completely nullified Kikuyu land rights and created a free market in land in the 'White Highlands' as they now became known. Previous laws had paid lip service to protecting the rights of Kikuyu to 'occupy' their land (Kilson, 1955, pp. 111–13), but ultimately the decisive influence in the shift to total land expropriation was the influence of 'big capital' from Europe and the key financial role it would play in stimulating land purchases and development (Berman, 1990, pp. 56–7). Again, we see the larger global structures at play. Given the precarious state of the colonial state's finances this was financial leverage that it could not afford to resist. Ultimately, the Kikuyu would lose upwards of 60,000 acres to the settlers (Elkins, 2005a, p. 12). In *Axis Rule*, Lemkin (1944, p. 83) described this as the *political* technique of genocide, in that it imposed the national pattern of the colonisers by way of removing the occupied peoples and their property – in this case the land of the Kikuyu – and allocating it to the settlers.

The native reserves, as they were known, which were the natural corollary of the 'land grab', were located in the Central Province districts of Kiambu, Fort Hill and Nyeri. The vast majority was not set aside, and their boundaries not defined till 1926 (Colony and Protectorate of Kenya, 1926). In the Native Lands Trust Ordinance, 1928 (Colony and Protectorate of Kenya, 1928), the demarcations would be confirmed and a 'Native Lands Council' established that ruled over all matters pertaining to native reserves. Naturally, it consisted of no African representatives. Over time the conditions in the reserves deteriorated due to severe overcrowding, to such an extent that a Kikuyu family would struggle to meet their basic subsistence needs.

In a memorandum submitted to the Kenya Land Commission (from here on in Land Commission), a body which from 1932 to 1934 would hear land disputes and receive various relevant memoranda and testimonies on the topic, otherwise known as the Carter Commission after its chair Sir William Morris Carter, the Kikuyu Central Association (KCA) were moved to comment on the abject state of land provision for the Kikuyu: 'Some of the districts in our province break the record of the density of the world population of any agricultural people and occupy perhaps third place in the record of the density of the world population notwithstanding the fact that our country is a purely agricultural country' (Colonial Office, 1934, p. 200). Meek (1949, p. 77) added that in 1944 'density figures of 1,100 and even 1,800 to the square mile have been reported'. By 1948, one and a half million Kikuyu were restricted to 2000 square miles, juxtaposed to the 30,000 white settlers who held 12,000 square miles, much of it the most fertile land (Newsinger, 2006, p. 185).

It is inconceivable that under such deleterious conditions the Kikuyu could furnish the necessary livestock to support their various cultural practices, let alone support their respective progression through initiation and the various status grades, which was so critical to the Kikuyu way of Life. Kilson (1955, p. 120) succinctly observed:

> Kikuyu society would be well-nigh impossible without an adequate supply of land upon which these animals could graze. And, if one would

couple this with the fact that extensive farming is another major aspect of Kikuyu society, one might conclude that to alienate land from the Kikuyu would be tantamount to *setting their socio-cultural system on the road to total disintegration.* [emphasis added]

The upshot of all these policies was to push the reserves to the brink of an ecological crisis, compounded by the polarisation of the Kikuyu between a tiny minority of rich Kikuyu chiefs who collaborated with the colonial authorities and the vast majority of the Kikuyu who were pushed further into penury and faced the double humiliation of loss of land and status under British colonial rule. The ensuring ecological meltdown would threaten the very survival of all who lived off the reserves (Elkins, 2005a, p. 23). Here we observe the technique of the destruction of the foundation of economic existence *and ecological destruction.* The effects of the British land policy eerily chime with Lemkin's (1944, p. 85) observation in *Axis Rule*:

> The destruction of the foundations of the economic existence of a national group necessarily brings about a crippling of its development, even retrogression. The lowering of the standards of living creates difficulties in fulfilling cultural-spiritual requirements. Furthermore, a daily fight literally for bread and for physical survival may handicap thinking in both general and national terms.

Secondly, the colonial government imposed a hugely burdensome 'hut tax' and 'poll tax' collectively equivalent to two months' wages at the local rate (Elkins, 2005a, p. 23). The combined effect of the land and tax policy was to force Kikuyu migration in search of work and land. This conditioned the rise of what became known as the *squatter* community (Tanogo, 1987), and the dispersal of tens of thousands of Kikuyu tribesmen in search of living on settler farms and plantations. By 1945 there were 200,000 registered squatters in the White Highlands, the vast majority of whom were Kikuyu (Curtis, 2003, p. 319; Tanogo, 1987, p. 126). The effect was to further undermine the group integrity of the Kikuyu, with all the attendant genocidal effects that would accompany it (Kilson, 1955, p. 121) even if it depended on adapting or exploiting structural features of Kikuyu society, namely the aforementioned *ahoi* system or 'Kikuyu expansionist dynamic' (Kanogo, 1987). Recall that the *ahoi* were tenants attracted to a larger property-owning clan or *mbari* (Muriuki, 1974, p. 114) who wanted to augment their authority and power by attracting non-clan or alien elements to their fold. The neo-feudal aspects of the squatter system resembled at least superficially this *ahoi* system (Jackson, 2017, p. 238).

This was an example of articulation and the partial preservation of the Kikuyu figuration.

The final screw in the first phase of genocide would come with the compulsory *labour policy* brought into being by master-and-servant laws that regulated, and ultimately coerced through penal sanction, Kenyan rural workers and farmers (Anderson, 2000). These labour ordinances had the effect (and intention) of forcing African peasants to pay for their tenancy rights through labour on the settler farms rather than cash payment, an obligation that was initially 90 days per year but by the 1930s had risen to between 240 and 270 days (Fibaek and Green, 2019, p. 93). Combined with the other labour laws, the labour control regime ensured a steady and reliable supply of labour on the settler farms and greatly reduced the operating costs for settler farmers, allowing them to capture a greater share of surplus value (Fibaek and Green, 2019).

In political-economic terms, the net effect of the articulation of the Indigenous peasant and settler modes of production on the Kikuyu – embodied in the land, tax and labour policy – was to ensure that 'the material conditions of reproduction in the reserves were insufficient to meet the needs of simple *reproduction*, commodity purchases, and tax payments' (Berman, 1990, p. 37) [emphasis added]. These were the mechanisms that forced the Kikuyu onto the labour market and meant they were paid below the value of commodity labour power and the market value of their cash crops. But given the paltry nature of the wages paid on the settler farms plus the meagre prices paid for the surplus product sold by the Kikuyu peasants – due to the aforementioned marketing boards – the vast majority of Kikuyu found it increasingly difficult to make up what Berman (1990, p. 37) described as the resulting 'reproductive gap'. The intention of these policies was to subordinate African peasant production to the settler economy and force African peasants into waged work. The effect was to slowly cripple the economic, political and cultural foundations of the Kikuyu.

The (lumpen) proletarianisation of Kenyan peasants was a natural corollary of primary accumulation. Lumpen to a degree, since not all of the peasants alienated from their land would become workers gainfully employed in factories and large workplaces. Some, due to the population dynamics of the capitalist economic system, as we saw in Chapter 2, and resultant creation of a reserved army of the unemployed, were compelled to scrape together a living in the informal economy as prostitutes, hawkers and the like (Elkins, 2005, p. 24). It compelled the migration of impoverished African peasants, who either failed to scrape a meagre living together on the reserves, or who hadn't managed to establish themselves as squatters on the White Highlands, into the increasingly overcrowded and depressed squalor of the urban centres in search of work. This was accelerated by ever increasing mechanisation of the settler estates, which forced thousands more to escape into the cities; the population of Nairobi doubled between 1938 and 1952 (Newsinger, 2006, p. 185). The unintended consequence of this was to foster the rise of popular discontent, not only among squatters and impoverished reservation workers in the country-side but an increasingly militant Kenyan working class and urban poor (Newsinger, 2006, pp. 186–7).

Here again we see, in a fascinating parallel with the Australian colonial space, the logic of (primary) accumulation, driving the logic of elimination: socio-economic processes which I earlier described as one of two key structures in the political economy of eco-genocide. In the context of British economic history, this first key structure gave rise to what was referred to as the 'enclosures' in Chapter 2, and the expansion into non-capitalist territory, 'into a world dense with cultural difference' (Smith, 2002, p. 79). This was a social cataclysm crippling the foundations of the Kikuyu, just as they crippled Indigenous life on the Australian Frontier and rural peasant life in Britain (Hobsbawm, 1959, p. 3), forcing the migration of some to the urban centres, where they were absorbed into the body of the nascent working class and urban poor. Once the stolen land and cheapened black labour was fully incorporated into the various industrial (and financial) processes operating within the expanded reproduction of the circuits of capital, the logic of the value contradiction at the heart of the political economy of capitalism, the *second* key structure nurtured the rise of class forces, which adopted 'European political technologies' and exhibited certain modalities of struggle commensurate with their class position, such as the formation of trade unions, strikes and other various forms of industrial action, as well as particular political programmes and political parties. These forms of struggle played a role in hastening the 'defeat' of the colonial authorities and the granting of independence, but not necessarily the end of relations of genocide for *all* Indigenous groups, as will be examined when we take a closer look at Kenya today. This unintended consequence, where the colonial authorities are concerned, is a function of what in Chapter 1 was described as the dialectic of the settler–Indigenous relations, where struggle against forms of colonial domination and genocide shift the terrain of genocidal techniques.

One fascinating distinction between the Australian case and the Kenyan settler–Indigenous dialectic is that although the forcible articulation of the Indigenous figuration with Australian settler capitalism drove radical economic and political transformations, giving rise to distinguishable class groups within the Indigenous community, such as an emergent rural and urbanised working class and urban poor, this did not give rise to, at least in the short term, internal class antagonisms within Indigenous nations or communities. By that I mean that there were not opposed class groups with irreconcilable class interests, but, by and large, rather class groups that did have material and political interests in common, as we saw in Chapter 2, with the rise of the pan-Indigenous movement. That is to say, with very few exceptions, the loci of the vast majority of Indigenous people were within classes that either had no access to, or control of land, or the other factors of production, such as capital or labour. They were rather either surviving in semi-feudal relations in the countryside, on the various settler farms, cattle stations and reserves, or joining the ranks of the urbanised working classes in towns and cities predominantly in the East, in the factories, the docks and so on. There would of course, over time, emerge a middle class of professionals, in sectors like law, academia or public administration, who also played a key role in organising Indigenous resistance. But this wouldn't be until much later in the twentieth century, and moreover, this class, in the main, would also *not be a property-owning class*. In other words, there was no substantial Indigenous atomised (petty) bourgeoisie.

In part, this was because Indigenous people in Australia, on the whole, were either wiped out or locked into a state of semi-permanent unemployment, underemployment and economic irrelevance. Of course, as we saw in Chapter 2, their employment, *inter alia*, as sheep herders, pearl divers, stockmen, miners, guides for explorers, domestic servants and even as agents of repression and domination were crucial for the success and viability of the settler-colonial project in the nineteenth and early twentieth centuries (Reynolds, 1990). But this was not to be the experience of the vast majority, who instead, once severed from their land, were either murdered, left to starve or corralled into reserves. This almost complete exclusion of Indigenous people from any form of meaningful right to property in land or land tenure or even common law rights to occupancy (barring those few Indigenous communities in the Northern territory and elsewhere who managed to maintain material-cultural ties to their land on colonial terms), endured until much later into the twentieth century, with the emergence of key milestone Indigenous land rights legislation in the Northern territories, the ARLA, and of course native title after the Mabo ruling. However, in Kenya and other colonial territories such as India, the colonists were a minority and so depended on Indigenous labour both as workers and consumers of manufactured goods for the reproduction of its economy, and for the maintenance of its polity more generally, on a far greater scale (Thorpe, 1992, p. 98). Moreover, the simple fact of the sheer demographic dominance of Indigenous people in Kenya meant that a significant proportion of land and resources would remain in the hands of the Indigenous of Kenya.

Above all, the differences in the class composition outlined above was determined by the fact that, in common with the Australian experience in Chapter 2, the forcible articulation of the settler with the Indigenous economic system is conditioned, in the initial stages at least, by the technical conditions in which settler capital historically finds Indigenous lifeways, or, as we saw earlier, what Hardt and Negri (1994, p. 15) called *foreign processes of production*. Unlike in Australia, Kenyan societies were composed of not just hunter-gatherer production relations but also pastoral and horticultural and agricultural economies. Therefore, the utility that these economies had to the settler economy and the possible ways in which they could be forcibly fused with it would, in the Kenyan settler-colonial space, give rise to *antagonistic* class divisions within Kenyan society and Kikuyu more specifically, almost from the very beginning of the life of the colony.

Tragically, the 'reproductive gap' imposed on the Kikuyu and other African peasants was, as has been revealed above, far from adequately filled. As Barta (1987, pp. 237–41) reminded us in his analysis of settler colonialism in Australia, colonisation established two 'incompatible forms of society and economy', in its quest to forcibly incorporate Indigenous society into the orbit of the global capitalist economy. The alienation of land had genocidal consequences for the Indigenous peoples of Australia. Barta understood genocidal intent as inherent in the policy of the metropolitan government, the local colonial authorities – in Kenya from the colonial governor all the way down to the district commissioners – and the settlers themselves who took the land, even when the horrific human consequences – the crippling poverty, the breakdown of their culture and the dissolution of the Kikuyu group – were foreseeable.

With the rise of open hostilities between the colonial authorities and the Indigenous peoples of Kenya, what would come to be known as the Mau Mau rebellion (1952–1960), the genocide would enter its second much more brutal phase, which I (Crook, 2013) have elsewhere described as the 'concentrated shock of genocide behind the "wire'. The Mau Mau insurrection was in essence a war between the British colonial authorities and the Kenya Land and Freedom Army (KLFA), an army dominated by soldiers from the Kikuyu as well as Meru and Embu (Osbourne, 2010). Discussion of this 'concentrated phase' is beyond the remit of this book, suffice to say that to defeat the Mau Mau resistance would take the complete 'obliteration of the Kikuyu domestic landscape' (Elkins, 2003, p. 217). The concentrated shock of genocide would reach its highest pitch in the villages, affecting a devastating toll on the Kikuyu way of life, decimating their economic, social, political and cultural foundations, hasten the end of the formal empire and usher in the era of formal independence. However, as we will see below, this would not fully purge the Kenyan state and society of its colonial legacy, with devastating consequences for its 'less civilised' remaining Indigenous people, such as the Sengwer.

Indeed, what of the fate of those considered less 'civilised' than the agriculturalists like the Kikuyu? What would become known as the 'Dorobo question' in administrative circles, perhaps better than any other case of 'civilising violence' (Cavanagh, 2016, p. 3), serves to underscore the crucial dialectical relationship between, on the one hand, the logic of capital accumulation, more broadly conceived as the changing imperatives of settler capitalism in Kenya, and the broader exigencies of the world market. On the other hand, Indigenous elimination made possible through the uneven racialised landscapes that 'othered' those categorised as 'Dorobo'. This dialectic is revealed once we consider the thinking of colonial officials tasked with solving the 'Dorobo question' and how the governance of forest-dwelling communities was reconciled with the ultimate exigencies of a settler economy ensconced in the political economic web of Pax Britannica. The biopolitical practices resolved to affect *total* cultural erasure of hunter-gatherer groups like the Sengwer, in order to 'integrate' them into the political economy, rather than, as we saw with the Kikuyu and other ethnic groups considered more civilised, bring about partial destruction of their economies and societies through forcible articulation with the settler-colonial system. The biopolitical practices of the colonial administration would deny the Sengwer and other forest dwellers any right to inhabit their forest dwellings as a sovereign cultural group, or to any land for that matter, and reinvent the Embobut Forest and the slopes of the Cherangani Hills, once again, as a blank map or palimpsest (Kostanski and Clark, 2009, p. 189), bereft of *productive* settlement: a reinscribing of a landscape that was already deeply etched with networks of Sengwer place names and pathways; this was *terra nullius*. They would be subject in the words of Cavanagh (2016, p. 3) to 'civilising violence ... to secure their liminal humanity', including forced assimilation, dispossession and the attendant social death, to once again make them fit and productive members of the colony and its political economy.

In its fundamentals, this process of cultural erasure, supported by the burgeoning science of planning, was remarkably redolent of those same processes that took place in Australia in the nineteenth and twentieth centuries. Once again, it would entail the defining, controlling and regulating of spaces with prescribed relations that governed who could and couldn't utilise the land and the forms of social life that could flourish within them (Jackson, pp. 72–3). What marked out these processes where the forest-dwelling communities were concerned was the deployment of a racialised *conservationist* logic, a form of 'green governmentality'

(Luke, 1997), that would leave a lasting legacy in the governance of Kenya's forest.

The question of the fate of the Sengwer would be determined by the imperatives of the colonial economy and the need to 'conserve' the forests and their ecosystem services for the benefit of white settler farmers and rationalise the top-down control of officially designated 'tribes' under British dominion. The forests became the focus of much concern for the colonial administration, in particular the material demarcation of forest reserves (Anderson, 1987). This included Crown Forest Reserves subject to the jurisdiction of the Forest Department, forest reserves given over to white settlement in the White Highlands, and forest reserves folded into reserves allocated to other non-Dorobo communities; a three-jawed pincer encircling and eroding the lifeways of forest-dwelling hunter-gatherer groups. These demarcated forests, too, were racially spatialised and considered either 'European' or 'African'. Just as with the native reserves, their demarcation fuelled conflicts and disputes around access, habitation and use of forest and grazing land resources (Anderson, 1987). Moreover, what was deemed by the colonial authorities the 'fiscally barren' nature of the Sengwer hunter-gatherer economy (Cavanagh, 2016, p. 10), meant that the only viable form of articulation as far as the colonial state was concerned would be Hartwig's third mode, namely the destruction of the hunter-gatherer mode 'such that the producers are "freed" of the means of production' (1978, p. 129). As we will see below, this logic will carry over to the postcolonial state in the present day.

Their fate would be decided like all of Kenya's Indigenous societies, through official committee hearings, in particular the landmark Land Commission and its subsequent report issued to London.[2] This administrative process marked a pivotal moment in the consolidation and deepening of the 'logic of elimination' (Wolfe, 2006). It would befall the Committee on the Dorobo Question, formed in March 1929, to interrogate this issue and submit a report to London, which was attached to the Land Commission report (Colonial Office, 1934). In a summary of the report of the Land Commission written for the *Journal of the Royal African Society*, former Chief Native Commissioner O. F. Watkins (1934, p. 213) captures the essence of the colonial administration's position as it bore on the question of the 'Dorobo problem' and the conservation of the forest, when he concluded that 'they cannot exist in the modern world as forest-dwellers *without danger to forest and so to water*, already a scarcening commodity in Eastern Africa' [emphasis added]. The anxiety evinced by this summary, which would be reflected in the conclusion of the commission, echoed a broader fear among colonial administrators about the sustainability of the Kenyan forests and the problem of how to both ensure the conservation of large swathes of it and ensure its continued exploitation for profitable ends (Ofcansky, 1984, p. 136). It was long understood by the colonial administration that the sustainable use of the forests was key to sustaining the white settler economy and its native timber industry, and that if exploitation and deforestation of the forest were not slowed, its crucial ecological role as a water catchment area and its vital role in soil conservation would be lost – an anxiety that will rear its ugly head once more when we turn our attention below to the present day. In a report on Kenyan forestry for the colonial authorities, British forestry expert Robert Scott Troup (1922, p. 10) observed that the 'limit has already been exceeded in respect of the destruction of forest on which the maintenance of the water supply depends'. After explaining the aforementioned ecological functions and the consequences of unchecked deforestation, he concluded, with a palpable sense of alarm, 'in this respect the forests of Kenya Colony, situated as they are for the most part on hilly country, exercise an important, not to say a vital, influence on the general prosperity of the colony' (Troup, 1922).

This was of a piece with the broader anxiety about environmental degradation and growing alarm at the rate of despoilation and degradation of soil and forests in the wake of the colonisation of Kenya (Anderson, 1984, p. 32), an ecological anxiety common throughout the European empires (Grove, 1995, p. 474, 1997; see also Crosby, 2004). Understood from this perspective, and as evinced by the evidence and conclusion of the Kenya Land Commission, forest-dwelling peoples, refracted through the prevailing discourse on race science, 'civilizational development' and African 'nature' more generally, and scientific forest management more specifically, were seen as ecological threats to the continued sustainability of the forests, and perhaps even an impediment to its continued profitable exploitation (Cavanagh, 2016, p. 11). A racialised political ecology secured through the bundle of racialised discourses on Africa's environment, discussed below, played a key part in reconstructing African non-human nature, as much as it did Africans themselves.

Forest-dwelling groups were not compatible with the prevailing scientific conservationist logic, or scientific conservation (Guha, 2000, p. 7), which suggested the necessity of their removal, a logic borne of an enlightenment tradition that instrumentalised nature as something to be 'mastered' and 'tamed' by the application of European reason (Adams and Mulligan, 2003, p. 5). But they were simultaneously deemed a threat to romanticised notions of the African 'wilderness' that saw all humanity as a blight on its continued flourishing (Neumann, 1996). This sentiment would prove central to the rise of a 'preservationist' movement across the European colonies (Neumann, 1996, 1998), one whose legacy, as we will see below, continues to this day and will prove decisive in shaping the biopolitical status of forest-dwelling Indigenous groups in Kenya and elsewhere.

What Marx (1988) called humanity's non-organic nature, with which humanity must maintain a constant dialogue, would be symbolically reconfigured through antecedent forms of 'green governmentality' (Luke, 1997), such that the Sengwer would no longer be able to converse with it; an eco-biopolitics that treated forest-dwelling groups and their forest dwellings as malleable clay. This was a racialised conservationist discourse that assumed as axiomatic that the Sengwer and all other forest-dwelling groups did not know how to live sustainably, within their dwelling places that they had lived in for hundreds of years. This 'correcting' of 'destructive' socio-ecological relations, or forms of 'environmental control' which Mackenzie (2000, p. 698) described as a 'conservationist ethic', eerily chimes with my definition of ecologically induced genocide, namely any ecologically destructive practice, or process, that forcibly controls the subject group's interaction with, ejects them from or prejudices or precludes the enjoyment of their land and the local "ecosystems (Crook and Short, 2020, p. 167)

Despite numerous testimonies from members of the Sengwer[3] and settler farmers[4] affirming and confirming their existence as a legitimate and viable socio-cultural unit, the committee would eventually decide the only solution was forcible assimilation. This solution to the 'Dorobo question' was one that would befall all those hunter-gatherer groups considered 'primitive', including the Ogiek of the Mau Forest (Kimaiyo, 2004). The committee in essence recommended that, 'wherever possible, the Dorobo should become members of, and be absorbed into, the tribe with which they have most affinity' (Colonial Office, 1934, p. 2133). Moreover, that through 'absorption', submission to the 'headman' or administrative chiefs of other tribes and 'intermarriage', they will gradually be assimilated into more 'advanced populations' (Colonial Office, 1934, pp. 2133–5). Suffice to say, these recommendations would be wholly adopted by the Land Commission.

In its final report to London, the commission, speaking of those forest-dwelling groups found in the Rift Valley, which included, *inter alia*, the Sengwer and Ogiek, echoed the stagist logic of colonial administrators and the majority of the submissions and evidence found in the Land Commission report when it observed that 'the passing of the game and forest laws interfered with the primitive mode of life led by the Dorobo' and acknowledged the sustained attempts by the colonial administration 'to induce them to become useful members of native society' by encouraging them to 'acquire stock and to cultivate'.[5] Of course 'induce' was putting it rather mildly. In reality, this euphemism concealed a multitude of sins including various forms of lawfare and coded threats of state violence (Cavanagh, 2019, p. 99). The commission, following the Dorobo committee and the prevailing wisdom in colonial administrative circles, argued, 'the Dorobo are most likely to progress and become useful citizens if they live side by side with communities who have *already advanced some along the road of orderly progress*' [emphasis added].[6] The conclusion drawn by colonial administrators was that Dorobo, like the Sengwer, should be assimilated via the technology of the reserve system into what Lord Frederick Lugard, treaty maker and colonial administrator, called more 'advanced populations' (1922, p. 200), or what Sir Charles Eliot, Commissioner of the East Africa Protectorate (1900–1904), called 'superior tribes' (1905, pp. 107–8) to accelerate their development. Indeed, by forcing them onto reserves much like we saw with the Kikuyu, they would, as Eliot (1905, p. 106) hoped, 'adopt fixed habitations' and thus be compelled to provide labour on the farms of white settlers and pay tax (Njonjo Commission 2002, pp. 25–6), as indeed many members of hunter-gatherer groups did (Hitchcock et al., 2015, p. 42).

This would bring about Hartwig's (1978, p. 129) third stage of articulation and 'free' the producers from the means of production and Rey's aforementioned third stage of articulation of the settler-colonial capitalism with Indigenous societies: 'the total disappearance of the pre-capitalist mode' (cited in Foster-Carter, 1978b, p. 218). Where hunter-gatherer groups were concerned, their level of 'development' would not permit any other form of articulation with the dominant settler-colonial system. Through the process of real subsumption of forest-dwelling labour to colonial capital, 'foreign processes of production' (Hardt and Negri, 1994, p. 15) would not be allowed to survive in any form, nor the corresponding communities permitted 'to maintain their connection to the territory and the past' (Hardt and Negri, 2017, p. 182).

The committee hearings would clearly demonstrate the biopolitics at work that attributed rights to the various groups according to their levels of advancement and mode of life, a normative vision that condemned lifeways that were not only not 'fit' enough, but, given the recurring financial crises of the Kenyan colonial state (Berman and Lonsdale, 1980), 'fiscally barren' (Cavanagh, 2016, p. 10). As we saw with the Kikuyu, the right to a reserve was tied to the political economic function of providing labour for the white settler farms on the White Highlands, valuable crops and tax for the colonial coffers.

However, the *total* destruction of the Sengwer would not come to pass. Though the remaining colonial records and oral evidence provide us with an incomplete picture, the forcible subsumption to colonial labour and integration into Eliot's (1905, pp. 107–8) 'superior tribes' would (under the auspices of the British) ultimately fail. In practice, as Cavanagh's (2008b, p. 308) exhaustive archival work has shown, despite official orders to transfer forest-dwelling populations and police access to those forests, officials occasionally opted to allow informal access for subsistence purposes. Nevertheless, as Card (2010) was keen to stress, social death does not mean an inexorable and permanent ending or finality. As the structural understanding of genocide *as a process* put forward in this book argues, genocide and its settler-colonial structure is not an event, a finite moment in time (Wolfe, 2006a, p. 163). If we understand relations of genocide or settler Indigenous relations as a dialectical phenomenon, then it is a continual process, with ebbs, flows and even reversals and regressions, unfolding through time. Ergo, the destruction of group life, or 'social vitality' is, similarly, a non-binary process stretched along the continuum of time which can be subject to reversals. As Card (2010, p. 262) herself argued, 'In genocides, survivors experience a social death, to a degree and for a time. Some later become revitalised in new ways; others do not.' The story of the struggle of the Sengwer would resume with the dawn of the new (post)colonial regime.

Architecture of dispossession then: racialised geographies and the cheapening of black bodies

The forcible articulation of different modes of production, upon which the new colonial political economy depended, hinged on racialised or 'imaginative geographies' (Said, 2003), just as did the colonial political economy in Australia. The aforementioned laws, and the segregation and racialised geography upon which they and the reserves were based, were predicated on the discursive creation of uneven racialised landscapes (and ecologies), on what I earlier described as racial spatialisation. These landscapes were key to the reproduction of racial capitalism, in that the latter assumed and depended on the cheapening of black bodies and their relocation and concentration for the successful reproduction of the settler-colonial economy (Berman, 1990, p. 59), as well as legitimating the colonial project in Kenya specifically, and Africa more broadly (Young, 1994, p. 74). Once again, genocidal techniques would include, as Wolfe (2006, p. 388) observed in other colonial contexts, a 'whole range of cognate biocultural assimilations' that would impoverish meaningful land rights and sovereignty and, at best, reduce Indigenous rights to that of occupancy and usufruct, whether they were agriculturalists like the Kikuyu, pastoralists like the Maasai or hunter-gatherers like the Sengwer.

By forcibly relocating ethnic groups and allotting some groups, land within strictly circumscribed socio-economic roles, like the Kikuyu, they were nurturing their 'development'. As we learned earlier, In the case of hunter-gatherer groups like the Sengwer, collectively known as 'Dorobo', commonly believed by colonial administrators to be 'pre pastoral', according to colonial records, or even 'pre tribal', given their hunter-gatherer figuration (Cavanagh, 2019, p. 93), by forcing their assimilation into other social groups they were accelerating their 'development'. Ultimately, they ensured the various ethnic groups contributed to the economic well-being of the colony. In other words, the reserves, in conjunction with the coercive legal measures and practices discussed above, were a biopolitical means of remedying the 'backward' nature of African peasants, by internalising new behavioural norms, conducive to the settler economy, and, like Indigenous peoples in Australia, initiating African people into the 'rites of white discipline' (Jackson, 2018, p. 80; Bernardi, 1997, p. 38). In this sense, the reserves were a crucial lynchpin in the fulfilment of the noble covenant of the British system of colonial governance, which was discursively and ideologically predicated on 'the dual mandate'. Stated briefly this mandate obliged colonial authorities to develop the colonies economically, in the interests of the metropole, *and* civilise and develop the African races and tribes. Indeed, as argued above, the reserves served as a crucial political economic mechanism in the creation of a ready supply of cheap black labour in the countryside and the cities in the myriad forms described above.

These 'imaginative geographies' (Said, 2003) in Kenya, unlike Australia, also depended on uneven racialised landscapes that *stratified* 'races' according to a racial and civilisational ladder. Those considered 'advanced populations' by Lugard (1922, p. 200) could be apportioned land on reserves and amenable to indirect rule through 'chiefs' such as the Bantu ethnic groups in Uganda which had developed to the 'kingdom stage' of development (Lugard, 1922, p. 68), or in Kenya the Kikuyu, whom Eliot (1905, p. 106) considered to be 'one of the most active and intelligent among the East African tribes' and who were 'almost certainly a comparatively recent hybrid between the Masai and a Bantu stock'. The latter two ethnic groups were considered to be 'superior tribes' by Eliot (1905, pp. 107–8) when compared to the acephalous or stateless hunter-gatherer groups, such as the 'Dorobo' like the Sengwer. In other words, races like the forest-dwelling Dorobo, or 'pygmies' or 'Bushmen', and the various tribes they were further subdivided into, were less 'racially potent' (Cavanagh, 2016, p. 96) and thought to exist in *hierarchical relation* to each other. Moreover, they existed on a point along a path of development marked by the capacity to develop and utilise technology, develop hierarchical and centralised forms of governance and, of course, the ability to accumulate wealth (Cavanagh, 2017, p. 292). Where possible, via the assistance of Lefebvrian spatial technologies such as the reserve system, the less advanced 'races' should be allowed to 'hybridize' with 'fitter stock' 'to the great advantage of the country' (Eliot, 1905, p. 107). In other words, Eliot (1905, pp. 106–7) argued a policy of absorption or assimilation could be applied to 'distinct races' depending on their level of development. Race was for Eliot (1905, p. 106) 'a hybrid and in a process of slow change' and to have different races 'blend' was 'nature's law'. It was therefore a 'sound policy to encourage the intermingling of different tribes and the formation of a *settled* and peaceable population' (Eliot, 1905) [emphasis added]. For Eliot and his peers, 'settled' and 'agricultural' modes of life and their associated economies were one step above hunter-gatherers in the ladder of civilisation. Therefore, those who were not advanced enough, such as the forest-dwelling Sengwer, would be absorbed into their more 'advanced' neighbours. This was of a type with the 'stagist' 'evolutionary' understanding of history we encountered in the Australian settler-colonial space and akin to Adam Smith's teleological stages of development (1978, p. 14). Tragically, this stagist thinking will live on in residual form in the postcolonial period and have grave consequences for the present juncture.

Speaking to the broader significance of the 'imaginative geographies' (Said, 2003), colonial discourses on race and the colonial governmentality of which they formed part, Young (1994, pp. 75–6) sharply observed their inner connections with the imperatives of the colonial political economy, averring '[t]he idea of progress, now at its zenith, and notions of African society as *malleable clay* in the hands of the colonizer, available for reshaping into new economic functions and social contours, suffused the colonial system' [emphasis added].

It was this notion of African society as malleable clay which powerfully conveys the centrality of biopolitics to the construction of the Kenyan colony. The demographic and racial categories furnished by the social Darwinian discourses facilitated the reengineering of Kenyan societies to suit the imperatives of the Kenyan settler class and ultimately the needs of the metropole. In other words, the reserves (and the colonial political economy more generally), were proto-eugenic laboratories that sought to mould Kenya's fluid ethnic mosaic into rigid fixed identities that tied them to portions of land in the pursuit of the virtuous and noble goal of 'protection' or 'improvement' (Cavanagh, 2019, p. 96). They also conveniently facilitated the cleansing of those most fertile portions of the land desired by the white settlers. In today's Kenya, as we will see below, the notion of malleable clay will still apply to some of its Indigenous denizens.

Taken together, these processes of biopolitical transformation visited upon both the forest-dwelling Sengwer and the agriculturalist Kikuyu, exhibit all the hallmarks of a 'logic of elimination' (Wolfe, 2006) or Barta's (1987) relations of genocide, if one remembers that culture is the master concept and the target of genocide is the structure or edifice of the group, not necessarily the individuals that form its constituent parts. The forcible subordination of African peasant production to secure its political economic articulation to the settler economy, what was earlier described as the two stages or structures of the political economy of genocide, and force African peasants into waged work, had the *effect* of slowly crippling the economic, political and cultural foundations of the Kikuyu. The forest in the Cherangani Hills was an integral part of the economy and society of the Sengwer and their culture. Their forcible excision from the forest amounted to domicide that menaced the group's cultural and biological integrity, given their territorially bounded nature (Abed, 2006, p. 326), and all the ways the Sengwer depend on the forests. Both cases are consistent with my definition of eco-genocide introduced in Chapter 1: the destruction of, or severance from the eco-systemic habitat of the group that leads to 'social death'. Arguably, hunter-gatherer societies like the Sengwer suffered more extreme forms of social death and certainly more forced assimilation and cultural destruction, or 'civilising violence', than any other lifeway, given they had much further to come to meet the biopolitical standards expected of British colonial authorities.

Nevertheless, in the final analysis the clay was not malleable enough. The contradictions in the particular economy examined above would eventually trigger open revolt against the settler-colonial state. The ensuing Mau Mau struggle and the genocidal war it unleashed would, however, hasten the end of the British colony, with London convinced that the writing was on the wall, forcing the colonial power to the negotiating table, and setting in train a period in which attempts at negotiation would ultimately see the defeat of white colonial settlerdom and the victory of African nationalism (Ogot, 1968, pp. 285–8). On 12 December 1963, Kenya would be officially independent and one year later become a republic. In the midst of a global decolonisation movement, the metropole had decided retreat and withdrawal would be the prudent thing to do. The political and economic benefits of the ailing Kenya colony simply did not outweigh its costs anymore. Critically, however, the British would leave in their wake a colonial legacy that would cast a long shadow over Kenya's postcolonial future, with devastating consequences for forest-dwelling peoples.

The legacy of colonisation, 'decolonisation' and decoloniality

As I argued in connection with Australian settler–Indigenous relations, the story of invasion, annexation and colonisation of land, and by extension, the imposition and extended reproduction of settler power, colonial economy and its corollary, relations of genocide, is just one side of the story; one side of the dialectic of settler–Indigenous relations. Struggle against these forms of colonial domination and genocide in Australia shifted the terrain of genocidal relations, in subtle yet profound ways. The 'logic of elimination' (Wolfe, 2006a, p. 387) would, in part due to resistance, mutate and transmogrify through various 'modalities, discourses, and institutional formations' (Wolfe, 2006a, p. 402). Relations of genocide in Kenya were not exempt from this dialectic. The Mau Mau struggle would precipitate the end of the colonial regime and usher in a new one led by Kenyan nationalists of the KAU and its leader Jomo Kenyatta. But this victory would be a pyrrhic one that would not end relations of genocide, at least not for all its citizens, principally because it would not fully purge itself of the legacy of colonialism and fully shake off what the Africanist Basil Davidson (1992) called 'the black man's burden'. Here, Davidson was principally speaking of the alien form, or what he called the 'curse' of the nation state and the imposition of 'divide and rule' tribal politics and racialised forms of Western governance, wholly divorced from precolonial African institutions and socio-political structures. The latter were more than capable of integrating themselves into a global order on their own terms; an opportunity squandered with the 'scramble for Africa', thus missing the 'road not taken' (Davidson, 1992, ch. 2). Comforted by the assumption that Africa had no history, or if they did it was distorted by Eurocentric and developmentalist assumptions – what Foucault (2002, pp. xxiii–xxiv) would have understood as an episteme that marred much of Western archaeology, colonial ethnography and anthropology (Davies, 2012) – European colonists felt entitled to subsume and reconstruct, and in some cases entirely liquidate, those precolonial institutions, to lift the veil of ignorance away from the 'backward' and undeveloped Africans forcibly and violently. As Shivji (2009, p. 2) put it so powerfully, all Africans were 'denominated as uncivilized, uncultured, undisciplined pagans whose souls needed to be saved and whose bodies needed to be thrashed'. Paradoxically, this reterritorialisation of African geographic and cultural space which conveniently placed African societies outside the 'family of lawful nations', to become wards of the colonial and settler-colonial states, was done in order to bring them back into the fold of the 'enlightened'.

The legacy of these processes, at least as they pertain to the structuring of the relations of genocide for those still considered Indigenous in Kenya today, would be threefold. Firstly, it would leave behind a political economic structure that by and large remained intact, with its skewed concentrations of wealth, maldistribution of land and resources and disfigured and dependant function as an economic auxiliary of the former colonial powers, through its forcible integration into the global capitalist economy, much as we saw with Australia. Though in the case of Australia, which, unlike Kenya, never experienced a return of the settler invaders to their mother country, the settler ruling class, and to lesser degree, the white settlers and their descendants who occupy lower positions in the class structure, would continue to benefit from the colonisation of the continent and its Indigenous people. Secondly, the structural and cultural 'baggage' of an inherited colonial state alongside its forms of racialised biopolitics and governmentality woven together with neocolonial discourses on development that, although ultimately coded for white privilege, due to its underlying axiom that there existed a *hierarchy* of races and tribes, could be readily adopted by new Kenyan political elites and pass over in residual yet important forms into the governmentality of the postcolonial period. Finally, the colonial lawfare and the socio-legal structures that left behind a poisoned soil, which forms a crucial substrate of the forms of governmentality, ideology and biopolitics; in short, superstructural relations of the postcolonial state. As Mignolo (2011a, p. 53) reminds us, there is a crucial difference between decolonisation, the formal process of acquiring political independence and sovereignty, recognised by international law, and decoloniality, which seeks to go beyond mere juridical forms and deconstruct, purge and heal the violence wrought by the 'colonial episteme', its associated institutions and forms of governance.

It is beyond the remit of this and the following section and indeed the book to give a full and thorough exploration of the social, political and economic history of the intervening period between the end of the colony and the present day. Instead, as I did with my analysis of the key antecedents that prefigured and overdetermined relations of genocide in modern day Australia, I illuminate the most important features, processes and structural dynamics of a given social formation analysed thus far that have survived and adapted, been repurposed and co-opted by new power structures and elites that ensure the relations of genocide endure into Kenya's present day. In other words, my analysis has more in common with what was earlier referred to as a 'history of the present' (Garland, 2014; Foucault, 1995).

The political economic inheritance

The political economic inheritance of the newly independent Kenya was manifold. Attempts were made to 'Africanise' the state and economy and purge it of its white ruling elements. This critically involved the much-vexed question of land reform begun in earnest in the wake of the Mau Mau rebellion under the British in the form of the African Royal Commission of 1953–5 and the Swynnerton Plan (Swynnerton, 1954; Ochieng, 1992). This programme served mainly to bequeath the economy to the rising Kenyan bourgeoise that had gestated within the womb of British colonialism (Swainson, 1977) – a class that had been originally mutated into, if not germinated, by the forcible articulation with colonial settler capitalism examined in the preceding sections.

Given the relative weakness of the African bourgeoisie or what Franz Fanon (1963, p. 119) called the 'national middle class', what has been described as the 'developmental state' would have to play a greater role. The African bourgeoisie Fanon (1963, pp. 119–20) argued were 'completely canalised into the activities of an intermediary type', principally merchant rather than industrial capital, with the psychology of a businessman not captain of industry. The 'developmental state' would therefore need to be leveraged to carve out a bigger economic role and accumulate some measure of power, compensating for centuries of colonial domination, redirecting some of the accumulation process to benefit the nascent capitalist class (Ake, 1981, p. 96). This would be done in Kenya through a variety of measures, such as the Trade Licensing Act 1967, which restricted trade of certain goods to Kenyan citizens, and the establishment of the Kenya Trading corporation (KNTC), which managed import-export trade and was used 'as an instrument by the emergent bourgeoisie to penetrate the wholesale and retail sectors, which had formerly been the exclusive preserve of non-citizens' (Swainson, 1977, p.41). The latter organisation and others, such as the Agricultural Finance Corporation (AFC), which helped purchase or rehabilitate farms, and the Industrial and Commercial Development Corporation (ICDC), as well as a whole host of cooperative societies, were used to move capital into the hands of the burgeoning Indigenous bourgeoisie (Ochieng, 1992, pp.266–7).

Nevertheless, unlike in many other African nations post-independence (Ake, 1981), the Kenyan state, aside from parastatals in key infrastructure such as post, telecommunications and transport (Grosh, 1987) would, with some exceptions, not embark on ambitious nationalisation programmes but, rather, the maintenance of a largely market-driven economy, even if state assisted and directed, particularly in the areas of agriculture and wholesale and retail trade. Attempts were also made at introducing 'African Socialism' by the newly minted KAU government, which sought to eschew the philosophies of the capitalist West and communist East. It broadly consisted of securing civil and political rights for all its citizens and the expansion of the democratic franchise, as well as the alleviation of the gap between the rich and the poor. Above all, independence was about rehabilitating the humanity and agency of Africans after centuries of colonialism and slavery. As the trade unionist and one of the founding fathers of the Kenyan republic Tom Mboya (1963, p. 13) proclaimed, independence meant 'rediscovery of Africa by Africans'.

Alas, the economy would be deeply etched with the marks of British capital and, despite the aforementioned measures, would remain, as it does to this day, an economy that carries with it a profound legacy. This legacy is the one of underdevelopment. As Ochieng (1992, p. 263) argues:

> Kenya's colonial economy has been moulded into a distinctive pattern by the long years of colonial rule. It displayed characteristics typical of an underdeveloped economy at the periphery: the preponderance of foreign capital, the dominance of agriculture and the limited development of industry and heavy reliance on export of primary products and on imports of capital and consumer manufactured goods.

What Ndege (2009, p. 8) called 'Colonial capitalism' 'provided the anvil on which the post-colonial social formation continues to be forged'. Through the forcible integration of the Kenyan economy and society into the Western-dominated global imperialist capitalist system and the forcible imposition of settler-colonial capitalism, Kenya's economy would be forced into a dependent export orientation, structurally dependent on, above all, the British economy. This would force it into a relationship of *complementarity* or *dependence* (Ake, 1980; Shivji, 2009), specialisation in the production of primary commodities and a particular international division of labour. Perpetuated and reproduced though an 'imperialism of trade' and foreign investment controlled by the Western capitalist powers, which hinged on securing a market for manufactured goods *as well as* a source of primary commodities, driven by a capitalist system that was 'struggling to defeat its internal contradictions' (Ake, 1981, p. 36), the radical social and economic transformations and forcible articulations discussed in detail in the previous sections took place, further binding post-independence Kenya's economic fortunes to the world imperialist and economic system. These forcible articulations are sometimes described as 'disarticulation' where various sectors and regions within the economy will suffer from a lack of linkages and complementarity and reciprocity with each other and a lack of what economists call forward and backward linkages (Ake, 1981, p. 43). Instead, the linkages and forms of complementarity will be externally geared towards servicing the former colonial powers.

In essence, Kenya remains an example of what Nkrumah (1965) called 'neo-colonialism': political independence *but economic dependence*, or what the historian Mark Curtis (2003, p. 330) wryly calls 'dependent independence'. The upshot of all these structural legacies for the economy for the purposes of analysis here, as it pertains to the unfolding of relations of genocide where the Sengwer are concerned, is the resultant huge reliance on overseas loans and aid finance, due to ever worsening current account and fiscal imbalances. This in turn, due to attached conditionalities, further integrate underdeveloped countries like Kenya into the economic and political orbit of the hegemonic capitalist states in the North, in particular, as we will see towards the end of this chapter, through aid finance directed towards *conservation of nature*. Crucially, the role of international debt financing has long since been understood to play a role in primary accumulation (Marx, 1976, p. 921), which today invariably includes Indigenous land and people.

But more than this was the bequeathing to the postcolonial regime a particular political economy of land. It was not simply a matter of its maldistribution. Recall that a cultivated Kenyan bourgeois elite was forged in the fires of colonial rule through the forcible articulation of Indigenous societies and economies with the settler-capitalist system. This was ultimately in the pursuit of primary accumulation and its corollary, the creation of a ready supply of cheap black labour. The vast majority of Kenyans would through this articulation be forced into sedentary agriculture in the service of the colonial economy where the extraction of cheap labour was the aim. This was the second of Hartwig's (1978, p. 129) three modes of articulation. The need to provide a supply of cheap black labour in the White Highlands would drive huge demographic changes with large migrations of Kikuyu and other tenant farmers and labourers, who would later reasonably make claim to land they laboured and worked on for decades, alongside the land claims made by those groups who were originally displaced to make way for the white settler farms (Cavanagh, 2018a, p. 126). This laid down the fertile soil for a politics of competing land claims in the future. For a minority it would be Hartwig's (1978, p. 129) first mode: the extraction of agricultural commodities; for even fewer, they would go on to benefit from the socio-economic differentiation that it fuelled and become the nucleus of a future capitalist class. Their rise would be accelerated by land tenure programmes such as the Swynnerton Plan (1954) and the preceding drives to modernise the economy and its agriculture base through what is now described in African historiography as the 'second colonial occupation' (Low and Lonsdale, 1976).

These programmes were designed to transform land held by the native population into *privately* owned formally registered land. This commitment to the individuation of landownership was officially continued by the postcolonial state only a few years into its existence, ironically under a policy declaration called 'African Socialism and Its Application to Planning in Kenya' (GoK, 1965). Critically, this entrenched a political economy of land in which 'collective' or 'community' land rights, those that accorded with the ontology and relation to land of forest-dwelling communities like the Sengwer, were largely marginalised (Musembi and Kameri-Mbote, 2013, p. 6). Due to negotiations between the departing British and Kenyan nationalists on the eve of independence over the redistribution of formerly controlled settler lands to Kenyan citizens, the majoritarian ethnic groups who dominated the nationalist movement benefited the most from the land redistribution agreements and not minority groups like forest-dwelling peoples (Kew and Lyman, 2016, p. 153), compounding the iniquitous effects of the colonial political economy of land. However, as we will see below, the precise configuration of this political economy of land and their associated historical land injustices would not have been possible but for the broader institutional legacies of colonial rule and their 'colonial land administration practises and laws' in particular (GoK, 2009, p. 42). To this legal legacy and its continued effects in the present juncture, we will return below. For now, we will turn to the evolutionist and developmentalist ideology that underpinned this prioritisation of particular forms of property and land regimes.

Developmentalism and the 'black man's burden'

In the decades that followed independence, right across Africa, intellectual debate raged on what national renewal and development meant and how to achieve it. There were those who situated themselves in the radical traditions of Marx, Lenin, Baran, Amin, Sweezy, Fanon, Frank and many more. They argued that African nations were beholden to a subordinate position as periphery to the dominant centres of the global capitalist economy which siphoned off accumulated surpluses and fuelled the continued development of the imperialist powers whilst conversely under-developing Africa; the prescriptions were therefore necessarily revolutionary. On the other hand were those intellectuals who embraced the mainstream Western understandings of developmentalism and Western-orientated 'modernization programmes' predicated on an 'almost mystical belief in the validity of one economic system' (Samson and Gigoux, 2016, p. 115): Western capitalism. The programmes sought to 'modernise' backward sectors of the economy and infuse the 'uncaptured peasantry' (Hyden, 1980) with an 'entrepreneurial spirit' (Shivji, 2009, p. 6). In essence, the programmes, which would spawn a rich new lexicon, sought to engineer the social and economic development of a large swathe of the world just emerging from the shadows of empire, dividing it into spatial regions according to levels of 'poverty', 'progress', 'economic wealth' and 'growth' (Chant and McIlwaine, 2009, p. 6). Moreover, these development discourses recast the role of former colonial powers, international financial institutions (IFI) and various nongovernmental organisations (NGO) based in the Global North as agents of progress and modernisation of the 'Third World', 'developing world', 'underdeveloped South'. This form of developmentalism is usually associated with President Harry S. Truman's inaugural address of the US in January 1949 in which he articulates his 'Four Point Plan', the fourth laying out his vision for post-war reconstruction in the context of decolonisation and the beginning of the Cold War (Chant and McIlwaine, 2009, p. 6–7). It is here that distinctions between 'underdeveloped' and 'prosperous' regions are first made, and where the former colonies were encouraged to emulate the paths of the development laid down by Europe and the US. Above all, this was an ideology that presupposed 'the accumulation of capital as the preordained direction of history' (Samson and Gigoux, 2016, p. 114).

Critically, these forms of developmentalism would bear the mark of their colonial roots. Arguably for two reasons. Firstly, as alluded to already, because they imposed a Eurocentric, unilinear and teleological model of development on the rest of the world, which presupposed that Western development paths were not only superior and more enlightened but the only path. Macekura and Manela (2018, p. 3) eloquently capture the loose bundle of ideas, assumptions and discourses:

> [D]evelopment in history has amounted to a loose framework for a set of assumptions – that history moves through stages; that leaders and/ or experts could guide or direct the evolution of societies through these stages; that some places and people in the world are at more advanced stages than others – that have structured how diverse historical actors understood their place in the world and sought to change it.

Secondly, because they are, as we will see below, woven into racist colonial assumptions examined above about the 'uncivilised' and 'primitive' nature of those still considered Indigenous people in modern-day Africa. Much as with the inherited colonial state more generally, this form of racialised developmentalism would not be confined to Kenya alone but shape the forms of racialised biopolitics and governmentality of many other African states in the postcolonial era (Samson and Gigoux, 2016, p. 117). This legacy will be key to our understanding of recent forms of 'green developmentalism' examined below. Both these two strands of development discourses would come together with devastating consequences for Indigenous peoples in Kenya. The aforementioned political economy of land hinged on a unilinear, developmentalist assumption that converting property and land to individuated, privatised land tenure was necessary to develop Kenya's agricultural base since it would be better suited to market relations, therefore allowing access for credit and most importantly providing a profit motive that would unleash the entrepreneurial spirit (Musembi and Kameri-Mbote, 2013, p. 6). By extension, those modes of life, and their associated cultures, based on collective forms of land ownership and an ontology of reciprocity with nature, were deemed less productive and inferior. Ultimately, in Kenya, it was this latter school of thought, that which embraced Western blueprints for development, that won the day. No doubt this was in part due to the hegemonic imperatives of US imperialism during the Cold War, which did not tolerate radical national alternatives (Blum, 1986). Indeed, post-independence Kenyan regimes under Kenyatta and Daniel arap Moi became 'compradors' of their imperialist sponsors (Shivji, 2007, p. 17). If radical alternatives did emerge, they were silenced through military coups and assassinations (Blum, 2001, pp. 125–67; Shivji, 2009, p. 7).[7] Moreover, as Eric Aseka (2000) argues, the ideology of 'African socialism' in Kenya was never intended to overcome the structural features of underdevelopment (least not in a way that would allow for 'autocentric' development), and nearly two centuries of 'moulding' to the priorities of the British Empire and British capitalism. On the contrary, it was oriented towards the *preservation* of the capitalist system. Successive governments from Kenyatta through to Moi and right through the present day have encouraged a deepening of economic integration into the global capitalist economy.

In fact, the 'curse' of the colonial state and the preservation of British interests and, ultimately, the interests of international capital after independence, was assured through British statecraft and 'substantial manoeuvring in the political and economic fields' (Curtis, 2003, p. 330). These 'manoeuvrings' included the land transfer schemes shortly before and after independence, including the aforementioned Swynnerton Plan (Swynnerton, 1954), which ensured that, as argued earlier, on the whole, only the rising Kenyan bourgeoise could purchase land. These land schemes, which intriguingly were funded by the World Bank and Britain's Commonwealth Development Corporation, an early harbinger of neocolonialism operating through international financial organisations and governance networks, were according to Wasserman (1975, p. 172) designed 'to bolster a moderate nationalist state and to preserve European economic (and political) interests'. By shoring up and consolidating the rising Kenyan middle class, it would ensure a powerful vested interest that would act as a bulwark against radical change. Through land titles and loan repayments, this new economic elite would be obliged to defend a largely market driven economy conducive to private investment, and dependent on European dominated capital agriculture and its associated infrastructure (Curtis, 2003, p. 332). Colonial interests were confident that through a means of social control other than formal political authority, such as instruments of trade, aid and debt, most of the advantages that accrued to colonial powers would survive independence (Wasserman, 1976, p. 11). In essence, decolonisation *preserved the colonial political economy* and, beyond that, integrated an Indigenous elite into positions of authority where they could protect the important interests of the colonial system' (Wasserman, 1976, p. 1) [emphasis added].

The 'black man's burden' would not finish here. The political economy of land would be further complicated by what was an already extremely complex politics of competing land claims entangled with a politics of ethnic clientelism and a party-political system organised along ethnic lines in the post-independence period (Kanyinga et al., 2020). Kenyatta's KAU party was despite its rhetoric of national unity allocating resources and land to its base in the majoritarian Kikuyu and Luo communities. With the election of Daniel arap Moi and his KADU party in 1978, this time the ethnic patronage favoured the Kalejin communities. As we saw, ethnic patronage as a system of political power played its part in the consolidation of the colonial political economy of land and the further economic marginalisation of minority Indigenous groups like the Sengwer. Indeed, the legacy of ethnic clientelism traces its lineage back to the divide and rule politics of the British colonial period in which attributing land and resources along tribal and ethnic lines was a form of colonial governmentality.

Colonial lawfare

But this would not be the only legacy. Kenya would have to contend with socio-legal blueprints carried over from its colonial past as well, legal blueprints which determined access and ownership rights over land. As a result of the Kenya Land Commission (Colonial Office, 1934) and the conclusions it drew regarding the biopolitical status of forest-dwelling communities like the Sengwer and the Ogiek, the ancestral land found in the forests and surrounding grazing lands would be demarcated and gazetted as protected areas or government forests or folded into reserves allocated to other non-Dorobo communities. Where the Sengwer ancestral land was concerned, in the following decades, the colonial government would gazette ten blocks of forest highland areas found in the Cherangani Hills, followed by a further two blocks by the post-independence government (Kenrick, 2020a, pp. 238–9). In fact, on the eve of independence, as much as 22,000 km² of forest and 'protected areas' throughout Kenya had been alienated for the purposes of conservation alone (Cavanagh, 2018a, p. 125). As we saw, some ancestral land would be absorbed into the reserves of other ethnic groups permitted only to occupy, the right of usufruct, and not own the lands under the provisions of the law pertaining to 'trust land' (Sorenson, 1967, p. 47; Ojienda and Okoth, 2011, p. 159; Cavanagh, 2017, p. 238); they would remain 'tenants-at-will of the Crown' (East Africa Protectorate, 1915).

The category of trust land carried over into the post-independence period, to be held 'in trust' by local county governments. In 1964, one year after independence, land designated as 'trust land' was officially declared national forest reserves, essentially state property. The precarious status of trust land would be further undermined with the passing of two new land laws in 1968 which permitted the dissolution of trust land in the event of governmental or individual registration of title (GoK, 1968a, 1968b). This enabled government-appointed 'trust land custodians' to extinguish Indigenous land tenure or 'set aside' land for their own enrichment or that of powerful elite and tribal interests, often displacing entire communities (Kew and Lyman, 2016, p. 154; Wily, 2018, p. 7). In fact, the first of these laws, known as the Trust Land Act of 1968 (GoK, 1968a), was modelled on British colonial legislation examined in the previous chapter, which demarcated and gazetted native reserve land and provided for powers to 'set aside' land and extinguish all customary rights (Wily, 2018, p. 3). Recall that these powers were invested in the loyal Indigenous political and economic elite cultivated by the colonial authorities. In the post-independence period, these powers would be transferred to local officials of county councils, who invariably were drawn from the same dominant ethnic majority communities. These councils in turn were centrally controlled by government ministers in Nairobi.

As Kenrick (2020, pp. 238–9) argues, these are laws rooted, at least ostensibly, and sometimes outright mendaciously, in the approach known as 'fortress conservation', which is the practice of 'fencing off' nature and forcibly displacing Indigenous people with the aim of setting up 'protected areas' and preventing assumed destructive local practices, all which restructure socioecologies. The observant reader will recognise the continuity of this approach with the British colonial period examined earlier, which refracted through a 'primitivist' discourse assumes as axiomatic the harmful impact of 'traditional' ways of life on forests (Neumann, 1997, p. 568). We will return to this notion of 'fortress conservation' below and see how once again this practice and its associated discourse are tied up with broader notions of development, only this time dressed up in the garb of sustainable development and climate change mitigation. What is important to understand here is that these laws are predicated on a 'conservationist ethic' (Fiona and Mackenzie, 2000, p. 698), which moulds certain spatial attitudes, or 'mental terrains' earlier described as racecraft (Fields and Fields, 2012: 18). This facilitates the carving out of racialised topographical features through the imposition of draconian and domicidal land management practices of a piece with what Vandergeest and Peluso (1995, p. 387) describe as 'internal territorialisation', and ensures the consolidation of (neo)colonial state formation and the expansion of state power into rural areas (Neumann, 1997). Recall that for Wolfe (2006a, p. 388), territoriality is the key motive force driving the logic of elimination.

Fundamentally, this tangled legal web is rooted in a colonial tradition that contained a 'dual bias' (Musembi and Kameri-Mbote, 2013, p. 6) in favour of both privatised individuated ownership of land as opposed to community or collective ownership *and* the colonial presumption that sedentary agriculture is superior to all other modes, embedded in the Swynnerton Plan (1954) and ultimately the legal architecture imported by the British dating back to 1899, rooted as we saw, in a episteme of *terra nullius*. In essence, the postcolonial government consolidated and extended the political economy of land and its associated property forms and 'production of space' inherited from the former colonial occupiers, which already excluded alternative life ways that based their economies on forms of subsistence dependent on food procurement (gathering and hunting) and not just food production (farming). Through this lawfare, the Kenyan state and its economic and political elites continued the onward march into *non-capitalist* territory, 'into a world dense with cultural difference' (Smith, 2002, p. 79), entrenching the 'facts on the ground' through the necessary legal and institutional architecture in the form of private property regimes (Busbridge, 2017) and consolidating *de jure* as well as *de facto* control of Indigenous land, mirroring Lemkin's second phase of genocide, the imposition of the 'national' pattern of the occupier. However, as argued before, this phase will only be completed once the non-capitalist territory, namely Sengwer ancestral land, is *fully* incorporated into the (global) circuits of capitalist production and subject to the reign of exchange value; as we will see, the Sengwer refuse to give up and repeatedly return to their forest dwellings, frustrating government attempts to complete this phase. Nevertheless, in more recent developments, colonial lawfare will play a key part in the denial of not just the collective land rights and suppression of Indigenous sovereignty of the Sengwer, but their alterity too. Ultimately, The Sengwer and their mode of life were marginalised legally and ultimately biopolitcally, through the deepening and consolidation of an inherited political economy of land understood as embodying the 'preordained direction of history' (Samson and Gigoux, 2016, p. 114).

Notes

1. For the war of 'pacification' see Mungeam (1966).

2. UKNA/CAB/24/248 – 'The Kenya Land Commission Report, 1934'.

3. See for instance the testimony by Arap Kamusein, UKNA CAB/24/248, Kenya Land Commission Report, Volume II, pp. 1992–1993.

4. Mr A. C. Hoey, UKNA CAB/24/248, Kenya Land Commission Report, Volume II, pp. 1993–2003.

5. Kenya Land Commission report, 1934, UKNA/CAB/24/248, p. 259.

6. Kenya Land Commission report, 1934, UKNA/CAB/24/248, p. 260.

7. For International development understood as a post-1945, Cold War doctrine see *Staging Growth: Modernization, Development, and the Global Cold War*, ed. David C. Engerman et al. (2003); Engerman, D. (2016).

Chapter 5

Kenya now: the architecture of dispossession

It seems the very same 'modernising' tendencies embodied in the former British colonial state machine have been imparted to the postcolonial regime. These were the tendencies, as we saw, that considered some peoples primitive, uncivilised and benighted who posed an unfortunate impediment to the development of the colony. In the present juncture, earlier described as the era of neoliberalism or 'globalisation' (Shivji, 2009, p. 10), the 'developmentalist' forces have re-emerged with a green sheen in the guise of environmental conservation and climate-change mitigation. The anti-ecological properties of the capitalist system have given rise to a new form of developmentalist genocide in the sphere of international relations and environmental governance. In this era, the 'developmental state', replaced by the neoliberal Kenyan state, first introduced in the lost decade of structural adjustment programmes (SAPs), would be repurposed 'to preserve law and order, to enforce private contracts, to foster competitive markets' (Friedman, 2002, p. 2), all in the pursuit of the *conservation* of nature.

The structures of discourse and underlying episteme of the new conservation and environmental movement are remarkably amenable to the presuppositions of the colonial discourse that condemned some social groups like the Sengwer as a barrier to progress and threats to the social and environmental order. The old forms of colonial governmentality and their concomitant discourse will, like the discursive equivalent of a zoonotic spillover, mutate into a viral form that adapts to its new host, the emerging environmental discourses in the age of neoliberalism known variously as 'market environmentalism', the 'Green Economy' or 'green growth'. Moreover, these discourses and the capitalist system that underpins it are not only *not* succeeding in averting or even mitigating climate change or the ecological crisis, and in some cases accelerating it, but given the ecocide-genocide nexus, they can, and are, driving the genocidal destruction of entire social groups. One case, the case of the Sengwer in Kenya, exemplifies this sinister process.

The Sengwer as obstacle to conservation

In 2018, the EU suspended funding for its 31 million euro Water Towers Protection and Climate Change Mitigation and Adaptation (WaTER) project in Kenya (EEAS, 2018). The project is designed to conserve and protect the water catchment system, otherwise known as the 'water towers', located in five areas including the Cherangani Hills and the Mau Forest complex (UNEP, 2012, p. 21), the ancestral homes of the Sengwer and Ogiek respectively. After repeated warnings from human rights and civil society organisations in Kenya and around the world (Kenrick, 2017), UN experts (OHCHR, 2018) and the affected Sengwer, the EU finally acted after the killing, on 16 January 2018, of forty-one-year-old Robert Kirotich, a member of the Sengwer community. He was killed during a raid by the EU-funded Kenya Forest Service (KFS), an agency overseen by the Ministry of Environment and Forestry, mounted in order to 'clear' the forests of what the Kenyan government see as illegal squatters, loggers, cattle ranchers and poachers, who it argues are criminal elements in the forest which must be flushed out' (Voice of America, 2018). These 'criminal elements', which include forest dwelling peoples like the Sengwer, the Ministry of Environment and Forestry claim are environmentally degrading the Mt. Elgon and the Cherangani Hills. The latter are two critical ecosystems for Kenya, vital for water and food security for the region and a host of dependent local species and the nation as a whole. In addition, these two areas, as well as the other water catchment sites – Mount Kenya, the Mau Forest complex and the Aberdares range – are responsible for 75 per cent of renewable surface water resources in Kenya and play a vital role in sustaining a number of key industries (UNEP, 2012, p. 8). This was just another episode in a long history of repeated violations of human rights and mass evictions of the Sengwer (at least thirteen such evictions since January 2014) and other Indigenous groups from their forest dwellings and destruction of their villages by the KFS, stretching back, as we will see below, decades.

These forced evictions violate not only the rights of the Sengwer to housing, and to their ancestral lands under international law and according to African Union human rights standards, but also their rights under the 2010

Constitution of Kenya, which recognises their right to live in their ancestral lands under Article 63.2.d.ii, as does the 2016 Community Land Act. These rights the Sengwer have pursued by petitioning the Kenyan Land Commission and Kenyan Environment and Land Court, so far to no avail.[1] Moreover, the project design and terms of reference for technical assistance laid out in the original tender embodied a model of conservation that was neocolonial in its conspicuous lack of any meaningful consultation with the Sengwer and other affected communities. This is a glaring oversight since *free, prior and informed consent* on development projects that affect Indigenous peoples is a fundamental right enshrined in the UNDRIP (UNGA, 2017), an international instrument which the EU itself pledged to honour in the EU Commission's *Implementing EU External Policy on Indigenous Peoples* document (EC, 2016), a pledge made in the same year the WaTER project was launched. The failure to consult also violates the EUs *Charter of Fundamental Rights and the 2015 EU Human Rights Action Plan* (EU, 2021). The terms of reference of WaTER did not even mention the Sengwer or other Forest communities, let alone make any attempt to implement a human rights impact assessment.

In fact, KFS actions arguably amount to forced or involuntary population transfers, defined by a report produced by the Council of Europe's Committee on Legal Affairs and Human Rights (2011) as

> a practice or policy having the purpose or effect of moving persons into or out of an area, either within or across an international border, or within, into or out of an occupied territory, without the free and informed consent of the transferred population and any receiving population. It involves *collective expulsions or deportations and often ethnic cleansing*. [emphasis added]

The International Criminal Court (ICC) (1998) includes 'deportation or forcible transfer of population' as one technique that falls under the definition of Crimes against Humanity; the phrase 'forcible transfer' was included to acknowledge that involuntary transfers of populations within a state's borders fall under the definition of 'deportations', which have long been recognised as an international crime (Lee, 2001, p. 86). This would amount to domicide and a *prima facie* violation of all of the three key rights articulated in the UNDRIP, and thus an attack on the structural integrity of group life. There was no FPIC (UNDRIP, Article 19), and by extension it constitutes a violation of their rights to sovereignty and, by severing their connection to the land, amounts to an assault on the ecological, economic and cultural integrity of the genos, corresponding to Lemkin's techniques, given the central role occupied by Sengwer land explored in detail below. This forced transfer within national borders, often targeting ethnic groups and involving collective punishment, chimes loudly with the forced evictions of Sengwer villagers at gun point and by way of burning down and destroying their villages.

The public record of the Kenyan government and the KFS of repeated evictions and human rights violations is well documented. As we saw above, not long after independence, with the Kenyan government consolidating the inherited political economy of land and by extension the discrimination of customary community forms of land control, ancestral land was now either given over to other ethnic groups or gazetted as 'protected areas' and legally declared state forests. This essentially outlawed Sengwer occupation of their land. By the 1970s, the evictions began to involve burning down of homes, but not all property and by the 1980s this developed into what could be described as a 'scorched earth' policy of burning *everything* down – entire villages (Sengwer elder Lukas Kiraton, quoted in Kenrick, 2020a, pp.238–9). KFS actions intensified throughout the 1980s. In the 1990s KFS tactics began to incorporate illegal redrawing of forest boundaries and the allocation of lands to other ethnic communities (Kenrick, 2020, pp.238–9). Here we see policies such as parcelling out of land to adjacent communities, redrawing of land boundaries and violent campaigns of 'pacification', all underpinned by a neocolonial legal architecture, which in their form and content bear a striking similarity to colonial-era policies explored in the previous chapter.

These mechanisms of control again raised their ugly heads with the launch of a World Bank-funded conservation and carbon offset project, known as the UN-authorised Reducing Emissions from Deforestation and Degradation (REDD+) programme, funded via the Natural Resource Management Programme (NRMP) (World Bank, 2007). Starting in 2007, the World Bank provided the KFS $64 million dollars to improve 'the management of water and forest resources in selected districts'. After initially including provisions that recognised the rights of forest communities like the Sengwer, they were later amended to remove all such references (Ahmed, 2014). The project lasted till 2013. Coterminous with this, in 2009, the Finnish government, arguably the most important international donor to the KFS, began its project (2009 to 2015) called *Miti Mingi Maisha Bora*, which translated means 'Many Trees, Good Life'. The project was predicated on the environmentally dubious notion that the most practical and efficient way of protecting the forests is to encourage fast-growing commercial plantations for profit, a model which has been imported from Finland, where it has been successful. However, the model is inappropriate for the Embobut since the forest is not fast-growing and ignores the criticality of protecting the fragile biodiversity of the Indigenous forests. Moreover, this model and its financing by the Finnish government fosters a particular structure and institutional logic in the KFS which predisposes it to pursuing perverse commercial incentives and, most saliently for this research, an incentive to evict forest-dwelling communities (Kenrick, 2020a, pp. 246–7). This perverse incentive to displace and commit domicide is arguably present in all the internationally financed projects, given the conspicuous elision of FPIC or even the lack of any reference to forest-dwelling communities at all in the planning documents, as we saw earlier, thus rendering Indigenous people invisible.

In 2009, not long after both projects had taken off, the government concluded that deforestation in the Embobut Forest was endangering water catchment functions of the forest and that *all* its residents would have to be resettled, failing to distinguish between Indigenous peoples who had historical attachments to the forest and newly arrived communities (AI, 2018, p. 6). This conclusion was based in part on the government-appointed Embobut Forest Task Force, which included representatives from civil society, forest communities, forest officials and politicians, and was tasked with assessing the state of the forest and consulting with forest residents to establish those eligible for resettlement. In its 2010 report, it concluded that the Sengwer were the most eligible group for resettlement, which was considered urgent (AI, 2018). Suffice to say, despite insistence from the KFS and the Ministry of Environment and Forestry that the Sengwer were fully consulted via the Embobut Forest Task Force process, three of its members interviewed by Amnesty International (AI) conceded that the decision to evict the Sengwer was taken *prior* to any consultation. Moreover, just as we saw with the EU-funded Water Towers Programme, there was an abject failure to provide FPIC (UNGA, 2017, Article 19) and a failure to engage with the Sengwer traditional decision-making structures, in violation of article18 (UNGA, 2017; anonymous, Sengwer, 18/03/2020). As the report (AI, 2018, p. 6) argued:

> Twenty-two community members interviewed said that they were not informed about consultation meetings. In some cases, forest residents were informed of the time, place and subject matter of meetings by word of mouth only, and only the day before the meeting, not allowing sufficient time to make arrangements (for example for childcare). Forest residents interviewed by AI reported a high degree of confusion and ignorance over the purpose of the process, the details of what was being proposed and what was ultimately agreed.

Moreover, a number of task force members are on record admitting that the Sengwer remaining in the forest was never an option (AI, 2018, p. 32).

Unsurprisingly, nearly every year of the World Bank and Finnish government-funded projects saw mass evictions of the Sengwer. The World

Bank's (2015) own Inspection Panel found the NRMP guilty of failing to take 'the proper steps to address the potential loss of customary rights' and enabling the evictions by failing to adequately identify or address that the institution it was funding, the KFS, was before, during and after the term of the NRMP ideologically committed to mass evictions. The report, however, ultimately exculpated the World Bank of the evictions directly, despite funding the agency that was responsible. Nevertheless, in the court of public opinion, culpability was clear. The World Bank and the Finnish government, just as the EU after them, employed a neocolonial model of conservation that ignored the rights of forest-dwelling Indigenous peoples and paid no heed to the devastating impacts the forced mass evictions would have on the viability and survival of their communities.

Once the World Bank-funded project had ended, the Kenyan government unilaterally decided that the most appropriate resolution to this problem was to provide financial compensation to the Sengwer and subsequently declare that this now extinguished their right and claim to the land.[2] Again, the Sengwer were not consulted over the compensation process, and, after senior politicians descended on Eldoret county, including the president, deputy president and the local senator, the message delivered was clear: either they accept the compensation or the full force of the state's paramilitaries would be levelled against them. Many were promised by local politicians that compensation would be for *past* historical injustices and not an implicit relinquishing of historical claims to land. Some legitimate Sengwer beneficiaries accepted the compensation under this proviso; many would subsequently receive nothing. Much of it was embezzled by non-Sengwer elites (Kenrick, 2020a, pp. 243–4; AI, 2018, p. 7). In early 2014, the convenient pretext of compensation would trigger yet another wave of evictions and mass displacement actions; this time the frequency of the evictions increased from anywhere between every few months to a year to every week (Kenrick, 2020a, pp. 243–4).

In order to strengthen the moral case for evictions, the government and the KFS often claimed that the Sengwer no longer resided in the Embobut Forest or were nothing more than criminal 'squatter' elements. Recall that dispossessed Kenyan peasants desperately searching for land and material security in light of their mass dispossession by British colonists and settlers, who eventually settled on white settler farms, were also labelled squatters. The label inherently implies a lack of legitimacy or permanency of residence and thus undercuts the historical claims made by Sengwer and other Indigenous people to their land so vital to Indigenous status under African regional law in the wake of the ACHPR ruling in 2010 that the Endorois community in Kenya are an Indigenous group (ACHPR, 2010). In a typical article published shortly after the wave of mass evictions began in 2014, as we saw earlier in the wake of the EU-funded Water Towers Programme, all the inhabitants of the Embobut Forest, with no distinction, were labelled squatters by the government, and *all* were accused of illegal farming, logging and charcoal burning and overgrazing (Suter, 2013). The overriding subtext of the article was that the amorphous mass of squatters were environmentally destructive. None of these suppositions were challenged or questioned by any of the quoted academics, local politicians, nor indeed by the journalist. It was not an editorial or opinion piece but the failure to provide any dissenting voices had the effect of reproducing and reinforcing this highly misleading and inflammatory dominant narrative.

Unlike the World Bank-funded project, the subsequent EU-funded WaTER project was not officially in aid of forest carbon offsets, but the direction of travel was clear. In a strategic ten-year 'Plan Period', published long after the ending of the controversial World Bank offset project in the Embobut Forest and Cherangani Hills, the Kenya Water Towers Agency (KWTA, 2019, P. 93) argued that in order to raise necessary finance to conserve the forest it would 'promote Payment of Ecosystem Service (PES) Schemes'. In a rather chilling Orwellian turn of phrase, it states that to secure the support or at least the acquiescence of effected communities it must 'sensitize the beneficiaries of the ecosystem service' and 'sensitize and build capacity [*sic*] the local community of carbon marketing' (KWTA, 2019). On its official government website it still uncritically presents the recommendations of a 2008 task force investigation into the Mau Forest complex, which concluded the forest and water catchment area could only be protected by moving from what it called a 'single-asset' system which only values it as a resource base to a 'multiple-asset' approach, 'which recognizes the wide variety of values of this ecosystem and diversifies revenue streams by capitalizing on ecosystem values, thereby maximizing both conservation and economic returns on the investment' (KWTA, 2020).

In May 2017, the self-defined 'non-profit scientific research organization', the Center for International Forestry Research (CIFOR), launched, alongside their partners, including Germany's Federal Ministry of Economic Cooperation and Development, a three-year project on the conservation of Kenyan water towers (CIFOR, 2017). Their main research focus is on the management of tropical forests. One component of their research is what they call 'Environmental services and landscape management', which essentially promotes mechanisms like PES and monetary valuation of nature more generally. Among their partners for the Kenyan water towers project include the now infamous KFS and the KWTA. Buried at the very end of the document detailing the proceedings of a workshop, under a section titled 'Suggestions on Areas of Collaboration', the CIFOR list 'Payment for Ecosystem (PES) Model: KEFRI is working on PES as a business model, which investors can adopt' (CIFOR, 2017, p. 17).

Sadly, the subterfuge has not ended there. According to Sengwer activist and community leader Elias Kimaiyo (author interview, 07/08/2020) the ministry of Environment and Forestry wrote letters to the relevant EU ambassador to lift the suspension of the funds for the WaTER project, fraudulently adding the co-signatures of community members. This letter, seen by the author, which calls on the EU to recognise a new group as the legitimate representatives of Sengwer community at a meeting in Maron primary school on the 27 May 2020, included the names of people Elias (07/08/2020) told me cannot even read or write. This person would be one of the new 'legitimate representatives'. One person who, according to the letter, attended the meeting, which alleges community leaders agreed to the lifting of the EU suspension, was compelled to sign his name to a handwritten letter, also seen by myself, refuting his alleged consent to lift the suspension. In a subsequent letter written on 10 June 2020 (Kimaiyo, 2020), written by Sengwer community leaders to the European Union in light of this manoeuvre, the letter clarifies that the Sengwer were never against the WaTER project in principle, only the lack of FPIC.

The United Nations Development Programme (UNDP) have also been important players in these unfolding events. Globally, they have been instrumental in REDD+ 'readiness' preparation schemes in sixty-five countries (UN REDD, n.d.), schemes that arrange the necessary institutional and legal regimes which make forest carbon offsets possible and provide funding, just as we saw under the EU and World Bank projects. What the Sengwer interviewee (author interview, 18/03/2020) was at pains to stress is that UNDP as a delivery partner, if successful, will ensure that Kenya will become a recipient of REDD+ funding, which in turn will provide finance to the Kenyan government and its agencies to continue their acts of domicide. More recently, they have been positioning themselves as replacements for the EU as major funders for forest conservation in Kenya (author interview, 18/03/2020; Kenrick, 2020b). As early as 2017, UNDP were invited by the Kenyan government to initiate a REDD+ programme. The UNDP are responsible for the initial stages of the project including identifying drivers of deforestation, land rights and developing safeguards and an information system (AI, 2018, p. 70). Ostensibly, these safeguards include not just compliance with national policies but respect for Indigenous people's rights, including right to land and protection against environmental destruction (AI, 2018).

However, despite assurances from the UNDP that Sengwer representatives have been included on the projects REDD+ steering committee and have been consulted regularly on the development of the project document known as the 'Draft PRODOC', which will define the projects, activities as well as its methodology, the Sengwer interlocutors interviewed by the author expressed concern this has not happened. Sengwer community representatives have consistently lobbied the UNDP since the beginning of the project, alerting the UN agency to the continued state violence and KFS eviction actions and urging the UNDP to address this fact, as well as open the consultation process more widely to the community as a whole. Unfortunately, it seems, KFS eviction actions and violence increase whenever meetings or consultations are organised between the Sengwer and international donors or partners, presumably to chasten such involvement. Indeed, a wave of KFS violence was unleashed on the eve of a World Bank-convened colloquium at Eldoret in March 2015, in light of the failure of the NRMP project (Kenrick, 2020a, p. 249).

In a letter, seen by the author, addressed to the head of UNDP in Kenya on 6 January 2020 (Kitum, 2020), the Sengwer community argued that until such assurances are given and the evictions and paramilitary violence ends, meaningful and constructive dialogue is impossible. In response, in a letter on 13 February 2020 (Badawi, 2020), the UNDP resident representative claimed that they were making every effort to consult relevant stakeholders, including Indigenous and community groups, but qualified this by reminding the Sengwer that the REDD+ project cannot contravene national law or court judgments which state *no Indigenous groups can occupy gazetted forests*, a clear signal that the UNDP takes the official government position. As we will see shortly, the Embobut Forest, according to Kenyan law, remains gazetted as a state forest and within the jurisdiction of the KFS, unless and until Sengwer tenure rights are finally recognised by the Kenyan Courts or government. Presumably, the UNDP are aware of this. In an interview with a Sengwer community member, I asked about the UNDP's position and response. They averred that this was 'a colonial mindset. They are only seeing the laws and wanted to push things their way. We told them [UNDP] the laws they are using, there are many challenges' (anonymous, Sengwer, 18/03/2020). Indeed, as we will see below, among the many challenges is the need to decolonise the law.

In meetings arranged by the UNDP between the local Marakwet County, the Ministry of Environment and Forestry and the Sengwer for the drafting of local forest laws and regulations, negotiations broke down due to intimidation at the hands of the UNDP representative and local government officials (Kenrick, 2020b). Moreover, Sengwer attendees spoke of being ordered to switch off phones to prevent recordings of the meetings, and last-minute changes of its location to areas where they didn't feel safe (Kenrick, 2020b). Reflecting on these 'dialogue processes', one interviewee (anonymous, Sengwer, 18/03/2020) described a Kafkaesque situation, 'they push us from one person to another. We approach UNDP, then UNDP says no, just go and plan with your County government, when we [*sic*] get County government they say "no you see we don't have jurisdiction over gazetted forest"'. As the interviewee explained, their forests, designated as public forest, are not devolved to county government jurisdiction under the new constitution, but they are still custodians of community and community lands, therefore they are effectively side-lined in county government plans despite being residents (anonymous, Sengwer, 18/03/2020). When they do finally meet, the interviewee added, 'when we meet today, what we decided today, what is being brought next time into the meeting is something totally different' (anonymous, Sengwer, 18/03/2020). They added (anonymous, Sengwer, 18/03/2020) that the consultations are just a 'trick ... to ask government institutions to come and talk to us so that they can record .... what they wanted is our presence but not what we are saying'. It is these kinds of Machiavellian tactics where the (neo)colonial authorities attempt to sow discord within Indigenous communities and frustrate attempts at genuine participation via administrative and bureaucratic processes, which by design create uneven fields of negotiation, that are precisely those documented in Australia in Chapter 3 in the period of recognition politics. It is perhaps no surprise then that despite the EU suspension, attempts at population transfer continue.

The forms of divide and rule and subterfuge evident in all the internationally financed projects and the construction of uneven fields of negotiation that they play out on, are underpinned by forms of colonial lawfare discussed in the previous chapter. In fact, in more recent years the Kenyan government has doubled down on the use of lawfare with the passing of the Forests Act of 2005 (GoK, 2005), which prohibits Indigenous groups living on their ancestral land, and the Wildlife Act of 2013 (GoK, 2013), which prohibits hunting and gathering practices deemed unsustainable and allows for the establishment of 'protected areas' without the necessity of FPIC. Without the latter, sovereignty, autonomy and meaningful land rights are impossible. Ergo, this cluster of laws will have genocidal consequences if enforced.

This is in spite of the new 2010 constitution (GoK, 2010), in large part written in the wake of intercommunal violence largely believed to be attributable to the divisive political economy of land (Cavanagh, 2018a), or what the 2009 National Land Policy (NLP)[3] described as 'present and historical land injustices' (GoK, 2009). Indeed, the new constitution specifically makes provision for 'community land' tenure and seeks to elevate it to the same legal status as that which is state or individually owned. These principles have required statutes to elaborate those provisions, like the Land Act of 2012 (GoK, 2012) and the Community Land Act of 2016 (GoK,

2016a). The former established that customary rights have equal legal weight as freehold or leasehold and the latter that community land does exist and is held 'in trust' by the local county government only until the relevant community formalises its tenure (Kenrick, 2020, pp. 249–50). Further, the new Forest Conservation and Management Act 2016 (from now on Forest Act) (GoK, 2016b) makes provision for community land to be transferred to communities such as the Sengwer or Ogiek. Unfortunately, the latter act also contains articles that contradict this aspiration. Although it recognises the category of 'forest community' (section 2)[4] and *community* forests, which includes 'forests on ancestral lands and lands traditionally occupied by hunter-gatherer communities' (GoK, 2016b, section 30(3)), It also states that *public* forests include any land that has already been gazetted as forest reserve, which, as we saw, includes Indigenous territory; the act stipulates public forests are managed by the KFS (GoK, 2016b, section 2). This is precisely the 'legal roadblock' evidenced in the UNDP involvement in REDD+ discussed above, and why one Sengwer activist asserted that the 2016 Forest Act was being used: 'if you go to the forest act then they don't allow us, we are nowhere. Now, the government uses the forest act instead of the constitution. When it comes to gazetted forest, that's out of the question. It leaves us in a dilemma' (author interview, 25/10/2021).

It is these sorts of 'ambiguities' or legal loopholes that Cavanagh (2018) likened to 'bureaucratic sabotage' that allows for the play of elite interests and the balance of power at any given moment to tilt the scales of justice in favour of those interests. Many in the Sengwer community are aware of the inherent colonial nature of Kenya's socio-legal system and its susceptibility to bureaucratic sabotage. One member of the Sengwer (author interview, 25/10/2021), referring to this 'ambiguity', argued, 'when you look at the constitution you look at it as something good, but when you go deep inside to get your rights you'll never get [*sic*], that is why I think it was delivered by elites to continue this'.

As argued repeatedly in this book, we must always pay attention to the manner in which rights are institutionalised (Freeman, 2002, p. 85). The convoluted and contradictory legal architecture allows for the dispossession of forest-dwelling communities and gives legal authority to agencies like the KFS to execute its exclusionary acts of displacement and 'relocation' of the Sengwer. The repeated wielding of symbolic violence through a discourse that both denies they reside in the Embobut Forest, as the KFS have done repeatedly and even denies their Indigenous status by discursively subsuming them within the category of ecologically destructive 'squatters' and criminals, ensures that even if the provisions within the 2010 constitution and the accompanying legislation were to be applied in good faith, the Sengwer would be denied entitlement to those provisions.

Indeed, Kenrick (2020a, pp. 253–5) argues that the denial of the habitation of the forests by the Sengwer is precisely designed to inhibit the ability of the independent National Land Commission (NLC) to adjudicate over Sengwer's case and the competing land claims made over the Embobut Forest. The NLC, enabled by parliament in 2012, derives its mandate to resolve historic injustices and concomitant competing land claims, and its powers from the 2010 constitution. Unfortunately, the constitution itself, and subsequent legislation, lacks clear guidance on how to achieve this, leaving room once again for 'bureaucratic sabotage' (Cavanagh, 2018a, pp. 137–8). Ultimately, the NLC, despite initial promises and rhetoric, issued an eviction notice and ordered Sengwer community members to leave, framing them as 'encroachers' (Rutto, 2016). In fact, one Sengwer community member (author interview, 25/10/2021) who attended a meeting hosted by the NLC in 2016 explained that the institution is in fact managed by state officials who hold deeply hostile attitudes that disparage the colonial legacy and its uneven impact on the Indigenous of Kenya, committing symbolic violence akin to other state agencies. He said the then chair of the NLC disputed the claim made by the Sengwer that they had been forcibly displaced by the British colonial authorities: 'he said [the chair] "you are pretending that you are not going out of the forests, your 'ancestral land'"'. The chair, according to my interviewee, claimed the Sengwer were in part to blame for their colonial encounter, 'you people who moved out their lands and paved way for colonial [sic] and that you people now are in a problematic situation ... but those who fitted the [colonial] system are okay'. The insinuation was that those who assimilated to the colonial system and its system of land tenure are now better off and that groups like the Sengwer would be wise to follow suit. The Sengwer community member continued 'the [Sengwer] community not [sic] even want to hear because they saw it as one way of oppressing them'.

Commenting on the Ogiek case and the Mau Task force report that had in part been set up to investigate the degradation of the forests in the Mau Complex *and* implement the African Court on Human and People's Rights (ACtHPR, 2017) ruling on the unlawful eviction of Ogiek from their ancestral lands (from now on the *Ogiek* case) (OPDP and Katiba Institute, 2020), a report that has still not seen the light of day, one community member of the Sengwer told me that these sorts of administrative measures and initiatives simply 'buy time, [sic] make excuse ... they come up with excuse to not help the Sengwer and Ogiek' (anonymous, 18/03/2020). Moreover, legislation has since moved the authority for the supervision of community land away from the semi-autonomous NLC back to the government ministry for lands (Wily, 2018, pp. 3–4). The history of the NLC is beset with attempts to undermine its functioning and independence by a parliament and executive unwilling to cede power (Kew and Lyman, 2016, p. 165). Nevertheless, by denying the habitation of the Sengwer in the Embobut Forest, the KFC were able to prevent the NLC from visiting the forests and meeting with the Sengwer.

This form of colonial lawfare and the accompanying discursive violence reconfigured the field of struggle and negotiation, facilitating legal and bureaucratic sabotage and empowering state paramilitaries. A petition filed to the Environment and Land Court in Eldoret on 22 March 2013, against intended evictions from Embobut Forest, argued that if carried out it would prevent the Sengwer from participating in their cultural life (in other words social death) in the interim, a series of injunctions were issued by the court demanding that all parties refrain from actions that would prejudice the case. Over time, the language of the injunctions evolved into a position that effectively gave the KFS latitude to continue its population transfer programmes. One injunction for instance in 2013 called on all parties to 'maintain the status quo'. The KFS would interpret this liberally in line with the dominant government discourse when they argued that the status quo was *no inhabitants in the forest* (cited in AI, 2018, p. 44). The court backpedalled when in 2016 it issued an injunction clarifying that no forest residents should be evicted, but still declared 'no new settlement to be allowed in the forest' (AI, 2018).

Unfortunately, a second stronger petition in 2018, which made a more detailed case based on the rights to community land tenure defined in the 2010 constitution, was dismissed on 13 May 2020 (Rutto, 2020). Justice Stephen Kibunja noted that the land had been gazetted as a National Forest by the colonial regime in 1954 and subsequently declared a central forest in 1964 and thus public land. He (quoted in Rutto, 2020) stated:

> The proclamation and subsequent gazettement of Embobut Forest as a forest reserve and thereafter as a central forest protected by the State has not been disputed. The forest having been proclaimed a forest reserve and gazetted as a central forest in 1964, then it forms part of *public land as defined by the Constitution.* [emphasis added]

The court went on to rule that no evidence had been presented to the court proving ownership of the forest by the Sengwer. Precisely how they would be expected to, given the nature of colonial and postcolonial dispossession, examined in this chapter and the previous chapter, and the lack of clear guidance in the 2010 constitution and subsequent relevant land laws, is left conveniently vague.

In the latest twist, a draft version of a new national forest policy by the Ministry of Environment and Forestry which sets out its new vision of forest governance, despite fine words about community participation, civil society organisations and local communities, makes clear its commitment to the development goals set out in vision 2030 and the importance of preparing the forests for inclusion within the global green economy, 'natural capital' and 'green accounting', (GoK, 2020, foreword, para. d). If there was any ambiguity about the role that forest communities like the Sengwer can play in this vision, they are put to rest in section 2.21.1 (GoK, 2020):

> Three of the five main water towers of Kenya host Indigenous communities. They are the Ogiek (Mt Elgon and Mau Forests Complex) and the Sengwer (Cherangani Hills). Their traditional way of life has changed and their livelihood activities now include livestock grazing and food crop production that are not compatible with forest conservation. *These livelihood activities have compromised the integrity of ecosystems and the services they provide*, such as water, to the communities in the lower catchment. [emphasis added]

What the above demonstrates is the fallacy that neoliberal reform means a weakening or diminishing in the power and role of the state. On the contrary, moves to privatisation, deregulation and marketisation of ever greater spheres of society and economy and the shrinking of 'the commons' are enabled and enforced by the power of the state. As Castree (2008, p. 142) points out, the setting up of commodity markets require legal regimes and 'market friendly re-regulation' enforced by the state, and as we saw, its various mechanisms for control, be it the use of neocolonial lawfare or the unleashing of violence at the hands of its paramilitaries; in every instance, the power of the state and its various agencies was crucial.

Greenwashed relations of genocide

A 2014 study of a similar conservation project in Kenya's neighbour Uganda, in the Bulakeba and Kachung districts, run by Norwegian company Green Resources, found local communities were disenfranchised and dispossessed and their access to food and water restricted, in order to orchestrate a land grab in aid of the conservation programme (Lyons and Westoby, 2014). The study found that the stated environmental targets were not met. Among the abuses committed by what the lead author of the report called the 'darker side' of the green economy, were the destruction of homes to make way for the monoculture plantations, planting trees on community land, confiscation of animals and forcing the local villagers to farm on ecologically sensitive land. The villagers had lost the primary means of income, access to medicine and firewood and water for their farm animals.

The environmentally, socially and culturally destructive pattern found in the forest plantation project in Uganda, where Indigenous and place-based peoples have been evicted from the land they have lived on for centuries, denied access to food, medicinal plants, firewood and the right to hunt or farm, the destructive pattern strikes a familiar and menacing chord with KFS actions in the Embobut Forest and Cherangani Hills in Kenya. Recall that the Sengwer have suffered forced mass evictions, which, properly understood, can only be described as a 'scorched earth' policy of ethnic cleansing that violently severs the community from its means of material subsistence, its medicine, its cultural identity and its *mode of life*. From what is a Lemkian perspective, by severing the connection the Sengwer have to their ancestral land, the site of their culture, identity and lifeway, the actions are genocidal. Speaking of the World Bank-funded NRMP project, during one field interview, Sengwer activist and community leader Paul Kibet (09/10/2016), at the forefront of the resistance to this 'creative destruction' said that the REDD+ project was inflicting irreparable and fatal damage to the life of the Sengwer *genos*:

> We are deriving our sources of life from the forests; shrines actually are in the forests. Our spirits always are in the forests. Actually, we normally pray in the forests. So, as they started actually to evict us since 2007 up to date [sic], they have completely actually interfered with our system of life. Many children of school-going age actually are dropping out from school, many old men and women have been exposed actually to cold because of [sic] destroying the homesteads and etcetera. So [sic] get a lot of people now suffering with pneumonia ... the whole system of life, actually people have been terrorized.

Reflecting on the evictions fuelled by the EU funded Water Towers Programme, Milka Chepkoir, a Sengwer activist, said (Muraya, 2018):

> We have repeatedly experienced forced evictions at the hands of KFS. Its wardens have regularly burned our homes, along with stores of food, blankets, school uniforms, and books. Over the years, they have made thousands of our people homeless in what at night can be a cold highland to have no home.

In a report written by Chepkoir on the impact these evictions have had on Sengwer women, she documents sexual abuse, psychological torture and extreme poverty (Kuto, 2016). The evictions and destruction of their homes, she argues, have a disproportionate impact on women since in

Sengwer culture it is these spaces that are normally occupied by women and children. As a result of the evictions and wholesale destruction of villages, men have left to find new land and build new homes for their families. This has undermined family life and, according to Chepkoir, led to the breakdown of the clan and kinship system, and traditional rules that govern marriage and other cultural practices. This is genocide in all but name.

When asked about the consequences of the evictions and destruction of villages, one Sengwer interviewee observed that it was driving *de facto* assimilation (anonymous Sengwer, author interview, 25/10/2021):

> When houses are abandoned several times, so people tend to go different ways into different communities, who are presumably outside the forest. And those communities are bigger communities like Marakwet and Pokot and the rest. So, when the children, as young as they are, they go in [*sic*] that schools, most of the languages that they speak are Pokot or Marakwet ... Sometimes students are 'pulled around' if they speak Sengwer. Other children laugh at them. These are traumatising cases because there is nothing you can do and you can't send away your children to another school ... so it's a genocide.

Here is evident not just the genocidal techniques that sever the link with land, economy and religion, Lemkin's (1944, pp. 82–90) fourth and seventh technique, and indeed the ninth ecological technique, but the destruction of the ultimate repository of culture, the third technique, and that which can sustain intergenerational vitality and group memory and thus the 'social vitality' of group life (Card, 2003, p. 63), the very language of the community itself.

In a chilling *de jure* example of cultural destruction, they (anonymous Sengwer, author interview, 25/10/2021) added that because the Sengwer are not recognised at the county or national government level as a distinct Indigenous group, they are forced to use identity cards that label them as members of larger adjacent communities like the Marakwet or Pokot. If they do not accept this labelling, they will be denied access to government services and job opportunities. Commenting on the cultural and psychological harms of this practice of assuming alien identities, he said, 'it is what is killing us slowly, it is what is killing our identity slowly'. The interviewee (anonymous Sengwer, author interview, 25/10/2021) reminded me that of course this was a technique the British colonial administration used; a method of colonial control familiar to the 'invented tradition' school (Iliffe, 1979, p. 324; see also Ranger, 2012), to control and consolidate systems of indirect colonial governance by imposing, co-opting and 'inventing' ethnic groups, tribes and their leaders. Ironically, despite

Lynch's (2016) assertion that what she calls 'the politics of naming' is used cynically and instrumentally by Indigenous groups like the Sengwer, it seems it is the Kenyan state, just like its colonial predecessor, that continues to impose, co-opt and invent in the furtherance of its goals. Commenting on the loss of identity, he (anonymous Sengwer, author interview, 25/10/2021) added, 'people will in twenty years' time only read about people living in forests who are called Sengwer in history books ... it [*sic*] will be hurting for some of our kids who will learn, reading in books while you are still existing, but without that identity'.

When asked if he and the Sengwer recognised this process of forcible eviction from the forest as genocide, as Lemkin understood the term, Elias (07/08/2020) replied: 'Yes exactly, that is really what I recognise, because *culture* is like a unifying factor between human beings *and its interaction with nature*' [emphasis added]. He (07/08/2020) added, 'There is nothing better than to call it genocide if you are deprived of your land and your culture.' In fact, he (07/08/2020) stressed:

> it is a kind of slow genocide which is worse than mass killing. It's a kind of trick so you [the international community] never see it. If it is mass murder, there will be uproar but what they [the Kenyan government agencies and various other complicit bodies] are doing now is strangling you slowly ... Our People say, if you want to kill a frog you don't throw it into boiling water; it will just jump out. You put it in lukewarm water and then increase the fire slowly.

When land and ecosystems are bound up with the culture of a *genos*, as they invariably are where territorially bounded Indigenous and place-based peoples like the Sengwer are concerned (Abed, 2006), dispossession, or 'domicide', involuntary population transfers, ethnic cleansing and their corollary ecological destruction, whether ostensibly in the name of conservation or not, degrades and destroys the 'national' pattern of the Indigenous group and drives 'social death'. 'When you destroy a tree, it is the same as when you destroy a Sengwer', one Indigenous interlocutor argued (author interview, Kimaiyo, 07/08/2020). He (author interview, Kimaiyo, 07/08/2020) added, 'a forest is like a womb to us. If you destroy a womb of a mother, then you cut off a generation.' The last observation speaks directly to the importance of both ecology and culture, perhaps better described as eco-culture, and the latter in maintaining intergenerational bonds and the integrity of the social group, just as Card argued (2003, p. 63). As one Sengwer community member (author interview, 25/10/2021) observed, 'this new era of colonisation in the name of conservation, is driving the last nail into the coffin of our identity, language and culture ... if they throw us out of the forest, where will we meet to speak our language?' In place of their culture: the green-washed socio-economic and cultural 'pattern' of a phalanx of international conservation NGOs, international financial and political institutions and (post)colonial state machines.

The political economy of ecologically induced genocide today

The laws of motion of the capitalist system in the current juncture in Kenya, where the case study is concerned, are broadly similar to those elucidated in Chapter 2 and in the current juncture in Australia in Chapter 3. Again, the ecocide-genocide nexus is driven by capitalist ecology for two structural reasons, namely the extra-economic processes of plunder, fraud or theft, from without the circuits of production and capital accumulation that bring about domicide and Lemkin's first stage of genocide, the destruction of the cultural pattern of the occupied. This is followed by the *second* structure known as a value-contradiction, 'capitalism's inner dialectic' (Harvey, 2003b, pp. 63–88), which operates once Indigenous land is fully incorporated via institutional and legal systems, within the expanded reproduction of the circuits of capital, 'capitalism's inner dialectic' (Harvey, 2003b, pp. 63–88). However, the precise form which both structures or stages take in the Kenyan case study demonstrate intriguing differences.

We saw the first stage of primary accumulation in the repeated attempts to domicidally sever the Sengwer and enclose Embobut Forest of the Cherangani Hills through the World Bank-sponsored NRMP project and the attempts at ethnically cleansing by the KFS. Sometimes the distance, in time or space, between the act of enclosure (the first stage) and the process of capital accumulation (the second stage) may be great, rendering the relation and connections between these two processes obscure or unclear (Kelly, 2014, p. 685); again, we saw this with the EU-funded project. Both projects involved attempts to forcibly control and ultimately eject the Sengwer from the land, consistent with the definition of eco-genocide here. Even the first stage of accumulation by dispossession is ecocidal, since it attempts to excise the Sengwer and their ecologically sustainable life modes, from the political ecology of the Embobut Forest. As argued in Chapter 2 and throughout this book, this process of primary accumulation is what drives territorial expansion and is a fundamental structural component of settler colonialism and arguably neocolonial modalities. Crucially, as we have seen in both sites of settler colonisation in previous chapters, the processes of accumulation by dispossession (Harvey, 2003b) necessarily involves the '"creative destruction" of pre-capitalist [Indigenous] ecological-political orders' (Havemann, 2016, p. 186).

Previously, I argued Coulthard's (2014, p. 12) adaptation of Marxist theories of political economy and primary accumulation, where 'state-formation and colonial-capitalist development required first and foremost land, and only *secondarily* the surplus value afforded by cheap, Indigenous labor' [emphasis added], although often true in colonial contexts, was not strictly accurate in the Australian and Kenyan context. In fact, as I demonstrated in Chapter 2 and elsewhere (Crook, 2013), Indigenous labour would be 'allowed to remain' (Lemkin, 1944, p. 79). Accordingly, when examining the 'subject position of the colonized vis-à-vis the effects of colonial dispossession' (Coulthard, 2014, p. 11) both the capital-relation and colonial-relation were constitutive. However, in the Embobut Forest it is the colonial relation that has proven decisive.

The second key structure is the law of value under the capitalist system which, as argued in Chapter 3 in Australia, and in Canada (Crook and Short, 2014), explains the ecologically destructive forces unleashed by capitalist extractive industries.[5] In Kenya, however, the narrow horizons of the commodity form embodied in exchange value underpin genocidal structuring dynamics as well, only this time as a primary driver of the eco-destructive tendencies of the capitalist mode of *organised social (re)production*. The transformation and fragmentation of nature into smaller, commensurable, alienable parts through the pricing of aspects or parts of nature applies equally to market environmentalism and the genocide of the Sengwer, where trading the right to pollute and carbon offsetting, governed by the law of value and money, appropriates natural conditions as means of production, in a manner that pays no heed to the ecological (and genocidal) consequences. Just as capitalism seeks to simplify and reduce labour to better exploit it through a division of labour, reducing it to a mere appendage of a larger system of social production, so it pursues a 'division of nature' (Foster, 1997a, p. 92; Burkett, 2014, p. 86) with grave ecological and socio-political consequences. To date, the Sengwer have successfully resisted this final stage in the political economy of genocide, by frustrating attempts of the Kenyan government, the KFS and the various other international financial, intergovernmental and NGO agencies, to first remove them from their land indefinitely and complete the process of accumulation by dispossession.

As before, the narrow horizon of exchange value which conditions capital accumulation, understood as an ecological process, will increase 'throughput of materials and energy' (Burkett, 2014, p. 112) at unsustainable rates, causing 'metabolic rifts' (Burkett, 2014; Foster, 2000, 2005; Stretesky et al., 2013). Thus, the capitalist metabolic order, given its anti-ecological properties, is genocidal for those social groups, like the Sengwer, living on the margins of the capitalist world. The expansion of the capitalist system into the realm of nature conservation will predictably have both ecological and genocidal consequences. When asked if the Sengwer agree with the Marxist analysis of the anti-ecological properties of the capitalist system, Elias (author interview, Kimaiyo, 07/08/2020) was quick to concur, saying, 'absolutely. What we are undergoing now is a 'greed capitalism'. There is a saying that there is plenty for everyone under the sun, but there is not plenty for everyone's greed.'

The conservationist mode of production: green accumulation by dispossession

Arguably, both conservation projects, and the mass evictions they fuelled and funded, are a form of accumulation by dispossession, since the mass evictions have the effect of dispossessing the traditional owner conservators, the Sengwer, undermining their customary rights and denying them access to sacred cultural sites, all in the name of preparing the land for conservation. As argued, accumulation by dispossession is the first of two key structures identified as part of the political economy of genocide, which affect the 'creative destruction' of non-capitalist [Indigenous] ecological-political orders; as a form of 'conservation' it is a uniquely twenty-first century modality of colonisation. According to Elias Kimaiyo (author interview, 09/10/2016) the conservation projects like the one funded by the World Bank or the EU were 'the new system of colonization, the new style'. The neocolonial model of conservation or conservationist mode of production is still a capitalist mode, only this time, rather than using nature as a bottomless resource (Brockington and Duffy, 2010), it seeks to valorise two things. Firstly, it valorises the eco-regulatory labour that nurtures the reproductive and rejuvenating role of nature, for example bee pollination of flowers or carbon sequestration by forests, as opposed to more conventional production of goods for the market. The category of eco-regulation refers to valorised labour, which is 'a labour of sustaining, regulating and reproducing, rather than transforming', which optimises the conditions of organic processes that are otherwise impervious to intentional modification (Benton, 1989, pp. 67–8). Where the conservation of the forests is concerned, it would presumably involve the kind of labour the Sengwer have done for centuries, including, *inter alia*, preventing forest fires, planting trees to replace log trees, controlling grazing and restricting habitation to the glades, restricting the degree of cultivation and protecting water springs (author interview, Kimaiyo, 11/08/2020). In other words, the exchange value is a function of the eco-regulatory labour, which stewards, conserves and monitors the 'self-organising' dynamics of ecosystems in order to harvest (pun intended) its infrastructural value.

Secondly, through the creation of artificial scarcity of legal carbon emission limits under international climate change and environmental treaties, as we will see later, the conservation projects which produce carbon credits effectively collect a form of rent, capturing a portion of surplus value, in much the same way that Marx (Marx and Engels, 2010, p. 464) argued landowners claimed a redistribution of surplus value 'arising from a monopolisation of a natural force'.[6] This process corresponds to the first and second stage of the political economy of genocide, which includes not only forcible enclosures and accumulation by dispossession, which secures *de facto* control, but also the elaborately erected edifice of property regimes which creates the artificial scarcity (made possible by the international climate change and environmental treaties discussed below) and secures *de jure* control. These are the laws of motion of a genocide machine manifested in a new guise: a 'conservation machine'.

This form of latter-day conservation, which, as we saw above, is predicated on the material and discursive excision of the Sengwer, clearly falls within the definition of 'fortress conservation' explored above, and by extension predicated on the colonial production of environmental knowledge explored previously. In other words, the 'conservationist mode of production', with its roots in the colonial period, has inherited the cultural practices and discourses of racial spatialisation discussed in the previous chapter, but adapted to the new regime of neoliberal environmentalism. Under the logic of neoliberal conservation, once again the geographical space, or the ancestral forests of Indigenous people are rebranded with the hot iron of exchange value, essential to facilitate the expansion of capitalism, only this time to valorise eco-regulatory labour and the collection of rent through the 'monopolisation of a natural force' (Marx and Engels, 2010, p. 464). This new form of the capitalist mode hinges on the 'spatial problematic' (Soja, 1985, p. 108) for its expansion and reproduction just as much as previous manifestations of the capitalist system. This is why 'territoriality is settler colonialism's specific, irreducible element' (Wolfe, 2006, p. 388). More specifically, what Harvey (2003b, p. 64) would go on to later define as a 'spatio-temporal fix' is more than simply 'temporal deferment and geographical expansion' (Harvey, 2003b, p. 65). In this case, it entails a particular racialised arrangement or production of space that allows for that expansion.

A report co-written by UN Special Rapporteur on Indigenous peoples, Victoria Tauli-Corpuz (Tauli-Corpuz et al., 2018), has predictably shown that this exclusionary practice has fuelled a plethora of human rights violations against Indigenous and place-based peoples all around the world. It also shows that this is vast practice spanning the globe driven by a coterie of states, multilateral organisations, NGOs and private donors, which has grown at an alarming rate in the last few decades (Tauli-Corpuz et al., 2018). One estimate has put the total global spending on 'protected areas' alone at US$13 billion (Balmford et al., 2003). In 1987, a report of the World Commission on Environment and Development recommended this exclusionary practice be substantially increased, in aid of protecting forests, mitigating climate change and biodiversity (WCED, 1987). These efforts were given further impetus by global commitments to protect biodiversity, enshrined at the 1992 Rio Summit where the United Nations Convention on Biological Diversity (UN, 1992) was ratified; CBD specifically calls for 'area based' conservation. Since then, the proportion of the earth's land surface covered by this exclusionary practice has tripled between 1980 and 2005 and now covers 15 percent of land surface, with the vast majority in the developing world (CBD, 1992, p. 6). Parties to the CBD reaffirmed and strengthened this commitment in 2010 with a pledge to increase this to '17 percent of terrestrial and inland water, and 10 percent of coastal and marine areas' (CBD, 2011). Furthermore, these efforts are considered a key part of meeting the commitments agreed at the Paris Earth Summit (UNFCCC, 2015) and the *2030 Agenda for Sustainable Development* (UNGA, 2015).

The political economy of climate change mitigation and the associated conservationist mode of production has engendered a rich lexicon to describe this neocolonial relation of power: 'carbon colonialism', 'carbon grab' and even 'green grabbing' (Fairhead et al., 2012). In essence, 'while colonialists took land to extract resources, conservationists take land to preserve it' (Kenrick, 2016). Fairhead et al. (2012, p. 238) defined green grabbing as 'the appropriation of land and resources for environmental ends'. The authors argue that this form of land alienation in the name of carbon sequestration or biodiversity is as we have seen, part of a history of colonial and neocolonial expropriation in the name of the environment, linking it to a broader cluster of conservation efforts such as the gazetting of national and wildlife parks, forest reserves and the prevention of assumed destructive local practices. As we saw in the previous chapter, the Sengwer and other forest-dwelling groups were indeed forcefully transferred by British colonial authorities in the interests of conservation. Recall that, just as now, it was ostensibly in the interests of forest conservation and water security. However, the forms of neocolonial expropriation in the name of conservation emerging in the era of the neoliberalisation of nature have in important respects departed from the logics that shaped older practices and discourses.

The questions that remain unanswered are what is driving this new modality of capitalism? How is the surplus value captured and created by this new industry realised? In other words, where does the market that purchases the various environmental commodities come from? And how does the value form embedded in the environmental commodity itself contribute to the eco-genocidal process?

Neoliberal globalisation and the commodification of nature as a vector of genocide

[T]he ecology of societies in which the capitalist mode of production appears as an immense collection of services. (Robertson, 2012)

Over twenty years on after the original Earth Summit the path to sustainable development and climate change mitigation has, it seems, taken on a rather different hue. Although the original Rio Summit and then the Kyoto Protocols ratified in 1997 attempted to deliver GHG emission reductions via the mechanism of the market, it did at least contain legally binding reduction targets. It seems the latter was discarded and we are now left only with the 'invisible hand' to guide us down the royal road to climate change mitigation. State-led and legally enforced solutions are off the agenda – the 'green economy' and market-driven solutions such as carbon trading and REDD+ 'offsets' have become the panacea (Crook and Patel, 2012). Instead, we are left with what the eminent climatologist Kevin Anderson (2016b) called 'techno utopias' such as 'biomass energy carbon capture and storage' (BECCS) or 'negative emission technology' and 'the political and economic dogma' of today's economic paradigm: market environmentalism. But what exactly are these paradigmatic solutions?

The World Bank NRMP and Green Resources genocidal conservation machines are part of a complex and convoluted intergovernmental architecture of climate change mitigation and nature conservation, sponsored by UN agencies like the United Nations Environment Programme (UNEP) and the UNDP, which began to push hard for what it called the 'Global Green New Deal' (UNEP, 2009). Underpinned by the philosophy of 'market environmentalism', 'green capitalism' or 'green neoliberalism' (Goldman, 2006; Heartfield, 2008), 'neoliberal nature', catalysed by the 2008 economic crisis, sought to fundamentally restructure socioecologies to make them more amenable to structural accumulation strategies, which includes a growing and bewildering proliferation of environmental commodities such as bee pollination, water purification, soil regeneration and, of course, as we saw with the World Bank-funded NRMP conservation project, carbon.

An essential background enabling factor to the rise of the green economy and neoliberal nature and the structural integration of developing countries like Kenya into its fold is, of course, the preceding history of the reorganisation of global capitalism referred to in Chapter 2 under the 'rubric of neoliberalism' (Harman, 2007). This history and the nature of neoliberalism will not be rehearsed again here. Suffice to say, the shift in conservation and environmental governance, which gave rise to a conservationist mode of production that attempts to value and assess 'non-human natures' as 'service providers' rather than simply as a source of resources or 'primary appropriation', is part of the broader 'neoliberal turn' in global economic governance, or globalisation in the mid-1970s which would eventually encompass other spheres of governance, like development, the environment, climate change and conservation practices. Concomitant to this is the discursive and material (re)production of nature as 'natural capital' or bioeconomy, rooted in the classical liberal belief that, as Adam Smith (1776) argued, we naturally 'truck, barter and exchange'. By extension, if we understand all of nature as a commodity then the efficient allocation of resources that proceeds from market relations will arrest the degradation of nature. The discursive (re)production under neoliberalism extended to *human* nature too. By extending the molecular process of the gradual commodification of new areas of social life, a key component of neoliberalism in its double movement (Davidson, 2013), human flourishing, which was predicated on liberating 'individual entrepreneurial freedoms and skills' (Harvey, p. 2), could be secured. As we will see later, the cross-fertilisation of this neoliberal episteme of nature with broader (neo)colonial development discourses, discursively restructures socioecologies such that Indigenous peoples will be erased as they had been under the British colonial authorities.

The same neoliberal globalisation process also stymied the development of and in some cases actually de-developed countries in the Global South (Hickel, 2017), leaving 'beneficiary' countries such as Kenya further under-resourced and dependant on privatised 'green' development to fund green development initiatives and address their respective environmental crises. In fact, the structural position of dependency of Kenya discussed earlier was compounded by what is often referred to as the 'lost decade' of the 1980s. It is this period which is generally understood as the dawn of neoliberalism on a global scale or 'globalization' and the beginning of the end of the 'developmental' state (Shivji, 2009, p. 9–10). Recall that the roots of what in the Australian context was described as a neoliberal transnational governance, via institutions like the WTO, IMF and the World Bank

(Sassen, 2010), are found in the external oil shocks of the 1970s and the global recessions of the same decade (Rono, 2002, p. 82). Moreover, it is these same 'mediating institutions' (Harvey, 2003a, pp. 127–30) through manipulation of credit and debt management that impose neoliberal reforms like SAPs and as we saw, the various conservation and REDD+ programmes. This is the form which latter-day capitalist imperialism takes. The territorial logic and Harvey's (2003b, p. 64) spatio-temporal fix still plays itself out only via these 'mediating institutions'. Recall also that 'formal sovereignty can easily coexist with coloniality' (Sassen, 2013, p. 27). Put bluntly, these institutions mediate capitalist imperialism. The external shocks inflicted a number of blows to the Kenyan economy, further compounding its position of dependency. These included erratic fluctuating prices for their major exports, a fall in GDP, decline in living standards and an increase in debt which coincided with widespread drought, famine, high population growth and rapid urbanisation, as well as the collapse of the East African Community's customs union and common market, of which Kenya was a part (Rono, 2002, p. 82). What followed was the implementation of the now infamous SAPs, conditionalities on World Bank and IMF assistance, which, in accord with the neoliberal ideology policy prescriptions described in Chapter 2 in the Australian context, required the Kenyan economy to, *inter alia*, reduce the budget deficit, including decreasing spending on essential social and welfare services, limiting wage increases, foreign trade 'liberalization', removal of price controls on key essential goods, deregulation of domestic marketing of agricultural commodities and deregulation of interest rates and foreign exchange rates. Not only did these SAPs have the opposite to their intended effect and lead to an increase in the debt burden of Kenya and an increase in the expenditure on repaying and servicing debts, leaving even less room for investment in development, but they predictably led to an increase in poverty, inequality, decrease in participation of women in the economy, rise in levels of crime and an acceleration in economic decline (Rono, 2002). This echoed the impacts of SAPs on Africa more generally (Chabal and Daloz, 1999, p. 120; Thomson, 2010, p. 194; Fatton, 1992, p. 130). Aside from these devastating consequences, SAPs would serve to more tightly weave Kenya into the structures of neoliberal globalisation and governance and compound their structural dependency.

Moreover, these new forms of environmental commodities, which ostensibly arose as a global governance solution to a growing environmental problem, ironically serve to further entrench ecological and environmental inequities on a global scale. That is to say, the architecture of neoliberal environmental governance allows Global North countries to escape their obligations under climate change treaties and exploit Global

South countries as sources of carbon credits and so allow them to continue to pollute in the North. The theory within environmental sociology known as *ecologically unequal exchange* can help us understand this dynamic (Jorgenson and Clark, 2009; Clark and Foster, 2009). It draws attention to not only the relationship between capitalism, economic growth and environmental degradation, as does Marxist ecology more generally, but focuses on a global distributive aspect to ecological relations between the global North and South. Specifically, it argues that largely through international trade, more powerful Global North countries gain unequal access to natural resources and what is known as sink capacity, otherwise understood as the ability of the environment to absorb waste products (Givens et al., 2019, p. 2). Further, this unequal access to resources and sink capacity is linked to all stages of global commodity chains, namely extraction, production, consumption and disposal (Givens et al., 2019). Critically, the resulting material flows disproportionately impact Global South countries in terms of environmental harms (Jorgenson and Clark, 2009). The system of neoliberal environmental governance and its associated carbon markets exacerbate these iniquitous material flows by providing Global North countries with more access to sink capacity through the acquisition of carbon credits and offsets. The valorisation of the Embobut Forest is predicated on its sink capacity, in terms of its ability to absorb and fix excess carbon. It is precisely through this ecologically unequal exchange that we can comprehend 'carbon colonialism' (Fairhead et al., 2012).

Key to the valorisation of the abovementioned environmental commodities and the neoliberalisation of nature is an institutional matrix that make the commodities alienable and commensurable; in other words, public and governmental bodies need to artificially create a market for these environmental goods. This is achieved through neoliberal environmental governance technologies, such as Payments for Ecosystem Services (PES),[7] where those who maintain and manage the aforementioned restorative and rejuvenating properties of nature are financially compensated, the United Nations programme for REDD+ and carbon and biodiversity offsetting (BDO) (Dunlap and Sullivan, 2019) and of course emissions trading, first set up on the international plane by the 1997 Kyoto Protocol to the UN Framework Convention on Climate Change (UNFCCC) (UN General Assembly, 1994). The NRMP and the Green Resources project fall under the UN's REDD+ programme,[8] first set up at the thirteenth session of the Conference of the Parties (COP) to the UNFCCC, in Bali, in 2007. The REDD+ programme in the Embobut Forest, like other REDD+ projects, set out to expand forest cover and protect ecosystems, in aid of producing what has become known as REDD+ 'Offsets'- the carbon credits that can be sold to compensate for carbon emissions elsewhere.[9]

It is the restructuring of socioecologies under the guise of conservation and climate change mitigation which constitutes genocide, since the Sengwer are continually excised from this new neoliberal socioecology. The manner in which this excision is secured is simultaneously material *and* discursive; the latter will be discussed in more length in the following section. It is material because what was earlier described as the first stage of political economy of genocide, the primary accumulation that entails forcible population transfer, is *prima facie* material. It self-evidently reorders the physical environment. But it is material in a further sense. The second stage of the political economy of genocide, when the land or the ecosystems have been incorporated into the circuits of capitalist production, entails a continual carving up of nature in the commodification process. Commodification of the restorative and metabolic function of any particular part of an ecosystem, just as we saw earlier with the commodity form more generally, is invariably done so in a manner that pays no heed to its relationship, to either the rest of the *local* ecosystem or the biosphere more generally. Reflecting on this aspect and effect of the extension of the value form exhibited by carbon markets and carbon offset projects, our Sengwer interviewee Kimaiyo (author interview, 11/08/2020) sardonically remarked 'how do you end up selling air when you are polluting the other side?'

Take for example, the growth of fast growing, large-scale tree plantations in low industrialised countries, which are used as carbon offsets made possible under provisions of the 1997 Kyoto Protocol, to compensate for carbon emissions produced elsewhere, often in the industrialised North (Nuñez and GenderCC, 2010, pp. 102–3). These monoculture tree plantations, made possible by first cutting down old growth bio-diverse forests, often have deleterious impacts on local ecosystems and enable the continuation of carbon emissions at source in the industrialised North, negatively impacting both the local ecosystems *and* the planetary carbon cycle. The case of the Sengwer exemplifies how the material restructuring of the socioecology also impacts the health of the local ecosystems given the loss of their role as traditional owner-conservators in maintaining those ecosystems and the pernicious impact on the planetary carbon cycle.

The discursive moment in the carving up of nature operates at multiple levels. There are the grand narratives discussed in the next section, about development and 'progress' and the racialised categories that help ruling economic and governing elites pursue these development projects, and then we have the more fundamental discursive operations involved in the carve up of nature into discrete packets which obscure the nature of the ecosystemic totality. This latter discursive move is what is commonly referred to as commodity fetishism. Where commodity fetishism takes hold, the real underlying relationships between human beings in social production are seen instead as 'the fantastic form of a relation between things', which not only obscures the type of labour that is necessary for the production of these commodities but *obscures or makes invisible the workers themselves* (Marx, 1976, p. 165). Accordingly, the social construction of abstract value inherent in the environmental commodity obscures both the ecosystemic totality (the true holistic ecological web in which the environmental commodities are embedded), and the relationship of human beings, such as the Sengwer, to nature in the social production of their existence. Instead, the valorisation process narrowly focuses on component parts of nature in abstraction from the ecosystemic whole, in its pursuit of a commodified system of abstract, uniform and tradable units of, ultimately, CO_2 reduction: in a word 'equivalence'. This equivalence, just like commodity fetishism more generally, acts like a sleight of hand obscuring real socioecological relations, which includes human cultures and their corresponding metabolic order, *like the Sengwer*, and the role they play in reproducing that metabolic order. It also obscures neocolonial relations that underpin the exchange of these carbon commodities, driving eco-genocide in the Embobut Forest and Cherangani Hills. On occasion, Indigenous peoples are allowed to take part in the eco-regulatory labour which forms a part of the valorisation of nature's rejuvenating properties. But all too often, as in this case, Indigenous peoples are not 'allowed to remain'. Ultimately, as Coulthard observed in the Canadian context, the colonial relation is decisive.

In essence, it is the logic of the value form under capitalism that is ultimately driving and organising the restructuring of socioecologies. Even the initial material phase of the predatory annexation of Indigenous land, the first stage of the political economy of genocide, one step removed from the normal production and exchange of commodities within the circuits of production and capital accumulation, is ultimately driven by this value logic. For the compulsion to expand in the first instance into non-capitalist territory is a function of the necessity to maximise the production of surplus value through the force of competition under the capitalist system. But this discursive operation at the level of the commodity form is merely the first most fundamental discursive operation.

Development ideology, green governmentality and racialised ecologies

In the aftermath of the Second World War, deep-rooted colonial discourses would become intertwined with a broad and malleable set of developmentalist and evolutionist discourses and institutional practices, no less Eurocentric and racist, only now more coded and insidious, that came to prominence in the wake of the decolonisation movement after the Second World War. This section seeks to draw on the post-development literature that understood development as a biopolitical discursive and institutional practice that (re)made the Global South into an object of intervention and reconstruction through its reinvention as 'underdeveloped' or less developed, and apply this framework to *all non-capitalist territory*, including Indigenous, but more specifically to the facilitation of the restructuring of socioecologies.[10] Development here is understood as a political economic structure with a 'discursive field or regime that sought but failed to impose Western modernity on the rest of the world' (Hodge, 2016a, p. 438). On varying scales, both local and international, a plurality of governance and development agencies, development programmes, strategies, and technologies are deployed to 'optimize' the development of populations, geographies and resources, and as argued above, even nature itself. In previous chapters we saw that the production of colonial knowledge about nature and its human denizens is a crucial element in colonial domination (Drayton, 2000). The Sengwer are well aware of the role of this discourse and its role in (re)framing responsibility for stewardship of the forest. Commenting on its significance Elias (11/08/2020) remarked, 'who says we are not developed! So long as God gave us our nature it is up to us!'

The various conservation projects, such as the EU, Finnish government and World Bank-funded projects examined above, were rationalised by the Kenyan government as vital to its development goals and cast in a developmentalist lexicon. In a report titled *The Landscape of Climate Finance in Kenya: On the Road to Implementing Kenya's NDC*, published by Kenya's National Treasury (Odhengo et al., 2021), funded by Germany's Federal Ministry of the Environment, Nature Conservation and Nuclear Safety, it notes (Odhengo et al., 2021, p. 1) that the Paris agreement (UNFCCC, 2015) set a goal to provide 100 USD billion per year by 2020 to support mitigation and adaptation activities in developing countries. A report by the UNEP, co-sponsored by the KFS and other Kenyan government agencies, argues that '[c]arbon-trading mechanisms provide an opportunity for the Government of Kenya to earn foreign revenue' (UNEP, 2012, p. 36). In order to take advantage of this new revenue stream 'the proper institutional and financial mechanisms must be in place so that resources are directed efficiently toward national climate and development priorities' (Odhengo et al., 2021, p. 1). Those arrangements are precisely those examined above which entail both phases of the political economy of genocide: the destruction of the cultural pattern of the Sengwer through domicide to establish *de facto* control, or accumulation by dispossession; followed by the erection of a legal and institutional architecture that produces both artificial scarcity in carbon molecules and *de jure* control and finally the incorporation of Indigenous land into the normal circuits of capitalist production and accumulation.

The report defines the success of its development goals, outlined in the Kenyan government's *Vision 2030* document (GoK, 2007), as achieving middle-income status to secure a high-quality life for if its citizens in an environmentally sustainable manner (GoK, 2007, vii). In fact, the water towers targeted in the aforementioned conservation projects are considered vital both directly and indirectly to Kenya's *Vision 2030* development goals: directly, to target the new ringfenced climate revenue streams from multilateral and bilateral donors or 'international support and [the] private sector' (GoK 2013, p. 154), which alongside ecotourism and sustainable agriculture will build the rudiments of a 'green economy' that will 'support the transition to low carbon climate resilient development pathway' (GoK 2013); indirectly to the economy as a whole. Indeed, the *Vision 2030* document targets 10 per cent annual growth (GoK 2013, p. 6) largely through the development of six sectors (GoK 2013, p. 30), four of which, namely agriculture, tourism, wholesale and retail trade, are dependent on Kenya's forests, reimagined as 'natural capital' (UNEP, 2012, p. 11).

What must be stressed here is what Kenrick (2016, pp. 249–50) calls the 'flawed global logic' at play. Global, since, as argued earlier, the role of 'mediating institutions' (Harvey, 2003a, pp. 127–30) like the World Bank or the EU, dominated by neocolonial states are decisive. In this case the 'mediating institutions' are central to the imposition of the 'green' developmentalist vision, aided and abetted by the political and economic elites in the Kenyan state, long since structurally integrated into the neoliberal global economy. Flawed, because it is rooted in the fallacy that action on climate change and ecological collapse must be taken, not for its own sake, or because of a recognition that socioecological relations in equilibrium with earth's systems are necessary to support human and non-human life, but because, as one document pertaining to the EU-funded Water Towers Programme argued, climate change 'hampers long-term growth' (Kenrick, 2016, pp. 249–50). This ontology sees growth as the only solution to poverty and marginalises alternative zero or low-carbon lifeways like the Sengwer's and indeed 'degrowth' approaches based on a more equitable distribution of wealth (Kenrick, 2016; see also Hickel, 2020). As Short (2016, p. 188) has sharply observed, in a finite world, growth-driven capitalism, which is to say capitalism *per se*, since all forms of capitalism are characterised by the drive to accumulate and spatio-temporal fixes

(Harvey, 2003b, p. 64), is inherently ecologically unsustainable, '"sustainable development" [is] a dangerous oxymoron' (Harvey, 2003b).

The fallacy of the neoliberal state taking a back seat has been here refuted. The power of the state and its monopoly of violence have played a crucial role. Discursive practices, of a piece with the kind we witnessed during the colonial era, are a crucial dimension to this power and the mechanisms of control it wields. Indeed, the new neoliberal discourses on the environment are crucial in reframing Kenya and its denizens as 'ripe for intervention'. This is what Goldman (2001, p. 499) describes as the 'new neoliberal practise of eco-government' where through new modalities of power/knowledge and their associated discourses of 'ecological improvement' the Kenyan government becomes remade as a 'transnationalised environmental state' complicit in the forms of what Luke (1997) called *green governmentality* orchestrated by a 'green' World Bank and other international and intergovernmental 'mediating institutions'. In short, the construction of new global 'truth' regimes of neoliberal nature makes possible the aforementioned institutional matrix and regulatory regimes that facilitate the alienation of nature and its commodification. By reframing nature *and* its denizens, they facilitate the opening up of Indigenous land and socioecologies to appropriation for green accumulation. Through the Foucauldian knowledge-power nexus nature is remade as environmental services (ES). Those who have lived there since time immemorial are either demeaned as resource custodians (Ojeda, 2012), or marginalised and displaced as irresponsible 'squatters', 'encroachers' and exploiters of their forest dwellings, as we saw with the Sengwer and the World Bank/ EU/UNDP-sponsored conservation projects, racialising ecosystems that remove black or Indigenous bodies from those colonised spaces. As Elias (07/08/2020) argued, scientists and conservationists 'don't see our ecosystem as a home'.

In fact, the very legibility of nature itself is a function of 'interrelated racial projects, including the *colonial productions of natural history*' (McCreary and Milligan, 2018, p. 6) [emphasis added]. One such discursive practice, evident in the case of the Sengwer, concerns the notion that nature is 'external', 'primaeval' and 'pristine' and must remain that way, embodied in the sign wilderness; notions that remain popular among Western environmentalist circles to this day (Braun, 2002, p. 12). These signifiers encode a nature that remains *outside* history, denying the inevitable intertwining of nature and society and erasing other histories of occupation of a *social nature* by Indigenous peoples. This discursive erasure will mean, as before under British colonial rule, the only viable form of articulation will be Hartwig's third mode, namely the destruction of the hunter-gatherer economy 'such that the producers are "freed" of the means of production' (1978, p. 129), and Rey's third stage of articulation of capitalist production with Indigenous systems: 'the total disappearance of the pre-capitalist mode' (cited in Foster-Carter, 1978b, p. 218). Once again, the Sengwer's level of 'development' will not permit any other form of articulation with the dominant capitalist system.

This social construction of nature as external to social relations plays a crucial mystifying role in the continued domination of nature and, if the reader recalls, this is uncannily similar to the discursive practice deployed in the colonial period by the British colonial authorities and the alliance of forest keepers and white settlers discussed in the previous chapter, which sought to construct a racialised political ecology that ensured African land and forests were kept free of human habitation to ensure its 'sustainable maintenance'. Just like then, today, forest-dwelling groups like the Sengwer and Ogiek are considered ecological threats and not compatible with the prevailing scientific forestry management practices, animated by romanticised notions of 'African wilderness' that presupposed all humanity an inherent ecological threat. Only this time, the bundle of racialised discourses include modern notions of development and the green economy.

As Fairhead et al., (2012) have shown, these new modes of appropriation are made possible by a green discourse interwoven with other pre-existing cognitive maps that underpin the new political economy in nature's restorative capacities. A discourse that has co-opted much of the green movement in its vision of 'ecological modernisation', which therefore can no longer be relied on to be implacably opposed to insatiable industrial growth. Conservation NGOs like the Worldwide Fund for Nature (WWF), Conservation International (CI) and the Nature Conservancy have embraced market environmentalism and PES as the solution to nature conservation and the climate crisis. Central to the development and construction of the various environmental commodities and the regimes of value, ownership and control they entail are the science-policy discourses that articulated them (Fairhead et al., 2012, p. 241). The carbon markets would not exist without the accompanying science-policy discourse, nor would BDO exist without the science-policy discourse that recognised its threatened status and allowed for systems of equivalence for their exchange (Corson and MacDonald, 2012). The very notion of treating nature not as a static reserve of resources but as 'service provider' (Sullivan, 2012b, p. 205), elucidated in the foundational science-policy assessment document Millennium Ecosystem Assessment (MEA, 2005), was crucial in the development, construction and institutionalisation of PES and markets for nature conservation more generally (Sullivan, 2012b, p. 205; McAfee and Shapiro, 2010; Kosoy, and Corbera, 2010; Nelson, 2015, p. 1). Essentially, the environmental commodity fetishism analysed in this chapter, which restructured the local socioecologies and extirpated the Sengwer in the process, hinged on a broader set of racialised Eurocentric narratives about nature which were given scientific credibility by the aforementioned science policy discourses. These in turn depended on a cluster of developmentalist and evolutionist discourses which traced their lineage to at least the beginning of the post-war period. It is through this cluster or bundle of discourses that the imposition of the cultural pattern of the occupier is achieved.

Resistance to relations of genocide

The resistance of the Sengwer and fellow forest-dwelling or Indigenous people like the Ogiek in Kenya is many ways reminiscent to that of Indigenous people in Australia. As we saw with some Indigenous Nations, who still had an organised relationship to their ancestral land, the Sengwer likewise resisted principally by refusing to be permanently severed from their forests, returning time and time again after forcible evictions by the Kenyan state. The significance of this cannot be overstated. By doing so the Sengwer repeatedly frustrated the ability of the KFS and other state agencies to complete the second phase of the political economy of genocide and fully incorporate the Embobut Forest into the circuits of capitalist production and trade. In a different political and historical context, black feminist Patricia Hill Collins (2000, pp. 201–2) argues 'survival is a form of resistance and ... struggles for *group survival* are just as important as confrontations with institutional power' [emphasis added]. When the balance of forces is arrayed so heavily against you, the mere act of surviving as a viable genos is indeed a form of resistance.

Like Indigenous people in Australia, Kenya's Indigenous people have also resorted, especially in the last few decades, to 'legal resistance', forms of lobbying and awareness raising, adopting what was earlier described in the Australian context as 'European political technologies' (Russell, 2005, p. 130), to counter the states lawfare, organising through various Indigenous umbrella organisations such as Forest Indigenous Peoples Network (FIPN), Pastoralist, Hunters and Gatherers and Ethnic Minority Network (PHGEMN) or the Kenya Pastoralist Development and Network (KPDN) and more recently Hunter–Gatherers Forum Kenya (HUGAFO–K) with some significant success. Networks like the FIPN and HUGAFO–K are founded on the recognition of a common historical experience of dependence on forests and structural oppression and marginalisation because of that dependence and their traditional livelihoods. Arguably, this represents the development of precisely the form of pan-national Indigenous consciousness I argued would emerge dialectically out of the struggle against settler colonisation, moving from a social collective in itself to a social collective for itself. One Sengwer interviewee, when asked if their community was organising with any other communities, stressed that although their collaborative organisations included pastoralist Indigenous communities, they were mostly made up of hunter-gatherer groups because they were the most marginalised and oppressed communities in Kenya (anonymous Sengwer, author interview, 18/03/2020). This speaks to the aforementioned common historical experience of dependence on forests and structural oppression.

These forms of organising and lobbying played a critical role in the 2010 constitutional reforms discussed above and in the various land commissions such as the Njonjo Land Commission (2002) and Ndung'u Commission (2004) that would feed into the constitutional review process on the question of land reform and the erection of new institutional frameworks (Simel, 2009, p. 16). The Ogiek also brought a case to the Land and Environment Court (2014), which once again involved the displacement of the community from their Mau homelands. This time, citing the 2010 constitution and the 2009 NLP, as well as a number of international instruments, the court found that the Indigenous community had special protections under national and international law and that the evictions from the Mau Forest constituted a violation of their rights to life, given it prevented the Ogiek from fulfilling their livelihoods in accordance with their culture. The court also found that settling non-Ogiek in the Mau Forrest was not legal and that the Ogiek community should be given priority when allotting land in the Mau Forest. Crucially however, the courts did not find that the Ogiek's customary occupation of the forests amounted to formal legal property rights. The conclusion of the Court was that the NLC was the constitutionally proper place to resolve this latter issue (Kew and Lyman, 2016, p. 167).

This form of 'legal resistance' would also take place in international fora, such as through engagement with the ACHPR. One landmark decision bears mention in this context. It was the *Centre for Minority Rights Development (Kenya) and Minority Rights Group International on behalf of the Endorois Welfare Council v The Republic of Kenya* (ACHPR, 2010). The Endorois won a landmark decision that they are indeed Indigenous and their eviction from their land violated a number of articles of the African Charter on Human and Peoples' rights (Charter), including their right to *collective* property (ACHPR, 2010, para. 162), culture, religion, health and natural resources and indeed their way of life (ACHPR, 2010, paras. 173,

251), and that the government must compensate them (ACHPR, 2010, Recommendation 1(c); Cerone, 2010; Kamga, 2011), and that indeed, it failed, just as with the Sengwer, to provide them with FPIC (ACHPR, 2010, para. 290). This was the first international human rights body to recognise African Indigenous people's rights over traditional lands and globally the first legal recognition of the violation of the rights to development (ACHPR, 2010, para. 298). The commission ordered that the government not only consult the community on future development on the land, including Lake Bogoria Reserve, but that they provide the community with royalties derived from economic activities on their land (ACHPR, 2010, recommendations 1(c) and 1(d)), such as the tourist industry, and grant them 'legal title' (ACHPR, 2010, para. 206). The Ogiek arguably achieved even greater success when via the Ogiek Peoples' Development Program (OPDP), together with Centre for Minority Rights Development (CEMIRIDE) and Minority Rights Group International (MRGI), they issued a communication to the ACHPR claiming that a number of provisions of the charter had been violated, including, *inter alia*, right to life, freedom of religion, the right to culture, property and the right to development. The commission later referred this to the African Court on Human and People's Rights, which ultimately issued a judgment upholding the land rights of the Ogiek and violations of all the rights alleged by the Ogiek (ACtHPR, 2017). Of particular importance to the analysis here, the Court concluded that the forcible separation of the Ogiek from their forests would have profound cultural implications for the group life of the Ogiek. In accord with the arguments of the UN Special Rapporteur on Indigenous peoples, Victoria Tauli-Corpuz (Tauli-Corpuz et al., 2018), the court also found that secure land tenure leads to better conservation outcomes. The implications for the Sengwer, who, as we have seen, face the same culturally destructive practices, and possible strategic litigation avenues, are clear. Moreover, these forms of resistance were greatly bolstered by working together with networks of international NGOs, activists and lawyers, such as Forest Peoples Programme (FPP), MRGI or the International Work Group for Indigenous Affairs (IWGIA). These networks would both raise the profile of their struggle, as well as provide them with the logistical and legal experience and expertise to engage in international and regional governance institutions and fora and build the relevant legal challenges.

However, both cases as well as the above discussed strategies of the Sengwer demonstrate the inherent limits of *legal* resistance or strategic human rights litigation and lobbying of government agencies. In the Endorois case, they still have not been provided with firm guarantees to collective tenure. The proximate cause is, as examined earlier, due to the failure to fully decolonise the legal system and 'bureaucratic sabotage' which endlessly postpone or stymie such attempts. Although they now do have access to Lake Bogoria for religious and cultural purposes in line with recommendation b (Tauli-Corpuz et al., 2018) and have been paid royalties for *some* economic activities, as Wilson Kipkazi, executive director of the Endorois Welfare Council (EWC)[11] asserted (ESCR-Net, 2019, p. 11), this was only due to sustained 'community pressure' and, indeed, ratcheting up of international pressure via the aforementioned international networks, and not strictly due to compliance with the ACHPR judgment. The failure to fully implement ACHPR's judgment comes despite the ACHPR (2013) issuing a resolution demanding that they implement all their recommendations and the UN Committee on Economic, Social and Cultural Rights (2016, para. 16) recommendation that they implement the court's decision 'without further delay'.

As for the Ogiek and the implementation of their case, on the domestic level, the ruling of Kenya's Land and Environment Court referred their case to the NLC, but, as we saw, 'bureaucratic sabotage' (Cavanagh, 2018a, pp. 137–8) and legal amendments have denuded the NLC and frustrated its attempts to fulfil its constitutional role. As for the ACtHPR ruling in 2017, the Kenyan state has still many years later failed to implement its recommendations, most importantly the formal recognition of collective land tenure (Forest Peoples Programme, 2020). As of writing, it still has not released the findings of the Mau Taskforce set up to facilitate the implementation of the African Court judgment (MRGI, 2020). Further, despite the landmark ruling by the ACtHPR (2017), the KFS in 2020, in the midst of the Covid pandemic evicted 300 Ogiek from their ancestral homes (Onyatta, 2020).

Likewise, the Sengwer have repeatedly petitioned their local environment court to no avail and, given the failure to fully decolonise its legal system, it may well have to exhaust all other legal domestic remedies, just as the Endorois did, before pursuing justice in an international legal forum like ACHPR. Whether this will deliver any meaningful prospect of resolution to the Sengwer's just claims for secure lands tenure and respect for their rights as a people, given the failure of just such a course evident in the other cases, is open to question. One Sengwer interviewee expressed doubts over just such a course. Commenting on the ACtHPR's decision on the *Ogiek* case in 2017, they observed, 'we learned from the Ogiek ruling ... they don't have powers to impose what they are ruling' (18/03/2020).

Decoloniality, unlike decolonisation, means not just moving beyond mere juridical and administrative forms but uprooting the 'colonial episteme' upon which it is grounded. That is to say, whilst decolonisation means formal independence, this will not deconstruct or fully purge a society of the forms of colonial governance, modes of thinking, intersubjective relations, cultural patterns, knowledge production and the episteme upon which they are founded that were forged and institutionalised under colonial occupation, because 'coloniality survives colonialism' (Maldonado-Torres, 2007, p. 243). This is undoubtedly true, but the forms of (colonial) political economy, its mode of production, circulation and exchange that structure a society's material reproduction and sustain its dialogue with nature, are also not tied to formal politico-juridical forms and can endure or linger under a variety of superstructures or 'political shells', including forms of political independence. In other words, decoloniality does not *just* mean moving beyond the 'colonial episteme', or what some have described as 'intellectual imperialism' (Alatas, 2000), where colonial domination is secured though colonisation of knowledge production and the creation of an 'epistemic hierarchy' leading to forms of 'global epistemicide' (Santos, 2014). This is a necessary but not sufficient condition; dismantling a political economy of knowledge through 'epistemic disobedience' (Mignolo, 2011b) must be accompanied by a wider 'disobedience' that dismantles the political economy of production, circulation and exchange more generally. It is to this 'moving beyond' that we will turn in the final chapter.

Notes

1. On 13 May 2020, the Kenyan Environment and Land Court in Eldoret dismissed a suit to degazette their Forest land in the Embobut Forest (The Standard, 2020).

2. The figure was 400,000 Kenyan Shillings per household, or 4,585 USD in 2013. This was only enough to purchase four cows and one acre of land (Tickell, 2014).

3. The 2009 National Land Policy was the culmination of decades of investigation into the country's historic land injustices. This was the first major land policy since the colonial era, and it set out to establish a number of principles in order to institute broad land reforms that would support Indigenous rights to land and collective land tenure.

4. According to the act, '"community" means a clearly defined group of users of forest land identified on the basis of ethnicity, culture or similar community of interests as provided under Article 63 of the Constitution'.

5. There is a long and drawn-out argument about labour theory of value (LTV) with many arguing it has been discredited or empirically invalidated. Why not just argue instead that the drive for profit and ceaseless growth explains the anti-ecological properties of the capitalist system? Of course, there are many Marxists who have refuted this claim. For a recent defence of LTV see Fine and Saad-Filho (2016), Grossman (2016) and Burkett (2018).

6. I'm indebted to the professor of economics and renowned Marxist ecologist Paul Burkett, whose generous patience in answering my questions in our correspondence helped me apply value analysis to the carbon markets in this novel way.

7. Payments for Ecosystem Services (PES) involves the valorisation of the aforementioned restorative and rejuvenating properties of nature discussed in reference to the conservationist mode of production.

8. The REDD+ project is an example of the Clean Development Mechanism (CDM) under the Kyoto Protocol, which allows countries from the developed world (Annex B Party) to implement an emission-reduction project in developing countries. For Eastern European economies 'in transition' it is called Joint Implementation (JI).

9. BDO is grounded in the same commodity logic, wherein methods for calculating systems of equivalence and commensurability between units of species and habitats under regimes of private property rights enable the trade in these units to 'offset' for 'unavoidable' harm due to development projects. The Business and Biodiversity Offsets Programme (BBOP), an international consortium, has developed international standards for biodiversity commodities (Dunlap and Sullivan, 2019, p. 10).

10. For work on development as a Foucauldian practice see Escobar (1984, 1995), Alvares (1992), Rist (1997), Nandy (1988) and Ferguson (1990).

11. The (EWC) is a registered civil society organisation founded in 1995 by elders from the Endorois community to organise against gross human rights violations.

Conclusion: a neo-Lemkian ontology in the age of the Anthropocene

The cases of the Sengwer in the Embobut Forest and the Gomeroi, Githabul and Wangan and Jagalingou nations in Australia manifestly exhibit Lemkin's (1944, p. 79) two-stage process. This same two-stage process mirrors the two structures identified in Chapter 1 as the political economy of genocide of a rather peculiar type in the age of the Anthropocene. Moreover, in all the examined cases the capitalist system was shown to be inherently ecologically destructive, violating 'the everlasting nature–imposed conditions of production' (Marx, 1976, p. 290). The 'treadmill of accumulation' (Foster, 2005) under conditions of competition, which imbues capitalist production with the imperative to expand, transgresses the 'metabolic interaction' between human beings and nature and expands into *noncapitalist* territory, 'into a world dense with cultural difference' (Smith, 2002, p. 79) giving rise to the extra-economic processes of plunder, fraud or theft, from *without* the circuits of production and capital accumulation. Ultimately, it is the value-contradiction embedded within the various industrial (and financial) processes operating within the expanded reproduction of the circuits of capital, 'capitalism's inner dialectic' (Harvey, 1981, p. 10), that elides nature's contribution to production of value and its role in social reproduction more generally. This accounts for the externalisation of environmental (and social costs) and this is why, as I have argued elsewhere, capitalist ecology is eco-criminogenic and eco-genocidal (Crook, Short and South, 2018).

The political economy of ecologically induced genocide, *of the type described above*, involves a process of, first, primary accumulation which facilitates and consolidates *de facto* control of Indigenous land by creating 'facts on the ground' through dispersal programmes, population transfers, extermination programmes and so on, or as we saw in Kenya with the gazetting of national or wildlife parks or conservation areas. In Australia, simply the threat of violence latently manifest in the ostensibly peaceful 'negotiations' under the 'Right to Negotiate' provisions of the NTA with Indigenous people, if not engaged with, could eventually lead to the loss of all customary land rights and the threat of eventual control and enforcement actions by law enforcement agencies. This facilitates the second phase of securing *de jure* control of Indigenous land by creating the necessary legal and institutional architecture in the form of private and state property regimes which invariably deny the collective common law tenure rights of the traditional owner-conservators and assert the legal and political jurisdiction of the relevant settler-colonial or 'postcolonial' state. This completes the incorporation of Indigenous land and territory into global circuits of capital; the various eco-destructive industrial processes, referred to earlier, then unfold.

A crucial part of accomplishing the second phase of 'imposing the national pattern of the oppressor' and achieving *de jure* control involves sophisticated ideological and discursive practices which in the modern era no longer resemble overtly racist exterminatory ideologies, but adopt racially coded developmentalist overtones, sometimes with a green hue – practices which play a crucial part in (re)imposing spatial relations that, as they did in the colonial past, are vital to facilitating *both* the reproduction of the capitalist system and accumulation of capital *and* the reproduction of the neocolonial state through continued 'internal territorialisation' (Vandergeest and Peluso, 1995, p. 387). Mathews (2011, p. 10) remind us that this process of state formation is never complete 'but requires continuous performance, a work that is always contested and never done'. Indeed, as we saw in both Australia and Kenya, in the past, and in the modern period through a global neoliberal logic, a number of agencies within the state apparatus, described by Cavanagh and Himmelfarb (2015, p. 62) as 'institutionalised assemblages of actors mobilised around a common territorial objective', pursue projects framed through discursive practices and enforced through the lethal threat of the monopoly of violence that continually 'perform' both objectives. In Australia, the cadastral technologies operating at various phases through its colonial history concentrated and segregated racialised populations, be it on reserves, cattle stations or, latterly, urban ghettos. In the current juncture, the behaviour and conduct of Indigenous peoples is spatially regulated through the racialised discourses or 'cultural imaginaries' (Mbembe, 2003, p. 26) of Indigenous rights and reconciliation in the post-Mabo era, compelling them to engage with colonial institutions like the NTA that facilitate the incorporation of their Indigenous lands into circuits of capital and further expand the internal territorialisation of the colonial state. In Kenya, the 'assemblage of actors' that included the KFS, county councils and the

Ministry of Lands and the Ministry of Environment, Water and Natural Resources, as well as the 'mediating institutions' like the World Bank and EU, which still have not shaken free from their colonial past, carry over forms of colonial lawfare, political economy of land and racialised discourses of development that treat Indigenous peoples as impediments to progress. Like their former colonial masters, the new political and economic elites seek to impose racialised productions of space that restructure socioecologies and once more facilitate the expanded reproduction of capital and territorialisation of state.

Indeed, in both cases, what I earlier described as the international chain of capitalist production and trade is being reproduced through a continual, contested and dynamic process of state formation. Mbembe (2003, p. 26) succinctly summed this process up when he observed:

> The writing of new spatial relations (territorialization) was, ultimately, tantamount to the production of boundaries and hierarchies, zones and enclaves; the subversion of existing property arrangements; the classification of people according to different categories; resource extraction; and, finally, *the manufacturing of a large reservoir of cultural imaginaries*. [emphasis added]

In the case of the Sengwer in Kenya, the cultural imaginary entailed a reframing of nature in a manner that cast them as irresponsible custodians or squatters, or simply reimagined socioecologies without them in. In Australia, the structure of rights possessing an intellectual lineage that stretches all the way back to the Enlightenment, bequeathed to it by the colonial state, in their colonial form presuppose the legitimacy of settler-colonial sovereignty, which excludes from view the long history of structural violence that was its *sine qua non*. In its current form, the Indigenous land rights offered under the NTA and all the other Indigenous land rights legislation, are still marked by racial elision, exclusion and exception, as human rights are more generally (Samson, 2020). Indeed, the broader liberal project has throughout its history been defined by a 'logic of exclusion' (Losurdo, 2011) that denudes or attenuates rights so they may be made compatible with what Adam Smith (1976, p. 687) argued was 'the obvious and simple system of natural liberty', namely the market.

This dynamic process of internal territorialisation is vital to facilitating the spatio-temporal fixes that Harvey (2003b, p. 64) understood were necessary to periodically resolving the contradictions that give rise to capital overaccumulation. This was most markedly the case in the age of neoliberalism, which as we saw brought in its wake radical transformations in the relations of genocide. Recall the observation that the various spatial practices and technologies that enable the 'production of space' (Lefebvre,

1974) and its rebranding with the hot iron of exchange value are 'the hand-maiden of property' (Blomley, 2003, p. 127). This is in the final analysis about the material processes of accumulation by dispossession and surplus value extraction, not as Cavanagh and Himmelfarb (2015, p. 61) claim, conversely, about colonial state formation. As these processes of territorialisation, state formation and capital accumulation take place, the symbolic and political processes may be dominant, but in the final analysis the economic proves decisive. The racialised productions of space that restructure socioecologies in both sites of colonisation, in Kenya under the auspices of *conservation*, and in Australia the incorporation of Indigenous land into the orbit of *extraction*, did, indeed, amount to internal territorialisation that expanded the frontiers of the Kenyan and Australian settler-colonial state. But ultimately these processes facilitated the continued expanded reproduction of colonial capitalism and extended the commodity form to as yet unchartered spheres of nature–society relations (Heynen et al., 2007, p. 10).

Capitalist production relations as the vector driving eco-genocide in Australia is not just an aberration or idiographic, but in fact, gives rise to many instances, interconnected by a thousand threads. In fact, the case of Kenya illuminates the interconnectivity, ontologically speaking, of the two cases. In other words, one gives rise necessarily to the other, where one form of commodification of nature in the sphere of *production* (Australia, pastoralism, mining and extreme energy) and its associated environmental externalities leads to another form of commodification of nature, as a compensatory stabilising measure, in the sphere of *reproduction* and conservationism (Kenya and market environmentalism). While one capitalist mode causes ecological ruptures, another, spawned by the first, seeks to 'fix' them.

The specificities and contingencies of each case notwithstanding, they represent but two manifestations of ecologically induced genocide, both driven, fundamentally, by the same genocidal structuring dynamics, and both connected historically by a global imperialist capitalist system (and the British empire more specifically). In fact, they are both settler colonies that were once part of the British empire that left a legacy of a global political economy determining their insertion into the international division of labour, which endures to this day: Australia is still dependent on agricultural, fossil and mineral exports and Kenya is still dependent on forestry, agriculture, fishing, tourism and increasingly on earning foreign currency exchange through neoliberal conservation, due in large part to its 'dependent independence' (Curtis, 2003, p. 330). Both form a part of a global chain of imperial production and trade and thus part of a 'global chain of genocide'. Finally, both emerged as dialectical responses to the ecological contradiction at the heart of the political economy of capitalism in different contexts, those contexts being transmitted by a settler-colonial past. This is *the engine of genocide*, an inescapable condition that would carry over into the modern post-Mabo and post-independence period.

Once the burgeoning settler-colonial society and state in both Kenya and Australia became firmly entwined with international market forces, this predatory and expansionist form of capitalism led to an inevitable clash of two different modes of life and ultimately the subsumption of one by the other. This forcible articulation takes many forms (Hartwig, 1978, p. 129) and is determined to a large extent by the technical conditions in which settler-colonial capitalism historically finds the Indigenous mode of life. To the extent that capital can make use of or valorise some aspect of Indigenous material culture, it will be preserved at least partially in a deformed state. It is this forced articulation or hybridisation on political economic grounds that is often overlooked by the genocide literature. Where the sites of colonisation and their respective relations of genocide differed was in the manner of this forced articulation. As we saw Kenya, relations of genocide were uneven, because the various Indigenous groups had differing economic systems, not all of which were found to be by the colonial authorities conducive to the development of the settler colony. The fate of forest-dwelling people in Kenya like the Sengwer and their biopolitical status was conditioned by their hunter-gatherer mode, subjecting them to arguably greater degrees of 'civilising violence' (Cavanagh, 2016, p. 3) to secure their 'liminal humanity' than those Indigenous groups like the Kikuyu who were considered more advanced according to colonial social Darwinist thinking. Unfortunately, the stagist thinking of Kenya's former colonial masters, the symbolic dimensions of colonialism, would prove adaptable to the current postcolonial juncture in the form of neoliberal environmentalism.

In Australia, an analogous process unfolded. In some cases, Indigenous people were able to adapt to the settler-colonial system, through various forms of articulation and hybridisation, in which elements of the settler economic system are fused with the largely nomadic Indigenous mode, but only with those industries that were compatible with those Indigenous communities, communities who were already destroyed in part by colonisation and its associated techniques of land theft, violence and disease. For the vast majority of Indigenous people, the more direct and unmediated dispossession and domicide reminiscent of the frontier violence stage took place. Paradoxically, articulation and hybridisation were made possible through relations of domination, subjugation and, ultimately, genocide, and yet this articulation allowed for the partial preservation of Indigenous connection to country and traditional modes of life. This seeming paradox is resolved once you understand that this state of affairs is only provisional and conditional on the continued viability of that particular colonial economy, or at least the viability of continued dependence on Indigenous labour, or, in the age of land rights, the Indigenous estate and the extraction of commodities and resources. Hartwig (1978, p. 129) argued the third mode of articulation was the destruction of non-capitalist societies and the freeing of the means of production. Arguably, the process of neoliberal assimilation in Australia examined in Chapter 3 may ultimately achieve this ontologically *if not* materially. In other words, some Indigenous people may still maintain ownership of land, but through a process of interpellation become transformed as entrepreneurs and rentiers. Remarking on these psychoactive affects in the Canadian settler colony, Coulthard (2014, p. 12) sharply observed 'the long-term goal of indoctrinating the Indigenous population to the principles of private property, possessive individualism, and menial wage work' would continue to be an important feature of Indigenous policy. This is not a foregone conclusion, however. As May (1983, p. 41) argues, even in extreme cases where domicide was the norm, Indigenous production relations were not completely destroyed. May (1983) has suggested the preservation of culture or its superstructure attests to the continued survival, in attenuated form, of the Indigenous mode of life; my research corroborates this, particularly those who resist these assimilatory and interpellating processes.

Indeed, the other side of this coin is Indigenous struggle, which, dialectically, alongside the evolving nature and composition of the Australian and Kenyan economy, shifted, as we saw, the settler–Indigenous struggle onto different terrain, and the relations of genocide into different modalities: in Australia, from frontier violence to the protection regimes, to land rights and NTA and what is called administrative genocide; in Kenya, from a settler-colonial society rooted primarily in white settler farming, to a post-independence regime that still 'others' Indigenous peoples as an obstacle to its full development. Ironically, from the vantage point of Kenya's Indigenous people, it has further to come to decolonise than Australia, since some Indigenous groups like the Sengwer are still not officially recognised either by government or Court ruling as Indigenous and entitled to full customary rights to its ancestral land. In other respects, it is has gone further, since its newly minted 2010 constitution recognises, at least in the abstract, Indigenous rights to ancestral land and the legal parity of collective tenure rights with all other forms of property.

At each stage, the degree of their articulation with and incorporation into the settler-colonial economy and civil society more generally would prove decisive in shaping the nature of that struggle and through the dialectic of struggle and the dialectic of colonial-Indigenous identity, the

CONCLUSION   187

development of their identity and consciousness. As Fanon (1963) ably argued, it is this struggle that would be necessary to purge their identity of any sense of inferiority. In the case of Australia, the resistance to settler-colonial domination would give rise almost immediately to a form of resistance which would eventually shape the development of a pan-Australian Indigenous consciousness, particularly in the twentieth century. In Kenya, a more complex discursive and symbolic terrain where Indigenous people are concerned, shaped in large part by the *uneven* nature of relations of genocide examined in Chapter 4, led to a stratified and hierarchical understanding of Kenya's cultural mosaic. This would have lasting legacies that only now in the last decade or so are being addressed, where those at the bottom of that hierarchy are concerned. The uneven nature of relations of genocide in Kenya would postpone the development of a comparable pan-Kenyan movement of its Indigenous peoples. Dovetailing with the rise of a global human rights system driven by globalising forces in the post-war era, Indigenous peoples in Kenya are now asserting their claims, with the help of international networks of human rights NGOs, to a unique and culturally distinct way of life, and only now beginning in recent years to forge pan-Kenyan forms of struggle.

The imperative of the capitalist mode to expand means expropriating Indigenous territory and incorporating it into the normalised sphere of capitalist production, circulation and exchange. But what is different now, in the post-Mabo phase of genocide, is that it is achieved via the absence of overtly violent coercive means, and it is in place the Trojan Horse of Indigenous rights. Even in Kenya, as we saw, the 'assemblage of state actors' feel obliged to pay lip service to Indigenous rights like FPIC, though the traditional top-down, juridical, forms of state violence are still central. Arguably, it is not enough to simply indigenise human rights law, as Samson (2020, p.162) argues, to address the aforementioned exceptions and elisions. Decoloniality must mean moving beyond the 'colonial episteme', of which colonial human rights is an expression. If, as Fanon (1967, p.84) recognised, colonialism has a dual structure which operates both on the psychological and economic terrain, then we must dismantle the latter to have any hope of addressing the former and purging human rights of its parochialism. Recall Coulthard's (2014, p.173) warning that 'for Indigenous nations to live, capitalism must die. And for capitalism to die, we must actively participate in the construction of Indigenous alternatives to it.' This is not to argue that any struggle short of dismantling capitalism is futile. The evidence of Indigenous struggles in Australia and Kenya do point to the partial victories that legal and extra-legal struggles can wrest from the settler-colonial system. But even these partial victories, whether they be Indigenous rights hard won under the land recovery regimes in Australia or legal and constitutional recognition in Kenya, ultimately serve to shift the 'structural target of the settler-colonial logic of elimination' (Strakosch and Macoun, 2012, p. 44) and reproduce genocidal structuring dynamics in different modalities.

The critique of human rights proffered by the Marxist canon is germane here. Contrary to popular belief that the Marxist tradition simply and one-sidedly repudiates the notion of human rights (Lukes, 1981), it is, in fact, much more nuanced. Whilst it is true there is no clear line on human rights within the works of Marx and Engels, one can construct a coherent and dialectically nuanced critique that is fruitful for our purposes here. Firstly, the dialectical method as employed within historical materialist framework treats all social phenomena as contradictory, interrelated and in a state of flux (O'Connell, 2017a). Therefore, any treatment of human rights which dismisses it as necessarily a tool of ruling elites in the maintenance of the status quo is one sided, which loses 'the potential contribution of rights, a potential contribution which coexists with their negative potential' (Sparer, 1984, p. 519). Put simply, human rights can be both emancipatory *and* a discourse and practice that reproduces the status quo. This was palpably demonstrated with the land recovery regimes and Indigenous rights systems in Australia in Chapters 2 and 3. As O'Connell (2017a) argues, 'human rights are neither emancipatory nor inherently conservative; they are a complex combination of both tendencies'. Whether human rights do ultimately play a progressive or reactionary role can only be determined by understanding the specific array of social forces in any given historical juncture where human rights play a decisive role.

Moreover, knowledge is vital to social action, which is to say that the point of understanding the world is to change it. This is exemplified in Marx's (1976b, p. 5) *Theses of Feuerbach,* where he famously asserted 'philosophers have only interpreted the world in various ways; the point is to change it'. For this reason, Marxist analysis privileges the role that human (and Indigenous) rights claims can play in advancing social struggle (O'Connell, 2017b), and recognises it as an important resource for marginalised and oppressed groups, as well as the terrain of political struggle, even if that terrain as we have seen is uneven. Critically, this critique appreciates how such a struggle over human and Indigenous rights can achieve partial victories and potentially be the prelude to a broader contestation of the social order. However, as Marx's (1975, pp. 146–74) critique of 'bourgeois rights' in *On the Jewish Question* suggests, although they constitute an advance, political emancipation falls short of addressing exploitation, which is ultimately rooted in the economic sphere. In other words, the structural impediments imposed by the 'laws of motion' of the capitalist system will, in the final analysis, militate against the full realisation of human and Indigenous rights. The experiences of Indigenous peoples in Kenya and Australia testify to this ontological reality. Therefore, to indigenise human rights we must also indigenise capitalist production itself. This is, I think, an oxymoron, if by indigenise (notwithstanding the recognition that, as argued above, there are Indigenous people who choose the 'market as the path to development') we mean a mode of organising a material culture in which labour and nature is not alienated. Arguably, given the threat to the biosphere posed by global capitalism (Crook and Short, 2014), and the expansion imperative of the capitalist system, even the potential for treaty negotiations which are taking place across Australia today with Indigenous communities (Wahlquist, 2018) may only ever be short lived in the long run. Perhaps it is the alliances forged across Indigenous and non-Indigenous communities, both locally and globally, which can, as we saw, impose material limits on the extent of capital accumulation, whether on the carbon commodity in Kenya or that of fossil capital in Australia.

The best effort of the Australian settler-colonial state to extinguish Indigenous land rights and Indigenous sovereignty is in a certain sense, dialectically, conditioning a renaissance in Indigenous culture and spiritual and ecological connection to land and the development of an Indigenous people for itself, cognisant of its interests on national and even global scales. Likewise in Kenya, the step change in the intensity of state repression of Indigenous sovereignty in recent decades has galvanised Indigenous groups fuelling a resistance that has led to their collaboration with international NGOs and activist groups like the FPP or the IWGIA. This could have truly global implications, due to its grounding in ecological sensibilities and collective notions of ecological responsibility as custodians of earth, much like that found in most 'cosmovisions' of many Indigenous societies around the world (Havemann, 2016). Just as Marx in the nineteenth century believed that Indigenous communities rooted in 'natural economies' in Russia could help Russian society move beyond a capitalist system which is both alienated from labour and nature (Harding, 1991), and is consequently capable of driving both ecocide and genocide, so too can the deep spiritual attachment that many Indigenous communities have to nature, and the ecological-political orders that they are premised on. These ecological-political orders implicitly offer us answers to many of capitalism's ills, not least its ecocidal character and the alienation from nature, as well as arguably lessons about alienated labour, a symptom also characteristic of developed capitalist economies. So today, too, we must learn from the Indigenous struggle and the black– green alliance emerging in Australia against the ecocidal war waged by capitalist production and elsewhere. Indeed, proposals put forward by a coalition of Indigenous and non-Indigenous activists in North America in a published book called the *Red Deal: Indigenous Action to Save Our Earth* (The Red Nation, 2021) argue that any movement to avoid catastrophic climate change and repair ecological destruction is necessarily coterminous with the struggle for Indigenous liberation, arguing that Indigenous resistance founded on the values of ecological justice and ecological responsibility as custodians of earth is necessarily revolutionary. As it argues, 'what's often downplayed is the revolutionary potency of what Indigenous resistance stands for: caretaking and creating just relations between human and other-than-human worlds on a planet thoroughly devastated by capitalism' (The Red Nation, 2021, p. 16).

Moreover, the potential for the Indigenous proletariat that played such a key role in the struggle of land rights and sovereignty in Australia, as we saw in Chapter 2, to once again leverage that structural power as part of the organised labour movement must be considered. As before, they can act as a transmission belt for ideas between Indigenous communities and the broader labour movement connected via an international chain of trade and production to the rest of the globe, only this time in the context of an emerging global environmental movement, must be considered. Although the politically driven neoliberal project in Australia wrought economic transformations that 'pacified' organised labour and suppressed levels of industrial struggle (Humphreys, 2018, p. 50), one cannot rule out a revival of industrial struggle. This could be a promising linkage precisely because of the structural power afforded by organised labour's strategic position within the structures of capitalist production. Moreover, the subject position of the Indigenous proletariat is not only compatible with Indigenous lifeways, as evidenced by the history of Indigenous struggle examined in Chapter 2, but recent pathbreaking research into 'fossil capital' (Malm, 2016) has shown that that from its very inception, the incipient industrial working class resisted as much the ecological degradation wrought by capital as it did its exploitation and alienation from work (Malm, 2016, ch. 10). In other words, there is a resonance between the subject position of what Foster (2010) calls an emerging 'environmental proletariat' disproportionately exposed to the externalities of a globalised ecological crisis and an Indigenous proletariat which still retains its spiritual attachment to country.

Indigenous people are at the sharp end of the ecocidal and genocidal properties of a global capitalist system. It is their struggle to preserve their connection to country and forest, and to nature more generally, that may prove humanity's last hope to awaken an ecological consciousness and remember its long since forgotten dependence on nature. For much of what is called the 'developed world', 'progress' has come at the expense of alienation from nature; this may prove its undoing. Instead, to reverse this alienation and restore our global ecology we must once again privilege our relationship with nature as the Indigenous people in this book do. As the Sengwer activist Elias Kimaiyo (author interview, 20/02/2018) affirmed, 'Sengwer and the Forests are one and inseparable.' It is this wisdom that must be rekindled.

Bibliography

Court cases

African Commission on Human and People's Rights (ACHPR) (2010) 276/2003: *Centre for Minority Rights Development (Kenya) and Minority Rights Group International on Behalf of Endorois Welfare Council v. Kenya*. Available at: http://www.minorityrights.org/i. [Accessed 17 December 2020]

African Court on Human and People's Rights (ACtHPR) (2017) *African Commission on Human and Peoples' Rights v. Republic of Kenya*, Application No. 006/2012. Available at: https://www.african-court.org /cpmt/storage/app/uploads/public/5f5/5fe/9a9 /5f55fe9a96676974302132.pdf. [Accessed 19 December 2020].

Burragubba v. State of Queensland [2016] FCA 984.

Burragubba v. State of Queensland [2017] FCAFC 133.

Burragubba & Anor v. Minister for Natural Resources and Mines & Anor [2016] QSC 273.

Burragubba & Ors v. Minister for Natural Resources and Mines & Anor [2017] QCA 179.

Land and Environment Court (2014) *Joseph Letuya & 21 others v. Attorney General & 5 others Civil Application*, No. 635.

Mabo & Others v. State of Queensland ('Mabo No. 2'). 107 ALR 1 (HC) (1992). Available at: http://www8.austlii.edu.au/cgi-bin/viewdoc/au /cases/cth/HCA/1992/23.html [Accessed 12 March 2018].

McGlade v. Native Title Registrar [2017] FCAFC 10.

Wien J. in *R v. Belfon* (1976) 3 All ER 46.

Wik Peoples v. Queensland ('Pastoral Leases case') [1996] HCA 40; (1996) 187 CLR 1; (1996) 141 ALR 129; (1996) 71 ALJR 173 (23 December 1996). Available at: https://www.informea.org/sites/default/files/court -decisions/Wik%20Peoples%20v%20Queensland.pdf. [Accessed 15 June 2018].

Constitutions, orders, regulations, declarations, ordinances, resolutions and domestic and international legislation

(ACHPR) African Commission on Human and People's Rights (2013) 257 Resolution Calling on the Republic of Kenya to Implement the Endorois Decision – ACHPR/Res.257(LIV)2013.

Aboriginal Land Rights (Northern Territory) Act (1976) [Australia]. Act No. 191 of 1976.

Aboriginal Land Rights Act (1983) [Australia]. No. 42 of 1983.

Aboriginal and Torres Strait Islander Heritage Protection Act (1984) (Cth) [Australia].

Colony and Protectorate of Kenya (1925) Master and Servants (Amendment) Ordinance. Nairobi: Government Printer.

Colony and Protectorate of Kenya (1926) Government Notice No. 394 of 1926. Nairobi: Government Printer.

Colony and Protectorate of Kenya (1928) Native Trust Land Ordinance, No. 203 of 1928. Nairobi: Government Printer.

Colony and Protectorate of Kenya (1930) Native Trust Land Ordinance, No. 9 of 1930. Nairobi: Government Printer.

CBD (Convention on Biological Diversity) (2011) Strategic Plan for Biodiversity 2011–2020, Including Aichi Biodiversity Targets. Available at: https://www.cbd.int/sp/ [Accessed 2 April 2021].

East Africa Protectorate (1897) East Africa Regulations, 1897. Mombasa: Government Printer.

East Africa Protectorate (1901) East Africa (Lands) Order-in-Council, 1901. The Official Gazette of the East Africa and Uganda Protectorates (1 October 1901). Mombasa: Government Printer.

East Africa Protectorate (1902) East Africa Order-in-Council 1902. London: HMSO.

East Africa Protectorate (1902) Crown Lands Ordinance, 1902. Mombasa: Government Printer.

East Africa Protectorate (1915) Crown Lands Ordinance, 1915. Nairobi: Government Printer.

East Africa Protectorate (1926) Colony and Protectorate of Kenya. Blue Book for the Year Ended 31st December, 1926. Nairobi: Government Printer.

European Union (EU) (2021, October 26) Charter of Fundamental Rights of the European Union. 26 October 2012, 2012/C 326/02. Available at: https://www.refworld.org/docid/3ae6b3b70.html [Accessed 17 September 2021].

Government of Kenya (GoK) (1965) Sessional Paper No. 10 of 1965 on African Socialism and Its Application to Planning in Kenya. Nairobi: Government Printer.

Government of Kenya (GoK) (1968a) Trust Land Act 1968. Nairobi: Government Printer.

Government of Kenya (GoK) (1968b) Land Adjudication Act 1968. Nairobi: Government Printer.

Government of Kenya (GoK) (2005) Forests Act 2005. Nairobi: Government Printer.

Government of Kenya (GoK) (2010) Constitution of Kenya. Nairobi: National Council for Law Reporting.

Government of Kenya (GoK) (2009) Sessional Paper no. 3 of 2009 on National Land Policy. Government Printer, Nairobi.

Government of Kenya (GoK) (2012) Land Act 2012. Nairobi: Government Printer.

Government of Kenya (GoK) (2013) Wildlife Act 2013. Nairobi: Government Printer.

Government of Kenya (GoK) (2016a) Community Land Act of 2016. Nairobi: Government Printer.

Government of Kenya (GoK) (2016b) Forest Conservation and Management Act 2016. Nairobi: Government Printer.

Great Britain (1842) *An act for regulating the sale of waste land belonging to the Crown in the Australian Colonies.* London: Printed by George E. Eyre and Andrew Spottiswoode.

Great Britain (1842) Australian Colonies, Waste Lands Act 1842 5 & 6 Vict c 36 (Imp)An Act for regulating the Sale of Waste Land belonging to the Crown in the Australian Colonies, and to make further Provision for the Management thereof 1842.

Great Britain (1846) Australian Colonies, Waste Lands Act 1846 9 & 10 Vict c 103–4 (Imp).

Native Title Act (1993) (Cth) [Australia]. Act No. 110 of 1993.

Native Title Amendment Act (1998) (Cth) [Australia]. No. 97 of 1998.

Queensland. Legislative Assembly. Agriculture, Resources and Environment Committee & Rickuss, Ian & Queensland. Legislative Assembly. Agriculture, Resources and Environment Committee. 2012, *Mines Legislation (Streamlining) Amendment Bill 2012 / Agriculture, Resources and Environment Committee.* Agriculture, Resources and Environment Committee Brisbane, Qld: Agriculture, Resources and Environment Committee. http://www.parliament.qld.gov.au/documents/committees /AREC/2012/MinesLAB/rpt7-16Aug2012.pdf [Accessed 7 November 2021].

UN Economic and Social Council (ECOSOC) (2016) Committee on Economic, Social and Cultural Rights: Concluding Observations on the Combined Second to Fifth Periodic Reports of Kenya of 6 April 2016, E/C.12/KEN /CO/2-5.

UN (1948) *Convention on the Prevention and Punishment of the Crime of Genocide.* United Nations, Treaty Series, vol. 78, p. 277, 9 December 1948. Available at: https://www.refworld.org/legal/agreements/unga /1948/en/13495 [Accessed 7 October 2024].

UN (1992) *The Convention on Biological Diversity*. Rio de Janeiro. Available at: https://treaties.un.org/pages/ViewDetails.aspx?src=TREATY&mtdsg_no=XXVII-8&chapter=27 [Accessed 27 August 2024].

UNFCCC (2015) *Adoption of the Paris Agreement*. 21st Conference of the Parties. Paris: United Nations.

United Nations General Assembly (UNGA) (1994) *United Nations Framework Convention on Climate Change: Resolution / Adopted by the General Assembly*. 20 January 1994. A/RES/48/189. Available at: https://www.refworld.org/docid/3b00f2770.html [Accessed 23 September 2021].

United Nations General Assembly (UNGA) (1998, Jul 17) *Rome Statute of the International Criminal Court art. 7:1*. (last amended 2010). Available at: https://www.refworld.org/docid/3ae6b3a84.html [Accessed 9 November 2020].

United Nations General Assembly (UNGA) (2015) Transforming Our World: the 2030 Agenda for Sustainable Development, 21 October 2015, A/RES/70/1. Available at: https://www.refworld.org/docid/57b6e3e44.html [Accessed 21 September 2021].

United Nations General Assembly (UNGA) (2017) *United Nations Declaration on the Rights of Indigenous Peoples: Resolution / Adopted by the General Assembly*. 2 October 2007. A/RES/61/295. Available at: http://www.refworld.org/docid/471355a82.html [Accessed 13 December 2016].

United Kingdom of Great Britain and Ireland (1890) *Foreign Jurisdiction Act of 1890*. London: HM Stationery Office.

Reports

(ACHPR) African Commission on Human and People's Rights (2005) *Report of the African Commission's Working Group of Experts on Indigenous Populations/Communities Submitted in Accordance with 'Resolution on the Rights of Indigenous Populations/Communities in Africa Adopted by the African Commission on Human and Peoples' Rights at Its 28th Ordinary Session*. Copenhagen: IWGIA.

CIFOR (2017) *The Water Towers of East Africa: Policies and Practises for Enhancing Code Benefits from Joint Forest and Water Conservation, Proceedings of the National Launch*. Nairobi: Center for International Forestry Research.

Colonial Office (1934) *Report of the Kenya Land Commission (and Evidence and Memoranda)*. Four volumes. London: HM Stationery Office.

Committee on Legal Affairs and Human Rights (CLAHR) (2011, 5 December) *Enforced Population Transfer as a Human Rights Violation*.

Strasbourg: Council of Europe. Available at: http://assembly.coe.int
/nw/xml/XRef/Xref-XML2HTML-en.asp?fileid=13204&lang=en
[Accessed 11 December 2020].

Fuglie, K. O. & Rada, N. E. (2013) *Resources, Policies and Agricultural Productivity in SubSaharan Africa*. Economic Research Report 145, U.S. Department of Agriculture, Economic Research Service.

Government of Kenya (GoK) (2007) *Kenya Vision 2030: A Globally Competitive and Prosperous Kenya*. Nairobi: Government Printer.

Government of Kenya (GoK) (2020) *Draft National Forest Policy, 2020*. 19 May 2020. Ministry of Environment and Forestry. Available at: https://policyvault.africa/wp-content/uploads/policy/KEN792.pdf [Accessed 25 October 2021].

Great Britain (1837) *Report of the Parliamentary Select Committee on Aboriginal Tribes (British settlements)*. London: W. Ball, A. Chambers, and Hatchard & Son.

IPCC (2007) Climate Change 2007: *Synthesis Report. Contribution of Working Groups I, II and III to the Fourth Assessment Report of the Intergovernmental Panel on Climate Change*. [Core Writing Team, Pachauri, R. K. and Reisinger, A. (eds.)]. Geneva, Switzerland: IPCC.

IPCC (2014) *Climate Change 2014: Synthesis Report. Contribution of Working Groups I, II and III to the Fifth Assessment Report of the Intergovernmental Panel on Climate Change* [Core Writing Team, R. K. Pachauri and L. A. Meyer (eds.)]. Geneva, Switzerland: IPCC.

KNCHR (Kenya National Commission on Human Rights) (2018) *The Report of the High-Level Independent Fact-Finding Mission to Embobut Forest in Elgeyo Marakwet County*. Nairobi: Kenya National Commission on Human Rights.

MEA (2005) *Millennium Ecosystem Assessment: Ecosystems and Human Well-Being*. Washington, DC: Island Press.

MEHI Centre (2021) *Pilliga Forest: Cultural Values and Threats from Coal and Gas*. MEHI Centre. Available at: https://www.wilderness.org.au /images/resources/Pilliga-Culture-Heritage-Report-2021.pdf [Accessed 4 December 2021].

Ndung'u Commission (2004) *Report of the Commission of Inquiry into the Illegal/Irregular Allocation of Public Land*. Nairobi: Government Printer.

Njonjo Commission (2002) *Report of the Commission of Inquiry into the Land Law Systems of Kenya*. Nairobi: Government Printer.

Odhengo, P., Korir, H., Muthini, D., Motur, W., Mazza, F., Van Caenegem, H., Bal, A., Mwangi, C. Mwithiga, L., Njoroge, S. and Wambua, M. (2021) *The Landscape of Climate Finance in Kenya on the Road to Implementing Kenya's NDC*. The Republic of Kenya: The National Treasury and Planning. Available at: https://www.climatepolicyinitiative.org/wp

-content/uploads/2021/03/The-Landscape-of-Climate-Finance-in
-Kenya.pdf [Accessed 10 October 2021].

Rumler, M. (2011) *Free, Prior and Informed Consent: A Review of Free, Prior and Informed Consent in Australia*. Melbourne: Oxfam, Australia.

Swammy, G. (1994) *Adjustment in Africa: Lessons from Country Case Studies*. Washington, DC: The World Bank.

Swynnerton, R. J. M. (1954) *The Swynnerton Report: A Plan to Intensify the Development of African Agriculture in Kenya*. Nairobi: Government Printer.

Taylor, C. and Meinshausen, M. (2014) Joint Report to the Land Court of Queensland on 'Climate Change – Emissions'. *Adani Mining Pty (Adani) v. Land Services of Coast and Country Inc & Ors.*

Troup, R. S. (1922) *Report on Forests in Kenya Colony*. London: Government of Kenya, by Crown Agents for the Colonies.

UN Environment Programme (UNEP) (2012) *The Role and Contribution of Montane Forests and Related Ecosystem Services to the Kenyan Economy*. Nairobi: UNEP.

UN Sub-Commission on Prevention of Discrimination and Protection of Minorities (1978, 4 July) *Study of the Question of the Prevention and Punishment of the Crime of Genocide*. Prepared by Mr. Nicodème Ruhashyankiko. E/CN.4/Sub.2/416.

Woodward, E. A. (1974) *Aboriginal Land Rights Commission: Second Report, April 1974*. Canberra: Australian Government Publishing Service.

World Bank Group (2015) *Kenya – Natural Resource Management Project: Progress Report to the Board of Executive Directors on the Implementation of Management's Action Plan in Response to the Inspection Panel Investigation Report*. Washington, DC: World Bank. Available at: http://documents.worldbank.org/curated/en/698141467987833169/Kenya-Natural-Resource-Management-Project-progress-report-to-the-Board-of-Executive-Directors-on-the-implementation-of-managements-action-plan-in-response-to-the-inspection-panel-investigation-report [Accessed 1 November 2019].

World Bank Group (2018) *Kenya Economic Update, April 2018, No. 17: Policy Options to Advance the Big 4*. Nairobi: World Bank.

Other primary sources

Adani. (n.d.) *Adani: We Help Build a Happy Nation*. Available at: https://www.adani.com/ [Accessed 19 October 2021].

Australian Bureau of Statistics (ABS) (2018a) *Life Tables for Aboriginal and Torres Strait Islander Australians.* Available at: https://www.abs.gov.au/statistics/people/aboriginal-and-torres-strait-islander-peoples/life-tables-aboriginal-and-torres-strait-islander-australians/2015-2017#acknowledgements [Accessed 1 September 2021].

Australian Bureau of Statistics (ABS) (2018b) *National Aboriginal and Torres Strait Islander Health Survey.* https://www.abs.gov.au/statistics/people/aboriginal-and-torres-strait-islander-peoples/national-aboriginal-and-torres-strait-islander-health-survey/2018-19#data-download [Accessed 3 September 2021].

Australian Bureau of Statistics (ABS) (2024) *Labour Force, Australia*, ABS. Available at: https://www.abs.gov.au/statistics/labour/employment-and-unemployment/labour-force-australia/jul-2024>. [Accessed 21 August 2024].

Australian Institute of Aboriginal and Torres Strait Islander Studies (AIATSIS) (2012) *Guidelines for Ethical Research in Australian Indigenous Studies: 2012.* Canberra: Australian Institute of Aboriginal and Torres Strait Islander Studies.

Australian Institute of Health and Welfare (AIHW) (2023) *Employment of First Nations people.* Available at: https://www.aihw.gov.au/reports/australias-welfare/indigenous-employment. [Accessed 21 August 2024].

Badawi, W. (2020) Letter to Kitum, 13 February.

Burragubba, A. (2018) High Noon in the Galilee. Aboriginal Law and Order, in Ritter, D. (ed.) *The Coal Truth: The Fight to Stop Adani, Defeat the Big Polluters and Reclaim Our Democracy.* Perth: UWA Publishing.

Burragubba, A. and Johnson, M. (2015) Letter to Ms. Victoria Tauli-Corpuz, Special Rapporteur on the Rights of Indigenous Peoples, 2 October. Available at: http://wanganjagalingou.com.au/wp-content/uploads/2015/10/Submission-to-the-Special-Rapporteur-on-Indigenous-Peoples-by-the-Wangan-and-Jagalingou-People-2-Oct-2015.pdf [Accessed 11 September 2021].

Collins, D. (1804) *An Account of the English Colony in New South Wales, from its first settlement in January 1788, to August 1801: with remarks on the dispositions, customs, manners, &c. of the native inhabitants of that country.* London: A. Strahan, for T. Cadell and W. Davies.

Commonwealth of Australia (2007) Parliamentary Debates, House of Representatives (2007, 7 August) Malcolm Brough, Minister for Families, Community Services and Indigenous Affairs and Minister Assisting the Prime Minister for Indigenous Affairs.

Department of Resources (2021, September) *Guide to Queensland's New Land Access Laws.* Brisbane: The State of Queensland. Available at:

https://www.resources.qld.gov.au/__data/assets/pdf_file/0018/1442223/guide-to-land-access-in-queensland.pdf [Accessed 27 November 2021].

Edwards, C. (2015) *Lighting Levels for Isolated Intersections: Leading to Safety Improvements* (Report No. MnDOT 2015–05). Center for Transportation Studies. Available at: http://www.cts.umn.edu/Publications/ResearchReports/reportdetail.html?id=2402 [Accessed 7 July 2020].

EEAS (1 January 2018) EU Suspends Its Support for Water Towers in View of Reported Human Rights Abuses [Press release]. Available at: https://eeas.europa.eu/headquarters/headquarters-homepage/38343/eu-suspends-its-support-water-towers-view-reported-human-rights-abuses_en [Accessed 31 July 2019].

Eliot, C. (1905). *The East Africa Protectorate*. London: Edward Arnold Grey, G. (1841). Journals of two expeditions of discovery in north-west and western Australia, Vol. II. London: T. and W. Boone.

European Commission and the High Representative of the Union of Foreign Affairs and Security Policy (EC) (2016, 17 October) *Implementing EU External Policy on Indigenous Peoples*. Available at: https://eeas.europa.eu/sites/eeas/files/swd_2016_340_f1_joint_staff_working_paper_en_v2_p1_865982.pdf [Accessed 10 September 2019].

IMF (2021) *IMF Executive Board Approves US$2.34 Billion ECF and EFF Arrangements for Kenya*. Available at: https://www.imf.org/en/News/Articles/2021/04/02/pr2198-kenya-imf-executive-board-approves-us-billion-ecf-and-eff-arrangements [Accessed 5 September 2021].

Johnston, H. (1902) *The Uganda Protectorate, Vols. I–II*. London: Hutchinson & Co.

Joseph, M. J. (2018, 4 January) Forest Is Our Ancestral Land, Sengwer Community Say Resisting Eviction. *Capital News*. Available at: https://www.capitalfm.co.ke/news/2018/01/forest-ancestral-land-sengwer-community-say-resisting-eviction/. [Accessed 16 July 2020].

Kimaiyo, E. (2020) Letter to Mr. Simon Mordue, EU Ambassador for Kenya, 10 June.

Kitum, P. K. (2020) Letter to Head of UNDP Kenya, 6 January.

KNBS (2020) *Economic Survey 2020, Kenya National Bureau of Statistics*. Available at: https://s3-eu-west-1.amazonaws.com/s3.sourceafrica.net/documents/119905/KNBS-Economic-Survey-2020.pdf [Accessed 10 August 2021].

KWTA (2019) *Elgeyo Hills Water Tower Ecosystem Conservation Plan: Plan Period Ten Years* (2020–2030) Nairobi: Kenya Water Tower Agency. Available at: https://watertowers.go.ke/wp-content/uploads/2021/02

/ELGEYO-HILLS-WATER-TOWER-ECOSYSTEM-CONSERVATION-PLAN
.pdf [Accessed 19 September 2021].

KWTA (2020, 1 October) *The Mau Task Force: Timeline Slider*. Nairobi:
Kenya Water Towers Agency. Available at: https://watertowers.go.ke
/timeline_slider_post/2008/ [Accessed 20 August 2021].

Lugard, F. D. (1922) *The Dual Mandate in British Tropical Africa*.
Edinburgh and London: William Blackwood and Sons.

Millennium Ecosystem Assessment (2005) *Ecosystems and Human
Well-Being: Current State and Trends*. Washington, DC: World
Resource Institute.

National Native Title Tribunal (NNTT) (2007) Githabul People's Native
Title Determination. National Native Title Tribunal. Northeaster New
South Wales, 29 November 2007. Available at: http://www.nntt.gov.au
/Information%20Publications/Determination%20brochure%20
Githabul%20people%20November%202007.pdf. [Accessed 23 May 2019].

Nature (1938) *An African Survey*, 142(3604), pp. 939–42.

NPI (n.d.) National Pollutant Inventory (NPI). Department of the
Environment and Energy. Australian Government, Canberra, ACT.
Available at: www.npi.gov.au. [Accessed 12 June 2020].

NSWALC (n.d.) *Land Rights: The Story So Far*. New South Wales
Aboriginal Land Council. Available at: https://alc.org.au/newsroom
/land-rights-the-story-so-far/ [Accessed 1 December 2021].

The Observatory of Economic Complexity (OEC) (n.d.) *Country Profile:
Kenya*. OEC. Available at: https://oec.world/en/profile/country/ken
[Accessed 10 August 2021].

OHCHR (2018, January 15) *Indigenous Rights Must Be Respected during
Kenya Climate Change Project, Say UN Experts*. Available at:
https://www.ohchr.org/EN/NewsEvents/Pages/DisplayNews.aspx
?NewsID=22584&LangID=E.

Pritchard, J. C. (1839) *On the Extinction of Human Races: The Practicability of
Civilizing Aboriginal Populations*. London: Aborigines' Protection Society.

The Queensland Cabinet and Ministerial Directory (2013) *Media
Statement*. Available at: http://statements.qld.gov.au/Statement/2013
/11/7/plan-todevelop-galilee-basin-unveiled [Accessed 5
September 2019].

Tauli-Corpuz, V. (2018) Report of the Special Rapporteur on the Rights of
Indigenous Peoples. Human Rights Council. 10 August 2018.
Available at: https://www.ohchr.org/Documents/Issues/IPeoples/SR
/A.HRC.39.17.pdf. [Accessed 4 November 2021].

Tauli-Corpuz, V., Alcorn, J. and Molnar, A. (2018) *Cornered by Protected
Areas: Replacing 'Fortress' Conservation with Rights-Based Approaches
Helps Bring Justice for Indigenous Peoples and Local Communities,*

Reduces Conflict, and Enables Cost-effective Conservation and Climate Action. [online] Rights and Resource Initiative. Washington, DC. Available at: https://rightsandresources.org/wp-content/uploads/2018/06/Cornered-by-PAs-Brief_RRI_June-2018.pdf [Accessed 21 September 2021].

UKNA/CAB/24/248 – 'The Kenya Land Commission Report, 1934'. Scribd [online] Available at: https://www.scribd.com/doc/74835533/CAB-24-248-The-Kenya-Land-Commission-Report-1934 [Accessed 6 August 2021].

UN REDD (n.d) *UN REDD Programme*. Available at: https://www.un-redd.org [Accessed: 7 October 2024].

UNEP (United Nations Environment Programme) (2009) *Global Green New Deal Policy Brief*. Geneva: United Nations Environmental Programme.

World Bank (2000) *Can Africa Claim the 21st Century?* Washington, DC.

World Bank (2007, 7 March) *Project Appraisal Document on a Proposed Credit in the amount of SDR 46.0 MILLION (US$68.5 million equivalent) to the Government of Kenya for a Natural Resource Management Project*. Available at: http://documents.worldbank.org/curated/en/584531468285619738/pdf/37982.pdf [Accessed 15 June 2020].

World Bank (2021a) *Country Profile. World Development Indicators: Kenya*. Available at: https://databank.worldbank.org/views/reports/reportwidget.aspx?Report_Name=CountryProfile&Id=b450fd57&tbar=y&dd=y&inf=n&zm=n&country=KEN [Accessed 21 August 2021].

World Bank (2021b, March 30) *Kenya Overview: Development, News, Research, Data*. World Bank. Available at: https://www.worldbank.org/en/country/kenya/overview [Accessed 6 August 2021].

World Bank (2021c) *World Development Indicators: Kenya*. Available at: https://data.worldbank.org/?locations=KE [Accessed 6 August 2021].

World Commission on Environment and Development (WCED) (1987) *Our Common Future*. Oxford: Oxford University Press.

Field interviews

Anonymous, Githabul elder, no. 1. Author interview, 23/01/2017.
Anonymous, Githabul elder, no. 2. Author interview, 23/01/2017.
Anonymous, Githabul elder, no. 3. Author interview, 23/01/2017.
Anonymous, Githabul elder, no. 4. Author interview, 23/01/2017.
Anonymous, Gomeroi elder, no. 1. Author interview, 27/02/2017.
Anonymous, Gomeroi elder, no. 2. Author interview, 21/03/2017.
Anonymous, member of the Sengwer. Author interview, 18/03/2020.

Anonymous, member of the Sengwer. Author interview, 09/12/2020.
Anonymous, member of the Sengwer. Author interview, 15/12/2020.
Anonymous, member of the Sengwer. Author interview, 24/12/2020.
Anonymous, member of the Sengwer. Author interview, 28/12/2020.
Anonymous, member of the Sengwer. Author interview, 25/10/2021.
Esposito, A. W&J Council's official advisor and spokesperson. Author interview, 10/02/2017.
Gaillard, I., Lismore carpenter. Author interview, 23/01/2017.
Gibson, P., historian of Australian labour and Aboriginal history. Author interview, 10/02/2017.
Hicki, V., Gomeroi woman, Walgett, NSW. Author interview, 06/02/17.
Jenkyn, J., local chinchilla farmer, QLD, Author interview, 07/03/17.
Kibet, P., member of the Sengwer. Author interview, 09/10/2016.
Kimaiyo, E., member of the Sengwer. Author interview, 07/08/2020.
Kimaiyo, E., member of the Sengwer. Author interview, 11/08/2020.
Lloyd-Smith, M., senior advisor to Australia's National Toxics Network. Author interview, 26/01/17.
McCarron, G., Western Downs GP, Australia. Author interview, 09/03/17.
Parker, G. P., Tara resident, Author interview, 03/03/17.

Secondary literature

Abed, M. (2006) Clarifying the Concept of Genocide. *Metaphilosophy*, 37(3–4), pp. 308–30.
Adams, W. and Mulligan, M. (2003) Introduction, in Adams, W. and Mulligan, M. (eds.) *Decolonizing Nature*. London: Earthscan Publications.
Adesina, J. O., Graham, Y. and Olukoshi, A. (2006) *Africa and Development: Challenges in the New Millennium*. London: Zed Books.
Adhikari, M. (2015) *Genocide on Settler Frontiers: When Hunter-Gatherers and Commercial Stock Farmers Clash*. Oxford: Berghahn Books.
Agbese, P. and Kieh Jr, G. (2007) *Reconstituting the State in Africa*. New York: Palgrave Macmillan.
Ahmed, N. (2014) Carbon Colonialism: How the Fight against Climate Change is Displacing Africans. *Vice*, 1 December. Available at: https://www.vice.com/en_us/article/kbzn9w/carbon-colonialism-the -new-scramble-for-africa [Accessed 10 June 2020].
Ahram, A. A. (2015) Development, Counterinsurgency, and the Destruction of the Iraqi Marshes. *International Journal of Middle East Studies*, 47(3), pp. 447–66.

AIATSIS (n.d.) *The Barunga Statement*. Available at: https://aiatsis.gov
.au/explore/barunga-statement [Accessed 31 October 2021].

Ake, C. (1981) *A Political Economy of Africa*. London: Heinemann.

Akinyi, C. (2021) Kenya's Public Debt Mountain: Is It Sustainable?
Business Daily, https://www.businessdailyafrica.com/bd/sponsored
/kenya-s-public-debt-mountain-is-it-sustainable–3246648 [Accessed
5 September 2021].

Alatas, S. F. (2000) An Introduction to the Idea of Alternative Discourses.
Southeast Asian Journal of Social Science 28(1), pp. 1–12.

Alfred, T. (1999) *Peace, Power, Righteousness*. Oxford: Oxford University
Press.

Alston, P. (1998) Individual Complainants: Historical Perspectives and
the International Convention of Economic, Social and Cultural Rights,
in Pritchard, S. (ed.) *Indigenous Peoples, the United Nations and
Human Rights*. Leichhardt, NSW: Federation Press.

Althusser, L. (1994) Ideology and Ideological State Apparatuses, in Žižek,
S. (ed.) *Mapping Ideology*. London: Verso.

Altman, J. (2005) Development Options on Aboriginal Land: Sustainable
Indigenous Hybrid Economies in the Twenty-First Century, in Taylor,
L., et al. (ed.) *The Power of Knowledge: The Resonance of Tradition*.
Canberra: Aboriginal Studies Press.

Altman, J. (2007) In the Name of the Market?, in Altman, J. and Hinkson,
M. (eds.) *Coercive Reconciliation: Stabilise, Normalise, Exit Aboriginal
Australia*. North Carlton, Victoria: Arena Publications.

Altman, J. (2009a) Indigenous Communities, Miners and the States,
in Altman, J. and Martin, D. (eds.) *Power, Culture, Economy Indigenous
Australians and Mining*. Research Monograph No 30. Centre for
Aboriginal Economic Policy Research (CAEPR) Australian National
University. Canberra: ANU E Press.

Altman, J. (2009b) Contestations over Development, in Altman, J. and
Martin, D. (eds.) *Power, Culture, Economy: Indigenous Australians
and Mining*, Research Monograph No. 30, Centre for Aboriginal
Economic Policy Research (CAEPR), Australian National University,
Canberra.

Altman, J. (2012) Indigenous Rights, Corporations, and the Australian
State, in Sawyer, S. and Gomez, E. (eds.) *The Politics of Resource
Extraction*. Basingstoke: Palgrave Macmillan.

Altman, J. (2013) Land Rights and Development in Australia: Caring for,
Benefiting from, Governing the Indigenous Estate, in Ford, L. and
Rowse, T. (eds.) *Between Indigenous and Settler Governance*. New York:
Routledge.

Altman, J. (2018) Raphael Lemkin in Remote Australia: The Logic of Cultural Genocide and Homelands. *Oceania*, 88(3), pp. 336–59.

Altman, J., Biddle, N. and Hunter, B. (2009) Prospects for 'Closing the Gap' in Socioeconomic Outcomes for Indigenous Australians. *Australian Economic History Review*, 49(3), pp. 225–51.

Altman, J. and Sanders, W. (1991) From Exclusion to Dependence: Aborigines and the Welfare State in Australia. *CAEPR Discussion Paper* (1). Canberra: Centre for Aboriginal Economic Policy Research, The Australian National University.

Altvater, E. (ed.) (1996). Ecological and Economic Modalities of Time and Space, in *Is Capitalism Sustainable?* New York: Guilford.

Alvares, C. (1992) *Science, Development and Violence: The Revolt against Modernity*. Oxford: Oxford University Press.

Amin, S. (1974) *Neo-Colonialism in West Africa*. Harmondsworth: Penguin.

Amnesty International (AI) (2018, May 15) *Families Torn Apart: Forced Eviction of Indigenous People in Embobut Forest, Kenya*. Amnesty International. United Kingdom. Available at: https://www.amnesty.org/en/documents/afr32/8340/2018/en/ [Accessed 9 August 2020].

Amnesty International Kenya (AI) (2020, July 13) *Burning of 28 Sengwer Homes in Embobut Forest, Elgeyo Marakwet. Amnesty International Kenya*. [Press release]. [online] Available at: https://www.amnesty kenya.org/burning-of-28-sengwer-homes-in-embobut-forest-elgeyo -marakwet/ [Accessed 13 May 2019].

Anaya, S. (2004) *Indigenous Peoples in International Law*. Oxford: Oxford University Press.

Anderson, D. (1984) Depression, Dust Bowl, Demography, and Drought: The Colonial State and Soil Conservation in East Africa during the 1930s. *African Affairs*, 83(332), pp. 321–43.

Anderson, D. (2000) Master and Servant in Colonial Kenya. *The Journal of African History*, 41(3), pp. 459–85.

Anderson, D. (2005) *Histories of the Hanged: The Dirty War in Kenya and the End of Empire*. London: Weidenfeld & Nicolson. [Kindle Edition].

Anderson, D. M. (1987) Managing the Forest: The Conservation History of Lembus, Kenya, 1904–63, in Anderson, D. and Grove. R (eds.) *Conservation in Africa: People, Policies, and Practice*. Cambridge: Cambridge University Press, pp. 249–68.

Anderson, D, M. (2016) The Beginning of Time? Evidence for Catastrophic Drought in Baringo in the Early Nineteenth Century. *Journal of Eastern African Studies*, 10(1), pp. 45–66.

Anderson, K. (2016a) The Hidden Agenda: How Veiled Techno-Utopias Shore up the Paris Agreement. [Blog] *kevinanderson.info*. Available at: http://kevinanderson.info/blog/the-hidden-agenda-how-veiled-techno -utopias-shore-up-the-paris-agreement/ [Accessed 3 December 2016].

Anderson, K. B. (2016b) *Marx at the Margins*. Chicago: The University of Chicago Press.

Angus, I. (2013) The Myth of 'Environmental Catastrophism'. *Monthly Review*. Available at: http://monthlyreview.org/2013/09/01/myth -environmental-catastrophism/ [Accessed 14 November 2016].

Angus, I. (2016a) *Facing the Anthropocene*. New York: Monthly Review Press.

Angus, I. (2016b) Planetary Crisis: 'We Are Not All in This Together', transcript, *Climate & Capitalism*, 7 May. Available at: https://climateandcapitalism.com/2016/05/25/planetary-crisis-we-are -not-all-in-this-together/ [Accessed 16 November 2016].

Angus, I. (2016c) 'Explaining the Anthropocene: An Interview with Ian Angus,' *Climate and Capitalism*. Available at: http://climateand capitalism.com/2016/05/18/explaining-anthropocene-interview-with -ian-angus/ [Accessed 20 November 2016].

Angus, I. (2016d) In Defense of Ecological Marxism: John Bellamy Foster Responds to a Critic. [online] *Climate and Capitalism*. Available at: https://climateandcapitalism.com/2016/06/06/in-defense-of-ecological -marxism-john-bellamy-foster-responds-to-a-critic/ [Accessed 5 August 2020].

Anthony, T. (2003) Postcolonial Feudal Hauntings of Northern Australian Cattle Stations. *Law Text Culture*, 7, pp. 277–307.

Anthony, T. (2004) Labour Relations on Northern Cattle Stations: Feudal Exploitation and Accommodation. *The Drawing Board: Australian Review of Public Affairs*, 4(3), pp. 117–36.

Anthony, T. (2007) Reconciliation and Conciliation: The Irreconcilable Dilemma of the 1965 'Equal' Wage Case for Aboriginal Station Workers. *Labour History*, 93, p. 15–34.

Anthony, T. (2007) Unmapped Territory: Indigenous Stolen Wages on Cattle Stations. *Australian Indigenous Law Review*, 11(1), pp. 4–29.

Apostolopoulou, E. and Adams, W. A. (2017) Biodiversity Offsetting and Conservation: Reframing Nature to Save It. *Oryx*, 51(1), pp. 23–31.

Arfat, S. (2013) Globalisation and Human Rights: An Overview of Its Impact. *American Journal of Humanities and Social Sciences*, 1(1), pp. 18–24.

Arrighi, G. (2007) *Adam Smith in Beijing: Lineages of the Twenty-First Century*. London: Verso.

Asch, M., et al. (2004) On the Return of the Native: Discussion. *Current Anthropology*, 45(2), pp. 261–7.

Aseka, E. (2000) The Post-Colonial State and the Colonial Legacy, Ogot, B. A. and Ochieng, W. R. (eds.) *Kenya: The Making of a Nation: A Hundred Years of Kenya's History, 1895–1995*. Maseno: Institute of Research and Postgraduate Studies.

Ashman, S. (2006) *Historical Materialism*, 14(4), pp. 301–7.

Attwood, B. (1994) The Paradox of Australian Aboriginal History. *Book Eleven*, 38(1), pp. 118–37.

Attwood, B. (2017a) The Founding of Aboriginal History and the Forming of Aboriginal History. *Aboriginal History*, 36, pp. 119–71.

Attwood, B. (2017b) Denial in a Settler Society: The Australian Case. *History Workshop Journal*, 84(1), pp. 24–43.

Austin-Broos, D. (2009) *Arrernte Present, Arrernte Past: Invasion, Violence and Imagination in Indigenous Central Australia*. Chicago and London: University of Chicago Press.

Austin-Broos, D. (2011) *A Different Inequality*. Crows Nest, NSW: Allen & Unwin.

Babington, C. (2005) Some GOP Legislators Hit Jarring Notes in Addressing Katrina, *Washington Post*, 10 September [online] Available at: http://www.washingtonpost.com/wp-dyn/content/article/2005/09/09/AR2005090901930.html [Accessed 29 November 2016].

Baker, E. (1989) 'A Scratch with a Bear's Paw': Anglo-Indian Land Deeds in Early Maine. *Ethnohistory*, 36(3), pp. 235–56.

Ballard, C. (2006) Strange Alliance: Pygmies in the Colonial Imaginary, *World Archaeology*, 38(1), pp. 133–51.

Balmford, A. et al. (2003) Global Variation in Terrestrial Conservation Costs, Conservation Benefits and Unmet Conservation Needs. *PNAS*, 100(3), pp. 1046–50.

Banner, S. (2005) Why Terra Nullius? Anthropology and Property Law in Early Australia. *Law and History Review*, 23(1), pp. 95–131.

Bargh, M. (2007) *Resistance: An Indigenous Response to Neoliberalism*. Wellington: Huia Publishers.

Barker, G. (2009) *The Agricultural Revolution in Prehistory*. Oxford: Oxford University Press.

Barnett, D. and Njama, K. (1966) *Mau Mau from Within*. London: Macgibbon & Kee.

Barta, T. (1987) Relations of Genocide: Land and Lives in the Colonization of Australia, in Walliman, I. and Dobrowski, M. (eds.) *Genocide and the Modern Age: Etiology and Case Studies of Mass Death*. New York: Greenwood Press.

Barta, T. (2007) On Pain of Extinction: Laws of Nature and History in Darwin, Marx and Arendt, in King, R. H. and Stone, D. (eds.)

Imperialism, Slavery, Race and Genocide: The Legacy of Hannah Arendt. New York: Berghahn.

Barta, T. (2008a). Three Responses to 'Can There Be Genocide Without the Intent to Commit Genocide?', *Journal of Genocide Research*, 10(1), pp. 111–18.

Barta, T. (2008b) They Appear Actually to Vanish from the Face of the Earth. Aborigines and the European Project in Australia Felix. *Journal of Genocide Research*, 10(4), pp. 519–39.

Barta, T. (2010) Decent Disposal: Australian Historians and the Recovery of Genocide, in Stone, D. (ed.) *The Historiography of Genocide.* Basingstoke: Palgrave Macmillan.

Bartlett, J. (2002) *Bartlett's Familiar Quotations.* Boston: Little Brown.

Bates, D. (1944) *The Passing of the Aborigines.* London: John Murray.

Bates, R. H. (1987) The Agrarian Origins of Mau Mau: A Structural Account. *Agricultural History* 61(1), pp. 1–28.

Bauman, Z. (1990) *Modernity and the Holocaust.* Ithaca, NY: Cornell University Press.

Bebbington, A. et al. (2008) Contention and Ambiguity: Mining and the Possibility of Development. *Development and Change* 39(6), pp. 887–914.

Beckett, J. (1988) Aboriginality, Citizenship and Nation State. *Social Analysis* 24, pp. 3–18.

Beckett, J. (1990) Welfare Colonialism: A Reply to Jeremy Long. *Oceania* 60(3), pp. 238.

Beckett, J. (1999) *Torres Strait Islanders.* Cambridge: Cambridge University Press.

Bedford, D. and Irving, D. (2000) *The Tragedy of Progress: Marxism, Modernity, and the Aboriginal Question.* Halifax: Fernwood.

Behre-Dolbear Group Inc. (2014) Ranking of Countries for Mining Investments: 'Where Not to Invest'. Available at: https://www.dolbear.com/wp-content/uploads/2016/04/2014-Where-toInvest.pdf. [Accessed 25 November 2021].

Beilharz, P. and Cox, L. (2007) Review Essay: Settler Capitalism Revisited. *Book Eleven* 88(1), pp. 112–24.

Bennett, S. (1991) *Aborigines and Political Power.* North Sydney: Allen & Unwin.

Benson, T. G. (1964) *Kikuyu-English Dictionary.* Oxford: Clarendon Press.

Bentley, G. C. (1987) Ethnicity and Practice. *Comparative Studies in Society and History* 29, pp. 24–55.

Benton, T. (1989) Marxism and Natural Limits. *New Left Review* 178, pp. 51–86.

Benton, T. (ed.) (1996) *The Greening of Marxism.* New York: Guilford Press.

Berg-Schlosser, D. (1994) Ethnicity, Social Classes and the Political Process in Kenya, in Oyugi, W. O. (ed.) *Politics and Administration in East Africa*. Nairobi: East African Educational Publishers.

Berman, B. (1990) *Control and Crisis in Colonial Kenya: The Dialectic of Domination*. London: James Currey.

Berman, B. and Lonsdale, J. (1980) Crisis of Accumulation, Coercion and the Colonial State: The Development of the Labor Control Systems in Kenya, 1919–1929. *Canadian Journal of African Studies* 14, pp. 55–81.

Berman, B. and Lonsdale, J. (1992) *Unhappy Valley: Conflict in Kenya and Africa*. London: James Currey.

Bernardi, G. (1997) The CDEP Scheme: A Case of Welfare Colonialism. *Australian Aboriginal Studies* 2, pp. 36–46.

Berry, S. (1992) Hegemony on a Shoestring: Indirect Rule and Access to Agricultural Land. *Africa* 62(3), pp. 327–55.

Bhambra, Gurminder K. (2014) *Connected Sociologies*. London: Bloomsbury.

Birdsell, J. (1970) Local Group Composition Among the Australian Aborigines: A Critique of the Evidence from Fieldwork Conducted since 1930. *Current Anthropology* 11(2), pp. 115–42.

Blackburn, R. H. (1974) The Okiek and Their History. *Azania* 9, pp. 139–57.

Blackburn, R. H. (1996) Fission, Fusion, and Foragers in East Africa: Micro- and Macroprocesses of Diversity and Integration among Okiek Groups, in Kent, S. (ed.) *Cultural Diversity among Twentieth-Century Foragers: An African Perspective*. Cambridge: Cambridge University Press.

Blaikie, P. and Brookfield, H. (eds.) (1987) *Land Degradation and Society*. London: Methuen.

Bloch, J. and Fitzgerald, P. (1984) *British Intelligence and Covert Action*. London: Brandon.

Blomley, N. (2003) Law, Property, and the Geography of Violence: The Frontier, the Survey, and the Grid. *Annals of the Association of American Geographers* 93(1), pp. 121–41.

Blum, W. (1986) *The CIA: A Forgotten History*. London: Zed Books.

Blum, W. (2002) *Rogue State, A Guide to the World's Only Superpower*. London: Zed Books.

Böhm, S. and Dabhi, S. (eds.) (2010) *Upsetting the Offset*. London: MayFly Books.

Bond, P. (2006) *Looting Africa: The Economics of Exploitation*. London: Zed Books.

Braun, B. (2002) *The Intemperate Rainforest*. Minneapolis: University of Minnesota Press.

Brenner, R. (2006) *The Economics of Global Turbulence: The Advanced Capitalist Economies from Long Boom to Long Downturn, 1945–2005*. Verso Books. London.

Brett, E. A. (1973) *Colonization and Underdevelopment in East Africa: The Politics of Economic Change, 1919–1939*. New York: NOK Publishers.

Brockington, D. and Duffy, R. (2010) Capitalism and Conservation: The Production and Reproduction of Biodiversity Conservation, *Antipode* 42(3), pp. 469–84.

Brook, D. (1998) Environmental Genocide: Native Americans and Toxic Waste. *American Journal of Economics and Sociology*, 57(1), pp. 105–13.

Broome, R. (1995) Victoria, in McGrath, A. (ed.) *Contested Ground*. St. Leonards, NSW: Allen & Unwin.

Brown, N. A. (2013) The Logic of Settler Accumulation in a Landscape of Perpetual Vanishing. *Settler Colonial Studies* 4(1), pp. 1–26.

Bryman, A. (2008) *Social Research Methods*. New York: Oxford University Press.

Buell, R. L. (1928) The Native Problem in Africa, Vol. I. New York: Macmillan.

Bukharin, N. (1929) *Imperialism and World Economy*. London: Martin Lawrence.

Burkett, P. (1990). Fusing Red and Green. *Monthly Review*. [online]. Available at: http://monthlyreview.org/1999/02/01/fusing-red-and -green/ [Accessed 12 December 2016].

Burkett, P. (1996) On Some Misconceptions about Nature and Marx's Critique of Political Economy. *Capitalism, Nature, Socialism* 7, pp. 64–6.

Burkett, P. (1997) Nature in Marx Reconsidered. *Organization & Environment* 10(2), pp. 164–83.

Burkett, P. (2014) *Marx and Nature*. New York: St. Martin's Press.

Burkett, P. (2018) Transformation Problem Unravelled. *Monthly Review*. [online] Monthly Review. Available at: https://mronline. org/2018/07/04/transformation-problem-unraveled/ [Accessed 12 February 2020].

Burnside, S. (2008) 'We're from the Mining Industry and We're Here to Help': The Impact of the Rhetoric of Crisis on Future Act Negotiations. *Australian Indigenous Law Review* 12(2), pp. 54–65.

Busbridge, R. (2017) Israel-Palestine and the Settler Colonial 'Turn': From Interpretation to Decolonization. *Theory, Culture & Society* 35(1), pp. 91–115.

Butlin, N. G. (1993) *Economics and the Dreamtime: A Hypothetical History*. Melbourne: Cambridge University Press.

Byrne, D. R. (2003) Nervous Landscapes: Race and Space in Australia. *Journal of Social Archaeology* 3(2), pp. 169–93.

Cain, P. J. and Hopkins, A. G. (1993) *British Imperialism: Innovation and Expansion, 1688–1914*. London: Longman.

Calleb, O. D. (2021) *Kenyan Debt Unsustainable and Has Reached a Crisis Level – Says Kenyan Peasants League: Via Campesina*. Available at: https://viacampesina.org/en/kenyan-debt-unsustainable-and-has-reached-a-crisis-level-says-kenyan-peasants-league/#_ftn2 [Accessed 5 September 2021].

Callinicos, A. (2009) *Imperialism and Global Political Economy*. Cambridge: Polity Press.

Campbell, A. (2005) The Birth of Neoliberalism in the United States: A Reorganisation of Capitalism, in Saad-Filho, A. and Johnston, D. (eds.) *Neoliberalism*. London: Pluto Press.

Campbell, C. (2007) *Race and Empire: Eugenic in Colonial Kenya*. Oxford: Manchester University Press.

Card, C. (2003). Genocide and Social Death. *Hypatia* 18(1), pp. 63–79.

Card, C. (2010) *Confronting Evils: Terrorism, Torture, Genocide*. Cambridge: Cambridge University Press.

Carraro, V. (2019) Promoting Compliance with Human Rights: The Performance of the United Nations' Universal Periodic Review and Treaty Bodies. *International Studies Quarterly* 63(4), pp. 1079–93.

Cassotta, S., Cueva, V. and Raftopoulos, M. (2021) Australia: Regulatory, Human Rights and Economic Challenges and Opportunities of Large-Scale Mining Projects: A Case Study of the Carmichael Coal Mine. *Environmental Policy and Law* 50(4–5), pp. 357–72.

Castan Centre for Human Rights Law (n.d.) What is the Northern Territory Intervention? *Monash University*. Available at: https://www.monash.edu/law/research/centres/castancentre/our-areas-of-work/indigenous/the-northern-territory-intervention/the-northern-territory-intervention-an-evaluation/what-is-the-northern-territory-intervention [Accessed 3 December 2021].

Castle, R., and Hagan, J. (1998a) Settlers and the State: The Creation of an Aboriginal workforce in Australia. *Aboriginal History* 22, pp. 24–35.

Castle, R., and Hagan, J. (1998b) Regulation of Aboriginal Labour in Queensland: Protectors, Agreements and Trust Accounts 1897–1965. *Labour History* 72, p. 66.

Castree, N. (2008) Neoliberalising Nature: The Logics of Deregulation and Reregulation. *Environment and Planning A: Economy and Space* 40(1), pp. 131–52.

Cavanagh, C. J. (2016) Anthropos into Humanitas: Civilizing Violence, Scientific Forestry, and the 'Dorobo Question' in Eastern Africa. *Environment and Planning D: Society and Space* 35(4), pp. 694–713.

Cavanagh, C. J. (2017) *Plague of Bureaucracies: Producing and Territorializing Difference in East Africa, 1888–1940* [PhD thesis]. Norwegian University of Life Sciences, Ås.

Cavanagh, C. J. (2018a) Land, Natural Resources and the State in Kenya's Second Republic, in Adeniran A. and Ikuteyijo L. (eds.) *Africa Now!* Palgrave Macmillan.

Cavanagh, C. J. (2018b) Critical Ecosystem Infrastructure? Governing the Forests – Water Nexus in the Kenyan Highlands, in Boelens, R., Perreault, T. and Vos, J. (eds.) *Water Justice*. Cambridge: Cambridge University Press.

Cavanagh, C. J. (2019) Dying Races, Deforestation and Drought: The Political Ecology of Social Darwinism in Kenya Colony's Western Highlands. *Journal of Historical Geography* 66, pp. 93–103.

Cavanagh, C. and Benjaminsen, T. A. (2014) Virtual Nature, Violent Accumulation: The 'Spectacular Failure' of Carbon Offsetting at a Ugandan National Park. *Geoforum* 56, pp. 55–65.

Cavanagh, C. and Himmelfarb, D. (2015) 'Much in Blood and Money': Necropolitical Ecology on the Margins of the Uganda Protectorate. *Antipode* 47(1), pp. 55–73.

Ceballos, G., Ehrlich, P., Barnosky, A., García, A., Pringle, R. and Palmer, T. (2015) Accelerated Modern Human–Induced Species Losses: Entering the Sixth Mass Extinction. *Science Advances* 1(5), pp. 1–5.

Cerone, J. (2010) African Commission on Human and Peoples' Rights: Centre for Minority Rights Development (Kenya) and Minority Rights Group International on Behalf of Endorois Welfare Council v. Kenya. *International Legal Materials* 49(3), pp. 858–906.

Chabal, P. and Daloz, J. (1999) *Africa Works: Disorder as Political Instrument*. Oxford: Oxford University Press.

Chang, C. (1982) Nomads without Cattle: East African Foragers in Historical Perspective, in Lee, R. and Leacock, E. (eds.) *Politics and History in Band Societies*. Cambridge: Cambridge University Press.

Chant, S. and McIlwaine, C. (2009) *Geographies of Development in the 21st Century*. Cheltenham, UK: Edward Elgar Publishing.

Charmaz, K. (2006) *Constructing Grounded Theory: A Practical Guide through Qualitative Analysis*. London: Sage Publications.

Chege, J., Ngui, D. and Kimuyu, P. (2014) Scoping Paper on Kenyan Manufacturing. *WIDER Working Paper* 2014/136. Helsinki: UNU-WIDER.

Chesterman, J. and Douglas, H. (2004) Their Ultimate Absorption: Assimilation in 1930s Australia. *Journal of Australian Studies* 28(81), pp. 47–58.

Chesterman, J. and Galligan, B. (1998) *Citizens without Rights*. Cambridge: Cambridge University Press.

Choonara, J. (2013) Neoliberalism and the British Working Class: A Reply to Neil Davidson, *International Socialism* 140 [online]. Available at: http://isj.org.uk/neoliberalism-and-the-british-working-class-a-reply-to-neil-davidson/#140hardychoonara3

Churchill, W. (2001) *A Little Matter of Genocide*. San Francisco: City Lights Publisher.

Clark, B. and Foster, J. B. (2009) Ecological Imperialism and the Global Metabolic Rift: Unequal Exchange and the Guano/Nitrates Trade. *International Journal of Comparative Sociology* 50(3–4), pp. 311–34.

Clark, B. and Foster, J. B. (2010) Marx's Ecology in the 21st Century. *World Review of Political Economy* 1(1), pp. 142–156.

Clark, B. and Foster, J. (2016) Marx's Ecology and the Left. *Monthly Review*. [online] Monthly Review. Available at: http://monthlyreview.org/2016/06/01/marxs-ecology-and-the-left/#fn32 [Accessed 11 December 2016].

Clark, B. and York, R. (2005) Carbon Metabolism: Global Capitalism, Climate Change, and the Biospheric Rift. *Theory and Society* 34(4), pp. 391–428.

Cleary, P. (2011) *Too Much Luck: The Mining Boom and Australia's Future*. Melbourne: Black.

Cleary, P. (2012) *Mine-Field: The Dark Side of Australia's Resources Rush*. Collingwood: Black Inc. [kindle].

Code, B. (2013) CSG protesters in the Northern Rivers have an opponent many didn't expect. The NSW Aboriginal Land Council wants to prospect for gas in the area, saying its people need a share of the profits from coal seam gas. *SBS News*, 28 August 2013. Available at: https://www.sbs.com.au/news/nsw-aboriginal-land-council-battles-for-csg-fair-share [Accessed 4 December 2021].

Collins, P. H. (2000) *Black Feminist Thought*. London: Routledge.

Cook, S. (2004) *Understanding Commodity Cultures*. Lanham, MD: Rowman and Littlefield.

Cooper, F. (2010) Writing the History of Development. *Journal of Modern European History* 8(1), pp. 5–23.

Coray, M. (1978) The Kenya Land Commission and the Kikuyu of Kiambu. *Agricultural History* 52(1), pp. 179–93.

Corbett, T. and O'Faircheallaigh, C. (2006) Unmasking Native Title: The National Native Title Tribunal's Application of the NTA's Arbitration Provisions. *University of Western Australia Law Review* 33(1), pp. 153–77.

Corfield, F. D. (1960) *Origins and Growth of Mau Mau: An Historical Survey*. Nairobi: Colony and Protectorate of Kenya.

Corson, C. and MacDonald, K. I. (2012) Enclosing the Global Commons: The Convention on Biological Diversity and Green Grabbing. *Journal of Peasant Studies* 39(2), pp. 263–83.

Coulthard, G. (2007) Subjects of Empire: Indigenous Peoples and the 'Politics of Recognition' in Canada. *Contemporary Political Theory* 6(4), pp. 437–60.

Coulthard, G. (2014) *Red Skin, White Masks*. Minneapolis: University of Minnesota Press.

Cowlishaw, G. (1992) Studying Aborigines: Changing Canons in Anthropology and History. *Journal of Australian Studies* 16(35), pp. 20–31.

Cowlishaw, G. (2006) On 'Getting It Wrong': Collateral Damage in the History Wars, *Australian Historical Studies* 37(127), pp. 181–202.

Cranstone, B. A. L. (1973) *The Australian Aborigines*. London: The Trustees of the British Museum.

Crook, M. (2013) The Mau Mau Genocide: A Neo-Lemkinian Analysis. *Journal of Human Rights in the Commonwealth* 1(1), pp. 18–37.

Crook, M. and Patel, R. (2012) *At Rio+20, the Green Economy Won't Save the Planet. But Green Democracy Will.* [online] Available at: https://sas-space.sas.ac.uk/4838/1/Opinion_piece_06_12.pdf [Accessed 4 December 2016].

Crook, M. and Short, D. (2014) Marx, Lemkin and the Genocide–Ecocide Nexus. *The International Journal of Human Rights* 18(3), pp. 298–319.

Crook, M. and Short, D. (2019) A Political Economy of Genocide in Australia: The Architecture of Dispossession Then and Now, in Bachman, J. S. (ed.) *Cultural Genocide: Law, Politics, and Global Manifestations.* London: Routledge.

Crook, M. and Short, D. (2020) Developmentalism and the Genocide–Ecocide Nexus, *Journal of Genocide Research* 23(2), pp. 162–188.

Crook, M. and Short, D. (2023) Greenwashed Relations of Genocide, in Long, A. M., Lynch, J. M. and Stretesky, B. P. (eds.) *Handbook of Inequality and the Environment*. Cheltenham: Edward Elgar Publishing.

Crook, M., Short, D. and South, N. (2018) Ecocide, Genocide, Capitalism and Colonialism: Consequences for Indigenous Peoples and Glocal Ecosystems Environments. *Theoretical Criminology* 22(3), pp. 298–317.

Crosby, A. (2004) *Ecological imperialism*. Cambridge: Cambridge University Press.

Crutzen, P, J. and Stoermer, E F. (2000) The Anthropocene, *Global Change Newsletter*, 1 May 2000.

Culhane, D. (1998) *The Pleasure of the Crown: Anthropology, Law and First Nations*. Vancouver: Talon Books.

Curthoys, A. (2012) Taking Liberty: Towards a New Political Historiography of Settler Self-Government and Indigenous Activism, in Fullagar, K. (ed.) *The Atlantic World in the Antipodes*. Newcastle: Cambridge Scholars Publishing.

Curthoys, A. (2015) Indigenous Dispossession and Pastoral Employment in Western Australia during the Nineteenth Century: Implications for Understanding Colonial Forms of Genocide, in Adhikari, M. (ed.) *Genocide on Settler Frontiers. When Hunter-Gatherers and Commercial Stock Farmers Clash*. Oxford: Berghahn Books.

Curthoys, A. and Docker, J. (2008) Defining Genocide, in Stone, D. (ed.) *The Historiography of Genocide*. London: Palgrave Macmillan.

Curtin, P. (1960). 'Scientific' Racism and the British Theory of Empire. *Journal of the Historical Society of Nigeria* 2(1), pp. 40–51.

Curtis, M. (2003) *The Web of Deceit: Britain's Real Role in the World*. London: Vintage.

Dadrian, V. N. (1975) A Typology of Genocide, *International Review of Modern Sociology* 5(2), pp. 201–12.

Darwin, C. (2009) *The Descent of Man and Selection in Relation to Sex*. Cambridge: Cambridge University Press.

Darwin, C. and Quammen, D. (2008) *On the Origin of Species*. New York: Sterling.

Davidson, A. (1987) *Reviews: Philip McMichael, Settlers and the Agrarian Question: Capitalism in Colonial Australia*. Cambridge: Cambridge University Press, 1984. *Book Eleven* 18–19(1), pp. 203–4.

Davidson, B. (1992) *The Black Man's Burden*. New York: Three Rivers Press.

Davidson, N. (2013) The Neoliberal Era in Britain Historical Developments and Current Perspectives. *International Socialism Journal* 139. [online]. Available at: http://isj.org.uk/the-neoliberal-era -in-britain-historical-developments-and-current-perspectives/ [Accessed 12 December 2016].

Davies, M. I. J. (2009) *An Applied Archaeological and Anthropological Study of Intensive Agriculture in the Northern Cherangani Hills, Kenya*. Unpublished DPhil thesis, University of Oxford.

Davies, M. I. J. (2012) The Archaeology of Clan and Lineage-Based Societies in Africa, in Mitchell, P. and Lane, P. (eds.) *The Oxford Handbook of African Archaeology*. Oxford: Oxford University Press.

Davis, M. (2004) Towards Cultural Renewal, in Hollier, N. (ed.) *Ruling Australia*. Melbourne: Australian Scholarly Publications.

Davis, M. (2010) Who Will Build the Ark? *New Left Review*, 61, pp. 29–46.

De Angelis, M. (2001) Marx and Primitive Accumulation: The Continuous Character of Capital's 'Enclosures'. *The Commoner* 2, September, pp. 1–22.

Denoon, D. (1983) *Settler Capitalism: The Dynamics of Dependent Development in the Southern Hemisphere.* Oxford: Clarendon Press.

Diamond, J. (2011) *Collapse.* London: Penguin Books.

Dickens, C. (2001) *Bleak House.* Ware, Hertfordshire: Wordsworth Editions.

Distefano, J. A. (1990) Hunters or Hunted? Towards a History of the Okiek of Kenya. *History in Africa* 17, pp. 41–57.

Dlugokencky, E. and Tans, P. (2016) ESRL Global Monitoring Division – Global Greenhouse Gas Reference Network. [online] Available at: http://www.esrl.noaa.gov/gmd/ccgg/trends/global.html [Accessed 14 November 2016].

Docker, D. (2008) Are Settler Colonies Inherently Genocidal? Re-Reading Lemkin, in Dirk Moses, A. (ed.) *Empire, Colony, Genocide: Conquest, Occupation, and Subaltern Resistance in World History.* Oxford, Berghahn Books.

Doherty, B. (2019) Queensland Extinguishes Native Title over Indigenous Land to Make Way for Adani Coalmine. *The Guardian*, 31 August 2019. Available at: https://www.theguardian.com/business/2019/aug/31/queensland-extinguishes-native-title-over-indigenous-land-to-make-way-for-adani-coalmine#:~:text=The%20Queensland%20government%20has%20extinguished,public%20announcement%20of%20the%20decision.&text=Seven%2C%20a%20majority%2C%20of%20the,claimants%20support%20the%20Adani%20mine. [Accessed 9 August 2020].

Drayton, R. (2000) *Nature's Government: Science, Imperial Britain and the 'Improvement' of the World.* New Haven: Yale University Press.

Dunlap, A. (2017) The 'Solution' is now the 'Problem:' Wind Energy, Colonisation and the 'Genocide-Ecocide Nexus' in the Isthmus of Tehuantepec, Oaxaca. *The International Journal of Human Rights* 22(4), pp. 550–73.

Dunlap, A. (2017b) A Bureaucratic Trap: Free, Prior and Informed Consent (FPIC) and Wind Energy Development in Juchitán, Mexico. *Capitalism Nature Socialism* 29(4), pp. 88–108.

Dunlap, A., & Sullivan, S. (2020). A Faultline in Neoliberal Environmental Governance Scholarship? Or, Why Accumulation-by-Alienation Matters. *Environment and Planning E: Nature and Space*, 3(2), 552–79.

Dunning, H. C. (1968) Law and Economic Development in Africa: The Law of Eminent Domain. *Columbia Law Review* 68(7), pp. 1286–315.

Edmonds, P. and Carey, J. (2017) Australian Settler Colonialism over the Long Nineteenth Century, in Cavanagh, E. (ed.) *Routledge Handbook of the History of Settler Colonialism.* London: Routledge.

Edwards, S. (1992) Floggings, in Shaw, B. (ed.) *When the Dust Come in Between*. Canberra: Aboriginal Studies Press.

Egede, L. E., Voronca, D., Walker, R. J. and Thomas, C. (2017) Rural-Urban Differences in Trends in the Wealth Index in Kenya: 1993–2009. *Annals of Global Health* 83(2), pp. 248–58.

Elbardan H. and Kholeif, A. O. (2017) An Interpretive Approach for Data Collection and Analysis, in *Enterprise Resource Planning, Corporate Governance and Internal Auditing*. London: Palgrave Macmillan.

Elkins, C. (2003) Detention, Rehabilitation and the Destruction of Kikuyu Society, in Odhiambo, E. S. A. and Lonsdale, J. (eds.) *Mau Mau and Nationhood*. Oxford: James Currey.

Elkins, C. (2005a) *Britain's Gulag: The Brutal End of Empire in Kenya*. London: Jonathan Cape.

Elkins, C. (2005b) Introduction Settler Colonialism: A Concept and Its Uses, in Elkins, C. and Pedersen, S. (eds.) *Settler Colonialism in the Twentieth Century*. London: Routledge.

Elkins, C. (2005c) Race, Citizenship, and Governance, in Elkins, C. and Pedersen, S. (eds.) *Settler Colonialism in the Twentieth Century*. London: Routledge.

Elkins, C. and Pedersen, S. (2005) *Settler Colonialism in The Twentieth Century*. London: Routledge.

Elton, J. (2007) *Comrades or Competition? Union Relations with Aboriginal Workers in the South Australian and Northern Territory Pastoral Industries, 1878–1957*. [PhD thesis]. Flinders University of South Australia.

Engels, F. (1958) *The Condition of the Working Class in England*. Stanford, CA: Stanford University Press.

Engels, F. (1964) *Dialectics of Nature*. Moscow: Progress Publishers.

Engels, F. (2016). *The Part Played by Labor in the Transition from Ape to Man*. [online] Available at: https://www.marxists.org/archive/marx/works/1876/part-played-labour/index.htm#nature [Accessed 14 November 2016].

Englert, S. (2020) Settlers, Workers, and the Logic of Accumulation by Dispossession. *Antipode*, 52(3) pp. 1–20.

Environmental Law Australia (n.d.) *Carmichael Coal Mine Cases in the Land Court and Supreme Court of Queensland*. http://envlaw.com.au/carmichael-coal-mine-case/ [Accessed 5 November 2021].

Eradicating Ecocide (2012). Closing the Door to Dangerous Industrial Activity: A Concept Paper for Governments to Implement Emergency Measures. Available at: http://eradicatingecocide.com/wp-content/uploads/2012/06/Concept-Paper.pdf [Accessed 20 November 2016].

Escobar, A. (1984) Discourse and Power in Development: Michel Foucault and the Relevance of his Work to the Third World. *Alternatives* 10(3), pp. 377–400.

Escobar, A. (1995) *Encountering Development: The Making and Unmaking of the Third World*. Princeton, NJ: Princeton University Press.

ESCR-Net (2019) *The Emerging Leadership of Endorois Women: An Indirect Impact of the Endorois Case*. Available at: https://www .escr-net.org/sites/default/files/the_emerging_leadership_of _endorois_women_-_en.pdf [Accessed 23 October 2021].

Evans, J., Grimshaw, P., Phillips, D. and Swain, S. (2003) *Equal Subjects, Unequal Rights: Indigenous Peoples in British Settler Colonies, 1830–1910*. Manchester: Manchester University Press.

Evans, R. (1984) 'Kings' in Brass Crescents: Defining Aboriginal Labour Patterns in Colonial Queensland, in Saunders, K. (ed.) *Indentured Labour in the British Empire, 1834–1920*. London: Croom Helm.

Evans, R. (2004) 'Plenty Shoot 'Em': the Destruction of Aboriginal Societies along the Queensland Frontier, in Moses, D. (ed.) *Genocide and Settler Society: Frontier Violence and Stolen Indigenous Children in Australian History*. New York: Berghahn Books.

Evans, R. (2008). 'Crime Without a Name': Colonialism and the Case for Indigenocide, in Moses, D. (ed.) *Empire, Colony, Genocide: Conquest, Occupation, and Subaltern Resistance in World History*. Oxford, Berghahn Books.

Fairhead, F., Leach, M. and Scoones, I. (2012) Green Grabbing: A New Appropriation of Nature? *Journal of Peasant Studies* 39(2), pp. 237–61.

Fanon, F. (1963) *The Wretched of the Earth*. London: Penguin.

Fanon, F. (1967) *Black Skin, White Masks*. London: Pluto Press.

Farrow-Smith, E. (2012) Aboriginal People Reject Native Title over Coal Seam Gas. *ABC News*, 14 December 2012. Available at: https://www .abc.net.au/news/2012-12-15/githubul-csg/4429486 [Accessed 4 December 2021].

Fatton, R. (1992) *Predatory Rule: State and Civil Society in Africa*. London: Lynne Rienner.

Fein, H. (1990) *Genocide*. London: Sage Publications.

Ferguson, J. (1990) *The Anti-Politics Machine: 'Development,' Depoliticization, and Bureaucratic Power in Lesotho*. Cambridge: Cambridge University Press.

Feshbach, M. and Friendly Jr, A. (1992) *Ecocide in the USSR*. New York: Basic Books.

Fibaek, M. and Green, E. (2019) Labour Control and the Establishment of Profitable Settler Agriculture in Colonial Kenya, c. 1920–45, *Economic History of Developing Regions* 34(1), pp. 72–110.

Fields, K. E. (1982) Political Contingencies of Witchcraft in Colonial Central Africa: Culture and the State in Marxist Theory. *Canadian Journal of African Studies* 16(3), pp. 567–93.

Fine, B. and Saad-Filho, A. (2016) Marx 200: The Abiding Relevance of the Labour Theory of Value. *Review of Political Economy* 30(3), pp. 339–54.

Fiona, A. and Mackenzie, D. (2000) Contested Ground: Colonial Narratives and the Kenyan Environment, 1920–1945. *Journal of Southern African Studies* 26(4), pp. 697–718.

Fletcher, R. and Neves, K. (2012) Contradictions in Tourism: The Promise and Pitfalls of Ecotourism as a Manifold Capitalist fix. *Environment and Society* 3(1), pp. 60–77.

Foley, G. and Anderson, T. (2006) Land Rights and Aboriginal Voices, *Australian Journal of Human Rights* 12(1), pp. 83–108.

Forest Peoples Programme (2020, 26 May) Press Release: Kenya's Mau Ogiek Remain Excluded from Ancestral Forest Three Years after Landmark Land Rights Win. *Forest Peoples Programme.* Available at: https://www.forestpeoples.org/en/Kenya-Ogiek-still-excluded-from-forest-three-years-after-land-rights-win. [Accessed 22 December 2020].

Foucault, M. (1991) Governmentality, in Burchell, B., Gordon, C., and Miller, P. (eds.), *The Foucault Effect: Studies in Governmentality.* Chicago: University of Chicago Press.

Foucault, M. (1995) *Discipline and Punish.* New York: Vintage Books.

Foucault, M. (1998) *The History of Sexuality Vol. 1: The Will to Knowledge.* London: Penguin.

Foucault, M. (2001) Truth and Power, in James D. Faubion (ed.), *Essential Works of Foucault 1954–1984, Volume 3: Power.* New York: New Press.

Foucault, M. (2002) *The Order of Things.* London: Routledge.

Foucault, M., Ewald, F., Fontana, A. and Senellart, M. (2014) *Security, Territory, Population.* Basingstoke: Palgrave Macmillan.

Foster, J. B. (1997a) *The Vulnerable Planet: A Short Economic History of the Environment.* New York: Monthly Review Press.

Foster, J. B. (1997b) Marx and the Environment, in Wood, E. M. and Foster, J. B. (eds.) *In Defense of History.* New York: Monthly Review.

Foster, J. B. (1999) Marx's Theory of Metabolic Rift: Classical Foundations for Environmental Sociology. *The American Journal of Sociology* 105(2), pp. 366–405.

Foster, J. B. (2000) *Marx's Ecology: Materialism and Nature.* New York: Monthly Review Press.

Foster, J. B. (2002) Capitalism and Ecology: The Nature of the Contradiction. *Monthly Review.* [online] Available at: http://monthlyreview.org/2002/09 /01/capitalism-and-ecology/ [Accessed 11 December 2016].

Foster, J. B. (2005) The Treadmill of Accumulation. *Organization & Environment* 18(1), pp. 7–18.

Foster, J. B. (2016a). The Anthropocene Crisis. *Monthly Review*. Available at: http://monthlyreview.org/2016/09/01/the-anthropocene-crisis/ [Accessed 4 December 2016].

Foster, J. B. (2016b). The Great Capitalist Climacteric by John Bellamy Foster. *Monthly Review*. [online] Available at: http://monthlyreview.org/2015/11/01/the-great-capitalist-climacteric/ [Accessed 7 December 2016].

Foster, J. and Magdoff, F. (2009) *The Great Financial Crisis*. New York: Monthly Review Press.

Foster-Carter, A. (1978a) The Modes of Production Controversy. *New Left Review* 1(107), pp. 47–77.

Foster-Carter, A. (1978b) Can We Articulate 'Articulation'?, in Clammer, J. (ed.) *The New Economic Anthropology*. London: Palgrave Macmillan.

Freeman, M. (2002) *Human Rights: An Interdisciplinary Approach*. Oxford: Polity.

Friedman, M. (2002b) *Capitalism and Freedom: Fortieth Anniversary Addition*. Chicago: University of Chicago Press.

Furedi, F. (1974) The Social Composition of the Mau Mau Movement in the White Highlands. *The Journal of Peasant Studies* 1(4), pp. 486–505.

Gallagher, J. and Robinson, R. (1953) The Imperialism of Free Trade, *Economic History Review* 6(1), pp. 1–15.

Gammage, B. (2011) *The Biggest Estate on Earth: How Aborigines Made Australia*. Crows Nest, NSW: Allen & Unwin.

Garland, D. (2014) What is a 'History of the Present'? On Foucault's Genealogies and Their Critical Preconditions. *Punishment & Society* 16(4), pp. 365–84.

Gathigira, S. K. (1952) *Miikarire ya Agikuyu*. London: Sheldon Press.

Givens, J., Huang, X. and Jorgenson, A. (2019) Ecologically Unequal Exchange: A Theory of Global Environmental in Justice. *Sociology Compass* 13(5), pp. 1–15.

Glassman, J. (2006) Primitive Accumulation, Accumulation by Dispossession, Accumulation by 'Extra-Economic' Means. *Progress in Human Geography* 30(5), pp. 608–25.

Goff, S. (2016) *Exterminism and the World in the Wake of Katrina*. [online] Available at: https://www.fromthewilderness.com/free/ww3/102305_exterminism_katrina.shtml [Accessed 20 November 2016].

Goldman, M. (ed.) (1998) *Privatizing Nature: Political Struggles for the Global Commons*. London: Pluto Press.

Goldman, M. (2001) Constructing an Environmental State: Eco-governmentality and other Transnational Practices of a 'Green' World Bank. *Social Problems* 48(4), pp. 499–523.

Goldman, M. (2006) *Imperial Nature: The World Bank and Struggles for Social Justice in the Age of Globalization*. London: Yale University Press.

Good, K. (1976) Settler Colonialism: Economic Development and Class Formation. *The Journal of Modern African Studies* 14(4), pp. 597–620.

Goodall, H. (1982) *A History of Aboriginal Communities in New South Wales, 1909–1939*. University of Sydney.

Goodall, H. (1995) New South Wales, in McGrath, A. (ed.) *Contested Ground*. St. Leonards, NSW: Allen & Unwin.

Goodall, H. (2008) *Invasion to Embassy: Land in Aboriginal Politics in New South Wales, 1770–1972*. Sydney, NSW: Sydney University Press.

Goodall, H. and Cadzow, A. (2009) *Rivers and Resilience*. Sydney: UNSW Press.

Gordon, T. (2006) Canadian Capitalism and the Dispossession of Indigenous Peoples. *New Socialist* 58, pp. 18–19.

Gordon, T. (2009) Canada, Empire and Indigenous People in the Americas. *Socialist Studies/Études Socialistes* 2(1), pp. 47–75.

Gorz, A. (1994) *Capitalism, Socialism, Ecology*. London: Verso.

Gramsci, A., Hoare, Q., Smith, G. and Nowell-Smith, G. (1999). *Prison Notebooks*. London: Lawrence & Wishart Ltd.

Green, R. (2015) The Economics of Reconciliation: Tracing Investment in Indigenous–Settler Relations. *Journal of Genocide Research* 17(4), pp. 473–93.

Grosh, B. (1987) Performance of Infrastructural Parastatals in Kenya since Independence: Transport, Communications and Electricity. *Working paper no. 451*, Nairobi: Institute for Development Studies, University of Nairobi.

Grossman, H. (2016) The Value-Price Transformation in Marx and the Problem of Crisis. *Historical Materialism* 24(1), pp. 105–34.

Grove, R. (1995) *Green Imperialism: Colonial Expansion, Tropical Island Edens and the Origins of Environmentalism, 1600–1860*. Cambridge: Cambridge University Press.

Grove, R. (1997) *Ecology, Climate and Empire*. Cambridge: White Horse Press.

Guha, R. (2000) *Environmentalism: A Global History*. New York: Longman.

Gupta, A. and Ferguson, J. (1997) Beyond 'Culture': Space, Identity and the Politics of Difference, in Gupta, A. and Ferguson, J (eds.) *Culture, Power, Place: Explorations in Critical Anthropology*, Durham, NC: Duke University Press, pp. 33–51.

Haebich, A. (2000) *Broken Circles: Fragmenting Indigenous Families, 1800–2000*. Fremantle: Fremantle Arts Centre Press.

Hagan, J. and Castle, R. (1998) Settlers and the State: The Creation of an Aboriginal Workforce in Australia. *Aboriginal History Journal* 22, pp. 24–35.

Hailey, L. (1938) An African Survey: A Study of Problems Arising in Africa South of the Sahara. *The Royal Institute of International Affairs*. New York: Oxford University Press.

Hall, S. (1996) When Was the Post-Colonial? Thinking at the Limit, in Chambers, I. and Curti, L. (eds.) *The Post-colonial Question*. London: Routledge.

Hallegatte, S. et al. (2016) *Unbreakable*. Washington, DC: World Bank Group.

Hannaford, I. (1996) *Race: The History of an Idea in the West*. Baltimore, MD: Johns Hopkins University Press.

Hansen, J. E. and Sato, M. (2016) Climate Sensitivity Estimated from Earth's Climate History. [online] Available at: http://www.columbia .edu/~jeh1/mailings/2012/20120508_ClimateSensitivity.pdf [Accessed 8 December 2016].

Harding, N. (1991) Russian Commune, in Bottomore, T., Harris, L., Kiernan, V. and Miliband, R. (eds.) *A Dictionary of Marxist Thought*. Oxford: Blackwell reference.

Hardt, M. and Antonio, N. (1994) *Labor of Dionysus: A Critique of the State-Form*. Minneapolis, MN: University of Minnesota Press.

Hardt, M. and Antonio, N. (2017) *Assembly*. Oxford: Oxford University Press.

Harman, C. (1998) *Marxism and History*. London: Bookmarks.

Harman, C. (2007) Theorising Neoliberalism. *International Socialism*, 117.

Hartwig, M. C. (1978) Capitalism and Aborigines: The Theory of Internal Colonialism and Its Rivals, in Wheelwright, E. L. and Buckley, K. (eds.) *Essays in the Political Economy of Australian Capitalism, Volume 3*. Sydney: Australia and New Zealand Book Company.

Harvey, D. (1981) The Spatial Fix: Hegel, von Thünen and Marx, *Antipode* 13(3), pp. 1–12.

Harvey, D. (1993) The Nature of Environment: Dialectics of Social and Environmental Change. *Socialist Register*, 29(29), pp. 1–51.

Harvey, D. (1996). *Justice, Nature and the Geography*. Oxford: Blackwell Publishers.

Harvey, D. (2001) *Spaces of Capital: Towards a Critical Geography*. Edinburgh: Edinburgh University Press.

Harvey, D. (2003a) The New Imperialism. Oxford: Oxford University Press.

Harvey, D. (2003b) The 'New' Imperialism: Accumulation by Dispossession, in Panitch, L. and Colin, L. (eds.) *Socialist Register.* Halifax: Fernwood.

Harvey, D. (2005) *A Brief History of Neoliberalism.* Oxford: Oxford University Press.

Havemann, P. (2016) Mother Earth, Indigenous Peoples and Neo-Liberal Climate Change Governance, in Lennox, C. and Short, D. (eds.) *Handbook of Indigenous Peoples Rights.* New York: Routledge.

Hawke, S. (2015) Metgasco Accepts $25m Buyback Offer, Flags Investment Outside NSW, *ABC News*, 16 December 2015. Available at: https://www.abc.net.au/news/2015-12-16/metgasco-not-confident-to -invest-in-nsw/7034640 [Accessed 15 July 2021].

Heartfield, J. (2008) *Green Capitalism: Manufacturing Scarcity in an Age of Abundance.* London: Mute Publishing.

Hedges, C., Sacco, J. and Williams, J. (2012) *Days of Destruction, Days of Revolt.* New York: Nation Books.

Hegel, G. (2006) *The Phenomenology of Mind, Vol 1.* New York: Cosimo Classics.

Heinlein, F. (2002) *British Government Policy and Decolonisation, 1945– 1963: Scrutinising the Official Mind.* London: Frank Cass.

Herzfeld, M. (2001) *Anthropology: Theoretical Practice in Culture and Society.* Oxford: Blackwell.

Heyer, J., Maitha, J. and Senga, W. (1976) *Agricultural Development in Kenya.* Nairobi: University of Nairobi.

Heynen, N., McCarthy, J. and Prudham, W. S. (eds.) (2007) *Neoliberal Environments: False Promises and Unnatural Consequences.* New York: Routledge.

Hickel, J. (2018) The Divide: A Brief Guide to Global Inequality and its Solutions. London: Windmill Books.

Hickel, J. (2020) *Less is More: How Degrowth Will Save the World.* London: Penguin.

Hitchcock, R. K., Sapignoli, M. and Babchuk. W. A. (2015) Settler Colonialism, Conflicts, and Genocide: Interactions between Hunter- Gatherers and Settlers in Kenya, and Zimbabwe and Northern Botswana. *Settler Colonial Studies* 5(1), pp. 40–65.

Higgins, P., Short, D. and South, N. (2013) Protecting the Planet: A Proposal for a Law of Ecocide. *Crime, Law and Social Change* 59(3), pp. 251–66.

Himbara, D. (1994) The Failed Africanization of Commerce and Industry in Kenya. *World Development* 22(3), pp. 469–82.

Hobsbawm, E. (1959) *Primitive Rebels.* Manchester: University Press.

Hobsbawm, E. J. (1975) *The Age of Capital*. London: Weidenfeld and Nicolson.

Hobsbawm, E. and Rude, G. (2014) *Captain Swing*. London: Verso.

Hodge, J. M. (2007) *Triumph of the Expert: Agrarian Doctrines of Development and the Legacies of British Colonialism*. Athens: Ohio University Press.

Hodge, J. M. (2016a) Writing the History of Development (Part 1: The First Wave). *Humanity: An International Human Rights, Humanitarianism, and Development* 6(3), pp. 429–63.

Hodge, J. M. (2016b) Writing the History of Development (Part 2: Longer, Deeper, Wider). *Humanity: An International Human Rights, Humanitarianism, and Development* 7(1), pp. 125–74.

Hodgson, D. (2002) Precarious Alliances: The Cultural Politics and Structural Predicaments of the Indigenous Rights Movement in Tanzania. *American Anthropologist* 104(4), pp. 1086–97.

Hogwood, B. W. and Peters, B. G. (1989) *The Pathology of Public Policy*. Clarendon Press: Oxford.

Holmquist, F., Weaver, F. and Ford, M. (1994) The Structural Development of Kenya's Political Economy. *African Studies Review* 37(1), pp. 69–105.

Horkheimer, M. and Adorno, T. (2001) *Dialectic of Enlightenment*. New York: Continuum.

Horner, J. C. (1994) *Bill Ferguson, Fighter for Aboriginal Freedom: A Biography*. Dickson, ACT: J. Horner.

Hornsby, C. (2012) *Kenya: A History since Independence*. London: I.B. Tauris.

Horowitz, I. (1982) Taking Lives: Genocide and State Power. New Brunswick, NJ: Transaction.

Howitt, R. (2001) *Rethinking Resource Management: Justice, Sustainability, and Indigenous Peoples*. London: Routledge.

Howlett, C. et al. (2011) Neoliberalism, Mineral Development and Indigenous People: A Framework for Analysis. *Aust. Geographer.* 42(3), pp. 309–23.

Howlett, C. and Lawrence, R. (2019) Accumulating Minerals and Dispossessing Indigenous Australians: Native Title Recognition as Settler-Colonialism. *Antipode* 51(3), pp. 818–37.

Hudis, P. (2015) Franz Fanon's Contribution to Hegelian Marxism. *Critical Sociology* 43(6), pp. 865–73.

Hughes, I. (1995) Dependant Autonomy: A New Phase of Internal Colonialism. *Australian Journal of Social Issues* 30(4), pp. 369–88.

Humphrys, E. (2018) Simultaneously Deepening Corporatism and Advancing Neoliberalism: Australia under the Accord. *Journal of Sociology* 54(1), pp. 49–63.

Hunt, J. (2016) Hunt Family Stands Up for Lawler's Well, *Green Left*, 18 November. Available at: https://www.greenleft.org.au/content/hunt -family-stands-lawlers-well [Accessed 8 October 2024].

Huseman, J. and Short, D. (2012) A Slow Industrial Genocide: Tar Sands and the Indigenous Peoples of Northern Alberta. *The International Journal of Human Rights* 16(1), pp. 216–37.

Igoe, J. (2006) Becoming Indigenous Peoples: Difference, Inequality, and the Globalization of East African Identity Politics. *African Affairs* 105(420), pp. 399–420.

Iliffe, J. (1979) *A Modern History of Tanganyika*. Cambridge: Cambridge University Press.

Ince, O. U. (2013) Primitive Accumulation, New Enclosures, and Global Land Grabs: A Theoretical Intervention. *Rural Sociology* 79(1), pp. 104–31.

International Commission on Stratigraphy (2016). *Subcomission on Quaternary Stratigraphy, ICS Working Groups*.

The International Service for Human Rights (2021, June 30) NGO Forum | Implementation of the African Commission's Decision on the Rights of the Endorois Indigenous People of Kenya. *The International Service for Human Rights*. Available at: https://ishr.ch/latest-updates/ngo-forum -implementation-of-the-african-commissions-decision-on-the-rights-of -the-endorois-indigenous-people-of-kenya/ [Accessed 23 October 2021].

Iorns, C. J. (1992) Indigenous Peoples and Self Determination: Challenging State Sovereignty. *Case Western Reserve Journal of International Law* 24(2), pp. 199–348.

Irving, T. (1994) *Challenges to Labour History*. Sydney: UNSW Press.

Jackson, J. A. (1969) *Societies, Schools and Progress in Kenya*. [PhD thesis]. Vancouver: University of British Columbia.

Jackson, S. (2018) The Colonial Technologies and Practises of Australian Planning, in Porter, L. and Johnson, L. (eds.) *Planning in Indigenous Australia*. New York: Routledge.

Jackson, S., Porter, L. and Johnson, L. (eds.) (2018) *Planning in Indigenous Australia*. New York: Routledge.

Jackson, W. (2017) Settler Colonialism in Kenya,1880–1963, in Cavanagh, E. (ed.) *Routledge Handbook of the History of Settler Colonialism*. London: Routledge.

Jacoby, R. (1983). Western Marxism, in Tom Bottomore (ed.) *A Dictionary of Marxist Thought*. Oxford: Blackwell, pp. 523–26.

Jalata, A. (2013) The Impacts of English Colonial Terrorism and Genocide on Indigenous/Black Australians. *SAGE Open* 3(3), pp. 1–12.

James, C. L. R. (2001) *The Black Jacobins*. London: Penguin Books.

Jennings, F. (2010) *The Invasion of America: Indians, Colonialism, and the Cant of Conquest*. New York: Norton.

Johnson, M. and Rowse, T. (2018) Indigenous and Other Australians since 1901: A Conversation between Professor Tim Rowse and Dr Miranda Johnson. *Aboriginal History Journal* 42, pp. 125–39.

Johnston, B. R. (2000) Human Environmental Rights, in Pollis, D. and Schwab, P. (eds.) *Human Rights New Perspectives, New Realities*. London: Lynne Rienner Publishers.

Jones, J. (2000) The Black Communist: The Contested Memory of Margaret Tucker. *Hecate* 26(2), pp. 135–45.

Jones, R. (1968) The Geographical Background to the Arrival of Man in Australia. *Archaeology and Physical Anthropology in Oceania* 3, pp. 186–215.

Jones, S. (1997) *The Archaeology of Ethnicity*. London: Routledge.

Jones, S. (2007) Discourses of Identity in the Interpretation of the Past, in Insoll, T. (ed.) *The Archaeology of Identities*. London: Routledge.

Jorgenson, A. K. and Clark, B. (2009) Ecologically Unequal Exchange in Comparative Perspective: A Brief Introduction. *International Journal of Comparative Sociology* 50(3–4), pp. 211–14.

Kamga, S. A. D. (2011) The Right to Development in the African Human Rights System: The Endorois Case. *De Jure Law Journal* 44(2), pp. 381–91.

Kanogo, T. (1987) *Squatters and the Roots of Mau Mau*. London: James Currey.

Kanyinga, K., Lynch, G. and Cheeseman, N. (2020) The Political Economy of Kenya: Community, Clientelism, and Class, in Kanyinga, K., Lynch, G. and Cheeseman, N. (eds.) *The Oxford Handbook of Kenyan Politics*. Oxford: Oxford University Press.

Kaplan, D. (2000) The Darker Side of the 'Original Affluent Society'. *Journal of Anthropological Research* 56(3), pp. 301–24.

Kauanui, J. (2016) 'A Structure, Not an Event': Settler Colonialism and Enduring Indigeneity. *Lateral* 5(1).

Keal, P. (2003). *European Conquest and the Rights of Indigenous Peoples: The Moral Backwardness of International Society*. Cambridge: Cambridge University Press.

Keen, I. (2003) Aboriginal Economy and Society at the Threshold of Colonisation. *Before Farming* 3, pp. 1–24.

Kenrick, J. (2016) Green Grabs Are Not the Solution to Land Grabs. *REDD-Monitor*, 7 July. Available at: https://redd-monitor.org/2016/07/07/green-grabs-are-not-the-solution-to-land-grabs/ [Accessed 3 May 2020].

Kenrick, J. (2017) *How can the EU WaTER Project Help Secure, Not Undermine, Human Rights in Kenya?* Forest Peoples Programme, 14 February. Available at: https://www.forestpeoples.org/en/public-sect

or-european-union-and-european-commission-world-bank/news
-article/2017/how-can-eu-water [Accessed 17 September 2018].

Kenrick, J. (2020a) Burning a Home That 'Doesn't Exist', Arresting People Who 'Aren't There': A Critique of Eviction-Based Conservation and the Sengwer of Embobut Forest, Kenya, in Bellier, I. and Hays, J. (eds.) *Scales of Governance and Indigenous Peoples*. New York: Routledge.

Kenrick, J. (2020b) *Sengwer call for end to human rights violations by Kenyan authorities following burning of 28 homes*. Forest Peoples Programme, 14 July. Available at: https://www.forestpeoples.org/en /sengwer-call-for-end-human-rights-violations-kenyan-authorities -after-burning-of-28-homes [Accessed 10 October 2021].

Kenrick, J., and Lewis, J. (2004) Indigenous Peoples' Rights and the Politics of the Term 'Indigenous'. *Anthropology Today* 20(2), pp. 4–9.

Kenyatta, J. (1938) *Facing Mt. Kenya*. London: Secker and Warburg.

Keogh, L. (2014) Frack or Frack-off? *Queensland Historical Atlas: Histories, Cultures, Landscapes*. Available at: https://www.qhatlas .com.au/frack-or-frack-off-coal-seam-gas [Accessed 2 November 2021].

Kershaw, G. (1997) *Mau Mau from Below*. Oxford: James Currey.

Kew, D. and Lyman, A. (2016) Long Road To Justice: Addressing Indigenous Land Claims in Kenya Lands, in Tidwell, A. and Scott, B. (eds.) *Indigenous Peoples and Conflict*. New York: Routledge.

Kidd, R. (2007) *Hard Labour, Stolen Wages*. Rozelle, NSW: Australians for Native Title and Reconciliation.

Kiernan, V. G. (1982) *European Empires from Conquest to Collapse, 1815–1960*. London: Fontana.

Kilson, M. L. (1955) Land and the Kikuyu: A Study of the Relationship between Land and Kikuyu Political Movements. *The Journal of Negro History* 40(2), pp. 103–53.

Kilson, M. L. (1966) *Political Change in a West African State: A Study in the Modernization Process*. Cambridge: Harvard University Press.

Kimaiyo, T. J. (2004) *Ogiek Land Cases and Historical Injustices*, 1902–2004. Nakuru, Kenya: Ogiek Welfare Council.

Kiriti-Nganga, T. (2020) Kenya – Economic Diversification, Challenges and Opportunities. *SSRG International Journal of Economics and Management Studies* 7(4), pp. 173–81.

Klare, M. (2013) *The Relentless Pursuit of Extreme Energy: A New Oil Rush Endangers the Gulf of Mexico and the Planet*, [online] Available at: http://extremeenergy.org/2013/03/12/the-relentless-pursuit-of -extreme-energy-a-new-oil-rush-endangers-the-gulf-of-mexico-and -the-planet/

Klein, N. (2007) *The Shock Doctrine*. London: Penguin Books.

Kliman, A. (2012) *The Failure of Capitalist Production*. London: Pluto Press.

Knaus, C. and Cox, L. (2021) NSW Sought to Have Narrabri Gas Project Removed from Scott Morrison's Fast-Track Approvals List. *The Guardian*, 25 October 2021. Available at: https://www.theguardian.com/australia-news/2021/oct/26/nsw-sought-to-have-narrabri-gas-project-removed-from-scott-morrisons-fast-track-approvals-list. [Accessed 4 December 2020].

Kosoy, N. and Corbera, E. (2010) Payments for Ecosystem Services as Commodity Fetishism. *Ecological Economics* 69(6), pp. 1228–36.

Kostanski, L., and Clark, I. (2009) Reviving Old Indigenous Names for New Purposes, in Koch. H. and Hercus, L. (eds.) *Aboriginal Placenames: Naming and Re-Naming the Australian Landscape*. Canberra: ANU E-Press.

Kovel, J. (2007) *The Enemy of Nature: The End of Capitalism or the End of the World?* London: Zed Books.

Krieken, R. (1999) The Barbarism of Civilization: Cultural Genocide and the 'Stolen Generations'. *The British Journal of Sociology* 50(2), pp. 297–315.

Krieken, R. V. (2004). Rethinking Cultural Genocide: Aboriginal Child Removal and Settler-Colonial State Formation. *Oceania* 75(2), pp. 125–51.

Krieken, R. V. (2008) Cultural Genocide, in Stone, D. (ed.) *The Historiography of Genocide*. London: Palgrave Macmillan.

Kühne, T. (2013) Colonialism and the Holocaust: Continuities, Causations, and Complexities. *Journal of Genocide Research* 15(3), pp. 339–62.

Kuper, A. (2005) *The Reinvention of Primitive Society: Transformations of a Myth*. New York: Routledge.

Kusimba, S. (2005) What Is a Hunter-Gatherer? Variation in the Archaeological Record of Eastern and Southern Africa. *Journal of Archaeological Research* 13(4), pp. 337–66.

Kuto, M. C. (2016, Oct 17) Sengwer Women's Experiences of Evictions and their Involvement in the Struggle for Sengwer Land Rights. *Forest Peoples Programme*. Available at: http://www.forestpeoples.org/topics/rights-based-conservation/publication/2016/sengwer-women-s-experiences-evictions [Accessed 12 July 2020].

Kwokwo Barume, A. (2014) *Land Rights of Indigenous Peoples*. Copenhagen: IWGIA, International Work Group for Indigenous Affairs.

Kymlicka, W. (1995) *Multicultural Citizenship*. Oxford: Clarendon Press.

Lambert, H. E. (1965) *Kikuyu: Social and Political Institutions*. London: Oxford University Press.

Lamphear, J. (1988) The People of the Grey Bull: The Origin and Expansion of the Turkana. *The Journal of African History* 29(1), pp. 27–39.

Langton, M. (2004) The 'Wild', the Market, and the Native: Indigenous People Face New Forms of Global Colonization, in Vertovec, S. and Posey, D. (eds.) *Globalization, Globalism, Environments, and Environmentalism.* New York: Oxford University Press.

Leach, M. et al. (2012) Green Grabs and Biochar: Revaluing African Soils and Farming in the New Carbon Economy. *Journal of Peasant Studies* 39(2), pp. 285–307.

Lee, R. (ed.) (2001) *The International Criminal Court: Elements of Crimes and Rules of Procedure and Evidence.* Ardsley, NY: Transnational Publishers.

Lemkin, R. (1944) *Axis Rule in Occupied Europe: Laws of Occupation, Analysis of Government, Proposals for Redress.* Washington, DC. Carnegie Endowment for International Peace Division of International Law.

Lenin, V, I. (1996) *Imperialism: The Highest Stage of Capitalism.* London: Pluto.

Lester, A. (2016). Settler Colonialism, George Grey and the Politics of Ethnography. *Environment and Planning D: Society and Space* 34(3), pp. 492–507.

Lester, A. and Dussart, F. (2014) *Colonization and the Origins of Humanitarian Governance: Protecting Aborigines Across the Nineteenth-Century British Empire.* Cambridge University Press: Cambridge.

Levene, M. (1999) The Chittagong Hill Tracts: A Case Study in the Political Economy of 'Creeping' Genocide. *Third World Quarterly* 20(2), pp. 339–69.

Levene, M. and Conversi, D. (2014) Subsistence Societies, Globalisation, Climate Change and Genocide. *International Journal of Human Rights* 18(3), pp. 281–97.

Levine, P. (2010) Anthropology, Colonialism, and Eugenics, in Bashford, A. and Levine, P. (eds.) *The Oxford Handbook of The History of Eugenics.* Oxford: Oxford University Press.

Levins, R. (2016) Is Human Behavior Controlled by Our Genes? Richard Levins Reviews 'The Social Conquest of Earth'. [online] *Climate and Capitalism.* Available at: http://climateandcapitalism.com/2012/08/01/is-human-behavior-controlled-by-our-genes-richard-levins-reviews-the-social-conquest-of-earth/ [Accessed 23 November 2016].

Lewis, D. (1997) *Community A Shared History. Aborigines and White Australians in the Victoria River District Northern Territory.* Darwin: Create-a-card.

Lewis, L. S. and Maslin, M. (2015) Defining the Anthropocene. *Nature* 519, pp. 171–80.

Leys, C. (1975) *Underdevelopment in Kenya: The Political Economy of Neo-colonialism, 1964–1971.* London: Heinemann.

Leys, N. (1934) Report of the Kenya Land Commission. New Statesman and Nation, July 28.

Liguori, G. (2016) *Gramsci's Pathways.* Chicago: Haymarket.

Lindgren, T. (2017) Ecocide, Genocide and the Disregard of Alternative Life-Systems. *The International Journal of Human Rights* 22(4), pp. 525–49.

Lipeitz, A. (2000) Political Ecology and the Future of Marxism. *Capitalism Nature Socialism* 11, pp. 69–85.

Lipson, E. (1953). *A Short History of Wool and Its Manufacture.* Cambridge, MA: Harvard University Press.

Lloyd, C. (2004) T*he 1840s Depression and the Origins of Australian Capitalism.* Working Paper, School of Business, Economics and Public Policy, University of New England, Armidale.

Lloyd, C. (2010). The Emergence of Australian Setter Capitalism in the Nineteenth Century and the Disintegration/Integration of Aboriginal Societies: Hybridisation and Local Evolution within the World Market, in Ian Keen (eds.) *Indigenous Participation in Australian Economies.* Canberra: Australian National University Press.

Lloyd-Davies, E. (2013) *Extreme Energy: A Process Not a Category.* Available at: http://extremeenergy.org/2013/07/25/defining-extreme -energy-a-process-not-a-category/ [Accessed 11 November 2019].

Lloyd, D., Luke, H. and Boyd, W. E. (2013) Community Perspectives of Natural Resource Extraction: Coal-Seam Gas Mining and Social Identity in Eastern Australia. *Coolabah* 10, pp. 144–64.

Lonsdale, J. (1977) When Did the Gusii (or Any Other Group) Become a Tribe? *Kenya Historical Review* 5, pp. 122–33.

Lonsdale, J. and Berman, B. (1979) Coping with the Contradictions: The Development of the Colonial State in Kenya, 1895–1914. *The Journal of African History* 20(4), pp. 487–505.

Losurdo, D. (2011) *Liberalism: A Counter-History.* London: Verso.

Loveday, B., Lipton, L. and Thomson, B. (2019) Pancreatic Cancer: An Update on Diagnosis and Management. *Australian Journal of General Practice* 48(12), pp. 826–31.

Lovelock, J. (2007). *Why the Earth Is Fighting Back – and How We Can Still Save Humanity.* London: Penguin.

Low, D. A. and Lonsdale, J. M. (1976) Introduction: Towards the New Order, 1945–63, in Low, A. and Smith, A. (eds.) *History of East Africa Vol. 3.* Oxford: Oxford University Press.

Löwy, M. (2010) Eric Hobsbawm, sociólogo do milenarismo campesino. *Estudos Avançados* 24(69), pp. 105–18.

Luke, H. (2017) Social Resistance to Coal Seam Gas Development in the Northern Rivers Region of Eastern Australia: Proposing a Diamond Model of Social License to Operate. *Land Use Policy* 69, pp. 266–80.

Luke, H. (2018) Not Getting a Social Licence to Operate Can Be a Costly Mistake, as Coal Seam Gas Firms Have Found. *The Conversation*, 23 March 2018. Available at: https://theconversation.com/not-getting-a-social-licence-to-operate-can-be-a-costly-mistake-as-coal-seam-gas-firms-have-found-93718 [Accessed 9 February 2018].

Luke, H., Rasch, E., Evensen, D. and Köhne, M. (2018) Is 'Activist' a Dirty Word? Place Identity, Activism and Unconventional Gas Development across Three Continents. *The Extractive Industries and Society* 5(4), pp. 524–34.

Luke, T. (1997) *Ecocritique: Contesting the Politics of Nature, Economy and Culture*. Minneapolis: University of Minnesota press.

Lukes, S. (1981) Can a Marxist Believe in Human Rights. *Praxis International*, 4, pp. 334–45.

Lunn-Rockliffe, S. (2018) Connecting Past and Present: The Archaeology of the Contemporary Past in the Glades of Embobut, Kenya [PhD thesis]. University of Oxford.

Luxembourg, R. (1963) *The Accumulation of Capital*. London: Routledge.

Lynch, G. (2011). Kenya's New Indigenes: Negotiating Local Identities in a Global Context. *Nations and Nationalism* 17, pp. 148–67.

Lynch, G. (2016) What's in a Name? The Politics of Naming Ethnic Groups in Kenya's Cherangany Hills. *Journal of Eastern African Studies* 10, pp. 208–27.

Lyons, K. and Westoby, P. (2014) The Darker Side of Green: Plantation Forestry and Carbon Violence in Uganda – The Case of Green Resources' Forestry Based Carbon Markets, *The Oakland Institute*. Oakland: Oakland Institute.

Lyons, K. (2018) Securing Territory for Mining when Traditional Owners Say 'No': The Exceptional Case of Wangan and Jagalingou in Australia. *The Extractive Industries and Society* 6(3), pp. 756–66.

Macekura, S. J. and Manela, E. (2018) *The Development Century*. Cambridge: Cambridge University Press.

Mackenzie, J. (1887) *Austral Africa: Losing It or Ruling It*. 2 vols. London: Sampson Low, Marston, Searle, and Rivington.

Mackenzie, J. M. (1987) Chivalry, Social Darwinism, and Ritualized Killing: The Hunting Ethos in Central Africa up to 1914, in Anderson, D. and Grove, R. (eds.) *Conservation in Africa: Peoples, Policies, and Practice*. Cambridge: Cambridge University Press.

Mackenzie, J. M. (1988) *The Empire of Nature*. Manchester: Manchester University Press.

MacKenzie, J. M. (1997) *Empires of Nature and the Nature of Empires. Imperialism, Scotland and the Environment*. East Linton: Tuckwell.

MacKenzie, J. M. (2007) General Editor's Introduction, in Campbell, C. (2007) *Race and Empire: Eugenic in Colonial Kenya*. Manchester: Manchester University Press.

Macoun, A. and Strakosch, E. (2013) The Ethical Demands of Settler Colonial Theory. *Settler Colonial Studies* 3(3–4), pp. 426–43.

Makki, M. (2015) *Coal Seam Gas Development and Community Conflict: A Comparative Study of Community Responses to Coal Seam Gas Development in Chinchilla and Tara, Queensland* [PhD thesis]. The University of Queensland.

Maddison, S. (2008) Indigenous Autonomy Matters: What's Wrong with the Australian Government's 'Intervention' in Aboriginal Communities. *Australian Journal of Human Rights* 14(1), pp. 41–61.

Maddison, S. (2009) *Black Politics*. Crows Nest, NSW: Allen & Unwin.

Maddison, S. (2017) Settler Australia in the 20th century, in Cavanagh, E. (ed.) *Routledge Handbook of the History of Settler Colonialism*. London: Routledge.

Magubane, Z. (2003) Simians, Savages, Skulls, and Sex: Science and Colonial Militarism in Nineteenth-Century South Africa, in Moore, D., Kosek, J. and Pandian, A. (eds.) *Race, Nature, And The Politics Of Difference*. Durham: Duke University Press.

Makkonen, T. (2000) *Identity, Difference and Otherness: The Concepts of 'People', 'Indigenous People' and 'Minority' in International Law*. Helsinki: University of Helsinki.

Maldonado-Torres, N. (2007) On the Coloniality of Being. *Cultural Studies* 21(2–3), pp. 240–70.

Malm, A. (2016) *Fossil Capital: The Rise of Steam-Power and the Roots of Global Warming*. Verso Books.

Mamati, K. (2018) An African Religious Worldview and the Conservation of Natural Environmental Resources: A Case Study of the Sengwer in Embobut Forest in Kenya. *FERNS* 1(1), pp. 28–59.

Markus, A. (1978) Talka Longa Mouth. *Labour History* 35, pp. 138.

Martin, D. (2011) Policy Alchemy and the Magical Transformation of Aboriginal Society, in Musharbash, Y. and Barber, M. (eds.) *Ethnography and the Production of Anthropological Knowledge*. Canberra: ANU E Press.

Martínez, J. (1999) *Plural Australia: Aboriginal and Asian Labour in Tropical White Australia, Darwin, 1911–1940*. [PhD thesis]. Doctor of

Philosophy book, Department of History and Politics, University of Wollongong.

Marx, K. (1904) *A Contribution to the Critique of Political Economy*. Chicago. Charles H. Kerr Publishing Company.

Marx, K. (1967) The Defence of the Moselle Correspondent: Economic Distress and Freedom of the Press, in Easton, L. D. and Guddat, K. H. (eds.) *Writings of the Young Marx on Philosophy and Society*. New York: Doubleday Anchor.

Marx, K. (1968) *Theories of Surplus Value, Vol. 2*. Moscow: Progress Publishers.

Marx, K. (1973) *Grundrisse*. London: Penguin Books in association with New Left Review.

Marx, K. (1975) On the Jewish Question, in Marx, K., and Engels, F., *Marx-Engels Collected Works*, vol. 3. International Publishers.

Marx, K. (1976a) *Capital, Vol 1*. London: Penguin Books in association with New Left Review.

Marx, K. (1976b) Theses on Feuerbach, in Marx, K., and Engels, F., *Marx-Engels Collected Works*, vol. 5. International Publishers.

Marx, K. (1988) *Economic and Philosophic Manuscripts Of 1844*. New York: Prometheus Books.

Marx, K. (1991) *Capital, Vol 3*. 1st ed. London: Penguin Books in association with New Left Review.

Marx, K. (2002) The Eighteenth Brumaire of Louis Bonaparte, in Cowling, M. and Martin, J. (eds.) *Marx's 'Eighteenth Brumaire': (Post)modern Interpretations*. London: Pluto Press.

Marx, K. (2012) *On Colonialism*. London: Forgotten Books.

Marx, K. and Elster, J. (1986). *Karl Marx*. Cambridge: Press Syndicate of the University of Cambridge.

Marx, K., and Engels, F. (1877) 1968. *Marx and Engels Correspondence*. New York: International Publishers. Available at: http://www.marxists.org/archive/marx/works/1877/11/russia.htm. [Accessed 3 March 2021].

Marx, K. and Engels, F. (1988) *Marx and Engels Collected Works*, Vol 30. Moscow: Progress Publishers.

Marx, K. and Engels, F. (1998) *The German Ideology*. New York: Prometheus Books.

Marx, K. and Engels, F. (2002) *The Communist Manifesto*. London: Penguin Classics.

Marx, K. and Engels, F. (2010) *Karl Marx, Frederick Engels: Volume 50, Letters 1892–95*. London: Lawrence & Wishart Electric Book.

Marx, K. and Simpson, R. (1969) *Theories of Surplus Value*. London: Lawrence & Wishart.

Mathews, A. S. (2011) *Instituting Nature: Authority, Expertise, and Power in Mexican Forests*. Cambridge: MIT Press.

Matthews, H., et al. (2014) National Contributions to Observed Global Warming. *Environmental Research Letters* 9(1), pp. 1–9.

May, D. (1983) The Articulation of the Aboriginal and Capitalist Modes on the North Queensland Pastoral Frontier. *Journal of Australian Studies* 7(12), pp. 34–44.

May, D. (1994) *Aboriginal Labour and the Cattle Industry*. Cambridge: Cambridge University Press.

Maynard, J. (2007) *Fight for Liberty and Freedom: The Origins of Australian Aboriginal Activism*. Canberra: Aboriginal Studies Press.

Mboya, T. (1963) *Freedom and After*. London: Andre Deutsch.

McAfee, K. and Shapiro, E. N. (2010) Payments for Ecosystem Services in Mexico: Nature, Neoliberalism, Social Movements, and the State. *Annals of the Association of American Geographers* 100(3), pp. 1–21.

McAuslan, P. (2007) *Land Law and the Making of the British Empire*, in E. Cooke (ed.), *Modern Studies in Property Law, Vol. 4*. Oxford: Hart Publishing.

McCarthy, F. M. et al. (2023) The Varved Succession of Crawford Lake, Milton, Ontario, Canada as a Candidate Global Boundary Stratotype Section and Point for the Anthropocene Series. *The Anthropocene Review* 10(1), pp. 146–76.

McCorquodale, J. (1987) *Aborigines and the Law*. Canberra: Aboriginal Studies Press.

McCreary, T. and Milligan, R. (2018) The Limits of Liberal Recognition: Racial Capitalism, Settler Colonialism, and Environmental Governance in Vancouver and Atlanta. *Antipode* 53(3), pp. 724–44.

McGill, V., and Parry, W. (1948) The Unity of Opposites: A Dialectical Principle. *Science & Society* 12(4), pp. 418–44.

McGrath, A. (1987) *Born in the Cattle*. Sydney: Allen & Unwin.

McGrath, A. (1995) A National Story, in McGrath, A. (ed.) *Contested Ground*. St. Leonards, NSW: Allen & Unwin.

McKenna, M. (2015) Indigenous Jobs Fears as Greens March in. *The Australian*. 14 August 2015. Available at: www.theaustralian.com.au/nationalaffairs/indigenous/indigenous-job-fears-as-greens-march-in/newsstory/10780449062e08709835ee550db0d417 [Accessed 20 September 2021].

McLellan, D. (2000) *Karl Marx: Selected Writings*. Oxford: Oxford University Press.

McLisky, C. (2007) 'All of ONE Blood'? Race and Redemption on Maloga Mission, 1874–88, in Boucher, L., Carey, J. and Ellinghaus, K. (eds.)

Historicising Whiteness: Transnational Perspectives on the Construction of an Identity. Melbourne: RMIT Publishing.

McMichael, P. (1980). Settlers and Primitive Accumulation: Foundations of Capitalism in Australia. *Review (Fernand Braudel Center)* 4(2), pp. 307–34.

McMichael, P. (1984) *Settlers and the Agrarian Question*. Cambridge: Cambridge University Press.

Meadows, D. H. et al. (1972) *The Limits to Growth*. New York: Universe Books.

Merlan, F. (1997) Reply to Patrick Wolfe. *Social Analysis* 40, pp. 10–19.

Merrilees, D. (1968) Man the Destroyer: Late Quaternary Changes in the Australian Marsupial Fauna, *Journal of the Royal Society of Western Australia* 51, pp. 1–24.

Mignolo, W. (2011a) *The Darker Side of Western Modernity: Global Futures, Decolonial Options*. Durham: Duke University Press.

Mignolo, W. (2011b) Epistemic Disobedience and the Decolonial Option: A Manifesto. *TRANSMODERNITY: Journal of Peripheral Cultural Production of the Luso-Hispanic World* 1(2), pp. 44–66.

Miller, C. (1971) *The Lunatic Express: An Entertainment in Imperialism*. New York: Macmillan.

Minority Rights Group International (MRGI) (2020, 18 December) Press release: UPDATE: One step forward for the Ogiek as Kenyan court issues conservatory orders, stopping government's titling process in Eastern Mau. *Minority Rights Group International*. Available at: https://minorityrights.org/2020/12/18/ogiek-update/ [Accessed 25 Sep 2021].

Moon, P. T. (1973) *Imperialism and World Politics*. Lincoln: Garland Publishers.

Moore, H. L. and Vaughan. M. (1994) *Cutting Down Trees: Gender, Nutrition, and Agricultural Change in the Northern Province of Zambia, 1890–1990*. London: James Currey.

Moran, A. (2009). Aboriginal Reconciliation: Transformations in Settler Nationalism. *Melbourne Journal of Politics* 25, pp. 101–31.

Moran, C. J. and Vink, S. (2010) *Assessment of Impacts of the Proposed Coal Seam Gas Operations on Surface and Groundwater Systems in the Murray-Darling Basin*. Brisbane: Sustainable Minerals Institute.

Moreton-Robinson, A. (1999a) Unmasking Whiteness: A Goori Jondal's Look at Some Duggai Business. *Queensland Review* 6(1), pp. 1–7.

Moreton-Robinson, A. (1999b) Imagining the Good Indigenous Citizen: Race War and the Pathology. *Cultural Studies Review* 15(2), pp. 61–79.

Moreton-Robinson, A. (2006) Towards a New Research Agenda? Foucault, Whiteness and Indigenous Sovereignty. *Journal of Sociology* 42(4), pp. 383–95.

Moreton-Robinson, A. (2007) Witnessing the Workings of White Possession in the Workplace: Leesa's Testimony. *Australian Feminist Law Journal* 26, pp. 81–93.

Moreton-Robinson, A. (2009a) *The White Possessive: Property, Power, and Indigenous Sovereignty.* Minneapolis: University of Minnesota Press.

Moreton-Robinson, A. (2009b) Imagining the Good Indigenous Citizen: Race War and the Pathology of Patriarchal White Sovereignty. *Cultural Studies Review* 15(2), pp. 61–79.

Morris, B. (1989) *Domesticating Resistance: The Dhan-Gadi Aborigines and the Australian State.* Oxford: St. Martin's.

Morton, A. (2021) Australia Shown to Have Highest Greenhouse Gas Emissions from Coal in World on Per Capita Basis. *The Guardian,* 11 November 2021. Available at: https://www.theguardian.com/environ ment/2021/nov/12/australia-shown-to-have-highest-greenhouse-gas -emissions-from-coal-in-world-on-per-capita-basis.

Moses, D. (2000) An Antipodean Genocide? The Origins of the Genocidal Moment in the Colonization of Australia. *Journal of Genocide Research* 2(1), pp. 89–106.

Moses, D. (2002) Conceptual Blockages. *Patterns of Prejudice* 36(4), pp. 7–36.

Moses, D. (2008a) Empire, Colony, Genocide: Keywords and the Philosophy of History, in Moses, D.(ed.) *Empire, Colony, Genocide: Conquest, Occupation, and Subaltern Resistance in World History.* Oxford: Berghahn Books.

Moses, D. (2008b) Genocide and Modernity, in Stone, D. (ed.) *The Historiography of Genocide.* Basingstoke, Hampshire [UK]: Palgrave Macmillan.

Moses, D. (2010a) Raphael Lemkin, Culture, and the Concept of Genocide, in Bloxham, D. and Moses, D. (eds.) *The Oxford Handbook of Genocide Studies.* Oxford: Oxford University Press.

Moses, D. (2011) Genocide and the Terror of History. *Parallax* 61(4), pp. 90–108.

Mullins, S. (2001) Australian Pearl-Shellers in the Moluccas: Confrontation and Compromise on a Maritime Frontier. *Great Circle* 23(2), pp. 3–23.

Mungeam, G. H. (1966) *British Rule in Kenya, 1895–1912: The Establishment of Administration in the East Africa Protectorate.* Oxford: Clarendon.

Munro, J. F. (1975) *Colonial Rule and the Kamba: Social Change in the Kenya Highlands, 1889–1939.* Oxford: Clarendon Press.

Muriuki, G. (1974) *A History of the Kikuyu, 1500–1900.* London: Oxford University Press.

Murphy, D. J. (2010) EROI, Insidious Feedbacks, and the End Economic Growth. Paper presented at the 6th Annual Conference of the Association for the Study of Peak Oil (ASPO). 7–9 October 2010. Washington, DC.

Murphy, J. (2016) Gomeroi Native Title Claim Votes out Applicants. *The Northern Daily Leader*, 27 July 2016. Available at: https://www.north erndailyleader.com.au/story/4058286/gomeroi-nation-change -leaders/ [Accessed 4 November 2021].

Musembi, C. N., and Kameri-Mbote, P. (2013) Mobility, Marginality, and Tenure Transformation in Kenya: Explorations of Community Property Rights in Law and Practice. *Nomadic Peoples* 17(1), pp. 5–32.

Mutiso, G. C. M. (1975) *Kenya: Politics, Policy and Society.* Nairobi: East African Literature Bureau.

Nadeau, K. (2010) Marxist Anthropology, in Birx, H. (ed.) *21st Century Anthropology.* Thousand Oaks, CA: SAGE Publications.

Nandy, N. (ed.) (1998) *Science, Hegemony and Violence: A Requiem for Modernity.* Oxford: Oxford University Press.

Nangulu-Ayuku, A. (2007) Reflections on the Postcolonial State in Kenya, in Agbese, P. and Klay Kieh, Jr., G. (eds.) *Reconstituting the State in Africa.* New York: Palgrave Macmillan.

Ndege, P. (2009) Colonialism and Its Legacies in Kenya. Lecture Delivered during Fulbright – Hays Group project abroad program: 5 July to 6 August 2009 at the Moi University Main Campus.

Neale, T. (2013) Staircases, Pyramids and Poisons: The Immunity Paradigm in the Works of Noel Pearson and Peter Sutton. *Continuum: Journal of Media and Cultural Studies* 27(2), pp. 177–92.

Nelson, S. H. (2015) Beyond the Limits to Growth: Ecology and the Neoliberal Counterrevolution. *Antipode* 47(2), pp. 461–80.

Neumann, R. P. (1996) Dukes, Earls, and Ersatz Edens: Aristocratic Nature Preservationists in Colonial Africa. *Environment and Planning D: Society and Space* 14(1), pp. 79–98.

Neumann, R. (1997) Primitive Ideas: Protected Area Buffer Zones and the Politics of Land in Africa. *Development and Change* 28, pp. 559–82.

Neumann, R. (1998) *Imposing Wilderness: Struggles over Livelihood and Nature Preservation in Africa.* Berkeley: University of California Press.

Newsinger, J. (2006) *The Blood Never Dried.* London: Bookmarks.

Nkrumah, K. (1965) *Neo-Colonialism: The Last Stage of Imperialism.* London: Heinemann.

Norman, H. (2016) Coal Mining and Coal Seam Gas on Gomeroi Country: Sacred Lands, Economic Futures and Shifting Alliances. *Energy Policy* 99, pp. 242–51.

Nuñez, R. and GenderCC (2010) Tree Plantations, Climate Change and Women in Böhm, S. and Dabhi, S., (eds.) *Upsetting the Offset*. London: MayFlyBooks.

Ochieng, W. R. (1985) *A History of Kenya*. London and Nairobi: Macmillan Publishers.

Ochieng, W. R. (1992) The Post-Colonial State and Kenya's Economic Inheritance, in Ochieng, W. R. and Maxon R. M. (eds.) *An Economic History of Kenya*. Nairobi: East African Educational Publishers.

O'Connell, P. (2017a) Marxism and Human Rights. Legal Form: *A Forum for Marxist Analysis and Critique*, 25 November 2017. Available at: https://legalform.blog/2017/11/25/marxism-and-human-rights-paul-oconnell/ [Accessed 3 December 2021].

O'Connell, P. (2017b) Human Rights: Contesting the Displacement Book. *Northern Ireland Legal Quarterly* 69(1), pp. 19–35.

O'Connor, J. (1994) Is Sustainable Capitalism Possible?, in Michael O'Connor (ed.) *Is Capitalism Sustainable? Political Economy and the Politics of Ecology*. New York: The Guilford Press.

O'Connor, J. (2001). Marx's Ecology or Ecological Marxism? *Capitalism, Nature, Socialism* 12(3), p. 125.

O'Faircheallaigh, C. (2006) Aborigines, Mining Companies and the State in Contemporary Australia: A New Political Economy or 'Business as Usual'? *Australian Journal of Political Science* 41(1), pp. 1–22.

O'Faircheallaigh, C. (2007) 'Unreasonable and Extraordinary Restraints': Native Title, Markets and Australia's Resources Boom. *Australian Indigenous Law Review* 11(3), pp. 28–42.

O'Faircheallaigh, C. (2011) Native Title and Australia's Resource Boom: A Lost Opportunity? *The Conversation*. http://theconversation.com/native-title-andaustralias-resource-boom-a-lost-opportunity-2725. [Accessed 9 May 2021].

Ofcansky, T. P. (1984) Kenya Forestry under British Colonial Administration, 1895–1963. *Journal of Forest History* 28(3), pp. 136–43.

Ogot, B. A. (1968) Kenya under the British, 1895 to 1963, in Ogot, B. A. and Kieran, J. A (eds.) *Zamani: A Survey of East African History*. Nairobi: East African Publishing House.

Ojeda, D. (2012) Green Pretexts: Ecotourism, Neoliberal Conservation and Land Grabbing in Tayrona National Natural Park, Columbia. *Journal of Peasant Studies* 39(2), pp. 357–75.

Ojienda, T. and M. Okoth. (2011) Land and the Environment, in Lumumba, P., Mbondenyi, M. K. and Odero. S (eds.) *The Constitution of Kenya: Contemporary Readings*. Nairobi: LawAfrica Publishing.

Okia, O. (2012) *Communal Labor in Colonial Kenya*. New York: Palgrave Macmillan.

O'Laughlin, B. (1975) Marxist Approaches in Anthropology. *Annual Review of Anthropology* 4(1), pp. 341–70.

Onyatta, O. (2020) State Turns Covid-19 into Season of Evictions. *The Star*, 14 July 2020. Available at: https://www.the-star.co.ke/news/big-read /2020-07-14-state-turns-covid-19-into-season-of-evictions/ [Accessed 10 Oct. 2021].

OPDP (Ogiek Peoples Development Programme) and Katiba Institute (2020) *Defending Our Future. Overcoming the Challenges of Returning the Ogiek Home a Report on Implementing the Ogiek Judgement in Kenya*. Katiba Institute, Nairobi.

Osborne, M. (2010). The Kamba and Mau Mau: Ethnicity, Development, and Chiefship, 1952–1960. *The International Journal of African Historical Studies* 43(1), pp. 63–87.

Overton, J. (1987) The Colonial State and Spatial Differentiation: Kenya, 1895–1920. *Journal of Historical Geography* 13(3), pp. 267–82.

Pakenham, T. (1991) *The Scramble for Africa, 1876–1912*. London: Weidenfeld and Nicholson.

Palmer, K. (2018) *Australian Native Title Anthropology*. Australia.

Pan African Climate Justice Alliance (2010). *African Climate Justice Manifesto*. Available at: https://ejcj.orfaleacenter.ucsb.edu/wp-content /uploads/2020/06/2010-African-Climate-Justice-Manifesto-PACJA.pdf [Accessed 8 October 2024].

Panter-Brick, C., Laydon, R., and Rowley-Conwy, P. (2001). Lines of Enquiry, in Panter-Brick, C., Layton, R. and Rowley-Conwy, P. (eds.), *Hunter-Gatherers: An Interdisciplinary Perspective*. Cambridge: Cambridge University Press.

Parsons, H. (ed.) *Marx and Engels on Ecology*. Westport, CT: Greenwood.

Patterson, O. (1982) *Slavery and Social Death*. Cambridge, MA: Harvard University Press.

Pearson, N. (2007) White Guilt, Victimhood and the Quest for a Radical Centre, 16, *Griffith Review*, pp. 3–58.

Pearson, N. (1999) Positive and Negative Welfare and Australia's Indigenous Communities. *Family Matters* 54, pp. 30–35.

Peck, J. (2013) Excavating the Pilbara: A Polanyian Exploration. *Geographical Research* 51(3), pp. 227–42.

Pels, P. (2008) What Has Anthropology Learned from the Anthropology of Colonialism? *Social Anthropology* 16(3), pp. 280–99.

Perelman, M. (1996). Marx and Resource Scarcity, in Benton, T. (ed.) *The Greening of Marxism*. New York: Guilford Press, pp. 64–80.

Peterson, D. J. (1993) *Troubled Lands: The Legacy of Soviet Environmental Destruction*. Boulder, CO: Westview Press.

Peterson, N. (1985) Capitalism, Culture and Land Rights: Aborigines and the State in the Northern Territory. *Social Analysis* 18(8), pp. 85–101.

Peterson, N. (2005) What Can the Pre-Colonial and Frontier Economies Tell Us About Engagement with the Real Economy? Indigenous Life Projects and the Conditions for Development, in Austin-Broos, D. and Macdonald. G. (eds.) *Culture, Economy and Governance in Aboriginal Australia*. Sydney: University of Sydney Press.

Porteous, J. and Smith, S. (2001) *Domicide*. Montreal, Quebec: McGill-Queen's University Press.

Posey, D. A. (ed.) (1999) *Cultural and Spiritual Survival of Biodiversity*. London: Intermediate Technology Publications/UNEP.

Povinelli, E. (1997). Reading Ruptures, Rupturing Readings: Mabo and the Cultural Politics of Activism. *Social Analysis: The International Journal of Social and Cultural Practice* 41(2), pp. 20–28.

Povinelli, E. (2007) *The Cunning of Recognition*. Durham: Duke University Press.

Powell, C. (2007) What Do Genocides Kill. *Journal of Genocide Research* 9(4), pp. 527–47.

Powell, C. (2011) *Barbaric Civilisation: A Critical Sociology of Genocide*. McGill-Queen's University Press.

Pradella, L. (2013) Imperialism and Capitalist Development in Marx's Capital. *Historical Materialism* 21(2), pp. 117–47.

Pratt, M. (1991) Arts of the Contact Zone. *Profession*, pp. 33–40.

Prendergast, D. and Adams, W. (2003) Colonial Wildlife Conservation and the Origins of the Society for the Preservation of the Wild Fauna of the Empire (1903–1914). *Oryx* 37(2), pp. 251–60.

Pretty, J., Adams, B., Berkes, F., Ferreira de Athayde, S., Dudley, F., Hunn, E., Maffi, L., Milton, K., Rapport, D., Robbins, P., Samson, C., Sterling, E., Stolton., S., Takeuchi, K., Tsing, A., Vintinner, E. and Pilgrim, S. (2008) *How Do Biodiversity and Culture Intersect? Plenary Paper for Conference: Sustaining Cultural and Biological Diversity in a Rapidly Changing World*, I.U.C.N – The World Conservation Union/Theme on Culture and Conservation. New York, 2–5 April.

Pulido, L. (2016) Flint, Environmental Racism, and Racial Capitalism. *Capitalism Nature Socialism* 27(3), pp. 1–16.

Putnam, L. and Banghart, S. (2017) Interpretive Approaches, in Scott, C., Lewis, L., Barker, J., Keyton, J., Kuhn, T. and Turner, P. (eds.) *The International Encyclopedia of Organizational Communication*. Chichester: Wiley.

Qureshi, S. (2013) Dying Americans: Race, Extinction, and Conservation in the New World, in Swenson, A, and Mandler, P. (eds.) *From Plunder* to *Preservation: Britain and the Heritage of Empire, 1800–1950.* Oxford: Oxford University Press.

Ranger, T. (2012) The Invention of Tradition in Colonial Africa, in Hobsbawm, E. and Ranger, T. (eds.) *The Invention of Tradition.* Cambridge: Cambridge University Press.

Rashed, H. and Short, D. (2012) Genocide and Settler Colonialism: Can a Lemkin-Inspired Genocide Perspective Aid Our Understanding of the Palestinian Situation? *The International Journal of Human Rights* 16(8), pp. 1142–69.

Rashed, H., Short, D. and Docker, J. (2014) Nakba Memoricide: Genocide Studies and the Zionist/Israeli Genocide of Palestine. *Holy Land Studies* 13(1), pp. 1–23.

Read, P. (1994) *A Hundred Years War.* Canberra: Australian National University Press.

Redclift, M. (1984) *Development and the Environmental Crisis.* New York: Methuen.

The Red Nation (2021) *Red Deal: Indigenous Action to Save Our Earth.* Common Notions.

Reece, B. (1987) Inventing Aborigines, *Aboriginal History* 11(1), pp. 14–23.

Reece, R. H. W. (1979) The Aborigines in Australian Historiography, in Moses, J. A. (ed.) *Historical Disciplines and Culture in Australasia.* St Lucia: University of Queensland Press.

Reinhardt, A. (2016) Red Skin, White Masks: Rejecting the Colonial Politics of Recognition. *Contemporary Political Theory* 15, pp. 52–5.

Reynolds, H. (1987) *Frontier.* Sydney: Allen & Unwin.

Reynolds, H. (1990) *With the White People.* New York: Penguin Books.

Reynolds, H. (1993) The Mabo Judgment in the Light of Imperial Land Policy. *UNSW Law Journal* 16(1), pp. 27–44.

Reynolds, H. (2001) *An Indelible Stain?* Ringwood, Victoria: Viking.

Reynolds, H. and May, D. (1995) Queensland, in McGrath, A. (ed.) *Contested Ground.* St. Leonards, NSW: Allen & Unwin.

Rice, S. (1989) An Ecological Interpretation of History. *Ecology* 70(4), pp. 1199–200.

Rich, P. (1983) Landscape, Social Darwinism and the Cultural Roots of South African Racial Ideology. *Patterns of Prejudice* 17(3), pp. 9–15.

Riley, H. L. (2013) *Monstrous Predatory Vampires and Beneficent Fairy-Godmothers: British Post-War Colonial Development in Africa.* [PhD thesis]. University College London.

Rist, G. (1997) *The History of Development: From Western Origins to Global Faith.* London: Zed Books.

Ritter, D. (2002) A Sick Institution? Diagnosing the Future Act Unit of the National Native Title Tribunal. *Australian Indigenous Law Reporter* 7(2), pp. 1–11.

Ritter, D. (2009) *Contesting Native Title: From Controversy to Consensus in the Struggle over Indigenous Land Rights.* Crow's Nest, NSW: Allen & Unwin.

Ritter, D. (2014) Black and Green Revisited: Understanding the Relationship between Indigenous and Environmental Political Formations. *Land, Rights, Laws: Issues of Native Title* 6(2), pp. 1–11.

Roberts, M. (2016) *The Long Depression.* Chicago: Haymarket Books.

Robertson, J. (2017) Adani Accused of Paying People to Stack Its Meeting on Crucial Mine Deal. *ABC News*, 1 December 2017. Available at: https://www.abc.net.au/news/2017-12-02/adani-accused-of-paying -people-to-stack-meeting-on-deal/9218246 [Accessed 5 December 2021].

Robertson, J. (2017) Adani's Compensation for Traditional Owners 'Well Below' Industry Standard, report finds, *ABC News*, 1 December. Available at: https://www.abc.net.au/news/2017-12-01/adani -compensation-well-below-industry-standard-report-finds/9212058 [Accessed 8 October 2024].

Robertson, M. (2012) Measurement and Alienation: Making a World of Ecosystem Services. *Transactions of the Institute of British Geographers* 37(33), pp. 386–401.

Robinson, R. and Gallagher, J. (1961) *Africa and the Victorians: The Official Mind of Imperialism.* London: Macmillan.

Robinson, C. (2000) *Black Marxism.* London: The University of North Carolina Press.

Rockström, et al. (2009) Planetary Boundaries: Exploring the Safe Operating Space for Humanity. *Ecology and Society* 14(2), p. 32. Available at: http://www.ecologyandsociety.org/vol14/iss2/art32/ [Accessed 15 November 2016].

Rono, J. K. (2002) The Impact of Structural Adjustment Programmes on Kenya Society. *Journal of Social Development in Africa* 17(1), pp. 81–98.

Rosberg, C. G. and Nottingham, J. (1966) *The Myth of Mau Mau: Nationalism in Colonial Kenya.* New York: The Hoover Institution.

Rose, C. (2004) Economic Claims and the Challenge of New Property, in Verdery, K., and Humphrey, C. (eds.) *Property in Question: Value Transformation in the Global Economy.* Oxford: Berg.

Routledge, W. S. and Routledge, K. P. (1910) *With a Prehistoric People, the Akikuyu of British East Africa.* London: E. Arnold.

Rowley, C. (1970) *The Destruction of Aboriginal Society.* Canberra: Australian National University Press.

Rowley, C. (1971a) *Outcasts in White Australia*. Canberra: Australian National University Press.

Rowley, C. (1971b) *The Remote Aborigines*. Canberra: Australian National University Press.

Rowse, T. (1987) 'Were You Ever Savages?' Aboriginal Insiders and Pastoralists' Patronage. *Oceania* 58(2), pp. 81–99.

Rowse, T. (2018) *Indigenous and Other Australians Since 1901*. Sydney: University of News South Publishing.

Rudy, A. (2001a) Marx's Ecology and Rift Analysis. *Capitalism Nature Socialism* 12(2), pp. 56–63.

Russell, P. (2005) *Recognizing Aboriginal Title: The Mabo Case and Indigenous Resistance to English Settler Colonialism*. Toronto: University of Toronto Press.

Rutto, S. (2016) Residents Walk out on NLC, Say They Should Be Let into Embobut Forest. *The Star*, 19 December 2016. Available at: https://www.the-star.co.ke/counties/rift-valley/2016-12-19-residents-walk-out-on-nlc-say-they-should-be-let-into-embobut-forest/ [Accessed 18 October 2021].

Rutto, S. (2020) Community Vows Not to Leave Forest Despite Order. *The Sunday Standard*, 12 June 2020. Available at https://www.standardmedia.co.ke/rift-valley/article/2001374834/community-vows-not-to-leave-forest-despite-order [Accessed 10 Oct. 2020].

Ryan, L. (2013) The Black Line in Van Diemen's Land: Success or Failure? *Journal of Australian Studies* 37(1), pp. 3–18.

Sahlins, M. (1961) The Segmentary Lineage: An Organization of Predatory Expansion. *American Anthropologist* 63, pp. 322–45.

Sahlins, M. (1968). Notes on the Original Affluent Society. In R. B. Lee and I. DeVore (eds.), *Man the Hunter*. New York: Aldine Publishing Company.

Sahlins, M. (2017) *Stone Age Economics*. Chicago: Aldine Atherton.

Said, E. (1994) *Culture and Imperialism*. New York: Vintage Books.

Said, E. (2003) *Orientalism*. London: Penguin.

Saito, K. (2016a) Marx's Ecological Notebooks by Kohei Saito | Monthly Review. [online] Monthly Review. Available at: http://monthlyreview.org/2016/02/01/marxs-ecological-notebooks/#fn56 [Accessed 12 December 2016].

Saito, K. (2016b) Learning from Late Marx. *Monthly Review*. [online]. Available at: http://monthlyreview.org/2016/10/01/learning-from-late-marx/#fn5 [Accessed 4 December 2016].

Saito, K. (2017) *Karl Marx's Ecosocialism: Capital, Nature, and the Unfinished Critique of Political Economy*. New York: Monthly Review Press.

Samson, C. (2020) *The Colonialism of Human Rights: Ongoing Hypocrisies of Western Liberalism*. Cambridge: Polity Press.

Samson, C. and Gigoux, C. (2016) *Indigenous Peoples and Colonialism*. Cambridge: Polity Press.

Samson, C. and Short, D. (2006) The Sociology of Indigenous People's Rights. In Morris, L. (ed.) *Rights: Sociological Perspectives*. New York: Routledge.

Sanders, W. (1985) The Politics of Unemployment Benefit for Aborigines: Some Consequences of Economic Marginalisation., in Wade-Marshall, D. and Loveday, P. (eds.) *Employment and Unemployment: A Collection of Papers*. Canberra: Australian National University.

Sansom, B. (1988) The Aboriginal Commonality. In Berndt, R. M. (ed.) *Aboriginal Sites, Rights and Resource Development*. Canberra: Academy of the Social Sciences in Australia.

Santos, B, S. (2014) *Epistemologies of the South: Justice Against Epistemicide*. New York: Routledge.

Sassen, S. (2010) A Savage Sorting of Winners and Losers: Contemporary Versions of Primitive Accumulation. *Globalizations* 7(1–2), pp. 23–50.

Sartre, J.-P. and Elkaïm-Sartre, A. (1968) *On Genocide: And a Summary of the Evidence and the Judgments of the International War Crimes Tribunal*. Boston: Beacon Press.

Sassen, S. (2010) A Savage Sorting of Winners and Losers: Contemporary Versions of Primitive Accumulation. *Globalizations* 7(1–2), pp. 23–50.

Sassen, S. (2013) Land Grabs Today: Feeding the Disassembling of National Territory. *Globalizations* 10(1), pp. 25–46.

Saugestad, S. (2001) Contested Images. First Peoples or Marginalised Minorities in Africa? in Barnard, A. and Kenrick, J. (eds.) *Africa's Indigenous Peoples: First Peoples or Marginalised Minorities?* Edinburgh: Centre of African Studies.

Scammell, W. H. (1968) *The London Discount Market*. London: Elek Books.

Schaller, D. (2008a) Colonialism and Genocide – Raphael Lemkin's Concept of Genocide and Its Application to European Rule in Africa. *Development Dialogue* 50, pp. 75–93.

Schaller, D. (2008b) From Conquest to Genocide: Colonial Rule in German Southwest Africa and German East Africa, in Dirk Moses. (ed.) *Empire, Colony, Genocide: Conquest, Occupation, and Subaltern Resistance in World History*. Oxford: Berghahn Books.

Schmidt, A. (1971) *The Concept of Nature in Marx*. London: New Left Books.

Schwandt, T. (2007) *The SAGE Dictionary of Qualitative Inquiry*. 3rd ed. London: SAGE Publications.

Sen, A. (2021) Embrace High Fossil Fuel Prices because They are Here to Stay. *The Financial Times*, 27 October 2021. Available at: https://www

.ft.com/content/a15e7ade-dad0-4ed3-a172-1974ac9d5b23 [Accessed 6 November 2021].

Servello, S. (2010) Australian Aborigines, in Birx, H. (ed.) *21st Century Anthropology*. Thousand Oaks, CA: SAGE Publications.

Seymour, F., La Vina, T. and Hite, K. (2014) *Evidence Linking Community Level Tenure and Forest Condition: An Annotated Bibliography*. Climate and Land Use Alliance. Available at: http://www.climateandlanduse alliance.org/wp-content/uploads/2015/08/Community_level_tenure _and_forest_condition_bibliography.pdf [Accessed 10 November 2020].

Shanin, T. (1983) *Late Marx and the Russian Road*. New York: Monthly Review Press.

Shaw, M. (2007) *What is Genocide?* Cambridge: Polity.

Shaw, M. (2012) From Comparative to International Genocide Studies: The International Production of Genocide in 20th-Century Europe. *European Journal of International Relations* 18(4), pp. 645–68.

Shivji, I. (2007) *Silences in NGO Discourse: The Role and Future of NGOs in Africa*. Nairobi: Pambazuka Press.

Shivji, I. (2009) *Accumulation in an African Periphery*. Dar es Salaam, Tanzania: Mkuki na Nyota Publishers.

Shields, R. (1988) An English Précis and Commentary on Henri Lefebvre's La Production de l'espace, in Sayer, A. (ed.) *Working Papers in Urban and Regional Studies* 63. Brighton: University of Sussex.

Short, D. (2003) Australian 'Aboriginal' Reconciliation: The Latest Phase in the Colonial Project. *Citizenship Studies* 7(3), pp. 291–312.

Short, D. (2007) The Social Construction of Indigenous 'Native Title' Land Rights in Australia. *Current Sociology* 55(6), pp. 857–76.

Short, D. (2008) *Reconciliation and Colonial Power: Indigenous Rights in Australia*. Aldershot: Ashgate Publishing Group.

Short, D. (2009) Sociological and Anthropological Perspectives on Human Rights, in Goodhart, M. (ed.) *Human Rights, Politics and Practice*. Oxford: Oxford University Press.

Short, D. (2010a) Australia: A Continuing Genocide? *Journal of Genocide Research* 12(1–2), pp. 45–68.

Short, D. (2010b) Cultural Genocide and Indigenous Peoples: A Sociological Approach. *The International Journal of Human Rights* 14(6–7), pp. 831–46.

Short, D. (2016) *Redefining Genocide: Settler Colonialism, Social Death and Ecocide*. London: Zed Books.

Simel, J. (2009) The Indigenous People's Movement in Kenya. *Indigenous Affairs* 3–4, pp. 10–19.

Singh, J. (2014) Recognition and Self-Determination: Approaches from Above and Below, in Eisenberg, A., Webber, J., Boisselle, A. and

Coulthard, G., (eds.) *Recognition versus Self-Determination*. Vancouver: UBC Press.

Smee, B. (2019) Adani Land-Use Agreement: Court Dismisses Indigenous Group's Appeal. *The Guardian*, 12 July 2019. Available at: https://www.theguardian.com/environment/2019/jul/12/adani-land-use-agreement-court-dismisses-indigenous-groups-appeal. [Accessed 10 October 2020].

Smith, A. (1776) *An Inquiry into the Nature and Causes of the Wealth of Nations*. London: W. Strahan and T. Cadell.

Smith, A. (1978) Lecture on Jurisprudence, in Meek, R. L., Raphael, D. D. and Stein, P. G. (eds.). *The Glasgow Edition of the Works and Correspondence of Adam Smith*. Oxford: Oxford University Press.

Smith, D. M. (2005). Marxism and Native Americans Revisited. In *Sixth Native American Symposium, Southern Oklahoma State University* (Vol. 10).

Smith, D. N. (2002). Accumulation and the Clash of Cultures: Marx's Ethnology in Context. *Rethinking Marxism* 14(4), pp. 73–83.

Smith, N. (2006) The Geography of Uneven Development, in Dunn, B. and Radice, H. (eds.) *100 years of Permanent Revolution*. London: Pluto.

Smith, N. (2008) *Uneven Development*. Athens, GA: University of Georgia Press.

Soja, E. (1985) The Spatiality of Social Life: Towards a Transformative Retheorization, in Gregory, D. and Urry, J. (eds.) *Social Relations and Spatial Structures*. London: Macmillan.

Sommer, B A. (1986) The Bowman Incident, in Hercus, L. and Sutton, P. (eds.) *This Is What Happened: Historical Narratives by Aborigines*. Canberra: Australian Institute of Aboriginal Studies.

Sorenson, M. P. K. (1967) *Land Reform in the Kikuyu Country: A Study in Government Policy*. Nairobi: Oxford University Press.

Sparer, E. (1984) Fundamental Human Rights, Legal Entitlements, and the Social Struggle: A Friendly Critique of the Critical Legal Studies Movement. *Stanford Law Review* 36(1/2), pp. 509–74.

The Standard (2020, Jun 12) Community Vows Not to Leave Forest Despite Order. *The Standard*. Available at: https://www.standardmedia.co.ke/rift-valley/article/2001374834/community-vows-not-to-leave-forest-despite-order# [Accessed 13 August 2020].

Stanner, W. E. H. (1979) *White Man Got No Dreaming*. Canberra: Australian National University Press.

Stanner, W. E. H. (2009) *The Dreaming and Other Essays*. Melbourne: Black Inc. Agenda.

Steffen, W. et al. (2015) The Trajectory of the Anthropocene: The Great Acceleration. *Anthropocene Review* 2(1), pp. 81–98.

Stepan, N. (1982) *The Idea of Race in Science: Great Britain, 1800–1960*. London: Archon.

Stevens, F. (1971) Aboriginal Labour. *The Australian Quarterly* 43(1), pp. 70–78.

Stewart-Harawira, M. (2005) *The New Imperial Order: Indigenous Responses to Globalization*. London: Zed Books.

Stichter, S. (1975) Workers, Trade Unions and the Mau Mau. *Canadian Journal of African Studies* 9(2), pp. 259–75.

Stockwell, S. (2017) 'Rushed' Native Title Changes Exclude Indigenous Australians, Critics Say. 13 March 2017. *Triple J Hack*. Available at: https://www.abc.net.au/triplej/programs/hack/native-title-changes -exclude-indigenous-australians-critics-say/8349448 [Accessed 9 October 2021].

Strakosch, E. and Macoun, A. (2012) The Vanishing Endpoint of Settler Colonialism. *Arena Journal* 37/38, pp. 40–62.

Strang, D. (1996) Contested Sovereignty: The Social Construction of Colonial Imperialism. In Biersteker, T. and Weber, C. (eds.) *State Sovereignty as Social Construct*. Cambridge: Cambridge University Press.

Stretesky, P. Long, M. and Lynch, M. (2013) *The Treadmill of Crime: Political Economy and Green Criminology*. Abingdon: Routledge.

Sullivan, S. (2012a) Financialisation, Biodiversity Conservation and Equity: Some Currents and Concerns. *Environment and Development Series* 16. Penang: Third World Network.

Sullivan, S. (2012b) Banking Nature? The Spectacular Financialisation of Environmental Conservation. *Antipode* 45(1), pp. 198–217.

Suter, P. (2013) Politicians 'SEE' Pain of Evictees as Squatters Go Up in Flames. *Daily Nation*, 26 January 2013. Available at: https://ifrapres sarch.nakalona.fr/items/show/90638 [Accessed 10 Oct. 2020].

Sutton, J. E. G. (1973) *The Archaeology of the Western Highlands of Kenya*. Nairobi: British Institute of East Africa.

Svirsky, M. (2014) The Collaborative Struggle and the Permeability of Settler Colonialism. *Settler Colonial Studies* 4(4), pp. 327–33.

Svizzero, S. and Tisdell, C. (2015) The Persistence of Hunting and Gathering Economies. *Social Evolution & History* 14(2), pp. 3–26.

Swain, T. (1997) *Place for Strangers*. Cambridge: Cambridge University Press.

Swainson, N. (1977) The Rise of a National Bourgeoisie in Kenya. *Review of African Political Economy* 8, pp. 39–55.

Sweezy, P. (2004) Capitalism and the Environment. *Monthly Review*. Available at: http://monthlyreview.org/2004/10/01/capitalism-and-the -environment/ [Accessed 9 December 2016].

Taiaiake Alfred (1999) *Peace, Power, Righteousness: An Indigenous Manifesto*. Don Mills, ON: Oxford University Press.

Tainter, J. (2011) *The Collapse of Complex Societies*. Cambridge: Cambridge University Press.

Tanogo, T. (1987) *Squatters and the Roots of Mau Mau, 1905–63*. London: James Currey.

Tatz, C. (1999) Genocide in Australia. *Journal of Genocide Research* 1(3), pp. 315–52.

Taylor, A. (2012). First Insights: Population Change for Territory Growth Towns, 2001 to 2011. *Northern Institute Research Brief Series* 7, pp. 1–9.

Taylor, C. (1995) *Philosophical Arguments*. Cambridge MA: Harvard University Press.

Te Ata O Tu MacDonald, L. and Muldoon, P. (2006) Globalisation, Neo-liberalism and the Struggle for Indigenous Citizenship. *Australian Journal of Political Science* 41(2), pp. 209–23.

Tennant, C. (1994). Indigenous Peoples, International Institutions, and the International Legal Literature from 1945–1993. *Human Rights Quarterly* 16(1), pp. 1–57.

Thomson, A. (2010) *An Introduction to African Politics*. New York: Taylor & Francis.

Thorpe, B. (1992) Aboriginal Employment and Unemployment: Colonised Labour, in Williams, C. and Thorpe, B. (eds.) *Beyond Industrial Sociology: The Work of Men and Women*. North Sydney: Allen and Unwin, pp. 157–221.

Thorpe, B. (1996) *Colonial Queensland*. St. Lucia, Queensland: University of Queensland Press.

Tickell, O. (2014) Kenya – Forest People Facing Violent Eviction. *The Ecologist*. Available at: https://theecologist.org/2014/jan/09/kenya-forest-people-facing-violent-eviction [Accessed 2 August 2021].

Tilley, H. (2011) *Africa as a Living Laboratory: Empire, Development, and the Problem of Scientific Knowledge*. Chicago: University of Chicago Press.

Tindale, N. B. (1974) *Aboriginal Tribes of Australia: Their Terrain, Environmental Controls, Distribution, Limits and Proper Names*. Berkeley: University of California Press.

Tocheva, D. (2018) Domestic Mode of Production, in Callan, C. (ed.) *The International Encyclopedia of Anthropology*. Hoboken, NJ: John Wiley & Sons.

Tonkinson, R. and Bernd, R. M. (2020) Australian Aboriginal Peoples – Traditional Sociocultural Patterns. *Encyclopedia Britannica*. [online] Available at: https://www.britannica.com/topic/Australian-Aboriginal/Traditional-sociocultural-patterns [Accessed 26 July 2020].

Trigger, D. S., Keenan, J., Rijke, K. D. and Rifkin, W. (2014) Aboriginal Engagement and Agreement-Making with a Rapidly Developing Resource Industry: Coal Seam Gas Development in Australia. *The Extractive Industries and Society* 1, pp. 176–88.

Tully, J. (2000) The Struggles of Indigenous Peoples for and of Freedom, in Iverson, D., Patton, P. and Sanders, W. (eds.) *Political Theory and the Rights of Indigenous Peoples*. Cambridge: Cambridge University Press.

Vandergeest, P. and Peluso, N. L. (1995) Territorialization and State Power in Thailand. *Theory and Society* 24(3), pp. 385–426.

Vattel, E., Kapossy, B. and Whatmore, R. (2008) *The Law of Nations, Or, Principles of the Law of Nature, Applied to the Conduct and Affairs of Nations and Sovereigns, With Three Early Essays on the Origin and Nature of Natural Law and on Luxury.* Indianapolis, IN: Liberty Fund.

Veracini, L. (2002) Towards a Further Redescription of the Australian Pastoral Frontier. *Journal of Australian Studies* 26(72), pp. 29–39.

Veracini, L. (2011) Introducing. *Settler Colonial Studies* 1(1), pp. 1–12.

Vergès, F. (2017) Racial Capitalocene, in Johnson, G. and Lubin, A. (eds.) *Futures of Black Radicalism*. London: Verso.

Vidal, J. John Vidal on the Great Green Land Grab, *Guardian UK*, 13 February 2008.

Vincent, E. (2016) Kangaroo Tails for Dinner? Environmental Culturalists Encounter Aboriginal Greenies, in Neale, T. and Vincent, E. (eds.) *Unstable Relations: Indigenous People and Environmentalism in Contemporary Australia*. Crawley: UWA Publishing.

Vincent, E. and Neale, T. (2016) Instabilities and Inequalities: Relations between Indigenous People and Environmentalism in Australia Today, in Neale, T. and Vincent, E. (eds.) *Unstable Relations: Indigenous People and Environmentalism in Contemporary Australia*. Crawley: UWA Publishing.

Vitoria, F. De. (1991) *Political Writings*. Cambridge. Cambridge University Press.

Voice of America (2018) *Kenya Flushes Out 'Criminals' in Forest Dispute after Sengwer Killing*. Voice of America. 18 January. Available at: https://www.voanews.com/africa/ kenya-flushes-out-criminals-forest-dispute-after-sengwer-killing.

Wahlquist, C. (2018) Victoria Passes Historic Law to Create Indigenous Treaty Framework. *The Guardian*, 21 June 2018. Available at: https://www.theguardian.com/australia-news/2018/jun/22/victoria -passes-historic-law-to-create-indigenous-treaty-framework [Accessed 22 August 2021].

Wallerstein, I. (1976) Three Stages of African Involvement in the World Economy, in Gutkind, P. C. W. and Wallerstein, I. (eds.) *The Political Economy of Contemporary Africa*. Beverly Hills and London: Sage.

Walter, M. (2007) Indigenous Sovereignty and the Australian State: Relations in a Globalising Era, in Moreton-Robinson, A. (ed.) *Sovereign Subjects: Indigenous Sovereignty Matters*. Sydney: Allen & Unwin.

The Wangan and Jagalingou Family Council (W&J FC) (9 April 2019) Federal Coalition Govt corrupts Adani water approval under political pressure from Qld LNP [Press release]. Available at: Federal Coalition Govt corrupts Adani water approval under political pressure from Qld LNP (wanganjagalingou.com.au) [Accessed 15 May 2020]

Washbrook, D. A. (1982) Ethnicity and Racialism in Colonial Indian Society, in Ross, R. (ed.), *Racism and Colonialism: Essays on Ideology and Social Structure*. Dordrecht: Springer.

Wasserman, G. (1975) The Politics of Consensual Decolonization. *The African Review: A Journal of African Politics, Development and International Affairs* 5(1), pp. 1–15.

Wasserman, G. (1976) *Politics of Decolonisation: Kenya, Europeans and the Land Issue 1960–1965*. Cambridge: Cambridge University Press.

Watkins, O. (1934) The Report of the Kenya Land Commission, September 1933. *Journal of the Royal African Society* 33(132), pp. 207–16.

Were, M. (2001) The Impact of External Debt on Economic Growth in Kenya: An Empirical Assessment. *Discussion Paper* 2001/116. Helsinki: UNU-WIDER.

White, R. (2015) Climate Change, Ecocide and Crimes of the Powerful, in Barak, G. (ed.), *Routledge International Handbook of the Crimes of the Powerful*. New York: Routledge.

Wilmot, E. (1985) The Dragon Principle, in McBryde, I. (ed.) *Who Owns the Past?* Melbourne: Oxford University Press.

Wily, L. A. (2018) The Community Land Act in Kenya: Opportunities and Challenges for Communities. *Land* 7(1), pp. 1–25.

Wise, L. E. (2017a) Social Death and the Loss of a 'World': An Anatomy of Genocidal Harm in Sudan. *International Journal of Human Rights* 21(7), pp. 838–65.

Wise, L. E. (2017b) *Social Death in Sudan: Towards an Ecology of Genocide* [PhD thesis]. King's College London.

Wolfe, B. D. (1967) Backwardness and Industrialization in Russian History and Thought. *Slavic Review* 26(2), pp. 177–203.

Wolfe, P. (1999) *Settler Colonialism and the Transformation of Anthropology: The Politics and Poetics of an Ethnographic Event*. London: Cassell.

Wolfe, P. (2001) Land, Labor, and Difference: Elementary Structures of Race. *The American Historical Review* 106(3), pp. 866–905.

Wolfe, P. (2006a) Settler Colonialism and the Elimination of the Native. *Journal of Genocide Research* 8(4), pp. 387–409.

Wolfe, P. (2006b) *Traces of History*. London: Verso.

Wolfe, P. (2008) Structure and Event: Settler Colonialism, Time, and the Question of Genocide, in Empire, in Dirk Moses, A. (ed.) *Colony, Genocide: Conquest, Occupation, and Subaltern Resistance in World History*. Oxford: Berghahn Books.

Wolff, R. (1977) *The Economics of Colonialism: Britain and Kenya, 1870–1930*. New Haven: Yale University Press.

Wolpe, H. (1975) The Theory of Internal Colonialism: The South African Case, in Ivar Oxaal, I., Barnett, T. and Booth, D. (eds.) *Beyond the Sociology of Development: Economy and Society in Latin America and Africa*. London and Boston: Routledge and Kegan Paul.

Wolpe, H. (1980) Capitalism and Cheap Labor Power in South Africa: From Segregation to Apartheid, in Wolpe, H. (ed.) *The Articulation of Modes of Production: Essays from Society and Economy*. London: Routledge & Kegan.

Wood, E. M. (2006) Logics of Power: A Conversation with David Harvey. *Historical Materialism* 14(4), pp. 9–34.

Woolford, A. and Jeff Benvenuto, J. (2015) Canada and Colonial Genocide. *Journal of Genocide Research* 17(4), pp. 373–90.

Young, C. (1994) *The African Colonial State in Comparative Perspective*. New Haven: Yale University Press, pp. 196–203.

Zierler, D. (2011) *The Invention of Ecocide: Agent Orange, Vietnam, and the Scientists Who Changed the Way We Think about the Environment*. Athens, GA: University of Georgia Press.

Zimmerer, J. (2008) Colonialism and the Holocaust: Towards an Archaeology of Genocide. *Development Dialogue* 50, pp. 95–123.

Zimmerer, J. (2014) Climate Change, Environmental Violence and Genocide. *The International Journal of Human Rights* 18(3), pp. 265–80.

Index

A

abiotic environment 1, 108
Aboriginal
  commonality 28, 244
  freehold 56
  participation 36
  problem 30, 42
  proletariat 46
Aboriginal and Torres Strait Islander
  Commission (ATSIC) 64
Aboriginal Land Councils 63, 66, 87, 93
Aboriginal Land Rights Act (ALRA) 63, 66,
  86, 194. *See also* Northern Territory
Aboriginal Reconciliation Act 1991
  (CARA) 51
Aboriginal tent Embassy 50
Aboriginal Treaty Committee (ATC) 51
Aboriginals Protection and Restriction of
  the Sale of Opium Act (1897) 42
Aborigines Progressive Association (APA)
  47
Adani Enterprises 72–78, 89, 91
administrative genocide 51, 65, 72, 186
advanced populations 125, 128
African
  peasants 41, 114, 118, 121, 128, 130
  socialism 134, 136, 138
  wilderness 174
African Royal Commission of 1953–5 133
Agenda for Sustainable Development 164
agrarian reforms 61
Agricultural Finance Corporation (AFC)
  133
ahoi system 117
air pollutants 80–1
Alfred, Taiaiake 16, 58
Amnesty International (AI) 147
ancestral law 29
Anderson, Kevin. B. 4
Anglo-Australian culture 46. *See also*
  Australia
animism 108
animistic philosophy 29
antagonistic class 121
Anthropocene 4, 14, 17, 19, 25, 101, 181
anthropogenic forcing 19
anti-colonial movement 49–50
anti-ecological nature 9, 89
anti-ecological properties 19, 143, 162, 179
architecture of dispossession 27, 32, 67,
  103, 112, 127, 143
Aseka, Eric 138, 207
assassinations 138

Australia
  architecture of dispossession now 32,
    67, 143
  architecture of dispossession then 27, 103
  colonial space 111, 115, 119
  economy 19, 36, 96
  experiences 121
  law 49
  mining capital 58
  settler capitalism 10, 28, 31–2, 34, 36,
    56, 119
  sites of continuing genocide 17
  See also Aboriginal
Australian Aboriginal Progressive
  Association (AAPA) 47
Australian Aborigines League (AAL) 47
Australian society on the cusp of colonisation 28
Australian Workers Union (AWU) 47
Australia's National Toxics Network 81,
  100, 203
auto-species extinction 4

B

Bantu ethnic groups 128
bargaining power 57, 65, 89
Barta, Tony 17
Barunga Statement 51
base metals 34
bee pollination 162, 165
Behre-Dolbear Group 55
Bentley Blockade 96, 99
biocultural assimilation 6, 16, 127
biodiversity loss 73
Biodiversity Offsetting (BDO) 168
biomass energy carbon capture and
  storage (BECCS) 165
biopolitics 14–6, 44, 59, 63, 65, 125–26,
  129, 132, 138
biosphere 1, 4, 8, 19, 71, 169, 189
biotic environment 1
Birdsell, J. 35, 92
black 14, 48–50, 82, 88–9, 97, 98–9,
  114–15, 119, 127–28, 131, 135–36, 139,
  173, 175, 189
  émigré 48
  Jacobins 14
  labour 114–15, 119, 128, 135
  man on country 88
  man's burden 131, 136, 139
  Marxism 14
  power 50
  rain 82

254   INDEX

black-green alliance 96, 99, 189
Black Panther Party 50
Blackburn, Justice 49
blue water 50
Bora rings 90
bourgeois rights 188
Brisbane 50, 81, 195
British East Africa Protectorate 104
British Empire 18–9, 22, 32–4, 103, 138, 184
bureaucratic
   apparatus 18
   ideology 76
   sabotage 153–55, 177–78
Burragubba, Adrian 73, 75–7
bush skills 37
Business and Biodiversity Offsets
   Programme (BBOP) 180

C

cadastral technologies 14, 182
Cape York Peninsula 61
capital accumulation 3, 5, 14, 19, 25, 31–2,
   35–6, 64, 68, 103, 122, 160–61, 170,
   181, 184, 189
capitalist ecology 3, 29, 68, 160, 181
Capitalist Mode of Production (CMP) 8
capitalist economic system 4–5, 9–10,
   12–4, 18–20, 25, 27, 29, 31–3, 39–41,
   44, 68–70, 88, 103, 115, 134–35, 138,
   143–44, 160–63, 170, 174, 179, 181–82,
   184, 189–90
carbon colonialism 164, 168
carbon cycle 19, 169
Caribbean 38
Carmichael Mine 72, 76–7
Carter, William Morris 116
cattle stations 37, 43, 46, 115, 120, 182
Cavanagh, C.J. 122–24, 126–29, 135, 140,
   152–54, 178, 182, 184–85
Center for International Forestry
   Research (CIFOR) 149
Centre for Minority Rights Development
   (CEMIRIDE) 176–77, 193
Chepkoir, Milka 157
Cherangani Hills 22, 107, 109, 122, 130,
   140, 144, 149, 156–57, 160, 170
Chieftainships 104
civilizational development 124
climate change 1–2, 17, 19, 73, 91, 141,
   144, 163–69, 172, 190
Climate Change Mitigation and
   Adaptation (WaTER) project 144
Coal Seam Gas (CSG) 17
   development 79–83, 86
   wells 80, 81
Cold War 58, 137–38, 142
Collins, Patricia Hill 175

colonial
   dilemma 61, 67, 74, 76, 84, 86, 94
   discourses 6, 13, 30–1, 129, 170
   encounter 13, 154
   episteme 132, 178, 187
   euphemism 76
   lawfare 57, 132, 139, 142, 152, 155, 183
   metropole 34
   occupants 23
   pastoralism 54
   state machine 12, 143, 160
colonial-era policies 146
colonial-relation 71, 161
colonialism 4–6, 11–2, 14, 16, 20, 34, 38,
   39–40, 45, 54, 59–60, 67–8, 86, 95,
   100, 104, 113, 121, 131–35, 139, 160,
   163–64, 168, 179, 185–86
colonised labour 38
commodification 4, 10, 53–4, 165–66, 169,
   173, 184
commodity fetishism 169–70, 175
Commonwealth 49, 55, 88, 98, 138
Commonwealth Development
   Corporation (CDC) 138
Community Development Employment
   Program (CDEP) 64
community land 145, 152–55, 195
Community Land Act (2016) 152, 195
community pressure 178
companion species 108
Conference of the Parties (COP) 168
Conservation International (CI) 174
conservation machine 163, 165
conservationist logic 122, 124
conservationist mode of production 20,
   162–64, 166, 179
constitutive logic of race 13
Corpuz, Victoria Tauli 163, 177
cosmovisions 189
Coulthard, Glenn 16
Council for Aboriginal Reconciliation
   (CAR) 51
creative destruction 34, 157, 161, 162
Crosby, Alfred 36
Crown Forest Reserves 123
Crown Lands Ordinance 115, 194
cultural assimilation 6, 43, 45, 62, 68.
   See also biocultural assimilation
cultural difference 4, 41, 119, 141, 181
cultural diffusion 62
cultural integrity 8, 12, 17, 24, 145
culture of poverty 63. *See also* poverty
Curtis, Mark 135

D

Darling Downs Hospital 83
Davidson, Basil 131

INDEX 255

Davies, Lloyd 70
Day of Mourning protest 48
de facto control 141, 163, 172, 181
de jure control 6, 67, 163, 172, 182
deleterious effect 110
dependent independence 135, 184
deterministic processes 96
developmental state 133, 143
developmentalism 2, 136–38
dewatering process 80
dialectical interaction 7, 28, 67, 103
dialectical relationship 13, 47, 122
disarticulation 134
dispersal campaigns 62
divide and rule 131, 139, 152
division of nature 161
domestic fallacy 25
domestication of animals 28
Doongmabulla Springs Complex 73
Dorobo question 107, 122–23, 125. *See also* ethnic groups in Kenya
Doubtful Creek 98, 100
draconian protection 46–7
drought 84, 167
dual bias 141

E

East African Protectorate 111
eco-criminogenic 8, 181
eco-genocidal destructive production 22, 36, 44
eco-regulatory labour 162–63
ecocentrism 9. *See also* anti-ecological nature
ecological
  catastrophe 1
  collapse 1, 4, 172
  completion 35
  consciousness 97, 190
  destruction 1, 8, 10, 13, 61, 69, 80, 117, 159, 190
  disaster 111
  inequity 1
  interconnections 3, 69
  modernisation 174
ecologically induced genocide 1, 8, 10, 13, 18, 22, 74, 125, 160, 181, 184
economic marginalisation 63, 74, 139, 244
ecosystemic laws 4, 29
egalitarianism 105
Eldoret country 148
Eliot, Charles 126
Embobut Forest 107–9, 122, 147–49, 151, 153–55, 157, 160–61, 168, 170, 175, 179, 181
Endorois Welfare Council (EWC) 178

energy return on investment (EROI) 71
entrepreneurs 63, 137–38, 186
environmental commodities 161, 165, 167–68, 170, 174
environmental
  control 125, 248
  degradation 9, 70, 97, 124, 168
  proletariat 190
  services (ES) 173
  sociology 4, 9, 12, 168
Environmental Law Australia 73, 78
epistemological trap 1
Esposito, Anthony 74
ethnic groups in Kenya 107, 110, 231
European expansion 28, 104
European political technologies 46, 119, 175
European Union (EU) 194
  Charter of Fundamental Rights 145
  Human Rights Action Plan 145
  Water Towers Programme 147, 149, 172
evangelical notions 30–1
Evans, Raymond 9
expanded reproduction 4, 5, 14, 35, 53, 58, 68, 119, 160, 181, 183–84
export-orientated extractivist 52
extra-human environment 7–8, 10, 12
extraction of commodities 40, 68, 96, 114, 186
extractive industries 9–10, 25, 55, 62, 68, 161
extractivist 52, 54–5, 68, 72
  mode of production in Australia 68
  state 52, 54–5, 72
extraeconomic processes of plunder 35. *See also* political economy
extreme energy 10, 17, 25, 69–71, 78–9, 87, 89–90, 184

F

Fanon, Franz 133
Federal Court 76–8, 101–2
Ferguson, Bill 47
fertile plains 36
final solutions 31
financial deregulation 53
fire-stick farming 28
fiscal independence 94
food procurement 141
Forest Conservation and Management Act (2016) 153, 195
Forest Indigenous Peoples Network (FIPN) 175
Forest Peoples Programme (FPP) 177
forest-dwelling communities 107, 122, 124, 136, 139–40, 147, 153, 164, 174
Fort Hill 116

256 INDEX

fortress conservation 140–41, 163
fossil capital 189–90
fossil fuels 1, 19, 40, 52, 54, 56, 69–70
Foster, J.B. 4, 9–10, 12, 38–9, 69, 126, 161, 168, 174, 181, 190
Foucault, Michel 15
Four Point Plan 137
Fourth World 49
Free Prior and Informed Consent (FPIC) 24, 75, 216
French
    colonies 33
    encroachment 111
    revolutionary traditions 59
frontier violence 6, 30, 33–4, 38, 45, 60, 185–86

G

Gaillard, Ian 99
Galilee Basin 73, 77, 91
Garland 7, 132
gas compression stations 79
genocidal effects 2, 117
genocidal processes 2, 13, 19–20, 27, 103
genocidal societies 2, 17–8
genocide, primary driver of 1, 3, 161
geo-political structures 24, 110
geostrategic logic 33
German encroachment 111
Githabul 2, 18, 22, 74, 77, 78–9, 85–9, 95–9, 181
global capitalism 18, 62, 67, 166, 189
global chain of genocide 184
global corporate interests 54, 72
global decolonisation movement 52, 130
global economic regime 54
    Global North 54, 137, 167–68
    Global South 52, 54, 166, 168, 171
global epistemicide 179
Global Green New Deal 165
globalization 166
Gomeroi 2, 18, 22, 74, 77, 78–9, 89–96, 99, 102, 181
Goodall, Heather 29, 47
Goulburn River National Park NSW 89
Gove case 49, 57
Governmentality 13, 15–6, 25, 51, 59, 64, 72, 122, 125, 129, 132, 138–39, 143, 170, 173
Gramsci, Antonio 58–9
Great Barrier Reef World Heritage Area 73
Great Depression 110
greed capitalism 162
green developmentalism 138
green economy 19, 143, 156, 165–66, 172, 174
green governmentality 122, 125, 170, 173

green neoliberalism 165
green theory 9
green-black alliance 96, 99, 189
greenhouse gases (GHG) 73, 165. *See also* climate change
greenwashing 156–60
Grey, George 31, 229
Gross Domestic Product (GDP) 167
guerrilla warfare 32, 45
Gurindji stockmen 48

H

Hardt, M. 41–2, 121, 126
Hartwig's third mode 123, 173
Harvey, D. 5, 33–5, 39, 54, 93, 163, 167, 183
Hawke, Bob 51
Hegel, G. 20–1, 222–23
hegemony of the mineocracy 85
herbal medicine 107
Hicki, Venessa 94
hierarchy of races 132
history of the present 7, 132
holocaust uniqueness 11
Holocene 19
homogeneity 3, 69
Horowitz, Irving 18
horse breakers 38
Howard government 61, 63–4, 76
Howlett, C. 54–5, 64, 72
humanitarian ethnography 31
hunter-gather mode 29, 38
Hunter–Gatherers Forum Kenya (HUGAFO–K) 175
hut tax 117
hybridisation 37, 40, 68, 114, 185
hybridity 62
hyperactivity 76

I

immigrant minority communities 16
Imperial British East African Company (IBEAC) 112
imperialism of trade 110, 134, 220
imperialism 33, 36, 110, 134, 138, 167, 179
indigeneity 14, 20, 46, 95
Indigenous alterity 6, 48, 64, 85
Indigenous figuration 29, 36, 38–9, 68, 114, 119
Indigenous genos 14
Indigenous groups
    Githabul 2, 18, 22, 74, 77–9, 85–9, 95–9, 181
    Gomeroi 2, 18, 22, 74, 77, 78–9, 89–96, 99, 102, 181
    Jagalingou 2, 18, 22, 72, 75, 77, 95, 101, 181

Kamba 105
Kikuyu 22, 104–7, 110, 113–19, 121–22, 126–30, 135, 139, 185
Luo 105, 139
Nandi 105
Sengwer 2, 17, 18, 22, 106–10, 115, 122–30, 135–6, 139–42, 144–64, 169–78, 181
Wangan 2, 18, 22, 72, 75, 77, 95, 101, 181
Indigenous Land Use Agreement (ILUA) 61
Indigenous liberation 190
Indigenous proletariat 44, 47, 71, 190
Indigenous sovereignty 6, 27, 30, 62, 65, 142, 189
Industrial and Commercial Development Corporation (ICDC) 133
institutionalisation of human rights 59
inter alia 5–6, 14–5, 18, 53, 81, 120, 125, 162, 167, 177
intergenerational relationships 21, 75, 92
intermarriage 125
internal citizenship 16
internal colonialism 6, 12, 38–40
internal territorialization 44
International Criminal Court (ICC) 145
International Monetary Fund (IMF) 54, 166–67
International Work Group for Indigenous Affairs (IWGIA) 177
interpellating processes 186
interpretive approach 21
invented tradition 158
invisible hand 165

J

Jagalingou 2, 18, 22, 72, 75, 77, 95, 101, 181
James, C. L. R. 14, 225
Jenkyn, John 80, 84
Johnson, Murrawah 73
Johnston, Harry 31
Joint Implementation (JI) 180
Jones, Rhys 28
juridico-political 29

K

Kalenjin 107–8, 151, 158, 197
Kamba 105
Keen, I. 29, 92
Kenya 7, 10, 17, 24, 33, 39, 42, 103–5, 113–14, 118–19, 121, 123–24, 126, 129–30, 132–36, 138–39, 141, 143–46, 148–52, 159–61, 167, 171–73, 175, 178–79, 184, 186–87
Kenya Forest Service (KFS) 144
Kenya Land Commission 116, 124, 139, 142, 145

Kenya Pastoralist Development and Network (KPDN) 175
Kenya Trading corporation (KNTC) 133
Kenya Water Towers Agency (KWTA) 149
Kenyatta, Jomo 131
kiama system 106
Kibet, Paul 157
Kikuyu 22, 104–7, 110, 113–19, 121–22, 126–30, 135, 139, 185
Kikuyu Central Association (KCA) 116
Kimaiyo, Elias 150, 162, 191
kingship network 46
kinship relations 29, 62, 92
Kipkazi, Wilson 178
Kirotich, Robert 144
Klare, Michael T. 69
Kymlicka, William 16
Kyoto Protocols 165

L

labour policy 118
Labour Theory of Value (LTV) 179
Lacey, Tom 47
Lake Bogoria 177–78
Lake Victoria 112–13
Land Act (2012) 152
land alienation 17, 115, 164
Land Councils 51, 57, 64, 66, 85–8, 94
Land Courts 83, 90, 145, 155, 176, 178–79
land grab 8–9, 17, 34, 54–5, 68, 114, 116, 156
laws of motion 2, 9–10, 31–2, 40, 160, 163, 188
leadership abolition 23. *See also* Lemkin's eight techniques
Leard Forest 89
Lefebvrian grid 42, 129
legal resistance 101, 175–77
legal roadblock 153
legalistic interpretation 11
Lemkin, Raphael 8, 22, 205, 236, 244
Lemkin's eight techniques 23
    biological 12, 42–3, 45, 130, 164
    ecological 158
    moral 23, 29, 38, 54, 65, 148, 226
    physical 6, 8, 11–2, 30, 49, 72, 117, 169
    religious 23, 29, 51, 109, 178
Lenin, Vladimir 5
Leys, Colin 114
liberalism 59
life-sustaining web 12, 69
liminal humanity 122, 185
liquefied natural gas (LNG) 81
Liverpool plains 89
Local Aboriginal Land Council (LALC) 10, 66, 93
local structural matrix 25

INDEX

loci of genocide 24
Lock the Gate Alliance 97, 99
Lockean property 31, 63
logic of elimination 6–7, 10, 13, 15, 18, 28, 44, 67, 95, 103, 113–14, 119, 123, 130–31, 141, 188
logic of exclusion 183
Lugard, Lord Frederick 126
Lunatic Express 112
Luo 105, 139
Luxemburg, Rosa 5
Lyons, K. 8, 54–5, 72–3, 76, 78, 156

M

Mabo case 32, 50, 60, 120, 243
Macekura, S.J. 137
Machiavellian tactics 152
MacIntyre river 89
Macklin, Jenny 63
Macoun, A. 7, 28, 188
Malcolm X 50
Malone, Patrick 75
Many Trees Good Life 146
market environmentalism 2, 17, 19, 143, 161, 165, 174, 184
market friendly re-regulation 156
Marx, Karl 101, 110, 112, 125, 135, 136, 161–63, 170, 181
Mau Forest complex 144, 149
Mau Mau 121, 130, 131, 133
Maules Creek Mine 89
Maynard, Fred 47–8
Maynard, John 47
mbari 105, 117
Mboya, Tom 134
McCarron, Geralyn 81–2
Merrilees, Duncan 28
Metagasco 98, 99
metaphysical obligation 49
Mignolo, W. 132, 179
Millennium Ecosystem Assessment (MEA, 2005) 174
mineral-dependent economy 55
Mines Legislation 83, 195
mining lobby 53, 57, 62, 77
Minority Rights Group International (MRGI) 176–77, 193, 235
Miti Mingi Maisha Bora 146
mixed economies 107
Mode of Production (MP) 2–3, 8, 13, 19–20, 22, 25, 28, 37–8, 40, 68, 72, 106–7, 112, 162–66, 179
modernization programmes 136
moheregu 105
monetary compensation 77
monopoly of violence 173, 182
Morrison, Scott 90

Moses, D. 11, 24, 30–1, 34
Mundunjudra 73
mythic geography 29, 91

N

Nabalco 49
Nairobi 113, 119, 140
Nandi 105
Narrabri Gas Project 90
National Aboriginal Conference 51
National Land Policy (NLP) 152
National Native Title Tribunal (NNTT) 74
Native Lands Trust Ordinance (1928) 116
native reserves 115–16, 123
Native Title Act 1993 (NTA) 52, 56
Native Title Amendment Bill (1997) 78
Native Title Claim Group 74, 77
Native Title Tribunal 74, 86
Natural Resource Management Program (NRMP) 146
nature-culture dualism 13
Nazis 11, 18
Ndung'u Commission (2004) 176
negative-emission technology 165
neo-colonialism 135
neo-feudal aspects 117
neo-Lemkian 10, 24, 28, 181
neoliberalism 5, 9–10, 17, 19, 25, 52–5, 63–5, 78, 87, 94, 143, 156, 163–69, 172–73, 182–86, 190
New South Wales (NSW) 22, 85
New South Wales Aboriginal Land Council (NSWALC) 66
Newtonian mechanics 93
Nile 111–12
Njonjo Land Commission (2002) 176
nomadic Indigenous mode 37, 185
non-capitalist modes of production 5
non-capitalist territory 4, 119, 141, 171
non-governmental organisations (NGOs) 137
normative hierarchy 27
Northern Land Councils 51
Northern Rivers 87–9, 96–100
Northern Territory 30, 37–8, 48–9, 57, 120
nyumba 105

O

octoroon 42
Ogiek Peoples' Development Program (OPDP) 177
ontological coin 11
outstation movement 57

P

Pacific trading hub 33
pacification 30, 113–14, 142, 146

pan-Indigenous identity 48
Paris Earth Summit 164
Parker, Dianne Glenda 82
pastoral economy 10, 43
Pastoralist, Hunters and Gatherers and Ethnic Minority Network (PHGEMN) 175
pastoralists 38, 43, 61, 83, 85, 127, 243
Pax Britannica 35, 122
Payments for Ecosystem Services (PES) 168, 179
peak oil 71, 237
pearl divers 120
Perry, Melissa 77
petite bourgeoisie class 114–15
Pilbara strike 48
Pilliga Forest 90, 91, 93–4, 197
Plan Period 149
political economy 2–4, 7, 10, 12, 14, 22, 24, 27, 29–30, 32, 35, 39, 44–5, 49, 52, 54, 58, 63, 68, 71, 94, 103–4, 106–7, 113, 119, 122, 127, 129, 135–39, 141, 146, 152, 160–64, 169–71, 174–75, 179, 181, 183–85
political geography 108
political jurisdiction 6, 182
political risk 55
poll tax 117
pollination 53, 108, 162, 165
Port Jackson 32
portmanteau biota 36
post liberal approach 11
post-independence period 139–40, 185
post-Mabo phase 187
poverty 63, 74, 82, 121, 137, 157, 167, 172
Powell, Christopher 21
pre-capitalist societies 5, 108
prima facie material 169
prima facie paradox 65
prima facie violation 145
primary accumulation 4–5, 36, 68, 114, 118, 135, 160–61, 169, 181
prime farmland 80
primitive accumulation 35, 39
private property 3, 6, 54, 59, 141, 180, 186
pro-Indigenous sentiment 47
production of space 141, 163, 183
productive settlement 122
prohibition of cultural activities 23
proletarianisation 39, 118
property-owning class 120
prostitutes 32, 118
protected areas 140, 146, 152, 164
protection 17, 30, 42–7, 60, 62, 92–5, 129, 144, 150, 176, 186. *See also* welfare
protection boards 30, 42, 47
protection regimes 42–6, 60, 186

proto-eugenic laboratories 129
pseudo-humanism 59–60
psycho-affective discourses 16

Q

qualitative variety of commodity 69
Queensland 22, 30, 33–4, 37, 42–3, 61, 66, 73, 76–80, 83, 102

R

racecraft 43, 141
racial apartheid 43
racial capitalism 14, 127
Racial Capitalocene 14
Racial Discrimination Act (RDA) (1975) 61
racial hierarchy 49
racial spatialisation 43–4, 88, 127, 163
racialised landscapes 14, 122, 127–28
rainbow serpent 73
raw materials 34, 40, 44, 70–1, 111
fossil fuels 1, 19, 40, 52, 54, 56, 69–70
subsurface minerals 40, 68
real economy 63–4, 96, 240
recognition paradigm 16, 57
reconciliation 16–7, 45–6, 51–2, 58–9, 65, 78, 96, 182
Red Deal 190
Red Skin, White Masks 16
Reducing Emissions from Deforestation and Degradation (REDD+) programme 146, 150, 165, 168
reflexive critical inquiry 2
Registered Native Title Claimants (RNTC) 74–6
regressive taxation 53
rehabilitate farms 133
relational approach 21
reproductive gap 118, 121
resource rush 55, 79
Rey, Pierre-Philipp 38
Reynolds, Henry 31, 33, 38, 66, 120
Rift Valley 125
right to negotiate 61, 75, 182
rights to land 24, 50, 179
rights to self-determination 24, 79, 89
Rio Summit 164–65
Robinson, Aileen Moreton 59
Robinson, Cedric 14
Robinson, Moreton 15, 39, 59, 65
rubric of neoliberalism 52, 166

S

sacrifice zone 81, 83
Said, Edward 15
Sengwer 2, 17, 18, 22, 106–10, 115, 122–30, 135–36, 139–42, 144–64, 169–78, 181

science-policy discourse 174
scientific impartiality 2
scorched earth 146, 157
Scott, Geoff 86
second colonial occupation 136
segmentary lineage system 105–6
segregation 30, 42–3, 45, 127
self-determination 6, 16, 24, 30, 49–50,
   57, 64, 79, 89–9
self-reliance 65
semi-arid zones 37
semi-feudal relations 41, 120
Senate Inquiry 78
settler-capitalist system 135
settler-colonial contexts 3, 68
settler-colonial courts 6
settler-colonial project 120
Shivji, I. 131, 134, 137–38, 143, 166
Short, Damien 9
Simpson, Audra 7
slavery 34, 38, 59, 134
Smith, Adam 129
Smith, Mariann Lloyd 100
Smithian economics 93
Snowball sampling 22–3
social cataclysm 119
social license 96, 231
social vitality 4, 11, 21, 38, 92, 127, 158
socio- cultural system 106
socio-ethical critique 9
sociology of genocide 9, 10, 12
solidaristic resistance 80
spatial practices 14, 183
spatio-temporal fix 5, 33, 163, 167, 172,
   183
sphere of pauperism 32
squattocracy 35
State Land Council 87, 94
Statutory Investment Funds 63–4
steam power 112
stewardship 90, 171
stigmatization 82
stolen generations 42, 82
structural adjustment programmes
   (SAPs) 143
subsumption of labour 41, 126
Suez Canal 111
suicide rose 83
Sultan of Zanzibar 111
superior tribes 126–28
Supreme Court 49, 102
Surat basin 79–80
sustainability 71, 108, 123–24
sustainable development 141, 164–65,
   173
Swynnerton Plan 133, 135, 138, 141

Sydney 32, 47–8, 50, 66
symbolic violence 14, 153–54

T

tailing ponds 80
Tara estate 82
Tarrawonga Mine 89
Taylor, Charles 16, 248
tenancy rights 118
territorialization 44, 183, 249
Thalia, Anthony 38
Thorpe, Bob 38
tipping points 90
Tongo State Forest 89
Toowoomba 84
Torres Strait Islander Heritage Protection
   Act (1984) 93–4
totemic geography 92
totemic relationship 29
Trade Licensing Act (1967) 133
Troup, Robert Scott 124
Truman, Harry S. 137
trust land 140, 194
tsunami 79

U

uncaptured peasantry 137
underemployment 38, 120
United Nations (UN) 23, 55, 61, 73, 150,
   164–65, 168
United Nations Declaration of the Rights
   Indigenous Peoples (UNDRIP) 23

V

vagabonds 32
valorisation process 170
Van Diemen's Land 32, 243
Vandergeest, P. 14, 44, 141, 182
victim groups 21, 23
violence 6, 14, 16, 21, 30, 33–4, 36–8, 45,
   60, 95, 113, 122, 126, 130, 132, 151–56,
   173, 182–83, 185–87
virtuous circle 105
volatile organic compounds (VOCs) 81

W

walkabout 37
Wangan 2, 18, 22, 72, 75–7, 95, 101, 181
Wangan and Jagalingou Traditional
   Owners Council 72
water catchment areas 80, 124, 144, 149
Water Towers Protection 144
Waterside Worker's Union 48
Watkins, O.F. 123
Wattie Creek 49

Wave Hill Strike 48
welfare 30, 42, 64–5, 86, 167, 176, 178
Werris Creek 89
West Pokot 108
White, Irene 75
Whitehaven coal 89, 92–5
Wik 10 Point Plan 61, 76
Wik peoples 61
Wildlife Act (2013) 152
Wolfe, Patrick 6
womb of feudalism 40–1

World Bank 138, 146–49, 157, 160, 162, 165–66, 172–73, 183
Worldwide Fund for Nature (WWF) 174

Y

Yolngu people 49
Yorkshire mills 34

Z

zoonotic spillover 143

www.ingramcontent.com/pod-product-compliance
Lightning Source LLC
Chambersburg PA
CBHW040744200525
26707CB00022B/14